B

BOETHIUS

THE CONSOLATIONS OF MUSIC, LOGIC, THEOLOGY, AND PHILOSOPHY

HENRY CHADWICK

CLARENDON PRESS · OXFORD

Oxford University Press, Walton Street, Oxford OX2 6DP
Oxford New York Toronto
Delhi Bombay Calcutta Madras Karachi
Petaling Jaya Singapore Hong Kong Tokyo
Nairobi Dar es Salaam Cape Town
Melbourne Auckland
and associated companies in
Berlin Ibadan

Oxford is a trade mark of Oxford University Press

Published in the United States by
Oxford University Press, New York

© Henry Chadwick 1981

First published 1981
First issued in Clarendon Paperbacks 1990
Reprinted 1992

All rights reserved. No part of this publication may be reproduced, stored in a retrieval system, or transmitted, in any form or by any means, electronic, mechanical, photocopying, recording, or otherwise, without the prior permission of Oxford University Press

This book is sold subject to the condition that it shall not, by way of trade or otherwise, be lent, re-sold, hired out or otherwise circulated without the publisher's prior consent in any form of binding or cover other than that in which it is published and without a similar condition including this condition being imposed on the subsequent purchaser

British Library Cataloguing in Publication Data
Chadwick, Henry
Boethius
1. Boethius   2. Philosophy, Ancient
I. Title
180'.937   B659
ISBN 0–19–826549–2 (Pbk)

Printed in Great Britain by
Biddles Ltd, Guildford and King's Lynn

HILARIAE

FILIAE DILECTISSIMAE

PREFACE

BORN fifteen hundred years ago (within a reasonable approximation), Boethius wrote one of the dazzling masterpieces of European literature. But he has been seldom studied as a whole, and has been seen more through the eyes of those whom he influenced than in relation to the writers whom he had read and who influenced him. The purpose of this book is to see the man in the setting of his own turbulent and tormented age, not to trace his large posterity in thought and literature. Moreover, the latter concern predominates in the collection of studies on Boethius by various authors, including myself, edited by Dr Margaret Gibson (Blackwell, 1981). Much is also said of that in the studies of Boethius by Pierre Courcelle (1967). Modern reappraisal of Boethius, especially since the work of Klingner (1921) and Courcelle (1948), has concentrated on his debt to the late Platonists of Athens and especially of Alexandria. The present book continues that line, and adds fresh Neoplatonist evidence for the interpretation of the five tractates on Christian theology. On the other side, I have also found more affinity with Augustine than has been generally recognized, and therefore conclude with a portrait of Boethius simultaneously more deeply Neoplatonic and more deeply Augustinian than has been acknowledged. I have also tried to integrate the various constituent elements in his intellectual achievement. The substructure of the *Consolation of Philosophy* is only clear when one has also seen something of his arithmetic, music, and logic, the last being the grand obsession of his mind. It is then possible to make a fresh attack on the question of his religious allegiance, debated since the tenth century when Bovo of Corvey asked how the evidently

Christian author of the theological tractates could write a work of so exclusively non-Christian inspiration as the *Consolation*. The examination in the first chapter of the political tangle between the Gothic kingdom of Theoderic the Great and the Byzantine ambitions of Justinian leads me to conclude that it is quite wrong to exclude religion from the causes of his tragic arrest and execution.

Parts of this book owe their first shape to lectures. Chapter IV began at the twelfth annual conference of the Medieval Association of the Pacific meeting in February 1979 under the learned presidency of Florence Ridley of the University of California, Los Angeles. Parts of chapters II, III, and V formed the Frederick Denison Maurice Lectures at King's College, London, in February 1980 under the Dean, Ulrich Simon. A valedictory lecture on taking leave of generous friends at Christ Church, Oxford in June 1979 has also been remade in these pages. On the margins of Boethian scholarship I have profited much from consulting others very learned in the subject: Professor J. M. Wallace-Hadrill, Dr A. M. Crabbe, Dr G. R. Evans, Dr M. T. Gibson, Dr D. P. Henry.

The book's appearance under the imprint of the Clarendon Press I owe to the gentle encouragement of Peter Spicer and Robin Denniston.

H. C.

CONTENTS

	ABBREVIATIONS	ix
	CHRONOLOGICAL TABLE	x
	INTRODUCTION	xi
I	ROMANS AND GOTHS	1
	Culture and the public service	1
	Symmachus	6
	The Neoplatonic schools	16
	Out of the ivory tower: John the deacon	22
	The hard road to church unity: the Acacian and Laurentian schisms	29
	Master of the Offices	46
	The collapse of toleration	56
	Boethius' sacrifice	66
II	LIBERAL ARTS IN THE COLLAPSE OF CULTURE	69
	Arithmetic	71
	Music	78
	Boethius' Treatise on Music and its sources	84
	Geometry and Astronomy	102
III	LOGIC	108
	Part of philosophy or a tool of all philosophy?	108
	Logic and rhetoric	111
	Porphyry	120
	Neoplatonists after Porphyry: Iamblichus, Syrianus, Proclus, Ammonius	127
	Boethius' commentaries on the *Isagoge*	131
	Translator of Aristotle	133
	The Ten Categories	141
	On interpretation	152

viii Contents

	Future contingents	157
	The monographs on logic	163
	Propositional logic and the hypothetical syllogism	166
IV	CHRISTIAN THEOLOGY AND THE PHILOSOPHERS	174
	Faith and history; *De fide catholica*	175
	The Person of Christ	180
	The Scythian Monks	185
	Nature and person	190
	Absolute and relative goodness	203
	God the Trinity	211
V	EVIL, FREEDOM, AND PROVIDENCE	223
	The Lady philosophy	225
	From Stoic moralism to Platonic transcendence	228
	O qui perpetua	234
	Degrees of perfection: the quest for the One	235
	Reminiscence: natural theology and the Bible	237
	The problem of evil	239
	Providence and fate	242
	Divine foreknowledge and free will	244
	The religion of Boethius	247

PRESERVATION AND TRANSMISSION	254
EDITIONS	258
BIBLIOGRAPHY	261
NOTES	285
INDEX	307

ABBREVIATIONS

ACO	*Acta Conciliorum Oecumenicorum*, edited by E. Schwartz (1914 ff.)
AL	*Aristoteles Latinus* (Leiden, 1961 ff.)
CAG	*Commentaria in Aristotelem Graeca* (Berlin, 1891 ff.)
CIL	*Corpus Inscriptionum Latinarum*
CLA	*Codices Latini Antiquiores*, edited by E. A. Lowe
CSEL	*Corpus Scriptorum Ecclesiasticorum Latinorum*
CTh	*Codex Theodosianus*
DTC	*Dictionnaire de Théologie Catholique*
ILCV	*Inscriptiones Latinae Christianae Veteres*, edited by E. Diehl
ILS	*Inscriptiones Latinae Selectae*, edited by H. Dessau
JTS	*Journal of Theological Studies*
MEFR	*Mélanges de l'école française de Rome*
MGH	*Monumenta Germaniae Historica*
PG	*Patrologia Graeco-Latina* edited by J. P. Migne
PL	*Patrologia Latina*
PLRE	*The Prosopography of the Later Roman Empire*, II, ed. J. R. Martindale (Cambridge, 1980)
PO	*Patrologia Orientalis*
PW	Pauly-Wissowa, *Realenzyklopädie für die classischen Altertumswissenschaft*
RAC	*Reallexikon für Antike und Christentum*
RHE	*Revue d'histoire ecclésiastique*
SB	*Sitzungsberichte*

CHRONOLOGICAL TABLE

SECULAR RULERS

East Roman emperors
Marcian 450–7
Leo I 457–74
Leo II 474
Zeno (first time) 474–5
Basiliscus 475–6
Zeno (second time) 476–91
Anastasius I 491–518
Justin I 518–27
Justinian 527–65

Barbarian kings of Italy

Odovacar 476–93

Theoderic 493–526

Athalaric 526–34
(Amalasuintha regent 526–35)

BISHOPS

Rome
Leo I 440–61
Hilarus 461–8
Simplicius 468–83
Felix III 483–92
Gelasius I 492–6
Anastasius II 496–8
Symmachus 498–514
(Laurentius 498, 501–6)
Hormisdas 514–23
John I 523–6
Felix IV 526–30
Boniface II 530–2
(Dioscorus 22 Sept.–
14 Oct. 530)

Constantinople
Flavian 446–9
Anatolius 449–58
Gennadius I 458–71
Acacius 472–89
Fravitas 489–90
Euphemius 490–6 (exiled)
Macedonius II 496–511 (exiled)
Timothy I 511–18
John II the Cappadocian 518–20
Epiphanius 520–35

Alexandria
Cyril 412–44
Dioscorus 444–51 (d. 454)
Proterius 451–7
Timothy Aelurus (first) 457–60 (Monophysite)
Timothy Salofaciolus (first) 460–75 (Chalcedonian)
Timothy Aelurus (second) 475–7
Peter Mongos (first) 477 31 July–4 Sept. 477 (Monophysite)
Timothy Salofaciolus (second) 477–82
John Talaia June–Dec. 482 (Chalcedonian)
Peter Mongos (second) 482–9

Thereafter a Monophysite succession at Alexandria; no Chalcedonian until 537.

PHILOSOPHERS

Ptolemy (Claudius Ptolemaeus) fl. AD 127–48
Nicomachus of Gerasa fl. c.150
Apuleius (Carthage) 123–c.180
Alexander of Aphrodisias (Athens) fl. c.200
Plotinus (Rome) 205–70
Porphyry of Tyre (Rome, Sicily) c.250–c.305
Iamblichus (Syria) c.250–c.325
Marius Victorinus (Rome) c.285–c.370
Syrianus (Athens) d. 437
Hierocles (Alexandria and Constantinople) fl. c.440–70
Proclus (Athens) 412–85
Ammonius son of Hermias (Alexandria) c.436–517 (or 445–526)
Martianus Capella (Carthage) fl. c.470 (?)
Damascius (Athens) fl. c.490–c.537–38
Simplicius (Alexandria, Athens) fl. 515–45 or later
Philoponus (Alexandria), Christian pupil of Ammonius c.490–c.570
Elias fl. c.550–c.600

INTRODUCTION

'LAST of the Romans, first of the scholastics': the tag echoes a famous judgement on Boethius by the humanist Lorenzo Valla in the fifteenth century. Valla saw in Boethius a man whose diction and philosophy were touched by barbarisms but nevertheless allowed him a claim to be the last classical writer in the Latin tongue. Renaissance humanism mixed its admiration for Boethius with the expression of occasional misgivings. Did his concept of education allow a sufficient place to literary values? Granted that he adorned the *Consolation of Philosophy* with a series of poems including some of real distinction, yet his prose is another matter; and he makes it clear that for him philosophy and theology are altogether more serious than the pleasures of the Muses who, in Platonic fashion, receive discourteous treatment in his pages. Renaissance men could also come to feel constricted by Boethius' writings on arithmetic, music, and dialectic which dominated the medieval schools. His studies in dialectic had in fact long been the object of mingled admiration and dislike, as one may see in John of Salisbury's *Metalogicon* of 1159, itself a classic of the twelfth-century renaissance. It was not, of course, a new thing in the fifteenth century that literary humanists should feel irritated by rigorous training in dialectic which could end by producing tiresome young nit-pickers who made the subject seem trivial.

As an educator Boethius consistently believes practice to be far less important than theory. His educational ideal is intended to produce men of understanding rather than of practical action and technique. The disciplines of moral philosophy, politics, and economics were held in respect and no doubt counted for much in public and political life; but the purer mental skills for Boethius, as for the Platonic schools of his time, lie in the natural sciences, mathematics, and metaphysics. And by the study of the natural sciences Boethius really meant the philosophical questions discussed in Aristotle's *Physics* (e.g. the nature of change, causation and necessity, the infinite, the definition of place and of time, the Prime Mover) or *De caelo*, on the heavenly bodies, or *De generatione et corrup-*

tione, on coming to be and passing away. Plato's *Timaeus* was also reckoned a primary text for the study of nature. Mathematical questions particularly interested Boethius because of their importance in Plato's scheme of education and the place that he assigned to mathematics in the construction of his metaphysics. Boethius provided the schools of the medieval West with standard handbooks on arithmetic and especially on music. He had a powerful interest in musical theory because he held Pythagorean and Platonic notions about musical proportion pervading the ordered structure of the universe. He does not write on arithmetic to help his readers with their accounts and tax returns; nor on music to assist them with the practice of the art which, like almost all ancient men, he regarded as no fitting occupation for a gentleman. His principal model in both arithmetic and music he found in Nicomachus of Gerasa, a Pythagorean of the second century AD whose writings sought to show how number and harmony are the key to understanding the cosmos. Nicomachus was held in the utmost admiration by the Neoplatonist philosophers of Boethius' time. His *Arithmetic* was expounded by Iamblichus; and Proclus believed Nicomachus' soul to be reincarnate in himself.

The curriculum of ancient schools was intended to provide what the Greeks called 'all-round education' (*enkyklopaideia*). For the Latin world Marcus Terentius Varro in the first century BC had set out to organize his prodigious erudition with an account of nine 'liberal arts', skills to be acquired by a gentleman. (The Latin phrase characteristically carries a 'class' overtone absent from the Greek equivalent.) His nine subjects were: grammar, dialectic, rhetoric, geometry, arithmetic, astronomy, music, medicine, and architecture. Shortly before Boethius' time the African pagan Martianus Capella wrote a handbook to the liberal arts, but dropping medicine and architecture to give a list of seven. Boethius thought the Latin world sufficiently provided with guides to grammar (Donatus in the fourth century and Priscian in his own time) and to rhetoric (Cicero and Quintilian). Vitruvius (first century AD) had written on architecture. But the Latin world seemed in need of better works on dialectic and on the four mathematical disciplines for which Boethius coined the term 'quadrivium', 'four ways'. The application of the word 'trivium' to grammar, rhetoric and dialectic became in medieval times a natural development from Boethius' 'quadrivium'.

Before Boethius the Latin West had almost no Plato in translation— only half the *Timaeus* in Cicero's version—and next to nothing of Aristotle, except a handbook by Apuleius and what little Marius Victorinus had been able to provide in the fourth century AD for the instruction of his aristocratic pupils in Rome. Boethius conceived the ambition of translating into Latin everything he could find of Aristotle and Plato. Since he rightly saw Aristotle to be almost unintelligible without explanations, he provided not only versions, which he then polished and revised, but commentaries of considerable length, and some monographs of his own. In practice his life, cut short in his mid-forties, allowed him time only to translate Aristotle's writings on logic, to which school tradition prefixed Porphyry's 'Introduction' (*Isagoge*) explaining the terms through which Aristotle thought 'definition' possible. Boethius wrote two commentaries on Porphyry, one on Aristotle's *Categories*, and two on *De interpretatione*; and much of the West's knowledge of Aristotelian logic for the next six hundred years depended on these works. He found almost all his Roman contemporaries unsympathetic and uninterested in these efforts. He tried to enlist their concern for logic in his long commentary on Cicero's *Topics*, which was designed to show the utility of dialectic for persuasive oratory, and then by a monograph 'On differences in topics', where he explained a method of distinguishing arguments suitable for public speaking from those which serve philosophical truth.

In his five tractates on theology, Boethius sought, as a layman trained in dialectic, to bring order to theological tradition with its confusing terminology of 'nature', 'person' and 'substance', the same terms being used in one sense of the Trinity, in another of the Person of Christ. The tractates manifest a deep knowledge of St. Augustine. At the same time they mark a stronger disjunction than Augustine would have wanted to see between the area of reason and the area of faith; there Boethius sees the authority of revelation and the Church as primary and decisive in matters where reason can have little or nothing to say. Medieval Christians sometimes felt that Boethius thereby set theologians on a road leading away from religious experience to a battlefield of disputation about technicalities. Nevertheless, Boethius' writings on Christian theology raise questions of permanent importance for the Church. He writes as one whose skill lies in dialectic and who sees some untidiness in the ecclesiastical garden, where he can offer a helping hand.

When he writes on Christian themes, Boethius is no dilettante, less than seriously engaged with the subject, passing an idle Saturday afternoon by penning a few reflections on the logical problems of coherence afflicting the language of customary usage. At the same time his mind is absorbed first and foremost by the problems of ancient Greek philosophy, especially as interpreted by the Platonic schools of his own time. Cicero and Seneca had done much to educate the Latin world in moral philosophy, but not much for dialectic, and here we have seen that Boethius found he had something to add.

Much of this study is given to the attempt to place Boethius in relation to his intellectual ancestry, so that the reader may be left with the impression that the hero of the book is hardly more than a diligent compiler and translator. That is in many ways a fair judgement, but it leaves out of account Boethius' own valuation of what was important and urgent to be done. The great Neoplatonist masters of his age, to whom he owed a profound intellectual debt, did not admire originality in the least. Quite as much as any Christian of the fifth century Proclus tended to see ideas in terms of orthodoxy and heresy. Heresy was synonymous with innovation. He understood his principal task as that of expounding the authoritative texts of Plato, with which Aristotle must be harmonized, and for which his logic was the preliminary tool. 'Scholasticism' ought not to be a pejorative term, in so far as it means the ordered presentation of human knowledge as it was taught in the schools. But if the term is used to imply deference towards venerable texts as providing an inspired canon, and requiring careful exegesis to give a harmonized picture, then Proclus is the archetypal 'schoolman', and Boethius is his grateful pupil.

Boethius' claim to a significant place in the history of thought rests on the works for which his mathematical and dialectical skills came to provide a scaffolding, namely the five theological tractates or *opuscula sacra*, and the masterpiece which he wrote in prison at Pavia in 524–5, the *Consolation of Philosophy*. Both the *Consolation* and the *opuscula* are pervaded by the teaching of Proclus and the Neoplatonists. Yet there is much in Proclus for which Boethius evidently finds little or no use. Boethius has woven, out of the material with which Proclus had provided him, a fabric of alternating highly compressed argument and fine poetry, an account of the moral problem of evil in a good Creator's world and of the reconciliation of an all-knowing providence with human freedom in a world of apparent contingency. Although he is a Christian, he wants to argue for providence exclusively on grounds of natural reason, deliberately setting aside any appeal to religious authority either in Christ or in the text of Scripture. Whatever we are to make of this work of extraordinary power and beauty, it cannot be rated either commonplace or merely derivative. 'A golden volume', felt Gibbon—even though qualified with the ironical touch 'not unworthy of the leisure of Plato or Tully.'

The figure of Boethius has been obscured by time, but an uncovering of the surface of his work at once reveals something of his interest and importance. As we dig deeper, we discover that there is more. The same is true of his place in the historical events of the declining western empire, where he was witness of much of long-term significance. That is where we must begin, with the Boethius of contemporary politics.

I
ROMANS AND GOTHS

Culture and the public service

ANICIUS MANLIUS SEVERINUS BOETHIUS was born into one of the powerful landed families of senatorial rank in fifth-century Italy. Some (not all) manuscripts spell his name Boetius; Romans had difficulty with the Greek theta. The exact year of his birth is not recorded. When he was executed in prison at Pavia in 525 or 526 he was not old. In the *Consolation of Philosophy*, written in prison awaiting execution, he laments that his troubles and imprisonment have brought premature old age (i m. 1, 7–12). When his two sons were nominated consuls in 522, they were still mere boys (ii, 3, 8). His early writings were already well known before the year 507 (Cassiodorus, *Variae* i, 45) but Ennodius of Pavia speaks of them as the works of a precocious youth 'teaching at an age when others are still learning'.[1] Accordingly, it seems reasonable to hold that his birth probably fell early in the 480s, and that his fifteen-hundredth anniversary falls at about the present time in the early 1980s.

Despite the turbulent age of the barbarian invasions, the old noble families of Rome manifested a remarkable capacity for survival. Barbarian army commanders and the fainéant emperors whom they made and unmade might come and go, but through it all the senators retained their land and power and made themselves indispensable to the administration. When the nominal line of western emperors ended, control by the wealthy senators continued much as before, in some respects their power being even enhanced by the removal of the western emperor. In 476 the barbarian soldier Odovacar decided to take the ornaments as well as the reality of power, and forcibly sent the emperor Romulus Augustulus into retirement at a pleasant estate near Naples. The senators were not slow to co-operate with Odovacar. They might have tax difficulties as when, about 486, he requisitioned a third of their

Italian land (their estates being very large) to provide for his army of Germanic soldiers.[2] After the elimination of Odovacar by Theoderic (493), the Ostrogothic king continued the system of co-operation—and imposed an income tax, in which matter Theoderic found the senators expert at tax avoidance.[3] But the replacement of a Roman emperor by a barbarian king at Ravenna, especially when that king was Theoderic who had been educated in Constantinople, had little more than a marginal effect on the dignity and ease of senatorial life. There remained many openings for them, on the civil side, in the bureaucracy at Ravenna. It became fashionable for them to edit revised texts of masterpieces of Latin literature; there was an important work of preservation to be done. They also edited Christian texts.

Odovacar's legitimate title was not accepted at Constantinople by the emperor Zeno. Even Theoderic found that with Zeno's successor Anastasius his status had to be negotiated painfully and with difficulty. At Ravenna Theoderic's title was king (*rex*), not western emperor, but he was allowed certain privileges such as that of nominating consuls for Byzantine approval. Theoderic was not treated by Byzantium as being in law western emperor, but in Italy Roman senators tended to speak of him as if he held this office.[4] A letter of the Roman senate to Anastasius of 516 writes of Theoderic as of 'domini nostri invictissimi regis Theoderici filii vestri'.[5] Boethius writes of Anastasius as 'emperor of the East', whose writ does not run in the West.[6] His contemporary Avitus of Vienne likewise speaks of Anastasius as 'king of the East' or 'Caesar of the Greeks', not emperor of all the Romans.[7] Greek East and Latin West have now become separate; 'utraque respublica' say the senate to Anastasius.[8]

Perhaps because Theoderic prized the culture, law, and administration of the empire, he did not desire the fusion of Roman and barbarian which Clovis' conversion to Catholicism would make possible for the Franks. ('Catholic' is here used to mark a contrast not between East and West, but between orthodox and Arian). Theoderic wished his Goths to retain their independent identity, assisted in this by the Arianism of their faith since the mission of Ulfila. He may also have seen that his rough soldiers, warlike, crude, and bibulous, would not be good for Roman culture. His policy has features reminiscent of Talleyrand's remark to the Russian Tsar Alexander: 'The French are civilized, their sovereign (Napoleon) is not. The sovereign of Russia is civilized, her people are not. Therefore the sovereign of Russia must be the ally of the French people.' No Roman might enter the army, no Goth a Roman school. The deliberate insistence on separate development was ultimately injurious to the cohesion of the Gothic kingdom in Italy, but at least had preservative effects on the old Roman way of life. The near-contemporary Ravenna chronicler called, after the name of his first editor, the second Anonymus Valesianus (61) attributes to Theoderic the remark: 'The poor Roman tries to live like a Goth, the rich Goth tries to live like a Roman.'[9] Naturally Theoderic's existence was resented by some old Roman families. The story circulated that the king was illiterate and signed state documents with a stencil. Procopius' *Secret History* records an almost identical story of the Greek emperor Justin, which casts strong doubt on its truth of either man.[10] It is possible that Theoderic was dyslexic which is far from incompatible with high education and intelligence, or that after an education at Constantinople his Latin was inferior to his Greek. His Arianism was a national identity-card for Goths, and was combined with strong adherence to toleration, leaving the Catholic churches of Italy unmolested. His mother Ereliliva was a Catholic who at baptism took the Roman Christian name Eusebia.[11] Theoderic had no time for one Catholic clergyman who thought to gain a wider sphere of usefulness by being converted to the Arian creed.[12] When in 500 he paid a ceremonial visit to Rome and was welcomed by the clergy and senators, he visited St. Peter's and venerated the apostolic shrine 'as if he were Catholic'.[13] It seems certain that it was on this occasion of his visit to Rome that Theoderic caused to be struck the fine gold medallion now in the National Museum at Rome, bearing a frontal portrait of the king making a stylized gesture with his right hand as the pacifier of the world, and carrying in his left a little Victory. The COMOB on the reverse indicates that it was issued 'within the palace' by the Count of the Sacred Largesses. The character of the medallion shows that it will have been one given out as a donative during the king's stay in the city. It bears on its face the legend REX THEODERICVS PIVS PRINC(EPS) I(NVICTVS) S(EMPER), and on the reverse REX THEODERICVS VICTOR GENTIVM. Below: COMOB [= comes obryziaci i.e. the official in charge of the assay office, responsible for the weight and value of the gold coinage.][14]

The portrait of Theoderic in the pages of Cassiodorus' *Variae* or Ennodius' *Panegyric* is one of a highly Romanized monarch, whose intervention in Italy against Odovacar has saved *Romanitas* to the rejoicing of all true Romans. It is far from clear that this is how Theoderic appeared to his own people; their ideal was of a warlike leader on horseback charging the enemy, which is indeed how Theoderic was represented (according to Agnellus) on the façade of his palace at Ravenna. Theoderic claimed descent from the semi-divine Amal dynasty, and his Gothic soldiers are not likely to have appreciated the forms of Roman officialdom with which he surrounded himself at Ravenna.

Theoderic needed the experience of the old Roman aristocracy for stable government. In return for granting recognition to Theoderic, the east Roman emperor Anastasius and his successor Justin desired that the Italian magistracies be filled by Romans, not by Goths. The arrangement could allow for exceptions, as in 519 when Justin, to please Theoderic, took the initiative in proposing that Eutharic Cillica, a Visigoth from Spain to whom he had given his daughter Amalasuintha in marriage in 515, be nominated to the prestigious office of the consulate. In the past there was plenty of precedent for appointing a barbarian to be consul; Theoderic himself had held the office in 484. Consuls had colourful ceremonial and ornamental duties, but did not exercise power. The main offices of state in Italy were retained by the Roman families. Praetorian prefects, the courts of the consistory controlling the treasury and the chancery, the mandarins of the civil service, continued to be recruited from those whom one of their number in the fourth century had described, with the confidence of a self-evident truth, as 'the best part of the human race'.[15] They took it for granted, and others shared their view, that the business of governing was their manifest destiny.

Boethius' father, himself probably the son of a Boethius who held a prefecture in 454 and in the following year went to his death with the great Aetius, had held a succession of high offices: prefect of the city of Rome, praetorian prefect, then in culmination the western consul (not recognized in the East) for 487. The ivory diptych bearing his portrait is preserved in the Museum at Brescia, and records his full name: N(onius) Ar(rius) [or An(icius) Aur(elius)?] Manl(ius) Boethius v(ir) c(larissimus) et inl(ustris) ex p(raefecto) p(raetorio) p(raefecto) u(rbi) sec(undo) cons(ul) ord(inarius) et patric(ius).[16] Although the functions were merely honorific, the consulship remained an office of the highest dignity. The holder's name appeared on the dating of all documents for the year. A young lad could perform the duties provided that his family was immensely rich and could pay for the consular games and the various ceremonies. The formula for consular appointments preserved in Cassiodorus (*Variae* vi, 1) lays stress on the splendid insignia, the happy freedom from any actual government responsibility, and the munificent generosity expected. The official duties were compatible with a dignified and learned leisure. During the year of his consulship in 494 Turcius Rufius Apronianus Asterius produced an edition of Vergil appending verses complaining of the distraction of consular games; and we know about his career thanks to the scribal subscription in the Medici codex of Vergil's *Bucolics* at Florence.[17] During his own consulship in 510 Boethius found time to work on his commentary on Aristotle's *Categories*, and explains, with conscious echoes of Cicero, that the instruction of his fellow citizens in how to use their minds is pertinent to his civic responsibility as consul, and indeed that, just as ancient Roman arms won an empire by appropriating other cities, so his own work furthers the enhancement of Rome's authority by translating Greek wisdom into Latin.[18]

Boethius' father died when his son was still a little boy, perhaps not long after the year of his consulship in 487. But the child was then taken into the even greater and more powerful household of Quintus Aurelius Memmius Symmachus, who had himself held the consulship together with Odovacar in 485 and whose father had been consul with Aetius in 446.[19] He belonged to the same family as the great pagan aristocrat of the

370s who unsuccessfully pleaded against Ambrose for the restoration of the Altar of Victory in the Senate House and for a policy of religious toleration based on the essential mysteriousness of divinity. The services of Q. Aurelius Memmius Symmachus as prefect of Rome are recorded on a surviving bronze tablet.[20] Through being taken into Symmachus' household the young Boethius was brought to a milieu of power and of high culture, sure to provide excellent opportunities for his career and comfort. Boethius held Symmachus in the utmost awe and affection. He grew up to marry Symmachus' daughter Rusticiana, and in his writings speaks of Symmachus as the judge whose criticism and approval he values most highly. It is therefore illuminating for the study of Boethius to inquire into Symmachus' political and cultural ideals as these are reflected in evidence taken from sources other than Boethius' writings.

Symmachus

Symmachus' eminence in Italian society as an arbiter of literary excellence is illustrated by the dedication to him of three works on Latin rhetoric by Priscian,[21] resident at Constantinople, who hoped to attract Symmachus' patronage on a visit that the senator paid to Byzantium about 500, probably as Theoderic's ambassador to the Byzantine court. In the West the ambitious, place-hunting Ennodius who, like Boethius, owed his upbringing and education to rich family friends, also dedicated to Symmachus a short tract written about 511 advising two aspiring young men, Ambrosius and Beatus, how to get on in society.[22] The tract ends with a request in verse to further Ennodius' own career. In alternating prose and verse Ennodius counsels the youths to love God and their neighbour, to study modesty, chastity, faith, grammar, and above all rhetoric. So they should follow the eloquence of the living masters in the present senate. And Ennodius names Faustus Niger (consul 490), his son Avienus (cos. 502) now at Ravenna; Festus (cos. 472) and Symmachus (cos. 485) at Rome; or Probinus (cos. 489) and his son Cethegus (cos. 504), the brilliant young Boethius (cos. 510), Agapitus (cos. 517) and Probus (cos. 525). Or if they seek feminine exemplars, there is Barbara the very flower of the Roman spirit, or Stephania (Faustus' sister,

Asterius' wife) the shining light of the Catholic Church. This instructive list of 'top people', whose patronage Ennodius would evidently be glad to enjoy, gives a noteworthy place to Symmachus and to Boethius. At the same time it is the kind of document that explains the coolness detectable in Boethius' attitude towards Ennodius' requests to him for help in prospering his career or solving his housing problems at Milan.

Ennodius' exhortation also presupposes the now intimate link between the great senatorial families and the higher clergy of the Church in Rome. Symmachus has a prominent position among these Catholic senators. According to the excerptor of a lost work of Cassiodorus entitled 'ordo generis Cassiodororum' (i.e. the fragment which Usener named after its discoverer *Anecdoton Holderi*),[23] Symmachus appeared to his contempories like old Cato the Censor: famous for his love of justice and hatred of humbug, his studies of Greek, his incorruptibility, and for such severity towards luxury as to bequeath the epithet 'censorious' to our language. But, says Cassiodorus, Symmachus 'transcended the virtues of the ancients by his most holy religion'. In this man classical and Christian virtues walked the earth together. When Boethius lay in prison awaiting his death, he felt grateful that at least no hand had yet been raised against his wise and saintly father-in-law. When Symmachus' fall eventually came, it was an evident case of guilt by association.

Symmachus shared in and admired that idealization of Rome's past glories and Neoplatonic mysticism to which Macrobius had given expression in his *Saturnalia* and his *Commentary on Scipio's Dream* from Cicero's *Republic*. The manuscript tradition of our text of Macrobius' commentary shows its dependence on a manuscript which Symmachus revised at Ravenna, at a date unknown, in co-operation with Macrobius Plotinus Eudoxius, *vir clarissimus*, whose name suggests that he was a member of the author's family. The subscription is at the end of the first book of Macrobius' commentary: AVR. MEMM. SIMMACKVS. VC. EMENDABAM VEL DISTVIN(guebam) MEV(m) (sc. exemplum) RAVENNAE CV(m) MACROBIO PLOTINO EVDOXIO. VC.

When Boethius came to write his first commentary on

Porphyry's introduction to Aristotelian logic, he drew attention to the value of Macrobius' work. How deeply Macrobius' study of Scipio's Dream entered into Boethius' mind is measured by the manifest borrowing in the second book of the *Consolation of Philosophy*, where ii pr.7 uses Macrobius with direct verbal echoes of *In Som.Scip.* ii, 9, 8 ff. If the borrowing was from memory, then Macrobius' text was well embedded in Boethius' consciousness.

Symmachus wrote a Roman History in seven books. The work is lost except for a single fragment, and attempts to discern elements of its ideology and standpoint by postulating its use in the *Romana* of Jordanes and in the chronicle of the Illyrian count Marcellinus, though attractive, are too speculative and vulnerable to be made the basis of serious reconstruction. Possibly Symmachus' History intended to express an attitude that all the greatness of Rome lay in the past, and that his dream for the future is to restore the imperial rule sadly lost in the West. Like Aurelius Victor, Eutropius, and the *Augustan History* in the fourth century, he saw the story of the empire as that of its emperors. The ending of the line of ghostly western emperors with Romulus Augustulus in 476 or Nepos in 480 was certainly regretted by Italian senators as marking a break in an institutional continuity whose symbolism they valued, even though substantially before 476 all actual power had irretrievably passed to the Germanic army commanders. Aetius' murder in 454 is marked by Marcellinus as the effective end of Roman power in the West. If one cannot have things in the way that they used to be, there may be some therapeutic reassurance in keeping at least the illusions of continuity to reconcile oneself to a world of terrifying changes. To Symmachus and his circle the domination of Italy and the sacred city (*sacratissima urbs*[24]) by a heretical Goth in royal insignia, acquiring in due course all the 'ornaments of the palace', could not but cause inward pain.

The fragment of the Roman History of Symmachus cited in Jordanes' *Getica* shows him borrowing from the *Augustan History* a significant anecdote about the third-century emperor Maximin the Thracian whose father was a Goth.[25] Symmachus' picture of Maximin is one of a crude barbarian naturally unsuited to the arts of good government, of whom, nevertheless, something could be made with Roman discipline and training. Just such a training had been given to Theoderic himself as a young man at Constantinople. Zeno had taught him respect for Roman ways and laws. The moral seems clear. Symmachus speaks for the Roman aristocrats who have no political alternative to collaboration, at least for the time being, and who see their co-operation with Arian Goths as the work of educating their new masters.

In the long citation from Symmachus' Roman History in Jordanes, it is twice emphasized that the reign of Maximin was cut short in consequence of his persecution of the Christians. Symmachus and his family take pride in their distinguished ancestors and especially in the eminent fourth-century orator Q. Aurelius Symmachus, but the family is now explicitly Christian and devotedly Catholic. Of Symmachus' daughters, Rusticiana married Boethius; Proba became a nun in Rome; a third daughter, Galla, was early widowed and childless after one year of marriage to a consul whose father had been a consul, and then became a nun at the monastery of St. Stephen by St. Peter's in Rome (a monastery still known in the eighth century as 'cata Galla patricia'). Gregory the Great tells of Galla's vision of the apostle Peter as she lay dying of cancer of the breast. Both Galla and Proba received letters from the eminent African theologian, Fulgentius bishop of Ruspe, then in exile in Sardinia. To Proba the presbyter Eugippius dedicated an anthology of excerpts from Augustine.[26]

During the long and agonizing conflicts between Pope Symmachus and his rival Laurentius competing for possession of the papal throne, which from 498 until 506 (and even later) divided the senators and clergy into two bitter factions in the city of Rome, the senator Symmachus appears to have been, at least initially, no supporter of his namesake. An undated letter sent probably about 502 or 503 in the name of the clergy of Gaul by bishop Avitus of Vienne, himself (as he pointedly stresses) of senatorial rank by birth, addressed to the senators Faustus (probably Faustus junior, prefect of Rome 502–3, not Faustus Niger) and Symmachus, implores them to give their support to Symmachus as the only lawful pope and thereby to show their love for Peter's see to be as great as their affection for the city of Rome.[27] The life of Pope Symmachus in the *Liber*

Pontificalis, which is a passionately anti-Laurentian piece, declares expressly that among the senators only Faustus Niger committed himself to Pope Symmachus' cause. The rest, no doubt including Symmachus the senator, must have either supported Laurentius or been neutral. Avitus' letter is generally taken to imply that at the time of writing Symmachus and Faustus junior had already given support to Pope Symmachus, but the text has too many subjunctives and optatives to make this interpretation plausible. More probably Faustus and Symmachus are addressed either because they are especially eminent neutrals not yet committed to the Symmachian cause or more probably because Avitus wishes to bring two highly respected Laurentian supporters over to the side of Pope Symmachus (below, p. 41).

In any event the correspondence puts beyond doubt Symmachus' standing and weight as a widely respected Christian senator with great moral authority. Of his interest in intricate questions of theology, especially those bearing on the disputes between East and West, Boethius' opuscula sacra give decisive testimony. To him Boethius dedicates his tract discussing the logic of the doctrine that the Trinity is one God, not three Gods.

From the time of Constantine onwards the higher clergy at Rome had led a movement to transform the look of their city.[28] Its landmarks hitherto had been its splendid temples and other powerful reminders of its pagan past and closely linked imperial greatness. The fourth-century Christians of Rome turned it into a Christian town studded with richly decorated shrines of the martyrs to which public processions could be held on their anniversaries or 'birthdays'. Wealthy founders were stimulated to vie with one another in the splendour of mosaic and marble adornment, and the master-calligrapher Filocalus was employed by Pope Damasus to inscribe verses on the martyrs' monuments in a style of high distinction. Sermons proclaimed that the city had now passed under the mighty protection of its glorious apostolic martyrs and 'founders' Peter and Paul with their great shrines on the Vatican hill and on the road to Ostia where they stand today. In the mid-fifth century Pope Leo the Great tells his flock that

Peter and Paul are now the guardians of their city, replacing those unsatisfactory characters Romulus and Remus.[29] When Alaric's Goths sacked the eternal city in 410, the cry went up 'Where are Peter and Paul?'[30] Christian preachers said that such sufferings were a just punishment both for the sins and failures of Christians and for the continued preference for the old pagan gods on the part of many citizens.

The Christianization of the city and, from the middle years of the fourth century, of its ruling class, resulted in the city being led by an oligarchic circle of aristocrats and higher clergy who, if not themselves members of the ruling class families like Felix III and his great-grandson Gregory the Great, were closely bound to the senators in a client–patron relationship. When Leo needed an inquisition to unearth crypto-Manichees who had infiltrated his congregation, it seemed natural to establish a tribunal of inquiry in which Christian senators and senior clergy sat together, the laymen acting as assessors in advising the episcopal court.[31]

Fourth-century senators were initially reluctant to do anything so unroman as to adopt Christianity, but their wives felt otherwise. Their successors soon found that they could be 'sons of the Church' without relinquishing any of their pride in Rome as 'head of the world'. Indeed the claims made for the Roman see's universal jurisdiction by Damasus and his successors imparted unprecedented dimensions to this civic and imperial pride. 'Thanks to Peter's see' (Leo tells the city) 'you have become *caput mundi*; you reign over a vaster empire by means of divine religion than by terrestrial supremacy. If by many victories you have extended your sovereignty over land and sea, what you have put under your feet by war and its toils is less than the *pax Christiana* has subjected to your sway' (*Sermo* 82). 'The Papacy', wrote Thomas Hobbes, 'is not other than the Ghost of the deceased Roman Empire sitting crowned upon the grave thereof'; and the remark would not be so irritating to all who care for the western Catholic tradition if it contained no element of truth. But Leo imparts a religious expression to the imperial domination. The Christian community at Rome is, for him, uniquely privileged among Christian churches: taught by Peter and Paul and grounded on the rock, predestined by God for its role of leadership, so protected from error as to be renowned for orthodoxy, this church's presiding bishop possesses jurisdiction (*plenitudo potestatis*) over all churches, not only his own. Only, Leo's senators would have found it hard to share his view that the grandeur of Rome had an exclusively Christian foundation to which the pagan past was irrelevant. They saw no reason why Romulus and St. Peter should not be equal sources of satisfaction to the city.

When an image of Minerva was toppled in consequence of public disorder in Rome, the restoration work was carried out under the authority of Faustus (albus, as Ennodius calls him to distinguish him from Faustus Niger), the city prefect of 502–3, and his care for the preservation of this relic of Rome's pagan past was recorded in an inscription (*CIL* vi 526 = 1664 = Dessau *ILS* 3132). He was not a pagan.

A letter in Cassiodorus' *Variae* shows Memmius Symmachus expending large sums on restoring classical buildings in Rome, including the theatre of Pompey.[32] Continuity with Rome's historic greatness was evidently important to him, and Theoderic's policy was to foster the restoration of cities throughout Italy.[33] At the end of the sixth century Gregory the Great's *Dialogues* (ii, 15, 3) attest how full Rome was of crumbling, collapsing stone, whose maintenance had been long neglected. No thunderbolt of divine displeasure was necessary to turn it into a ruin.

Fifth-century senators did not see their adhesion to Christianity as requiring the application of surgery to the old Roman calendar of pagan celebrations and carnivals. Filocalus' almanack published at Rome in 354 juxtaposes the pagan and Christian festivals and records side by side lists of consuls and bishops. Under Odovacar the senator Andromachus served for a time as Master of the Offices. He was without ambiguity a Christian by profession, and represented the Roman Church on a mission to Constantinople about 488 in connection with the Acacian schism. In a letter of 492 Pope Gelasius (492–6) speaks of Andromachus as 'my son'.[34] Yet Andromachus was soon to distress Gelasius by leading the senate in a decision to maintain the ancient annual festival of the Lupercalia on 15 February.[35] This was an archaic carnival of fertility and purification, at which men in wolf masks hilariously stripped and flagellated women suspected of illicit love affairs, and at which obscene songs were traditionally sung with the apotropaic purpose of averting storms and hail from the crops and of keeping the empire free of pestilence.[36] Gelasius urges that not only recent natural disasters and plagues in the provinces but also the sad loss of Roman imperial rule in the West since 476 have resulted from the continued toleration and support of such unseemly pagan festivals by Christian senators. Against the pope Andromachus protests that the well-tried and venerable rites are for the good of society. Their continued maintenance is felt to be a symbolic gesture that even under the new Gothic management old Rome's ways are unchanged. After 476 the senate was self-conscious of these things. It is the time when they began to mint large copper coins showing the helmeted bust of ROMA INVICTA, with the she-wolf suckling Romulus and Remus on the reverse.

Gelasius accuses Andromachus and his fellow senators of being 'neither Christian nor pagan' (p. 603 Thiel). The words have the ring of an ironic quotation from an apologia by Andromachus, conceding that the Lupercalia is not a Christian festival but denying that there is anything specifically pagan about it, since there is no sacrifice offered to a heathen deity. It is all as neutral and harmless as a Christmas tree in the twentieth century. On the other hand, it would not be quite true to maintain that for Andromachus the festival had a scarcely stronger pagan association than morris dancing on May Day or a Siena palio. The senators valued the archaic ceremonies because they were a characteristically Roman thing to do, and they saw no reason why such festivities should be regarded as incompatible with Christian faith or offensive to a Christian conscience. But unless Gelasius unscrupulously misrepresents them, they were also inclined to the opinion that such observances assisted in keeping heaven propitious and in averting pestilence and famine. Gelasius directly accuses them of encouraging a ceremony in honour of Castor and Pollux, patrons of sailors; perhaps returning mariners after a hazardous voyage were still inclined to make their offerings at the Twins' temple at Ostia, and the senators were disinclined to stop them. The Twins' festival at Ostia on 27 January was still being annually celebrated in the fifth century, as we know from Polemius Silvius.

Nevertheless Andromachus evidently denied with heat that in the Lupercalia or other venerable customs in the form still being preserved there is anything specifically pagan. It is disturbing and significant, Andromachus suggested, that Gelasius should be trying to abolish a custom in which loose sexual morality is subjected to mockery and discipline at a time when the bishop of Rome himself is treating with notorious laxity a clergyman known to have fallen into fornication. With such charges and countercharges tempers began to run high.

It is impossible to believe that Gelasius could have enjoyed much success in his struggle to suppress the Lupercalia. Perhaps the practical effect of his protest was merely to weaken the respect in which his official teaching authority was held. He conspicuously failed to carry with him the consciences of the Christian senators, and must have realized this only too well. His letter to Andromachus concludes a lengthy attack by conceding that his predecessors had raised no public objection to the festival (perhaps, he hopes, they privately made unsuccessful representations in imperial ears), and by declaring that at least he has now discharged his conscience. The tone is one of resignation, as if he hardly hoped for any practical action. However, Gelasius could write collects for the masses for February and March, in which the texts of the prayers carry scarcely veiled allusions to his desire that his flock would eschew those things that are contrary to their Christian profession.

Similarly the July games at Rome in honour of Apollo, of whose importance Livy and Macrobius had written, continued in full currency during Boethius' time. In his commentary on Aristotle's *Categories*, he speaks of the festival as the present custom.[37]

The capacity of the old senatorial aristocracy to combine adhesion to the Church (which they seem to have felt was much too serious a matter to be left to the bishops) with a desire to maintain the fine old traditions of the past may perhaps by illustrated by a further fact. About 500 a complete edition of the letters of the fourth-century pagan senator, Symmachus, was produced by some admiring member of the family.[38] In other words, there was not the least desire to disown distinguished ancestors who, in past conflicts between paganism and Christianity, had been on the other side from that occupied by their descendants. The bonds of class and wealth are altogether too powerful. The aristocrats' love of the classical past emerges to a striking degree in the compositions of Ennodius whose early hopes of a successful marriage to a wealthy girl foundered, so that he had to seek a career as a cleric, at Milan until 513, then bishop of Pavia until his death in 521. All his writing is dominated by the values of rhetoric, with an artificial employment of classical images blended with Christian themes, with an absence of any reserve towards the erotic or the obscene, and with a mannered style which makes almost every sentence as hard as a nut but too frequently deficient in any real kernel of serious meaning. His life of his predecessor Epiphanius of Pavia shows that he knew what a bishop ought to be. But the ruling passion of his life lay in classical literature, allusions to which abound in his rococo pages. For stylistic rhetoric he had no more favourite model than Symmachus, the fourth-century pagan.

The conversion of the educated aristocratic families brought with it an affirmative attitude to the literature and thought of antiquity. In North Africa Fabius (or Flavius) Claudius Gordianus Fulgentius, *vir clarissimus*, wrote a commentary on Statius' poetry, an exposition of the first two books of Martianus Capella (below, p. 21), a glossary of rare words, an allegorical interpretation of fifty mythological fables (dedicated to a presbyter of Carthage named Catus), and an epitome of world history. It is very possible that he is identical with the bishop of Ruspe, author of weighty works of Augustinian theology, who also had some correspondence with two sisters of Boethius' wife Rusticiana. Fulgentius read the *Aeneid* as an allegory of the spiritual life. This Christian love of the past, even when associated with some of the external forms of pagan ceremony, is of some importance as background for estimating the position of Boethius and his circle between classical culture and Christian belief. He belongs to a community which values both and does not wish to be told that they ought to be making a choice.

Symmachus' influence on Boethius is of major consequence

in a further practical respect. Symmachus knew Greek[39] and had a deep interest in Neoplatonic philosophy. His circle is comparable to the Christian/Neoplatonist group at Milan, led by the presbyter Simplician and the layman Manlius Theodorus, with whom Augustine had close links when he moved to Milan in 384, and through whom he came to read Marius Victorinus' translations of Plotinus and Porphyry. Although a knowledge of Greek was less common among the Italian senators of this time (sufficiently so for their knowledge often to be a matter of record),[40] Symmachus and his friends desired to keep open contacts with Constantinople and the Greek empire. Symmachus would naturally have set Boethius on the course of assimilating the highest culture available in the Greek world of his time.

This culture was to be found in the Greek Neoplatonic schools.

The Neoplatonic schools[41]

The old debate concerning the disagreements between Plato and Aristotle came to be intensified during the third century AD. About 200 Alexander of Aphrodisias in Caria had taught in Athens as a professional teacher of Peripatetic philosophy, and composed voluminous (partly extant) commentaries, which posterity valued highly, on Aristotle's *Prior Analytics*, *Topics*, and *Metaphysics*; *On the Soul*; also monographs *On fate* and *On providence* (this last surviving only in Arabic). Some reaction to this fresh impetus in Aristotelianism can be discerned in Plotinus' wrestlings with the application of the ten categories to the higher Platonic world of supra-sensible reality (*Enneads* vi, 1–3). Plotinus' biographer and editor Porphyry vigorously argued the essential underlying harmony of Plato and Aristotle, and thereby made it necessary and right for the Platonists to study Aristotelian logic, a subject for which Porphyry felt high enthusiasm and on which he composed detailed expositions. A generation later, in the time of Constantine the Great, the Syrian scholar Iamblichus of Chalcis composed a lengthy commentary on Aristotle's *Categories*, incorporating its logic into a Platonic metaphysical scheme. Iamblichus also wrote an influential exposition of the handbook to arithmetic by the second-century Neopythagorean Nicomachus of Gerasa, whose work enjoyed huge authority in the Neoplatonic schools.

The Platonists of Boethius' time had their two principal schools in Athens and Alexandria. At Athens the Neoplatonic metaphysics were taught by Plutarch of Athens who died in advanced old age in 432, and by his pupils Syrianus (d. 437), Hierocles, and Proclus the Lycian (412–85). Hierocles (mid-fifth century) moved to Alexandria to lecture on Plato; he wrote a surviving commentary on the *Golden Verses* of Pythagoras and a work on providence known through two summaries in Photius' *Bibliotheca* (214 and 251). Syrianus remained at Athens to write commentaries not only on Plato's *Phaedrus* and *Parmenides* (lost except for some fragments) but also on four books of Aristotle's *Metaphysics* in which the uneasy relationship to Platonism occupies the centre of the stage. His pupil Proclus wrote particularly voluminous works including extant commentaries on Plato's *Republic*, *Timaeus*, and *Parmenides*; on the first book of Euclid's *Elements*; on Ptolemaic astronomy; and systematic treatises—one on the *Theology of Plato* in six books (nine were intended, but the last three either became lost or were never completed), and another being a series of axiomatic propositions in Neoplatonic metaphysics entitled *The Elements of Theology*. A poor epitome of this last work passed into Latin, anonymously, under the title *Liber de causis*, but was recognized to be Proclus' work by Thomas Aquinas in his commentary on the Latin text. Proclus also composed three tracts on providence and evil. Throughout Proclus writes as an enraged pagan, slipping in quiet references to Christianity in a tone of cold anger, as if 'the prevalent opinion' were a kind of intellectual Black Death that somehow had to be endured, and if possible survived, by wise men. His own role is not that of an original or creative thinker but largely that of a systematizer of prodigious diligence (his biographer Marinus says that he used to give five classes and write 700 lines every day); a schoolman setting out to reconcile all his authorities with one another, holding pagan faith in harmony with reason, and seeing dialectical skill as a preparation of mind and spirit for theology.

Proclus' commentaries on Aristotle's logical treatises have

not been preserved. His expositions of Porphyry's *Isagoge*, the *Categories, Interpretation*, and both *Analytics* continue to be occasionally cited by Alexandrian exegetes of the next century. In the main the chances of transmission have given us the Athenian school's commentaries on Plato and the Alexandrian school's commentaries on Aristotle. Perhaps chance is not the sole factor in this division, which could foster the illusion that at Athens Plato was exclusively favoured, at Alexandria Aristotle. The texts show that the Alexandrians prized Proclus as an exegete of the Organon, but also suggest that there was a slight difference of emphasis between the two schools. Aristotle's philosophy concerns this visible world, of natural science and of human moral relationships, and in comparison with Plato has relatively less to say about the religious nature and destiny of man or about the divine presence in the order of creation. An exegetical preference for Aristotle would be less likely to precipitate a sense of rivalry with Christian theology, whereas Proclus' detailed system of Platonic dogmatics easily appears as if it were almost intended as an alternative to Christian doctrine.

Proclus' lecture room attracted many pupils, though he was sad to see how, under Christian influence, Athens had become a small place. His successors as heads of the Athens school lack distinction until Damascius in the early decades of the sixth century. Damascius presided over the Platonic Academy in a spirit of conscious independence over against Proclus with whose dogmatic theology he was in some degree of disagreement. But he fully shared Proclus' militant hostility to Christianity, thereby helping to provoke the emperor Justinian's decision in 529 to close down the Athenian school and to take over its rich endowments.

At Alexandria the Neoplatonic school consistently appears less militantly and overtly anti-Christian than that at Athens. Perhaps Hypatia's murder by enraged monks in 415 encouraged the philosophers to be careful and to keep off dangerous subjects. Bishop Cyril of Alexandria (412–44) has no fame for tolerating paganism, but his writings show him to know his way in Aristotelian logic and Platonic metaphysics. After Hierocles, whose doctrines of providence have sometimes been mistakenly supposed to manifest Christian influence, the main

The Neoplatonic schools 19

Alexandrian teacher was Proclus' pupil Ammonius the son of Hermeias. Born about 435–45, Ammonius died between 517 and 526. His period of greatest activity therefore falls at the time when Boethius' education is in progress, and at a time when the Athenian school was being led by mediocre figures. On contemplating the massive literary output of Proclus, Ammonius may well have felt that he did not need to write so much. Damascius' biography of his own predecessor at Athens, Isidore, speaks of Ammonius with contempt, accusing him of having been led astray by avarice and of surrendering to the pressures of the bishop of Alexandria; i.e. of having been baptized not from conviction but from expediency. This conversion story is curiously borne out by a dialogue entitled *Ammonius* composed early in the sixth century by Zacharias Scholasticus. The dialogue (*PG* 85) is based on some evidently historical disputations at Alexandria between Christian and pagan, and concerns the creation of the world in time and the destructibility or everlastingness of the cosmos, especially the heavenly bodies. The dialogue concludes with Ammonius conceding victory to his Christian opponent.

Ammonius' Alexandrian pupils include two major figures, whose writings contain numerous passages that illuminate matter in Boethius. In the 520s John Philoponus, a Monophysite Christian, wrote a vehement attack on Proclus' opinions about the eternity of the world. He also composed commentaries on Aristotle with acknowledgements to his notes of Ammonius' lectures. Ammonius' other principal pupil, Simplicius, remained intransigently pagan, and came to find it better to leave Alexandria. He joined Damascius at Athens from where he could more easily indulge in polemic against John Philoponus. Like Proclus, Simplicius tends to be long-winded and voluminous, but his works are a mine of information for the history of later Greek philosophy. His commentary on the *Categories* used two sources also available to Boethius, Porphyry and Iamblichus, and often provides indispensable clues to Boethius' meaning and background. In addition to his long commentary on the *Categories*, Simplicius composed expositions of Aristotle's *Physics* and *de Caelo*, in part designed to combat Philoponus' shocking Christian opinions that between the divine Creator and this created world there is a great gulf fixed, and that the physics or chemistry of stars and celestial bodies is identical with that of the earth. Simplicius' most rewarding and instructive work, however, is his commentary on the handbook (*Enchiridion*) of Epictetus, in effect a sustained essay on the moral life and on providence. It contains a full onslaught on the dualist Manichee solution to the problem of evil, and at one point a remarkable, even strident assertion of the indispensable social role of the philosopher in society.

To turn from any of Boethius' works, and especially from the theological tractates and the last three books of the *Consolation of Philosophy*, to a study of the Athenian and Alexandrian Neoplatonists is to be immediately aware of his intimate intellectual affinities with them. Much in Boethius which at first appears to modern readers obscure or even obfuscating looks rational and unsurprising when placed in the cultural context of the contemporary Greek philosophers. Although Proclus is never mentioned by name, Boethius' direct familiarity with many of his extant writings is easily demonstrated. He may also have known some of Ammonius' expositions of Aristotle and of Porphyry's *Isagoge*; but the case for asserting immediate dependence is not coercive as it is for Proclus. There is no way of proving the hypothesis, long sustained through an erudite series of books and articles by Pierre Courcelle, that in his adolescence Boethius studied at Alexandria under Ammonius. Nor, on the other hand, is there any improbability about the conjecture. At this period a young, intellectually ambitious Roman would think Alexandria an attractive place for philosophical study. The Roman pagan Messius Phoebus Severus moved from Rome to study at Alexandria early in the 460s, to be recalled by the emperor Anthemius in 467 to become city prefect and then in 470 consul, which led pagans (attested in Damascius' *Life of Isidore*) to dream of a revival of the old religion at Rome, about a decade before Boethius' birth. What stands beyond controversy is that Boethius' literary and educational programme is a faithful reflection of the assumptions and teaching practice of the contemporary Platonic schools of Athens and Alexandria, the latter being of much higher standing after Proclus' death in 485. In these schools, as the Greek texts make clear, young students were introduced to arithmetic through Nicomachus of Gerasa, to harmony through Nicomachus and Ptolemy, to geometry through Euclid, to astronomy through Ptolemy's *Syntaxis* (the 'Almagest'); then the Organon of Aristotle to which Porphyry's *Isagoge* is prefixed, together with specialized monographs on unconditional and conditional syllogisms; finally up to metaphysical questions such as evil and providence or the supreme God at the apex of Platonic theology.

Boethius was not the only Latin writer of his age to share the enthusiasms of the Greek Platonists. Apuleius, Marius Victorinus, Calcidius, and Macrobius, among others, anticipated many of Boethius' concerns. In Vandal Carthage probably in the 460s or 470s Martianus Minneus Felix Capella composed his bizarre and curiously fascinating work *The Marriage of Philology and Mercury*, written in alternating prose and verse—that is, in the literary genre of 'Menippean Satire'. Its genre is a likely model for Boethius' *Consolation of Philosophy*. The last poem in Martianus' work suggests that he had held office as proconsul and wrote in old age for his son's instruction. His work begins with two books of neoplatonizing, semi-gnostic fantasy which show him to be profoundly impregnated with Platonic mysticism of a type akin to that of Proclus. He also shows a little of Apuleius' liking for the erotic. Martianus was a student of the pagan gnostic verses called *Chaldean Oracles* which Proclus held in the utmost veneration as the directly revealed word of God, and his Greek reading almost certainly included much Porphyry and Iamblichus, whom he refers to as 'a certain Syrian'. Within a framework of pagan myth and allegory he portrays the way in which the love of learning in seven of Varro's nine liberal arts (in the order Grammar, Dialectic, Rhetoric, Geometry including much geography, Arithmetic, Astronomy, Harmony—omitting Medicine and Architecture) can become a pathway up to the company of heaven; Mercury being the mediator between human and divine and making possible, with the help of the nine Muses, the lady Philology's ascent through the seven planets to join the gods above. Much of the seventh book of Martianus depends on Nicomachus' *Arithmetic*, but with additions from Euclid. For Music he makes use of the neoplatonist Aristides Quintilianus (below, p. 83). Unlike Boethius Martianus betrays no touch of Christian influence. The symbolist and ironic style of his writing, together with the allusiveness and difficulty of his outré Latinity which often defeated his medieval scribes, enabled him to present polytheistic and astrological material in a manner that Christian commentators from Carolingian times could interpret as acceptable. A few verbal parallels in the verses of the *Consolation of Philosophy* suggest that Boethius had read his work (below, p. 297 n. 10); if so, he will have discerned more quality in Martianus' verses than modern critics have been able to discover.

In his commentaries on Aristotle all Boethius' sources are pagan, and he stands fully within the cultural tradition that they represent. As late as 515 in the mature second commentary on *Interpretation*, he has no inhibitions about writing that the sun and stars are 'divine bodies', immune from change other than movement because they are not susceptible of admitting contraries (*Perih.* ii, 238, 22 ff.; 244, 26; 249, 18–22). On the other hand, in the same work he later defines as 'divine' those incorporeal entities which undergo no movement or growth or diminution, but in the fullness of their nature are 'tota ubique' (ii, 459). The contrast in this last passage should not be attributed to inward pressure from, or sensitivity to, Christian insistence on the creaturely status of celestial bodies, for the same antithesis appears as a school commonplace in Ammonius' commentary on *Perihermeneias* (p. 243, 35–244, 1—heavenly bodies move, while unmovable entities are the divine causes in the intelligible world). Nevertheless even in Boethius' Aristotelian commentaries there is a sense of keeping the pagan religious tradition at arm's length. In the second commentary on Porphyry he describes the naming of this world as a god or Jove as language used by the 'ancients', *veteres* (*CSEL* 48 p. 208, 22); and the ascription of the divine title to sun and stars is accepted usage in 'the veneration of antiquity' (p. 259, 21).

Out of the ivory tower: John the deacon

Boethius' youthful writings on arithmetic and music attracted attention, and gained an immediate public reputation for him: 'for the liberal arts without a parallel.' Soon Theoderic was asking him, through a letter drafted by Cassiodorus, to design for the Burgundian king a sundial and, for night or indoor use or for rainy days, a waterclock. These were evidently intended as specimens of advanced Roman technology to impress and to gain the alliance of unsophisticated but dangerous Gallic tribesmen. (That Boethius possessed the practical technical competence must be very doubtful.) He was similarly asked to select a harpist to be sent to the Frankish king Clovis, no doubt in the hope that soft music would do something to tame his aggressiveness. Cultural exchanges may contribute to détente. Boethius' arithmetical fame even led Theoderic to ask his advice about the proper exchange rate between copper denarii, at this time much devalued, and the gold solidus, a question which arose out of complaints by palace soldiery that their pay in denarii was unfair.[42] As an outward sign of recognition Boethius was granted the title 'patricius' already by the year 507. In the same year Ennodius writes addressing him as 'magnitudo tua'. Looking back on his youth in the *Consolation of Philosophy* (ii, 3, 7) he realized that he had received honours then such as are denied men at the end of their careers.

Admiration came to the young Boethius partly because of the immense influence of Q. Aurelius Memmius Symmachus (in the *Consolation* Boethius is very frank about the assistance that Symmachus was able to give him in promoting his interests), and partly because of his cultivated learning. Cassiodorus mentions a bucolic poem by Boethius (*condidit et carmen bucolicum*, says the *Anecdoton Holderi*). The opening poem of the *Consolation of Philosophy* recalls how as a young man he used to write poetry. The various metres, and innumerable literary allusions and reminiscences, of the thirty-nine poems in this work richly illustrate both Boethius' love for the classical tradition in Latin poetry and also his own skill and sensitivity as a poet in his own right. Phrases from Vergil, Ovid, Horace, Seneca, Lucan, Statius, Prudentius, and Claudian are often woven together to make a fresh and brilliant tapestry. Joachim Gruber (1978) has remarked on the ingenious way in which the various types of metre are distributed through the work, taking *O qui perpetua* (iii m. 9) as the central climax and halfway point, on each side of which Boethius allocates the most frequent metres, but avoiding repetition of the same metre twice in any one book. Moreover, each poem has some link connecting it with the immediately adjacent prose section of the *Consolation*, and is no mere intermezzo in the argument but actually carries the thought and argument further on its way. As a poet Boethius may not merit the highest acclaim, but his best is remarkably good, vastly superior to Martianus Capella.

Boethius' labours on Aristotelian logic earned him less popularity. Formal logic, even when expansively illustrated and explained by Boethius' rich store of examples, seemed too technical and esoteric a discipline to interest Roman aristocrats, conditioned by Cicero and the long traditions of public life to think of oratory as the principal thing. Dialectic could be worth studying if it helped to win a case in the law courts. But logic pursued for its own sake was not a Latin predilection. Boethius frequently mentions unkind critics who bitingly suggest that his publications in this area, which cost him much sweat, are for ostentation rather than use. These references to malicious critics look more than a mere literary convention.

Boethius' elevation to the consulship is to be seen as a recognition of his rank and capacity to pay rather than as a decision to emerge from his library to take active part in the business of government. Nevertheless, even as consul his conception of his duties was more than merely ceremonial. With considerable courage in 510 he opposed the eminent and senior praetorian prefect Faustus Niger when, at a time of severe famine, Faustus proposed the compulsory purchase of food in Campania at low prices which would have reduced the farmers to destitution. Theoderic was impressed by Boethius' arguments and Faustus suffered a defeat.[43]

Three or four years later he was again deeply immersed in his long exposition of Aristotle's difficult treatise on *Interpretation*. So far as the evidence goes, it seems to have been a growing interest in the contemporary problems of the Church which led him, if not out of his private study, at least into writing a work with a practical consequence for the Roman church's policy in approaching the Greek churches. This work is the fifth but earliest of the five theological tractates or opuscula sacra. It was occasioned by his intellectual impatience with the terminological chaos of the debates, then racking the Greek churches, whether Christ's double being, as both divine and human, should be expressed in terms of 'two natures but one person' (as the Council of Chalcedon formulated it) or as 'one person, therefore one nature' (as the Monophysites of Egypt and Syria insisted). The fifth tractate shows Boethius being drawn out of his ivory tower to take sides in a complex debate whose intricacies he is well able to grasp. The formula which his argument favours, though not at that time the one smiled upon by the then Pope Hormisdas and his principal advisers among the higher Roman clergy, is that which was soon to receive the public backing of Justinian. A detailed study of the fifth tractate shows Boethius building a bridge to the ecclesiastical policy of reconciliation between Chalcedonian and Monophysite which Justinian would pursue throughout his career. The subject had the attraction for him that he could continue in his library, all dedicated to closeness and the bettering of his mind, while at the same time making a much needed contribution to the clarification of very confused issues.

To the historian it is convenient to use the labels Chalcedonian and Monophysite, the former label to describe those who, with whatever qualifications, stood by the definition of the council of 451 that Christ is one person and one hypostasis but known *in* two natures; the latter label to describe those who rejected Chalcedon and taught that, if Christ is one person and one hypostasis, he must also be one nature as incarnate Lord, though '*of* two natures'. In the fifth and sixth centuries each side called its own position 'orthodox', and 'Monophysite' is the Chalcedonians' term for describing their opponents. Both sides were less than fair to their antagonists, the Chalcedonians persistently refusing to acknowledge any clear distinction between a doctrine in effect merely verbally Monophysite (as in Severus of Antioch) and a radically Monophysite position such as that of the archimandrite Eutyches, condemned at Chalcedon in 451, denying that the humanity of Christ is of one substance with ours. Severus unremittingly disowned and condemned Eutychian doctrines as much as any Chalcedonian. On the other hand, Severus and his party refused to concede any clear distinction between the Chalcedonians (of any shade) and the radically diphysite Nestorians, for whom the unity of the person of Christ seemed secondary to the duality of the natures constituting the incarnate Lord.

The western churches were profoundly attached to the Christological definition of Chalcedon because it enshrined and acknowledged the doctrine of Pope Leo the Great's Tome. Chalcedon was valued not only as a statement of dogmatic truth but also as a recognition of Rome's primatial teaching authority by the Greek churches. But in Egypt and parts of Syria the open welcome given to the Chalcedonian definition by theologians suspected of Nestorian sympathies caused the utmost alarm; the see of Rome had no authority to foster heresy. Greek theologians anxious to defend the decisions of Chalcedon easily came to feel that Rome's interventions in the East were not marked by the highest sensitivity. To the Byzantine East Rome seemed to lack a theologian of quality to explain the issues. The fifth tractate in Boethius' opuscula sacra first changed this situation.

The fifth tractate, against Eutyches and Nestorius (below, p. 180), is dedicated to Boethius' friend and spiritual father John the deacon of Rome. John is the name of one of the seven city deacons during the troubled times of the conflicts between Pope Symmachus and Laurentius for possession of the Roman see. A deacon of this name appears in the lists for Symmachus' synod of March 499 (both presence and subscription lists) and also that of 6 November 502 which Symmachus presided over after his formal 'acquittal' of the charges against him, if that is a correct description of the October synod's denial of its own competence to judge them. After 502, however, the fearsome conflicts in the city streets and Pope Symmachus' loss of moral authority seem to have made John turn towards the episcopal visitor Peter of Altinum (Altino immediately north of Venice airport, then a substantial town on the coast of the lagoon) whom Theoderic had put in to hold the ring between the two contestants for the see. John the deacon collaborated with Peter for time. On 18 September 506, after the king's verdict for Symmachus, he put to the Pope a paper formally withdrawing his acknowledgement of the visitor's authority, and resubmitting himself to Symmachus' lawful jurisdiction. John the deacon's position during the troubled years did not diminish his high standing among the Roman clergy. He was of good repute for learning. Boethius was not the only Roman senator to look to him for instruction. A letter is preserved (*PL* 59, 399) which John addressed to Senarius, a Roman friend perhaps of Germanic ancestry and relative of Ennodius (*ep.* i, 13; v, 15–16). Senarius held a post in the court bureaucracy at Ravenna. He was sufficiently trusted by Theoderic to be sent on embassies both to the Byzantine court (*Variae*, v, 3–4) and to more distant Germanic princes (Ennodius, *ep.* v, 15–16). His extant epitaph expatiates on his pride in a wide diplomatic experience. (This out-of-the-way text is printed in Mommsen's *Cassiodorus* p. 499.) Renatus, *vir spectabilis*, conveyed from Senarius to John a letter inquiring about various liturgical customs of the Catholic Church, especially those of baptism for which he sometimes finds no biblical authority. The end of John's reply is lost. At the point where the manuscript breaks off, he is giving additional evidence of his obsession with logical questions, already evident from Boethius' opuscula dedicated to him. The body of the letter provides a major source of information for Roman baptismal customs early in the sixth century. It is perhaps more than a conventional turn of phrase when John congratulates Senarius that he has not 'concealed his zeal' for these matters of Catholic usage; in view of his position at the Arian court, this is perhaps more than stereotyped flattery, especially if Senarius (as his name suggests) is of Germanic origin. In any event, the letter to Senarius is good evidence of the high reputation enjoyed by John the deacon as a man of serious scholarship. The bringer of the letter, the senator Renatus, is also attested on a visit to Constantinople about 508–11 where, in fluent Greek, he engaged in controversy on the Christological problem with no less an antagonist than Severus of Antioch. At Constantinople also, perhaps on a later visit, Renatus (p. 256) commissioned an eminent scribe Theodorus to copy for him a collection of Boethius' dialectical writings; the corpus collected in Renatus' codex survives in a Fleury manuscript of the eleventh century now divided between Orléans and the Bibliothèque Nationale in Paris.

Pope Hormisdas (514–23) did not entrust responsibility to John in the course of his prickly negotiations with Constantinople in 515, 517, and 519–20. Nevertheless John the deacon, friend of Boethius, is likely to be identical with Hormisdas' successor, Pope John I (523–6). His personal associations with Boethius and his intellectual interests would make him favour close relations between old and new Rome, orthodoxy being assured after the reunion of 519. In 523 the Roman clergy and senators would see no hazard in electing a pro-Byzantine candidate to the papacy. And at the time of his election Theoderic also would have thought John a congenial figure in high ecclesiastical office. The re-establishment of communion between Rome and Byzantium in July 519 changed the complexion of the pro-Byzantine party at Rome. Before 518 its policy had been to find some ground for theological agreement with the emperor Anastasius and his patriarch, which necessarily meant some working acceptance or toleration of the Henoticon (p. 30, below). After 519 to be pro-Byzantine in Italy meant the opposite in theology to what it had meant previously. One would now be for rapprochement with the East if one was a zealous Chalcedonian. In 530 the pro-Byzantine group, in a contested election for the papacy, elected and consecrated the ex-Alexandrian deacon Dioscorus (below p. 65) who cordially hated the least concession to the critics of Chalcedonian Christology and who had long experience as a diplomat, first on behalf of Pope Symmachus in successful negotiations with Theoderic in 506, then on behalf of Hormisdas during his delicate negotiations with the East. Similar forces are likely to have been in operation on the death of Hormisdas in 523, which would make the election of the deacon John more rather than less probable. And with Boethius in high office at Ravenna, any advice tendered to Theoderic would obviously be favourable to John's election receiving the king's approbation.

There is inherent probability in the hypothesis that Boethius' fourth tractate *De fide catholica* reflects the catechetical instruction given to him by John. Of the way in which John's friendship and guidance became important to Boethius we have no evidence. But it is certain from the third theological tractate, likewise dedicated to John, that this distinguished

Roman cleric possessed a strong interest in intricate questions of Neoplatonic logic where they touched on matters of metaphysics and theology. Boethius' acknowledges himself to be John's 'son', in matters of spirituality and religion under his direction and pastoral care. In the second tractate he seeks to disentangle for John a major logical problem concerning the doctrine of the Trinity, namely whether or not the terms 'Father' and 'Son' are terms expressing 'substance'. He concludes with the request that John will judge whether Boethius' position is sound and 'of the faith' and that, where he dissents from Boethius, he will consider Boethius' argument with care and sympathy and reflect whether it is otherwise possible to conjoin faith and reason. The first tractate is a much fuller examination of the logic of Trinitarian language, and of theology in general, dedicated to his father-in-law Symmachus, with whom alone (he says) he discusses these delicate questions. The tractate begins with the important remark that it is the fruit of a very lengthy pondering of the questions at issue; it comes out of prolonged reflection on the writings of Augustine.

The eastern Church debates about the unity of the person of Christ entailed cognate questions concerning the doctrine of the Trinity, and at Rome itself anxious discussions took place about 519–20 inquiring into the legitimacy of a Greek liturgical acclamation 'One of the Trinity was crucified for us'. Can the Holy Trinity be separately numbered? Boethius sees the discussion in relation to Neoplatonist logical inquiries into questions of identity and difference: to say that x and y are 'the same' also implies that there is some kind of distinction between them, or the assertion of their identity would hardly be interesting. Moreover, the theopaschite assertion that the divine being 'suffers' might be tolerable in the language of devotion and adoration, but needed elaboration if it were to be proposed in a formal theological statement designed to bring divided Christians together.

The hard road to Church unity:
the Acacian and Laurentian schisms[44]

Since the Council of Chalcedon (451) ecclesiastical dissension had come to have social and political consequences for relations between East and West. In 482 a new Chalcedonian bishop of Alexandria, John Talaia, turned out to be politically unacceptable to the emperor Zeno; ejected by the Monophysite majority, who restored the moderate anti-Chalcedonian Peter Mongos who had briefly held the see in 477, he fled to Rome. Acacius, patriarch of Constantinople (482–9) re-established communion with Alexandria's new patriarch Peter on the basis of the Henoticon, Zeno's edict of union, designed to exclude Nestorianism as Leo's Tome and the Chalcedonian definition did not. As a gloss on Chalcedon the Henoticon might have stood, though it conceded that some at Chalcedon held heretical opinions. As a substitute for Chalcedon, even though it condemned Eutyches along with Nestorius, it offered inadequate defence against radically Monophysite positions. Pope Simplicius, while uncommitted to John Talaia, knew he could not accept Peter Mongos, and felt insulted that in so weighty a matter Acacius ignored him. But he died in 483 and left it for his successor Felix III (483–92) to break communion with Acacius on the ground that it was intolerable, in disregard of Roman authority, to establish communion on the ground of a document sanctioned by no synod and capable of being construed not merely as a supplement to but also as a subtle censure of the Chalcedonian definition that Christ is 'in two natures'. Felix's successor Gelasius (492–6) vehemently asserted Rome's rights of jurisdiction and, in spiritual matters, the superiority of his see to any emperor. The standing of the second see of Christendom in Alexandria (Constantinople 'the royal city' being in Gelasius' view an upstart) was for the first see to determine; moreover, popes could act on their own without needing synods to give validity to their decisions. In theology, however, Gelasius took cautious conciliatory moves, disguised as polemic, towards placating the more moderate critics of Chalcedon.

Under the brief pontificate of Anastasius II (496–8) secret moves of a more drastic rapprochement with the Alexandrians were made, politically linked with Theoderic's desire for recognition from the emperor Anastasius (491–518). But the leaking of the proposals, under which the West might accept the Henoticon as a gloss on Chalcedon and Leo if the East dropped the mention of Acacius' name at the eucharistic memorial, aroused alarm. At Rome it provoked the emergence of a hard-line opposition to détente with Constantinople and in November 498 impassioned rivalry for the papal succession. The pro-Byzantine Laurentius would have continued Pope Anastasius' soft approach. He was an ascetic commanding the suffrage of almost all senators and many parish clergy in the city. The anti-Byzantine party preemptively elected Symmachus, a Sardinian outsider, a convert from paganism, and one of the seven city deacons (a group often unloved by the parochial clergy jealous for the independence of their old title-churches, each with its endowments). Symmachus survived unhurt from the angry shower of stones that greeted him from his opponents. His policy was to make no concessions in theology or otherwise, and to assert Rome's universal jurisdiction with unrelenting fortissimo. By huge largess he won both the Roman plebs and the Ravenna officials. Theoderic decided for Symmachus whose consecration had preceded that of Laurentius by an hour or so, and the Italian bishops followed the king's lead. Another see, at a price, was found for Laurentius near Naples, and peace was sufficiently restored for the king himself to stay in Rome in 500, there to be received by Symmachus at St. Peter's where Theoderic conducted himself with every sign of devotion. On 1 March 499 Symmachus presided over a hastily assembled synod of Italian bishops, by way of establishing his authority. He sought agreed canonical procedures for episcopal elections at Rome when a pope dies ('quod absit') without having designated his successor. The ostensible intention was to avert the unedifying tumults that accompanied the double election of November 498. The main motives, however, seem to have been to keep out lay influence and to imply that under normal procedures and precedents the reigning pope possesses by divine right such absolute powers that he may nominate his successor without looking to any legitimation from the election or consent of plebs or clergy.

Symmachus offered too many hostages to his opponents. In 501 with probably deliberate and, if so, foolish defiance, he used the old Roman 84-year cycle to compute the date of Easter on 25 March. By the Alexandrian computation, also upheld in Pope Leo I's time by the table of Victorius of Aquitaine, Easter for 501 fell on 22 April, this date being kept not only by the Greeks but by northern Italy and by the Gothic churches. The king asked the Pope to come and discuss the divergence. Symmachus was kept waiting at Rimini for a summons to join the court. Walking there on the shore he saw a group of women also *en route* for Ravenna, and realized that Easter was not the only subject on Theoderic's agenda. That night he secretly left for Rome and sought asylum in St. Peter's. At Ravenna Theoderic and his nobles heard grave charges which the nocturnal flight to Rome seemed to confirm.

The Pope had sold church property to provide funds for Rome's poor, to win support among African refugees from Vandal persecution now settled in Trastevere, and frankly to bribe the court. (Some years later Ennodius writes begging an influential friend to cajole Symmachus into repaying a loan of 400 gold solidi provided by the bishop of Milan on Ennodius' guarantee for the sweetening of officials 'whose names it would not be safe to mention'.) But now the Laurentian party was dramatically assisted by rouged lady-friends of Symmachus' intemperate, pagan past, including a courtesan popularly known as Spicy (Conditaria). Slaves of Symmachus' household were questioned—without torture which, in accordance with normal Roman usage in sexual cases, Theoderic forbade; they testified to the Pope's continued association with Spicy. Theoderic realized that Symmachus was becoming hard to support. The refusal to come to Ravenna seemed an admission of guilt. Soon there was disagreement whether or not Theoderic had already expressed a verdict at the preliminary hearing at Ravenna. The king was aware that the case must be remitted to a synod, and that it would be politically explosive for him to adjudicate in an ecclesiastical matter. Yet the charges of immoral life were already leading to a massive loss of confidence in the Pope among the Roman clergy. The king was personally persuaded of Symmachus' guilt, or at least of the impossibility of his continuing in office, and felt it to be his duty to act in protection of the Catholic Church.

When in 418 two rivals had been elected pope, the emperor Honorius had expelled both from Rome and temporarily entrusted the Easter baptisms and care of the church property to the bishop of Spoleto, pending clarification. Following this precedent, at the request of a substantial group of Roman clergy and senators, Theoderic appointed a visitor, Peter of Altinum, to celebrate Easter at the Lateran basilica and baptistery and to be responsible for the church estates and revenues. This procedure was often adopted by popes themselves during Italian vacancies, as is plentifully illustrated in the correspondence of Gregory the Great. Theoderic explicitly ruled that until Symmachus had answered his accusers face to face, his position was in suspense, and he could exercise no rights over the revenues and temporalities of his office. This procedure, however, implied that in the king's eyes the see of Rome was still vacant. It was unlikely to be approved by the Italian bishops for whom Symmachus' lawful tenure had been settled in 499, Laurentius concurring, and for whom intervention by the king was in principle objectionable.

In 502, at the request of senators and clergy alienated from Symmachus but with the written consent of the Pope himself, Theoderic instructed a large number of Italian bishops to meet in synod at Rome under the presidency of Milan, Ravenna, and Aquileia; the last being sympathetic to Laurentius' cause, the first two being at first impartial and hesitant, but then persuaded that they must uphold Symmachus. The king committed authority to this synod to review the charges, setting aside without prejudice the preliminary hearing at Ravenna in Symmachus' absence which at least showed there was a case to answer. The synod was directed to examine 'all relevant witnesses', to invite Symmachus to state his defence, and then to reach a decisive verdict in the solemn awareness that only so could public order be restored to the city where the streets were becoming hazardous. But what was the basis of the synod's authority?

At the first session, not long after Easter, Symmachus himself appeared from his sanctuary at St. Peter's. No tumult attended his presence. He made a carefully planned declaration: that no synod could validly meet without papal consent and ratification; that the present synod was one that he welcomed and accepted, subject to its procedure being in strict accord with canon law; and that he would attend for an examination of the charges against him if and when the king's visitor Peter of Altinum was withdrawn so that there would be no questioning of his legitimacy as pope. A majority of the synod thought this reasonable and wrote to Theoderic to ask for this to be done. But Theoderic refused to withdraw the visitor and to restore the temporalities to Symmachus until, after due process, he had been declared innocent by the synod. It then appeared that in any event Symmachus interpreted canon law to grant no power to a synod to judge the legitimate holder of the primatial see. Most of the bishops had no desire to prove the contrary. A threat to the pope was felt to menace the authority of the entire episcopate and its independence of secular government as taught by Pope Gelasius. The synod therefore found itself in a paralyzing position: called into being by the Arian king and in canon law held impotent to act in the matter remitted to it. The strictest supporters of Symmachus held that, unless the synod were called and directed by the pope himself, it had no authority to meet at all, and would cause nothing but confusion by attempting to hold any sessions. After a series of dithering consultations through the hot Roman summer and amid growing violence in the city, which led a number of bishops to sneak away quietly, the surviving rump sadly came to feel themselves pawns in a lay conflict between rival city factions and even the mere tools of Theoderic's will, since the king laid full responsibility for a verdict on the synod's shoulders, but made no secret of his opinion that this pope was guilty. 'Priestly simplicity', they wrote to Theoderic in a report (probably mid-September) 'is no match for secular cunning.'

At a second session of the synod assembled at the king's express order on 1 September, an unheralded Symmachus suddenly arrived from St. Peter's with a crowd of supporters and protested that his legitimate rights had not yet been restored so that in his eyes the synod had lost all validity as an ecclesiastical assembly; the king could of course do whatever he wished. An affray broke out in which some were wounded and others died. But Symmachus' appearing prevented any possibility of action against him for contumacy. He retired to St. Peter's once more, bruised but morally in the ascendant. The synod was now in despair, its pleas to the senators ignored, its admonitions of dissident clergy simply scorned, its authority as a court successfully denied by the defendant on grounds which many of the bishops believed correct. Symmachus ignored all summons. At last Theoderic allowed them to express their verdict without having brought the Pope to meet his accusers, and on 23 October the synod (many bishops being absent) formally declared Symmachus not indeed to be morally innocent, which God alone could judge, but to be the canonical occupant of Peter's see immune from the sentence of inferior bishops. Acting not under canon law but under the royal mandate and claiming both Roman and canon law to justify their refusal to accept slaves' evidence as admissible, the synod refused to condemn. This refusal presupposed Symmachus' undisputed legitimacy as pope. Theoderic had already agreed that, if the synod acquitted, the Lateran and the church chest should be restored to him. The synod therefore asked for the restoration to be implemented. So in practice, not in principle, the king's wishes were defied. The synod noted that Symmachus enjoyed the support of 'almost all the plebs' whose anger it was unwise to incur and whose accurate aim with stones some had had opportunity to verify.

The left-handed acquittal was in law a triumph for Symmachus, but did nothing to assist his moral standing. It therefore failed conspicuously to restore the 'civilitas' which Theoderic felt to be the mark of his reign and which he had particularly charged the synod to restore to the dangerous streets of the 'royal city' of Rome. There the effect of the synod's judgement was to heighten the tension to explosive force and soon to make it seem that all hell had been let loose. Theoderic saw no good reason for handing over to Symmachus either the Lateran or the church treasury at the bidding of a synod that had so signally failed.

With Symmachus in control of St. Peter's at the Vatican and Peter of Altinum at St. John Lateran, the tension profoundly disrupted the normal liturgical life of the Christian community. Devout Laurentians could not visit the shrine of St. Peter, and had to be content with the old third-century shrine dedicated to both St. Peter and St. Paul on the Via Appia, now San Sebastiano. This Laurentian difficulty may explain a famous crux, viz. the omission of the shrine on the Vatican hill from the entry for 29 June in the 'Depositio Martyrum' in the

Liberian Catalogue or chronograph of 354: 'III kal.Iul. Petri in Catacumbas et Pauli Ostense Tusco et Basso cons' [AD 258]. Our transmitted text of the Depositio Martyrum, with the remaining items in the calendar of 354, depends on Renaissance copies at Brussels and Vienna of two eighth- or ninth-century manuscripts, one of which has been lost since the seventeenth century while the other now survives only in a few fragments at Berne. But both copies agree in all essentials of the entry for 29 June. The silence about the Vatican shrine is so extraordinary that it is usual to assume an accidental corruption of an original identical with the entry for 29 June in the sixth-century *Martyrologium Hieronymianum* ('Peter at the Vatican, Paul on the road to Ostia, both at Catacumbas'). But the transmitted text would be natural enough if the Carolingian manuscripts were dependent on a model written in the Laurentian camp about 502–6, at a time when the faithful were not encouraged to include the Vatican in their lengthy processions on the city's patronal festival. During this period of four years the opponents of Symmachus could celebrate St. Peter only at the 'basilica of the apostles' on the Via Appia by the place Catacumbas which gave its name to the catacombs.

The almanack of 354 is characterized by its quiet juxtaposition of calendars of pagan and Christian festivals, with lists of emperors, consuls, and popes. Its contents would make it a congenial text deserving of careful preservation in the senatorial circle supporting Laurentius.

On Symmachus' side the archivists were also kept busy forging documents in his interest with bogus Acta censuring the senate as inherently pagan, attacking the Easter table of Victorius of Aquitaine, fictionally recounting the vindication of an earlier pope, Xystus III, from a malicious charge of adultery, and asserting the transcendence of Peter's successor over all synods to be venerable tradition and no innovation.

For the Laurentians supreme ecclesiastical authority resided in episcopal councils, not, as for Symmachus and his party, in the pope apart from a council. But now the synodical weapon they had themselves asked for had backfired with an 'incongruous acquittal' cast in terms unlikely to persuade alienated presbyters in Rome's title-churches to obey their bishop in all things lawful and honest. Support for Symmachus among both presbyters and even deacons became further eroded, and he had to ensure enough friends by ordaining replacements in exceptional numbers. He shut himself up in St. Peter's as a citadel, leaving Peter of Altinum at the Lateran and the city churches to the Laurentians, Laurentius himself being now back in Rome evidently with a much irritated king's permission. On 29 June, feast of St. Peter and St. Paul, as Ennodius makes clear, rivalry was acute between Rome's two apostolic shrines. At this time the basilica of St. Paul's was decorated with papal portraits including a medallion of Laurentius visible as late as the seventeenth century when a surviving copy was made for Cardinal Francesco Barberini. Paradoxically the Laurentians' claims for the recognition of their candidate as morally true pope were undermined by the continuing presence in Rome of Peter of Altinum, whom Theoderic did not withdraw until 506. Ennodius takes ironic pleasure in observing that Peter had originally been appointed on royal authority at the petition of the Laurentians and that, though his role as visitor was unacceptable both to Symmachus and to the king's synod of 502, he equally prevented Laurentius from gaining control of the chest or recognition outside Rome. Unintentionally, therefore, Peter served Symmachus' cause more than that of Laurentius.

Relations between Ravenna and Constantinople cooled sharply after 505 when conflict broke out in Illyricum, and in 508 the Byzantine fleet harassed the Italian Adriatic coast (reported by Marcellinus Comes). Clovis' conversion to Catholicism and the ensuing alliance between Franks and Byzantines made Theoderic feel encircled by the emperor Anastasius' plots. So, after a dreadful four years of gang warfare, sectarian killings, and mob violence, Theoderic came to think even a discredited pope better than murderous chaos, especially if his record showed him to be cool towards the Greeks. Symmachus' cause was successfully pleaded by an Alexandrian deacon at Rome named Dioscorus, a man with thorough understanding of Byzantine church affairs and vehemently opposed to Anastasius. In September 506 Theoderic's verdict went in favour of Symmachus, the senators being instructed to restore his rights over the Lateran and city churches. Laurentius at once retired to a hermitage on the estates of his leading senatorial supporter Festus, ending his days in severe mortifications.

An overt move on Laurentius' behalf by the emperor Anastasius would clearly have been counter-productive. On the other hand the emperor's letter to Pope Symmachus, which he answers in the undated but probably late *ep.* 10, refuses to acknowledge Symmachus' legitimacy, treats him as an avowed enemy of the emperor's policy, and blames him for a cold rebuff which that policy has received from the Roman senators. The emperor also accuses Symmachus of being a Manichee, a charge which is probably an allusion to the attacks on the Pope's salon of feminine friends, since a standard accusation against Manichees is that outwardly they profess to live frugal ascetic lives and secretly indulge in unacceptable erotic practices. This correspondence presupposes an alliance in policy towards the East between Symmachus and the Roman senate. It must therefore be later than 506 and may be as late as 512.

The conflicts at Rome were far more than a quarrel between those Italians who favoured and those who opposed an accommodation with the Greek Church and empire, so that it is a delicate question to determine whether the disagreement under Pope Anastasius II was more an occasion than a fundamental cause of the Roman schism. Explosive local tensions of a social character almost wholly submerged the issue of the Acacian schism and how Rome should deal with it. The pro-Symmachus documents of the time (the synodal acts of 502, Ennodius' defence of the synod's verdict against a Laurentian pamphlet, and the Life of Symmachus in the *Liber Pontificalis*) never directly accuse his opponents of compromise with Eutychian heresy; it is hard to believe they would have failed to do so had the charge been plausible. It is as if the issue of a monstrous control over the Church by the king or by lay senators, or the dread of a possibly adulterous pope, so frightened the combatants that they quite forgot the origin of their quarrel.

Symmachus enjoyed the support of many of the plebs. The synod of 502 exaggerates in claiming 'almost all', since for the session on 1 September they asked Theoderic to provide an armed guard to conduct Symmachus safely from St. Peter's to their meeting-place in 'Jerusalem the basilica of the Sessorian palace'. But Symmachus' generous largess, and the hopes of the poor for more, ensured him a large following among the populace. He also had behind him at least two-thirds of the Italian bishops present at Rome in 502, including the bishops of Milan and Ravenna who played a leading role. The bishops were concerned for their independence of the Gothic government and of all lay interference, both in episcopal elections and in control over income and endowments. Symmachus' supporters included Cresconius of Todi who in 497 had been entrusted by Pope Anastasius II with his embassy to Constantinople to try to end the schism; Cresconius gave vocal support to Symmachus' opposition to lay interventions in ecclesiastical affairs. The senators were naturally unsympathetic to the clerical desire to exclude them from an effective say, whether in elections or in finance (which they or their ancestors had provided), and backed Laurentius together with a steadily increasing number of the city clergy in the title-churches, perhaps motivated by anxiety at Symmachus' centralizing control over their endowments. The position of Peter of Altinum, whom Ennodius scorns as a 'simple person', must have been almost impossible from the start. Installed by the king after a Laurentian petition, he was rejected by Symmachus and the synod of 502 and then, as the street-fighting became intolerable, stayed on in Rome no doubt in well-meaning hope that his presence could do something to moderate the tensions, but in fact blocking Laurentius' chances of acknowledgement. From 506 until his death on 19 July 514 Symmachus retained inglorious but undisputed possession of the papacy. Ascetics with good memories refused to have anything to do with him as a saunterer and voluptuary using worldly means to gain support. It must be conceded that in his extant letters there is nothing to impart any touch of grandeur to him as a man. But the poor and the refugees loved him. As in later times, they felt no warmth for their parish clergy; but this pope was their own.

The contemporary collection of papal biographies, the *Liber Pontificalis*, survives in two contrasting versions, one of which comes from a circle where Symmachus is accepted as canonical bishop of Rome but shamed by deplorable behaviour in himself and his supporters. This is the so-called Laurentian Fragment printed in the editions of the *Liber Pontificalis* by Duchesne and by Mommsen, contained in the Verona codex XXII (20) written about 555. (A facsimile of fo. 2r can be seen in E. Carusi and W. M. Lindsay, *Monumenti paleografici Veronesi* i, 1929, plate 6.) Since Symmachus has died but the Acacian schism has not yet ended, the fragment must be dated between July 514 and March 519. The author gives high praise to Pope Anastasius II's moves to end 'the wicked schism' with Constantinople. The Symmachian version, on the other hand, which achieved official acceptance in the record as part of the full *Liber Pontificalis*, places the blame for the troubles on the compromises with the East under Pope Anastasius II, whose removal by sudden death in November 498 is seen as an act of negative assistance by the Holy Spirit intervening to preserve Peter's see from falling into heresy. The incorporation of this severe judgement on Anastasius II into Gratian's *Decretum* gave it the widest currency. Dante found Pope Anastasius in hell (*Inferno* XI, 8 f.) and, since his account of Pope Agapetus converting Justinian from Monophysitism in 535 is taken from the *Liber Pontificalis* (*Paradiso* VI, 16–18), the poet no doubt used a manuscript of this collection of papal biographies.

The Symmachus biography in *Liber Pontificalis* sees the homicidal conflicts in the city as the consequence of senatorial rivalries, and reflects the Pope's bitterness that he found support only in the solitary figure of Faustus Niger. The senatorial opposition to Symmachus can have been reconciled only with difficulty. Gregory the Great records in his *Dialogues* (iv, 42) that Laurentius' supporters included a deacon Paschasius, an ascetic, friend of the poor and of monks, author of a book on the Holy Spirit. It is a tell-tale signpost to the sympathies of Boethius and of his father-in-law Symmachus that Paschasius was a close friend of Eugippius of Lucullanum, who dedicated to Paschasius in 511 his famous biography of St. Severinus of Noricum. Eugippius stood in a close relationship to Proba and Galla, sisters-in-law to Boethius, and also to Fulgentius of Ruspe. There is therefore strong probability that these personal connections justify the deduction that the family of Symmachus the senator favoured the Laurentian cause. One would not expect men of Boethius' and Symmachus' pro-hellenic prejudices (if given a choice) to uphold a pope known to be dedicated to an anti-Byzantine stance. These considerations have to be added to the evidence, considered earlier (p. 9 above), of the letter of Avitus of Vienne to Faustus Albus and Symmachus seeking to enlist the support of these senators for Pope Symmachus. But no doubt they were not militant for Laurentius, like Festus and Probinus, or Boethius might not have been honoured by the consulship in 510. That even then old wounds were still being nursed may be discerned in Boethius' conflict with Faustus Niger over the compulsory purchase of food in Campania in 510 (above, p. 24).

Boethius never makes the least allusion to the troubles, though the continued tensions cannot have failed to concern him during his year of office. From 506 the declared policy of Theoderic was to ask everyone to accept Symmachus as canonical pope without further dispute. The senate in effect had suffered a substantial defeat, leaving the position of both king and pope enhanced.

Peace was restored to Rome's streets in 514 by Pope Symmachus' faithful deacon and successor Hormisdas (514-23) whose policy towards the East was identical but whose moral character was beyond reproach. With a Ciceronian touch Cassiodorus, consul for 514, also claims in his *Chronicle* to have some credit for the happy reconciliation. To Ennodius the peace was a masterstroke of Theoderic's statesmanship. Nevertheless among both the senators and the clergy at Rome there continued to be differences of opinion about the proper policy in relation to the Greek emperor and the eastern churches. The so-called Laurentian fragment shows that feeling about the past divisions continued to provoke brooding resentments. The point, however, on which all at Rome came to be agreed was the absolute authority of a canonically elected pope as juridically valid without the need for any episcopal council. Gelasius had already proclaimed the theory, under pressure to explain how Rome could come to excommunicate Acacius without any synodical action. The decision, or rather deliberate indecision, of the Roman synod which in effect defied Theoderic in 502 was a thorough application of Gelasian principles of the Church's radical independence from secular authority in the governing of its affairs and of the highest possible claims for papal authority. It was now to be put to the test whether these claims would be a help or a hindrance in re-establishing communion between the Latin West and the Greek East.

Hormisdas' prime task was once more to negotiate peace with the East. With Theoderic's consent legates were twice sent to Constantinople, in 515 and 517, one legate on each visit being Ennodius, now bishop of Pavia, whose brief no doubt included a watch for the Gothic king's interests. The emperor Anastasius, whose exchanges with Pope Symmachus make painful reading, was disappointed with Hormisdas' manner which he felt to be overbearing and autocratic. He declined to accept the Roman view that the Henoticon implied a rejection of Chalcedon and of Leo (a view shared by moderate Monophysites), and the renewed conversations ended in a dangerously embittered deadlock in July 517. Anastasius' last letter told Hormisdas 'I can tolerate being insulted but not being ordered about'. The emperor saw, rightly, that the Roman terms for reunion would lead to riots and bloodshed which he had some duty to avoid. Throughout the negotiation the Roman position was consistent and uncompromising, and predictions from the Greek East (to be fully verified in 519–20) that a hard line would cost lives passed unheeded. Was it not better to be dead than a heretic? For Rome to stand firm for truth and principle whatever the human consequences?

For Anastasius the prime overriding issue was the possibility of recovering the unity of the empire, East and West together in 'one body' (*unum corpus*) under his own supremacy. To his grand design the schism in the Church was a thorn. With Pope Anastasius in 497 he had nearly won the acceptance of the Henoticon, understood certainly as a gloss on, and not as a rejection of, Chalcedon and Leo. At the same time he granted a recognition to Theoderic, with all the 'ornaments of the palace' (*Anon. Vales.* 64), no doubt in the expectation that Theoderic would lend the weight of his authority to the healing of the schism. The first letter in Cassiodorus' *Variae*, addressed from Theoderic to Anastasius, shows that Anastasius' hopes of Theoderic had been dashed. Theoderic makes it clear that he does not think his independent rule of Italy, in which Romans are governed impartially (*aequabiliter*), in any way disrupts the harmony of the two *respublicae* in peace and unity. He has carefully heeded Anastasius' frequent exhortations to love the Roman senate and to show affection for the city of Rome. Theoderic's letter is of about the year 508. At about this time Priscian at Constantinople delivered a panegyric before the emperor in Latin verse in which he explicitly refers to the well-known ambitions of Anastasius to reunite the barbarian West under his authority and jurisdiction together with the Greek East. It is hardly surprising, therefore, that Theoderic gave his verdict for Symmachus in the Laurentian schism.

Pope Symmachus' hostility to any proposals for conciliation with the Greek churches, except on terms they would be bound to regard as insulting and theologically dangerous, accordingly presented a grand obstacle to the emperor's design. Roman intransigence made it certain that political unity would be possible only hand in hand with an ecclesiastical reunion based upon Chalcedon and Leo in Christology and upon Greek recognition of papal jurisdiction over the universal Church. Disillusioned by the riots provoked by his support for the Monophysites in the years 508–12, Anastasius was open to persuasion. With pressure from powerful Chalcedonians such as his own nephew Hypatius and especially the Goth Vitalian (until his military defeat in 515), Anastasius began to move hesitantly towards a much less anti-Chalcedonian view, combined with an interpretation of the Henoticon as consistent with diphysite Christology; but he then found that Pope Hormisdas' demands were hardly less than those of Symmachus, and that he could gain unity with the West only at the price of widespread unrest in the East.

But on 9 July 518 the old emperor Anastasius suddenly died aged 88. He was succeeded by Justin, a Latin-speaking Balkan soldier who, with the advice of his clever nephew Justinian, was from the start determined to restore church unity with the West, no doubt from religious conviction but also because, however costly and impossible it seemed, it was an indispensable first move, *le premier pas qui coûte*, on the path towards Byzantine domination in Italy. The top posts in the palace bureaucracy were filled by sound Chalcedonians, and the hitherto all-powerful chamberlain Amantius paid for his outspoken opposition to Justin's new church policy by being sent to his execution. With the new emperor pressing his bishops to accept virtually anything the bishop of Rome might ask for, Hormisdas was in a powerful negotiating position. He had sent with his legates in 515 a careful formula, prepared in Greek as well as in Latin, to be proposed for signature by the emperor Anastasius, by the patriarch, and by all others wishing to enter into communion with Rome. Anastasius had dismissed it as impracticable. But now in 519 Hormisdas' legates were easily able to gain the emperor's signature; soon that of the patriarch of Constantinople, after some foot-dragging over the unpopular dropping of Acacius' name from the recital of the departed saints in the liturgy; and thereafter a growing number of Greek bishops, other than the most intransigent.

The formula of Hormisdas is the work of a canonist rather than a theologian, and is designed to reduce debate about the intricacies of Christology to the absolute minimum. It has nothing to say about nature or person or any other technical term of the Christological debate, and sticks to matters which have been decided by ecclesiastical authority on which further discussion would be out of place. The formula censures by name not only Nestorius and Eutyches but also four prominent past critics of Chalcedon, viz. Dioscorus, Timothy Aelurus, Peter Mongos of Alexandria, and Peter Fullo of Antioch, together with Acacius who had insulted Rome by establishing communion with them. None of these names may be recited at the liturgical memento of the departed. This exclusion Hormisdas extends to the names of all successors of the four prominent Monophysites and of Acacius (though well aware that two of Acacius' successors at Constantinople had suffered for their Chalcedonian sympathies), and indeed of all dead bishops who had been in communion with those on his black list. (This hounding of the dead naturally encountered emotional resistance mostly in Asia Minor and Syria, and especially at Jerusalem; and at Constantinople it was not thought a wise or humane policy.) The signatories to the formula also approve 'all the letters which the blessed Pope Leo wrote about the Christian faith' (a phrase subtly modified by the patriarch of Constantinople to read 'all that Leo wrote about the orthodox faith' which allowed some independent assessment), in particular the notoriously diphysite Tome. Above all, they request communion with Peter's see, the place where the Catholic religion always remains intact. The wording of this famous formula (with an omission of a phrase about 'following the definitions of the fathers') is echoed in the constitution of the first Vatican Council of 1870 in its attempt to define 'papal infallibility'. In 519 it would have been hard for the Pope to realize that he was being hugged now only that he and his successors might be the better squeezed by Justinian later.

Church unity was formally restored in 519, admittedly in an atmosphere of wary smiles and affectionate distrust. Gradually it came to have political consequences. Under Theoderic Italy was not governed as part of the Roman empire, though some Roman senators no doubt liked to talk as if it were still so. Independence from Byzantium was much enhanced by the long schism from 484 to 519, though successive bishops of Rome vainly tried to persuade the emperor Anastasius to pay heed to papal authority and church unity. In 494 Gelasius had even appealed to him on the ground that one with the title of Roman emperor should value and respect a bishop of Rome who was himself a 'born Roman' (*ep.* 12, 1). The ending of the schism reopened communications not only in the church but also in secular affairs, and therefore reduced Italian independence. At Constantinople it would come to seem natural for the now orthodox eastern emperor Justin to be deemed protector of the Catholic churches in Italy rather than to expect this role to be fulfilled by an Arian Goth even of the most benevolent impartiality. Until 523 relations between Theoderic and Constantinople were good; so much so that for the year 522 the two consuls appointed by the Byzantine emperor were Boethius' two young sons, named Symmachus and Boethius. It is hardly possible to suppose that this can have taken place unless Boethius' name was talked about in the court at Constantinople as a figure of weight in the background of the ecclesiastical and political rapprochement from the western side. Boethius was accordingly marked out as a man congenial to Justin and Justinian. This would prosper his affairs at Ravenna so long as Theoderic remained on excellent terms with Byzantium but would have the opposite effect if the relationship were to turn sour.

Boethius' interests may have been promoted by a distant lady relative, also a member of the Anicii family, Juliana, who was resident at Constantinople. Daughter of Olybrius who had become western emperor in 472, she was widow of Areobindus who in 512 had been acclaimed emperor by a faction opposed to Anastasius but had gone into hiding. The correspondence preserved in the Avellana collection (*CSEL* 35) shows her to be very active in 519–20 in promoting ecclesiastical reunion with the West.

Master of the Offices

In 522 on the occasion of his sons' installation at Rome Boethius delivered a panegyric on king Theoderic, no doubt by way of returning thanks to the king for the immense honour thereby conferred on him and on his family. The panegyric does not survive, but was known to Cassiodorus and therefore enjoyed some circulation for a time. After 525, however, one cannot imagine Boethius' family or friends taking any steps to see that it was preserved.

From 1 September of the same year Boethius took up the important administrative post of Master of the Offices, a position without precise parallel in modern western governments. The Mastership of the Offices was originally created by Diocletian to provide a linchpin for the various departments in the imperial court. Since Diocletian's court was a mobile military camp, the Master's functions were originally more military than civil. But soon civil functions predominated, except that the Master of the Offices retained responsibility for the household guards and the arsenals, and was in effect head of the intelligence service. He had both administrative and judicial functions. He saw that documents were prepared for the emperor's consideration, and that the emperor's decisions were then carried out. He controlled the public posts and had unique access to information. A holder of the post normally proceeded even higher to the rank of praetorian prefect. In this post, therefore, Boethius stood very close to the king, virtually under his daily surveillance. He also had extensive powers in relation to other senators, controlling access to the king and his consistory, introducing foreign embassies, and regulating the appointment of provincial governors. Theoderic's formula for the appointment is in Cassiodorus, *Variae* vi, 6.

In the *Consolation of Philosophy* Boethius looks back on his elevation with mingled pride and regret. He was drawn out of his library, he says, by altruism (ii, 7, 1) and by Platonic notions of the desirability of philosopher-rulers (i, 4, 5). His motive in accepting office was not the glory—though its sudden loss taught him that he was not as indifferent to that as he would have wished, and the nomination of his young sons to the consulate gave him exquisite pleasure. A man of conscience, he sought to 'follow God'; he fought for integrity and compassion in government against both rapacious Goths and oppressive prefects among the roman senators. Corruption in the imperial bureaucracy had long been endemic in the Roman empire, where it was essential to obtain a position of authority to be able to protect oneself in the jungle, and where success depended on the right patrons and on appropriate tips to the principal officials. If a post is obtained by outbidding others in gifts to those whose voice counts in the disposal of the prizes, the winner of the office will take it for granted that he is entitled to take advantage of his position to recoup his outlay and, in addition, to provide a surplus for the day when political change will thrust him out of office. Cassiodorus (*Var*. iii, 12) implies that under Odovacar corruption at court had been particularly bad, and therefore that under Theoderic a conscious effort was being made to clean up the Ravenna bureaucracy. Boethius may have had the illusion that in his high-minded stand he could be sure of enjoying the support of the king. In practice he gained many enemies among the dark figures whom he calls 'the court dogs', *palatinae canes*.

It is mistaken to see Boethius as a Roman at Ravenna supported by other Romans in a struggle with crude Goths. Among those whose grasping cupidity he succeeded in frustrating he mentions two Goths—Cunigast (who also turns up in Cassiodorus, *Var*. viii, 28) and Trigguilla whom Cassiodorus spells Triuuila (*Var*. iii, 20); he is Triggua in Ennodius (*ep*. ix, 21) and Triwanus in the Anonymus Valesianus (82).

Far more serious for him were the enemies he made among his fellow Romans. He began his tenure of the Mastership of the Offices by refusing to work with Decoratus whom he scorned as 'a clown and informer'.[45] Decoratus was a successful advocate in Rome. In his youth he had gained office through the patrician Faustus Niger, and aspired to the Quaestor of the Palace, an official with high rank as *vir magnificus* and having daily dealings with the Master of the Offices. He was eventually appointed in 524 after Boethius' fall, but soon death removed him.

Boethius found that as Master of the Offices he was able to protect from the palace dogs some of his senatorial friends. The dogs already had their teeth in the immense wealth of Paulinus (consul 498) when Boethius recovered his estates for him. In general, he concedes, his relations with Ravenna courtiers, the *aulici* whom he failed to keep sweet with favours, were disastrous. When the storm broke, his accusers were all Romans.

The attack upon him came indirectly as a consequence of a denunciation before Theoderic of the senator Albinus by Cyprian who held office as *referendarius* or private secretary. Rich and devout, Albinus had enjoyed a career of distinction: consul in his youth (493), praetorian prefect about 500–3, then a participant in the negotiations for church unity at Byzantium under Pope Hormisdas. The *Liber Pontificalis* records that he and his wife built a church to St. Peter on their estate near Rome and asked Pope Symmachus to consecrate it.[46] Cyprian discovered him to be corresponding with persons close to the emperor Justin in a manner amounting to treasonable conspiracy against Theoderic's kingdom. Albinus denied the charge, but Theoderic was in a mood to believe it true, and at Verona Albinus was declared guilty by the king without the legality of a proper trial. Boethius was distressed at the disregard of legal procedure, and boldly spoke in defence of Albinus before the king: 'Cyprian's accusation is false. But if Albinus did it, both I and all the senate have acted with a single counsel. It is false, my lord king.' So Boethius is reported in the later Ravenna chronicle or *Anonymus Valesianus* (85).

According to Boethius' own account Theoderic himself took Albinus' treason to be a conspiracy in which the entire senatorial order was implicated, and did this deliberately, being avid for an excuse to liquidate them all. It was Cyprian who extended the accusation against Albinus to include Boethius by declaring that Boethius had known about Albinus' disloyal correspondence but had suppressed the damning evidence. In Boethius' account the accusations he has to meet are (1) that of trying to suppress the evidence against Albinus; (2) having himself written letters expressing hopes of 'Roman liberty', evidently from Gothic domination. Boethius refuses to concede that any such letters are genuine, but the mildness of the language about 'Roman liberty' does not seem difficult to envisage as being close to what he could have thought and said. (3) Perhaps the most damaging and fatal charge arises from the interpretation of his obscure studies in 'the secrets of nature' and in pagan philosophy as black magic designed to further his ambitious designs—'vilissimorum spirituum praesidia' (i, 4, 39). This charge he thinks contemptible, but it is easy to understand how quickly it might be suggested. Later in the *Consolation* (iv, 6, 13) Boethius considers it possible that 'fate operates through certain divine spirits acting as servants of providence'. And in late antiquity the record includes several instances where charges of treason and of sorcery appear together.[47] The latter accusation imports an element of irrational panic to which no reasoned demonstrations of innocence can hope to reply. One can stand up to revolutions planned by merely human conspirators more easily than to the dire infernal powers invoked to help them.

In 510 two senators, Basil and Praetextatus, had been arraigned for sorcery before the prefect of Rome and a court of five other senators[48] with a Gothic count Arigern acting as assessor, magic being forbidden (says Theoderic's letter, *Variae* iv, 22) in Christian times. The panic reaction to this dabbling in sorcery by two senators is shown by the subsequent story for which details appear in Cassiodorus and Gregory the Great. Basil and Praetextatus succeeded in escaping from the prison where they were being held (*Variae* iv, 23). Basil disguised himself as a monk and fled to Amiternum in Valeria (near L'Aquila), where he won the confidence of the bishop and was personally conducted by him to the monastery of the holy abbot Equitius. Equitius' gift of spiritual discernment made him suspicious, and his fears were fully confirmed when a pretty nun in the convent under Equitius' care fell sick and, in the heat of her fever, specifically asked for the good monk to come and visit her; a request contrary to the rule of the house and clear evidence that Basil was the devil in disguise. Accordingly Basil was expelled, conducted back to Rome and there, in a fierce demonstration of zeal by the people, burnt alive (Greg. M. *Dial.* i, 4).

There is no evidence of Boethius' interest in magic. Nevertheless, the second commentary on *Interpretation* (ii, 231) allows substantial place to the determining power of the stars over animal life, and over human life as well, in so far as the area in which free will operates is severely constricted. In the *Consolation* the immutable order of the stars is contrasted with the disruptive freedom of man (i m. 5) and Boethius more than once declares that his philosophical studies have led him to careful study of the celestial order (i, 4, 4; i m. 2). The example of Proclus perhaps led Boethius to a private study of horoscopes which, at the crisis of his life, could have added fuel to Theoderic's suspicions that here was a man 'transported and rapt in secret studies' to the great danger of his kingdom.

In the year 519 a comet had passed across the heavens, visible both in Rome and in the East. Its course made sufficient impact to be recorded both in the *Paschal Chronicle* (612 PG 92, 859B) and also in a source used by the Monophysite chronicler Michael the Syrian (ii, 170 tr. Chabot). Comets were generally interpreted in antiquity to presage a change of dynasty or some impending disaster, as we are expressly told by Origen in his *Contra Celsum* (i, 59). That of 519 is sure to have precipitated secret speculation about the stability of the Gothic kingdom. It may well have contributed to Theoderic's feeling of insecurity, surrounded by a growing atmosphere of secret discussion about the future of Italy. In the Greek East it was interpreted as a sign of celestial displeasure at the new ecclesiastical policy of Justin and Justinian. To the Ravenna chronicler (*Anon. Vales.* 84) the comet's appearance during a whole fortnight was one among many portents of doom for Theoderic and his dynasty. So an insinuation of occult skills in the interpretation of celestial signs would have been very dangerous for Boethius.

As the bandwagon gathered momentum, Cyprian was supported by other malcontents in the move against Boethius, namely his own brother Opilio, by Basil (Opilio's father-in-law), and by Gaudentius who had been a business associate of Opilio (the name Gaudentius appears for the *consularis Flaminiae* in a papyrus of 517–18). All three recruits to Cyprian's cause had blots on their record which they now saw a chance to efface. Basil had at one time been in the king's service but suffered dismissal. He needed money to pay his debts and would be well rewarded for his pains in denouncing Boethius. Opilio and Gaudentius had been recently arrested for fraud and sentenced to exile by Theoderic. When they thereupon fled for asylum to a church in Ravenna, Theoderic directed that, unless they left by a prescribed date, they should be branded on the forehead and forcibly expelled. At this critical moment they saw a lifeline in Boethius' embarrassments. By instantly submitting a formally signed bill of accusations against the unhappy Master of the Offices, they won their reprieve. Of the later career of Gaudentius we hear nothing. But Cyprian and Opilio had successful careers after Boethius' fall, Opilio appearing in more than one document as a pillar of the Church. Letters in Cassiodorus (*Var.* viii, 6–7) defend Opilio from aspersions of avarice and delation, which is Boethius' portrait of the man. Cyprian was particularly trusted by Theoderic. He could speak Gothic as well as Latin and Greek. Before 1 September 524 Cyprian had been appointed to the major financial post of 'comes sacrarum largitionum' or treasurer to the royal household, and later rose to be Master of the Offices. Cyprian seemed to Theoderic a model of loyal service. He even brought up his children to play with Goths.[49] The probable date for these dramatic events is late in the year 523 or early 524.

During 522 and 523 Theoderic had suffered serious disappointments and troubles. Probably during 522 he suffered the loss of Eutharic Cillica, the Visigoth who came from Spain to marry Theoderic's daughter Amalasuintha in 515. Eutharic held the consulship on Justin's nomination for 519, and his installation at Rome was celebrated with popular games in the amphitheatre and splendid donatives to Goths and Romans alike. Cassiodorus dedicated his dry chronicle to Eutharic in

519 just to add to the festivity of this occasion. No doubt Eutharic was intended by Theoderic to ensure the continued survival of his dynasty. In the *Anonymus Valesianus* (80) Eutharic is remembered to have been an Arian marked by strong suspicion of Catholic intentions. Within a year or so of Eutharic's death perhaps Theoderic may have felt that his son-in-law was right.

That even before 521 there was gossip about the future of Italy after Theoderic is implicit in a letter of Ennodius assuring the king not only that it was marvellous for the Catholic Church to be under his benign rule but also that nothing would be more congenial than a successor exactly like him pursuing a similar policy (*ep.* ix, 30).

Eutharic Cillica's death enhanced the itch for speculation about the succession. His son Athalaric was merely seven years of age, and, although, when the time came, the transference of power took place without riot or revolution, Cassiodorus (*Var.* viii, 16, 5) explicitly attests that the succession was a matter of much uncertainty. In the circumstances there was strong temptation for Roman senators with a nostalgia for the forms of the Roman empire to be in dangerous correspondence with Byzantium about the future government of Italy.

In 522–3 there were other troubles and disappointments for Theoderic. Early in his reign he had built up an elaborate network of dynastic marriages with other western barbarian princely families, to ensure the political independence of Italy. These arrangements now began to break up. His nephew Sigeric, son of the Burgundian king Sigismund who had been converted from Arianism to Catholicism, became suspected of disloyalty to his father and was murdered.[50] Tension between Theoderic and the Burgundians led to war. Meanwhile in Vandal Africa Thrasamund (Theoderic's brother-in-law), king since 496, died on 6 May 523, to be succeeded by Hilderic son of Huneric and Eudokia, daughter of Valentinian III. Hilderic's mother influenced him in the direction of sympathy for Catholics. The dying Thrasamund extracted from Hilderic a promise on oath that he would never show kindness to Catholics or allow the many exiled clergy to return. Hilderic, however, at once allowed the exiles back and entered into a close alliance with Byzantium, to Theoderic's certain

Master of the Offices 53

distress.[51] Hilderic imprisoned Theoderic's sister Amalafrida (Thrasamund's widow), and Ostrogothic-Vandal relations were very bad.

Nearer home Theoderic had lost important supporters among the Catholic clergy in Italy. Ennodius of Pavia had died on 17 July 521.[52] On 6 August 523 Pope Hormisdas died,[53] to be succeeded by John I who may be identical with the Roman deacon to whom Boethius dedicated three of his theological tractates. (The name John is unfortunately too common at this time for the assertion of identity to be made with complete confidence.) Pope John appears to belong to the pro-Byzantine circle among the Roman clergy (above p. 28), perhaps nursing the illusion that achievements such as the formula of Hormisdas should lead to a practical exercise of jurisdiction by the Roman see in relation to the Greek churches. John may have owed his election to a word in Theoderic's ear from the Master of the Offices. The king is unlikely to have regarded the papal election as none of his concern.

Theoderic was past seventy years of age, and coming to feel vulnerable and encircled. The sudden revelation that a respected, presiding member of the senate was in treasonable contact with Byzantium, that the Master of the Offices (the king's very eyes and ears) knew of it and suppressed the evidence, and that this official could then blandly claim that Albinus had written whatever he had written in a representative capacity speaking for all his fellow senators, produced an intelligibly fierce reaction. Albinus and Boethius were arrested and taken first to a Verona baptistery (one wonders if they were there required to take oaths of innocence before the shrine of a saint such as Zeno), but then moved to prison, Boethius to Ticinum (Pavia), south of Milan. Of Albinus' fate we hear no more. Theoderic summoned from Rome the prefect of the city, Eusebius, to preside over the process. Boethius was never called to defend himself. The verdict went against him and the death sentence was passed by a senatorial court sitting nearly 500 miles distant, i.e. at Rome (not at Pavia as the *Anonymus Valesianus* might be taken to imply).[54] Boethius thought it pathetic timidity that the senators should abjectly decree their sentence against a man whose fault had been to protect their interests. He was replaced in the post of Master of the Offices by Cassiodorus, and Decoratus advanced to his coveted quaestorship.

In prison at Pavia (house arrest is unlikely, but he need not have been in the worst dungeon) Boethius composed his jewel and masterpiece the *Consolation of Philosophy*. Unless Theoderic should die, no reprieve is expected. The first book contains a protestation of innocence of treason and sorcery, and expresses his resentment that among the senators only Symmachus continued to stand by him. The rest scuttled for cover before Theoderic's sudden reign of terror. The *Consolation* is a polished work of literature in high style as well as an impassioned discussion of the logical problems of providence, freedom, and evil. It was not the work of a few days. Boethius was certainly a long time in custody, and the degree of discomfort suffered is likely to have varied with the barometer of Theoderic's relations with Byzantium. We do not know when Boethius died. In the late medieval calendar of Pavia St. Severinus is commemorated on 23 October. But this date coincides with St. Severinus of Cologne (on this day in the Roman Martyrology), so that confusion is very possible. In the ninth century Ado of Vienne, who knew Pavia, records in his chronicle that Boethius and Symmachus died 'for catholic piety' (*PL* 123, 107C), but does not include them in his calendar of saints. In 1330 an anonymous chronicler of Pavia alleges that 'until almost his own time' the autograph of the *Consolation of Philosophy* had been preserved in Pavia, transcribes the inscription on Boethius' tomb in the church of St. Peter in Caelo Aureo, and adds that after decapitation Boethius carried his head to the church. The same church had acquired the relics of Augustine of Hippo during the eighth century. Evidently the immense medieval popularity of the *Consolation*, interpreted as a Christian work, encouraged Boethius' veneration as a martyr and even his inclusion among the popular cephalophorous saints.

Nor is it possible to be certain in what year Boethius lost his life. The chronicler Marius bishop of Aventicum (Avenches), who died in 601, seems to have drawn on some Italian annals. He is decisive in recording under the year 524 that 'in that year Boethius the patricius was killed in Milanese territory', and likewise under the year 525 that Symmachus died at Ravenna.

But other annalistic chroniclers, perhaps less reliable, assign Boethius' death to 523 or 525. 523 is certainly too early, but 525 or even early in 526 is not necessarily too late. We shall see that there is some probability favouring 525; but 524 or early in 526 remains possible.

Boethius' long imprisonment is capable of many interpretations. Theoderic may have been still uncertain about his guilt and in search of additional evidence. Perhaps he hoped that under torture Boethius might disclose further clues to the ramifications of the treasonable conspiracy of the pro-Byzantine senators who had been implicated by Boethius' bland assurances that Albinus spoke and wrote for all the senate. Perhaps, more formidably, Theoderic was using Boethius' life as a weapon in the struggle against Justin and Justinian and against their friends in the Roman senate. At Pavia Boethius wrote his *Consolation of Philosophy* as a personal and private confession of humanist faith and of confidence in divine providence. The work betrays no inkling in its author's mind that there may have been a larger game going on in which he was hardly more than a pawn. A horrible note in the Ravenna chronicle of the *Anonymus Valesianus* records that in the prison 'in agro Calventiano' (either the quarter of Pavia called Borgo Calvenzano or, less probably, Calvenzano near Melegnano between Pavia and Milan), Boethius was subjected to ferocious tortures. A cord was twisted round his head many times for a very long period so that his eyeballs started from their sockets; blows from a club finished off the shattered wreck. The torture story cannot be literally correct since the application of such severe constriction to the head as to fracture the skull or the orbit at the back of the eye would clearly cause death before the eyeballs could fall out. But the story of the anonymous chronicler is corrected, and so confirmed, through an equally spine-chilling piece in the *Secret History* of Procopius, where he says that on Theodora's orders a young man accused of homosexual practices was subjected to torture by leather being twisted round his temples 'until he felt as if his eyeballs had jumped out'.[55] This is evidently the method applied to the wretched Boethius. The torture was so painful and frightening to him that his autonomic nervous system reacted, producing dilation of the pupils and retraction of the eyelids with the appearance of protruding eyeballs to the observer.

The process against Boethius also brought high risks to his family circle: to Rusticiana and her two sons and to his father-in-law Symmachus. On the final execution Symmachus' grief was not sufficiently concealed. Though now occupying the major office of 'head of the senate', he was taken under guard from Rome to Ravenna. Theoderic was afraid that Symmachus too might conspire against the Gothic kingdom, and on some charge or other he sentenced this very distinguished figure to execution.[56]

According to the first edition of the *Liber Pontificalis*, a nearly contemporary source, Theoderic ordered the bodies of Boethius and Symmachus to be hidden. If this is correct, it offers important evidence that Theoderic was becoming aware of the high risks attaching to his policy of terror against leading Roman senators. Symmachus and (through the publication of his *opuscula sacra*) Boethius were prominently associated with the Church. Their execution by an Arian king was sure to be seen by Catholics as religious martyrdom. A place in church calendars could be won by being a victim of secular tyranny without one's cause being specifically religious. Ammianus Marcellinus records how three civil servants unjustly executed by Valentinian I were remembered by the Christians of Milan.[57] Nevertheless, in the case of Boethius and Symmachus the importance of the religious element in the alienation between Theoderic and the Roman senators is not to be discounted.

The collapse of toleration

Theoderic's over-reaction to the discovery of the 'conspiracy' (on which Boethius cites Canius' words to Caligula 'Had I known of it, you would not') pushed him further and further, willy-nilly, in a direction having the reverse effect to that desired. He had thought to retain the loyalty of the Romans in Italy by separate development and conciliation. He treated the senate well and entrusted high responsibilities to the great aristocrats of the beau monde who felt they had a hereditary right to these offices. In strong contrast to Vandal Africa, he adopted a religious toleration which favoured and honoured the Catholic Church, even though Theoderic was not and did not wish to be a member of it. In 502 (for example) to the bishops assembled in Rome to adjudicate in the process of Pope Symmachus, he writes of 'your religion and mine' as distinct social entities, each with its own episcopate side by side. Even at the height of the troubles in Rome, he was careful to remain neutral between the parties. He insisted repeatedly that it was exclusively for the synod, not for him, to reach a verdict on the rightfulness of Symmachus' occupation of the papal throne. The synod was expressly told it was free to reach its own decision without fear of the king and solely in the fear of God. Theoderic's precepts to the synod show him much aware of the risks of intervening in church affairs. Symmachus' party was especially sensitive to this.

Under Odovacar when Pope Simplicius died in 483, the praetorian prefect Caecina Decius Basilius junior had met the Roman church authorities in the Theodosian mausoleum by St. Peter's and, claiming that he spoke in accordance with an admonition of Pope Simplicius, charged them on the king's behalf to elect no new pope without consulting him and to allow no sales of church property during the vacancy of the see. This lay ruling was appealed to in 502 as conceding the principle that the king could intervene in assigning control of the revenues to a visitor and in inviting the synod of 502 to meet. After the 'incongruous acquittal' on 23 October 502 Pope Symmachus reconvened the bishops on 6 November, re-enacting the provisions of Basil's instruction regarding church property but stressing that as a lay directive it possessed no authority until agreed by the pope in council. The feeling expressed in this apparent rigmarole was one to which Theoderic showed some sensitivity.

As long as the Acacian schism kept Rome and Constantinople apart the policy of royal non-intervention in ecclesiastical affairs worked well. Conversions from Catholicism to Arianism or vice versa were frowned upon as productive of ill will. But Theoderic's toleration also had other limits. The Manichees are recorded in the *Liber Pontificalis* to have suffered expulsion from Rome and the burning of their books in the times of Gelasius, Symmachus, and Hormisdas. The

Jews did better. North Italy had long contained substantial Jewish communities. Theoderic's dealings with them cannot be described as positively benevolent, but he rejected forced conversions. In one distinctly unfriendly letter he ends by assuring the Jewish community of Genoa that this is his conviction.[58] Some time between 515 and 522 social relations between Jews and Christians at Ravenna became strained to the point of mutual insults, which ended in riots and the burnings of synagogues in Ravenna and Rome. Theoderic not unreasonably required the churches in these cities to make restitution from their substantial resources; but this decision was not welcome to those who thought that a Christian ruler, even if an Arian and a barbarian, ought not to show sympathy for those who possessed the sacred scriptures but were regarded as having refused the light lightening the Gentiles.[59] Intolerant Catholics in Italy might naturally look to Byzantium to find there a model for greater strictness in dealing with such unassimilated dissidents. Justin and Justinian fully shared the opinion of the Italian Catholics that in an orthodox Christian empire the duty of the civil power is to uphold the truth and to make life at least a little difficult for persons who persist in error. Hormisdas hails Justin as 'schismatum et superbiae dissipator' (*ep.* 140, 21).

In 518 Justin's regime in the East was new, with many internal problems to solve. By 523-4 the central authority of Justin was becoming well established, and it was time to begin to put pressure on the heretics who pullulated throughout the Byzantine dominions; above all the monophysite critics of Chalcedon, but also many others. These others included Arian communities, many of which were of Gothic race situated in or near Constantinople and in Thrace. Arian Goths in the East would naturally look to Theoderic as their protector. Conversely, however, reaction at Constantinople to the arrest of Albinus and Boethius would easily encourage Justin and Justinian to look about for ways of bringing counter-pressure to bear on Theoderic and to harass these Gothic communities. Probably early in 525 reports were reaching Ravenna of forced conversions to orthodoxy and of the expropriation of Arian ecclesiastical buildings to orthodox use, creating a wave of alarm and anger. Theoderic can only have been furious.

In Italy Theoderic's policy of mutual non-interference had worked well. At Ravenna itself the Arian Goths had six or seven churches, some being magnificently decorated, and built a baptistery with exquisite mosaics, certainly of higher aesthetic quality than those of the rival Catholic establishment. Theoderic built his own palace church, again adorned with mosaic figures of the highest artistry. The apse bore the inscription 'Theodericus rex hanc ecclesiam a fundamentis in nomine domini nostri Yhesu Christi fecit.' Rededicated to St. Martin about 561, and taken over for Catholic use, it was later dedicated to St. Apollinaris and is now S. Apollinare Nuovo.[60] Wherever in Italy there was any substantial Gothic garrison, the Arians had their own church buildings. In Rome itself Gregory the Great tells us of two. One, which he restored and rededicated with relics of St. Agatha, had been on the slope of the Quirinal since the fifth century, and had been adorned by none other than Ricimer: FLA. RICIMER V.I. MAG. VTRIVSQVE MILITIAE EXCONS.ORD. PRO VOTO SVO ADORNAVIT, declared the old inscription, still visible in the sixteenth century but now destroyed. A second Arian church in Rome stood on the Coelian and Esquiline near the Lateran palace in what had been the old military zone and became the Gothic quarter of the city. Gregory the Great says the church lay 'iuxta domum Merulanam regione tertia'. Later it was taken over for Catholic use and dedicated to St. Severinus.[61] In the Greek East also the Arians possessed some churches with fine decoration. Procopius suggests that Justinian's motive for harassing the sects was avarice, since many of the sects enjoyed wealth, and Arian churches were particularly rich.[62]

Justin's move against the Arians in the East seemed intolerable to Theoderic, who began to think relations with Byzantium were on the path towards war. If Boethius was still alive at Pavia, Theoderic now had a strong motive for execution. He decided to send an embassy to Constantinople which would threaten bloody murder for the churches in Italy unless Justin ordered the immediate cessation of all harassment of the Arians, the restoration of the church buildings that had been taken over, and the sending back to their communities of the Arians who had been pressed into conversion to the orthodox faith. This embassy,[63] he decided, should be led by Pope John I in person, accompanied by five other bishops, including Ecclesius of Ravenna (whose portrait in mosaic is familiar from his church of S. Vitale), Eusebius of Fano in Apulia and Sabinus of Canosa. In addition, four of the most senior and august senators were sent: Theodorus, consul in 505, with his brother Importunus, consul in 509; Agapitus, consul in 517 (who about 510 had been sent by Theoderic on an embassy to Anastasius and had already played some role for Pope Hormisdas in 520 in negotiations with Constantinople);[64] and another Agapitus with the rank of patricius. The latter Agapitus died at Thessalonica on the return journey.

Pope John set out in sickness and in tears. He took the shortest route via Corinth, where an eminent citizen lent him a horse for the next leg of his journey (to Cenchreae across the isthmus) and then found the horse refusing to take his wife as rider after having carried so holy a burden (Gregory the Great *Dial.* iii, 2 tells the story as a charming miracle). But perhaps the Pope rode it too hard. There was urgency to his journey. At the fifteenth milestone from Constantinople the papal party was met with a procession carrying candles and crosses in honour of St. Peter and St. Paul. They entered by the Golden Gate where John restored a blind man's sight. At the meeting between pope and emperor, Justin bowed with a deep prostration and exchanged a kiss of greeting. The Greek capital felt it to be a great thing that, for the first time, a bishop of Rome should come to their city. The pope, says the Latin chronicler Count Marcellinus, who was in Constantinople, 'was received with wonderful honour'.[65] John was seated on the emperor's right in the church, and celebrated mass in Latin 'with full voice' on Easter Day. The *Liber Pontificalis* records that John even placed the crown upon the emperor's head—his second coronation, since a vivid account of his coronation in 518 by the patriarch of Constantinople has been preserved in Constantine Porphyrogenitus (*De Caerimoniis* i, 93). What Theoderic thought of this act by the pope is not recorded but can be readily imagined, especially on the analogy of Byzantine reactions to the papal coronation of Charlemagne, to which the episode is a startling inverted parallel.

The ambassadors explained their sad commission and, according to the first edition of the *Liber Pontificalis*, here a

The collapse of toleration 61

contemporary source, they obtained all for which they asked. But the second edition omits this statement, and the omission is borne out by the Ravenna chronicler, the *Anonymus Valesianus* (91), according to whom Justin conceded everything to save Italian lives except one thing which was asking too much, namely that there should be a returning to their communities of Arians who had been received into the orthodox church.

It is possible that there is an echo of the western embassy's pleas in Justin's edict against heresies of 527, where one clause expressly excepts the Goths from the severity of the edict (*Cod. Just.* i, 5, 12, 17). But that clause says nothing about the restitution of buildings already taken over.

When the western ambassadors found their way to Ravenna, the contrast between their enthusiastic reception at Constantinople and the atrabilious reaction from Theoderic was sharp. The *Anonymus Valesianus* says that Theoderic gave order for Pope John to be *in offensa sua*, a technical term of Germanic law for withdrawal of the king's favour in cases of disloyalty.[66] The *Liber Pontificalis* explains the hard facts: the ambassadors were put in prison and tortured and would have been put to the sword if Theoderic had not feared the reaction of the eastern emperor. But John died in Theoderic's dungeon at Ravenna. He could not have done more harm to the Gothic cause in Italy if he had lived on in office for another twenty years. At his funeral at Ravenna one of the crowd fell in an attack of 'demon-possession', but as the bier came to where he was he suddenly stood up in good health. The people and the senators tore pieces of his vestments as relics, and the procession passed on to the tomb outside the city with wild rejoicing. In a word, John died and was buried with full honours as a true martyr at the hands of 'a tyrant, not a king' (*Anon. Vales.* 94). John's death is dated by the *Liber Pontificalis* on 18 May 526. If he had been at Constantinople for Easter Day on 19 April, his return journey was made with all possible speed. Aelius Aristides in the second century AD attests a windy journey from Rome to Miletus via Corinth, achieved in 14 days (*Orat.* 24, pp. 305 f. Jebb = 48, pp. 409–10 Keil). Even so John's journey was fast and therefore attended with an exhaustion that is likely to have contributed to his death.

The urgency and speed of the journey of the embassy to and from Byzantium and the loss of Agapitus by death in the East may suggest that Pope John and his colleagues were in a hurry to return to save lives among the Catholics of Italy. We have already noted that we do not really know when Boethius died or how long he was kept in custody at Pavia. It is unhappily possible that first he and then Symmachus were hostages for the success of the papal mission, and that their execution, on ground of complicity in the conspiracy of Albinus, was intended as exemplary, as a warning of what could become of other distinguished buttresses of the Church in Italy if the eastern emperor continued to treat Arian Goths badly. The *Liber Pontificalis* may not be far out in dating the deaths of both Boethius and Symmachus during the absence of the papal party, in the early months of 526. Or were the papal ambassadors given urgency for their journey by their knowledge that one or perhaps two of their friends had already been executed before they started out from Italy, and that others might be sent to join them before they returned?

Theoderic's dissatisfaction with the outcome of the embassy remained extreme. A hundred days after John's death, an edict was published in Ravenna that on the ensuing Sunday, 30 August 526, the Arians would take possession of the Catholic churches of the city. But on that very day, the Ravenna chronicler declares, the king died of a painful stomach complaint. (The manner of his death is assimilated to that of Arius, of which it is tempting to recall Gibbon's remark that the historian has a choice between miracle and poison.) Before he died he had time to appoint his grandson Athalaric to succeed him, the boy's mother Amalasuintha acting as regent. During his lifetime he had already constructed his mausoleum; unfinished, but remarkable Germanic architecture and an object of wonder and admiration to contemporaries as to all visitors to Ravenna since.

Pope John's body was translated to Rome on May 27, probably a year later; admittedly the *Liber Pontificalis* places the translation to Rome only nine days after his death at Ravenna and explicitly dates it in 526.

In his *Dialogues* (iv, 31) Gregory the Great records a story, which he heard from Julian 'defensor' of the Roman Church, about a hermit on the island of Lipari who at the very hour of

Theoderic's death saw a vision of the king, stripped of the insignia of his girdle and his shoes, and with his hands bound, being taken by Pope John and Symmachus and dropped into the 'cauldron of Vulcan' (*Vulcani olla*), evidently a nearby volcano (Vulcano or Stromboli?) regarded as one of the chimneys of hell.

The Ravenna chronicler, the *Anonymus Valesianus*, sees the killing of Boethius, Symmachus and Pope John, as the culmination of a Homeric tragedy in which Theoderic was deprived of his wits. He is a chronicler with a thesis, namely that Theoderic was a great ruler of a peaceful and prosperous Italy, but his Arianism robbed him of judgement and turned him into a man impelled to act as an enemy to God's law.[67]

In the Byzantine world Procopius, writing wholly without a theological *parti pris*, similarly reports in glowing terms on the remarkable achievements of Theoderic as king. He sees him as a great man who somehow came to make the fatal mistake of executing Boethius and Symmachus and became undone in consequence. Procopius tells a macabre, Macbeth-like story of Theoderic being served at dinner with the head of a great fish which seemed to the king to resemble the head of Symmachus newly killed, the eyes fixing him with a manic, grim stare, so that he had to retire to his chamber in terror to collect himself. He then died in bitter remorse for the wrong done to Boethius and Symmachus.[68] Even in Byzantium, therefore, Theoderic's death was immediately linked with the drama of Boethius and his father-in-law. That Theoderic felt the remorse Procopius attributes to him is more than doubtful. What is clear is that popular opinion interpreted his death as being somehow associated with, or a consequence of, the action he had taken against Symmachus, one of the most admired and respected of the Roman senators.

When Jordanes (*Getica* 59, 304) ascribes to the dying Theoderic an exhortation to the Gothic counts and princes 'that they should honour the king [his grandson Athalaric] and love the Roman senate and people', he is no doubt expressing the view of the collaborationist Romans who had good reason to regret the Byzantine invasion of Italy, and in Jordanes' time may have been tempted to make common cause with Totila until his defeat and death in 552.

De Rossi found in a Paris manuscript (Paris. lat. 8071) a

mutilated cento of eight lines occurring among a group of texts taken from inscriptions once in the atrium of St. Peter's, Rome. It is therefore a presumption that it is the epitaph of a pope. The seventh line indicates that this 'bishop of the Lord fell as Christ's sacrificial victim'. The only pope buried at the atrium of St. Peter's to whom this line evidently applies is John I. A less mutilated text than that in the Paris manuscript was later found by W. Levison at Cambridge, giving the text:[69]

> Quisquis ad aeternam festinat tendere vitam
> hoc iter exquirat qua licet ire piis,
> tramite quo fretus caelestis regna sacerdos
> intravit meritis ante parata suis.
> M(en)te magis vivens commercia grata peregit,
> perdidit ut poss(e)t semper habere De(u)m.
> Antistes Domini procumbis victima Christi
> pontifici summo sic placiture Deo.

In the western hagiographical tradition Pope John's heroic confrontation with the Arian tyrant and martyrdom at his hands became built up remarkably quickly into a purely Latin story, in which the eastern emperor played no part at all. In Gregory of Tours' *De gloria martyrum* 40, written a generation or so later probably on the basis of oral tradition, the initiative in the orthodox onslaught on error and the devil is taken *motu proprio* by the pope, and no trace remains of the quiet coexistence between Catholic and Arian which actually prevailed for the greater part of Theoderic's reign in Italy, and which very well suited the see of Rome at that time.

During the weeks between Pope John's death and his own, Theoderic had time to intervene directly in the next papal election to ensure that the new pope belonged to the pro-Gothic party. Felix IV (526–30) was elected on 12 July on the express nomination of Theoderic according to the first edition of the *Liber Pontificalis*, here confirmed by a letter of Athalaric to the senate (*Var.* viii, 15) congratulating them that the election of their new bishop 'corresponded to the decision of our glorious lord and grandfather'. Athalaric is pleased to remind the senate that, 'although of another religion', Theoderic's care had been that all churches should have good bishops. The Romans now have a man approved by divine

The collapse of toleration   65

grace and recommended by the king after due examination. The remainder of the letter, however, clearly implies that there was a rival candidate with powerful support whose appointment had been excluded by the king's direct command; 'ex iussu Theoderici regis' says the first edition of the *Liber Pontificalis*.
The division in the Roman Church continued. When Felix IV felt his end to be near (he died on 20 September 530) he took steps to make a formal designation of his successor, Boniface II, the archdeacon and a man of wealth whose father Sigibuld bore a Germanic name but whose family (if connected with Sigisvult, consul for 437) had long been romanized. The action was controversial, however; the senate entered formal protest, and Boniface found himself opposed by a rival pope, the old Greek deacon Dioscorus with the support of sixty presbyters and the majority of the people. Dioscorus had come to Rome from Alexandria as an impassioned hater of the Henoticon and of all critics of Chalcedon. Deeply hostile to the emperor Anastasius he could alert Pope Hormisdas to every Byzantine move in the game of negotiation. With the accession of Justin his passionate Chalcedonianism turned him round into a prominent pro-Byzantine among the Roman clergy. High preferment had been forecast for him, Justin proposing him for the patriarchate of Antioch; Hormisdas wanted him for Alexandria. In 530 his ambition was to be briefly granted. But Boniface was inevitably more acceptable to Athalaric and the Gothic government at Ravenna. Felix IV may well have seen that only a pope acceptable to Athalaric would now be allowed, and in these circumstances it would be preferable for the departing pope to nominate than for the Gothic Arian king to do so. In the event the schism was healed by the rapid death of Dioscorus on 14 October, only 28 days after his consecration. (Dioscorus was laid under formal condemnation by Boniface, an act that generated continued resentment until it was removed by Pope Agapetus in May 535.) Soon Boniface II died also, in October 532, to be succeeded by John II from 2 January 533, after long and bitter conflicts over the succession, which was decided only after Athalaric's arbitration and huge bribes to the plebs requiring the sale of sacred vessels. When Athalaric died as an alcoholic wretch on 2 October 534, the stage was already set for Justinian's armies to plan their inter-

vention in Italy to overthrow Gothic power and to subject the papacy to Justinian's intricate ecclesiastical policies.

Amalasuintha, acting as regent for her son Athalaric, quickly realized the mistake which Theoderic had made and the dangerous bitterness that his actions had introduced between Romans and Goths. Her policy became one of friendly alliance with Byzantium, the support of Justin being needed to maintain her own power and authority. Procopius claims that so long as she ruled, no Roman was touched or fined. She restored the confiscated estates of Symmachus and Boethius to their children. Boethius' widow Rusticiana, however, did not forgive or forget what Theoderic had done. When the Byzantine armies invaded, Rusticiana had all the statues of Theoderic in Rome smashed, which put her in jeopardy after Rome fell to the Gothic army under Totila on 17 December 546. She was reduced to penury but Totila saved her from angry Goths.[70] Of Boethius' two sons, the younger, Boethius junior, perhaps married a lady from Sicily named Helpis.[71] In the time of Gregory the Great the senatorial circle includes a Symmachus living at Rome and a lady Rusticiana who moved to Constantinople to become one of the western aristocrats at the court of the emperor Maurice, the Lombard invasion having made Italy very uncomfortable. These are no doubt Boethius' grandchildren. Rusticiana junior married off her daughter to Apion III, a wealthy man from Oxyrhyncus who lived much in Constantinople.[72] Rusticiana is also mentioned in a poem on Christ's Nativity that once stood on an inscription in Rome.[73]

Despite Amalasuintha's attempts to heal the breach, the damage was already done. The conflict gravely weakened the position of Gothic power in Italy, and prepared the way for the wars of Justinian against the Goths, ending in the destruction of their kingdom after twenty long years of terrible suffering for the Italian population, who must have looked back on Theoderic's reign as a golden age of peace and plenty.

Boethius' sacrifice

A question that the historian is left asking at the end of the narrative is how far Justinian foresaw the outcome, so greatly to the advantage of the Byzantine empire. If at Constantinople it seemed reasonable to hope that from 519 the Catholic churches in Italy might prefer to look towards an orthodox Roman emperor rather than towards an Arian barbarian king, then, to exploit the political advantages, Justinian needed to find a way of undermining the general admiration for Theoderic's government prevailing in Italy. Justinian was possessed of a subtle and scheming mind (as his elaborate negotiations with the Monophysites richly illustrate), and it would not have taken him long to realize that the loyalty commanded by Theoderic in Italy could be corroded by harassing the Gothic Arians in Constantinople and Thrace within the Byzantine empire. It must have been obvious that Theoderic and his Gothic advisers would be angry, would not think it an immediate ground for war, but would retaliate by harassing Catholics in Italy with the desirable consequence that Italy would begin to look towards Byzantium for protection against heretical tyranny. The moves in the game of chess are not numerous in this case, and, as has been noted already, there is some evidence to suggest that Theoderic himself began to realize what was being done to him. The hypothesis requires that Justinian also calculated that the Catholics in Italy would lose a few prominent figures in the persecution that retaliation would bring, but thought that the loss of some of his friends, Boethius, Symmachus, or even the Pope, was a price worth paying to win the hearts of the Italian Romans. The immense welcome given to Pope John at Constantinople and the invitation to crown Justin can hardly have been stage-managed without Justinian being aware that to the degree the barometer soared in the East, it would plunge low in the West. He was not a stupid man. It is not necessary to ascribe to him all the Stalin-like qualities attributed to him in the pages of Procopius' *Secret History* if one is tempted by the hypothesis that the deaths of Boethius and Symmachus and John were a necessary part of Justinian's designs, and by the assumption that Justinian thought such casualties had to be accepted, in the cause of his reconquest of the West for Roman unity and for orthodoxy.

These sombre considerations may appear to put in a grey light the long debated question whether or not Boethius was truly a martyr for the Catholic faith and merits the commemoration in the Pavia calendar on 23 October, which was formally approved at Rome by a decree of the Congregation of Rites of 15 December 1883 and then confirmed by Pope Leo XIII (*Acta Sanctae Sedis* XVI 302 f.). Reaction against the Christianizing interpretation of the *Consolation of Philosophy*, and against the natural Catholic desire to claim so great a man among the Church's confessors, has led to an equally distorted opinion that there was no religious ingredient at all in the tensions that cost Boethius his life. Politics and religion were not such separate entities in the sixth century, either for Justinian or for Theoderic. Boethius' desire had been to further the reunion between Rome and the Greek orthodox churches, and everything in his senatorial background made him sympathetic to the political link with the East Roman empire that naturally accompanied the achievement of church unity. In simple terms he was no plain martyr for the faith before heretical tyranny. But that his death was seen by his contemporaries as a crucial incident in a conflict between Gothic Italy and the East Roman empire precipitated by a religious disagreement seems, beyond question, the conclusion that the ancient evidence imposes.

The question must recur when we come to consider the question of Boethius' personal religion in the light of the *Consolation of Philosophy*.

II
LIBERAL ARTS IN THE COLLAPSE OF CULTURE

ARISTOTLE observes in the *Categories* that if something is to be known, it must be knowable; conversely something can be knowable without anyone actually knowing it, either because it has not yet been discovered (such as the method for squaring the circle) or because it has sadly been forgotten and then by much effort needs to be rediscovered. This last observation fascinated Boethius, and his commentary on this passage treats it as a word for his own times. It is his great fear that amid the general collapse of higher studies in his time, the knowledge acquired by the philosophers and scientists of classical Greece may simply be obliterated by a failure in transmission.[1] Books may lie in libraries but, if they are to survive for more than a generation, they need users who understand and value their contents or they will rapidly suffer from neglect, and the valuable space they occupy will be applied to other purposes. 'It is one thing to have reason, another to use it', he writes. 'To abandon the stretching of one's mind's power is to lose it.' Or, with a sharper point, 'Men who have long been idle in using their minds adopt positions from which they never move, and learn nothing until their old age.'[2]

The Latin world possessed good guides in grammar and in rhetoric. In the middle of the fourth century Jerome himself had been among those who sat at the feet of the famous grammarian Donatus whose works have been preserved. Donatus seemed to Boethius a scholar and teacher fit to be compared with the great Alexandrian scholar Aristarchus in the Greek world. Moreover, his own contemporary Priscian, who taught a more advanced grammar than that of Donatus, was busy teaching Latin at Constantinople, dedicating works on style to Boethius' father-in-law, and composing treatises on Latin grammar which became indispensable in medieval schoolrooms. In rhetoric there was the incomparable model of Cicero, whose treatises on rhetoric explained the tricks of the trade. An allusion in the *Consolation of Philosophy* (iii, 5, 11) shows that Quintilian is still read. The fourth century had had a prominent orator in Marius Victorinus, an African who moved to Rome to become tutor to the sons of the great aristocrats. In the *Confessions* Augustine reports Simplician of Milan's vivid account of the explosive impact on Roman society of his decision to become a Christian. Victorinus wrote extant treatises on the art of public speaking, and also composed works on dialectic of which more must be said later. Boethius never takes Victorinus seriously as a philosopher, but has high respect for him as the greatest master of rhetorical skills in recent times (below, p. 115). His books were evidently still much in use in Boethius' time.

The points at which the Latin equipment was weak seemed to Boethius to be in the mathematical disciplines, that is, in Arithmetic, Music, Geometry, and Astronomy; and in the higher studies of philosophical logic. His effort is therefore concentrated in these areas. Roman lack of interest here is also deplored in Cassiodorus, *Variae* iii, 52.

In the generation immediately preceding Boethius, the African Martianus Capella had sought to present the four mathematical *artes* in a way attractive to Latin taste. Some important Platonic matter on these subjects had been set out by Macrobius in his *Commentary on Scipio's Dream*, where the treatment of astronomical geography is particularly extensive; and tough constitutions could learn about the higher flights by reading Calcidius' commentary on Plato's *Timaeus* composed late in the fourth century. Something on mathematics by Apuleius survived to be known to Cassiodorus, but has left no other trace. Cassiodorus says that Apuleius adapted a treatise by the Pythagorean Nicomachus which Boethius also used for his own work on Arithmetic.

For the Platonic tradition the four mathematical disciplines form a connected group occupying a central place both in our understanding and in the structure of things. Plato himself took this quartet as ways of training the mind to deal with concepts that transcend the physical world of sense-perception. Thinking about pure numbers can elevate the soul to an understanding of its own nature. Geometry may begin as a practical skill for measuring land, but the examination of the nature of a triangle or square or polygon will lead the mind to recognize that the boundaries of a geometrical figure are not physical but abstract concepts. In the case of music and astronomy the abstraction is less obvious. Plato thought that musical education should not be in the practical arts of flute or reed-pipe or lyre but rather in the abstract theory which alone is a proper concern of philosophers. As for the stars, the fact that they move shows they can serve as imperfect approximations guiding the mind up to the immutable truth about solids.

Plato's notions of the role of mathematics in education are akin to those associated with the Pythagoreans. Its concerns are not this physical world but a higher realm beyond space and time. In *Metaphysics* M Aristotle set out to try and refute this position. But the Neopythagoreans remained unconvinced.

Arithmetic

Nicomachus of Gerasa (Jerash in northern Jordan, a few miles south-east of the Sea of Galilee) lived in the middle of the second century AD and took Pythagoras as his guide to life. He wrote a tract on the Pythagorean order of daily living, later used by Porphyry and especially by Iamblichus.[3] In this tract Pythagoras' life and wonder-working career are held up as an example of moral and personal discipline; for Pythagoras suffered misunderstanding and attack, descended to the underworld and returned, and called an intimate group of disciples to observe ritual instructions, to heed his gnomic maxims, and to begin and end each day with special chants and prayers of self-examination.

Nicomachus' *Introduction to Arithmetic* achieved the status of being a standard textbook in the Neoplatonic schools of Athens and Alexandria. The work survives in its original Greek. First printed at Paris, 1538, it was last edited by Hoche in the Teubner series (1866), and has received an English translation and full commentary by M. L. D'Ooge, F. E. Robbins and L. C. Karpinski (1926 repr. 1972). It received commentaries, also extant, from Iamblichus in the fourth century, from Asclepius of Tralles, and from Philoponus in the sixth century.[4] A commentary by Proclus has unfortunately not survived, but passages in Proclus' *Commentary on the Timaeus* contain numerous mathematical expositions akin to Nicomachus' spirit. Proclus believed that Nicomachus' soul had become reincarnate in himself, which indicates the depth of the bond he felt towards his works.[5]

Nicomachus' Introduction to Harmony is not extant as a whole. Its main lines may be reconstructed partly from some surviving excerpts, partly from a brief *Enchiridion* summarizing the salient points for an aristocratic lady (who is promised a larger essay in due course),[6] and partly from Boethius' adaptations in his *De institutione musica*.

Nicomachus also wrote a work with great influence on the Neoplatonists called *Theological Arithmetic*, that is, on the mysteries of numerology as a clue to the meaning of the universe. This also is lost, and our knowledge of the content is derived from two sources, one hostile, one friendly. The erudite patriarch Photius in the ninth century gives a short and unsympathetic summary in his *Bibliotheca*, codex 187. A better idea of its character is derived from the *Theologoumena Arithmeticae*, a Neoplatonic compilation on the mystery of numbers and ratios which is likely to have come from the school of either Iamblichus or Proclus. The manuscripts ascribed it to no named author (Falco's Teubner edition suggests Iamblichus). It is noteworthy that Boethius, who owed Nicomachus a large debt, never makes use of these more mystical speculations. But he found congenial matter in Iamblichus' commentary on Nicomachus.

To Nicomachus Pythagoreanism is not simply a mathematically based philosophy. It has the merit of offering a synthesis of science and religion, combining exact mathematical theory with a belief that the harmony apparent in the cosmos is the same that binds together soul and body in man. The four mathematical disciplines he calls *methodoi*, paths or methods for proceeding upwards in a steady progress towards higher knowledge. The standard Neopythagorean order is Arithmetic, Music, Geometry, Astronomy which are described, in a text ascribed to Pythagoras himself in the *Theologoumena Arithmeticae* (p. 21, 7 ff. Falco), as 'steps' to wisdom trodden in this ordered progression.

Arithmetic 73

This is also the order pursued by Boethius. He begins his *Arithmetic*[7] with an elaborate dedication to Symmachus, hoping it will have the approval of his wise judgement that he has adapted the work from the Greek of Nicomachus; he recalls that Symmachus himself is very expert in both Greek and Latin. So Boethius submits to his scholarly opinion these firstfruits of his labour (*laboris mei primitias*). The four mathematical sciences are a *quadrivium*, a group of four ways by which, through the study of mathematical immutables, the mind may rise to the peak of perfection and learn to see the divine mathematics in creation. They are four progressive steps (*gradus*) liberating the eye of the soul (as Plato has put it) from corporeality. Arithmetic is the foundation without which the other three could have no standing. But the subject matter of each science is distinct. We have to distinguish (with Aristotle's *Categories*, chapter 6) between magnitude and multitude. Aristotle had explained that there are two kinds of being (a) that which is continuous with its constitutive parts, as a tree or a rock, and possesses magnitude; (b) that which consists of many parts and is a collective, as a flock, people, chorus, heap; these are multitudes. Magnitudes divide into those which move and those which do not. Multitudes divide into (a) those that are plural in themselves, as 3 or 4 or a tetragon, or any number which is dependent on no other for its existence; (b) those which depend on something else, as double or half or some proportion. On this classification, Arithmetic studies multitude in itself, while Music studies it in relation to something else (*ad aliquid*). Geometry studies immovable magnitude, Astronomy movable. The first and third sciences are pure, the second and fourth applied, and it is clear why the traditional order of study came into being. The principles of harmony govern the movements of the stars, but Arithmetic as the science of number lays the foundation of all else.

Boethius' *Arithmetic* closely follows his Greek model step by step. Since he has no algebraic symbols and sets out everything in continuous prose, it is not the easiest mathematical book to read, but he supplies many diagrams to help the reader along. Following Nicomachus, he begins from the basic division of numbers into even and odd. Then he examines the unique properties of the number 1, alone among whole numbers in not being the mean between two other numbers in an arithmetical series, and not to be reckoned among the odd numbers from which its behaviour differs. The next chapters explore sets of numbers, both even and odd, and subdivisions such as 'evenly odd', 2 (2n + 1). Odd numbers are then divided into (a) prime numbers, excluding 2; (b) numbers of which the factors are both odd and prime, as 9, 15, 21, 25, 35, 39; (c) numbers not prime in themselves but prime to one another, as 9 and 25 which have no common measure except 1.

From Nicomachus (i, 13) Boethius reproduces 'Eratosthenes' Sieve', by which prime numbers, if not too large, can be identified by taking the series of odd numbers and deleting first every third number beginning with 3, every fifth beginning with 5, every seventh beginning with 7—and so on. He also gives the explanation how to divide numbers into Abundant (where the sum of all possible factors including 1 exceeds the number itself), Deficient (where the sum of all possible factors is less than the number itself), and Perfect (where the sum of all possible factors is identical with the number itself). The perfect numbers known in antiquity are few (6, 28, 496, [8,128]) and it is suggestive of mystery that there is one each in the groups 1–10, 11–100, 101–1,000 and 1,001–10,000. Boethius mentions only the first three.

Numerical ratios then take the centre of Boethius' stage. The subject was especially interesting to Pythagoreans because their observation that musical concords depend on simple ratios is cardinal to their belief in the structural harmony of the cosmos. Three main types of ratio are distinguished, following the introduction to the *Sectio Canonis* ascribed to Euclid where it is explained that the first two types of numerical ratios form musical consonances. The ratios are all of greater to lesser. Boethius makes it all look simpler than it is.

(*a*) where one quantity is a simple multiple of that with which it is being compared;
(*b*) where one number is greater than the other in such a way that the greater contains the lesser plus *one* part of the lesser. 16 contains 12 plus one-third of 12. 36 contains 30 plus one-fifth of 30. (The ratios for the basic musical consonances are formed by very simple numbers, the

difference between them being one; as for example 3:2, 4:3.) For this type of ratio the Greeks used the term *epimorios*, a technical term which may have come from the ancient calculation of interest rates on loans. Boethius' rendering is 'superparticularis'. Individual ratios of this type may have their own technical epithets: *sesqualter* for 3:2, *sesquitertius* for 4:3. Boethius calls the greater number *dux*, the lesser *comes*, which may perhaps reflect his awareness that under the Gothic regime the military commander exercised greater authority than the civil administrator, reversing the original Roman precedence of count before duke (to bring about the protocol which still holds good today);

(c) where one number is greater than the other in such a way that the greater contains the lesser plus *more than one* part of the lesser. 25 contains 15 plus two-thirds of 15. 81 contains 45 plus four-fifths of 45.

The Greeks called this type of ratio *epimeres*. Boethius' word for it is 'superpartiens'. Aulus Gellius (*Attic Nights* xviii, 14) knows of no Latin equivalent for the Greek terms; so it is probable that the Latin words are Boethius' coinage.

The final chapter of Boethius' first book reminds the reader, who may be so unmathematical as to find all this rather dry, that these investigations have ethical and metaphysical significance. Goodness itself is a matter of definition and falls under knowledge. The first nature (i.e. God) can be imitated and perceived by the human mind. Evil is unprincipled and anarchic, and strays from the definiteness of the Good. Yet it is held in check by providence just as the mind controls excessive cupidity and anger. Boethius' moralizing is rather less lucid than his original model in Nicomachus, where the sense is clearer. The insistence on the 'definite' character of goodness is to mark a contrast with the indefinite dyad, which for the Pythagoreans symbolizes evil because it marks the beginning of multiplicity over against the One. The knowable and therefore limited is prior to the unlimited and therefore unknowable. Whatever is indeterminate is without identity and is in permanent flux.

The paragraph has the interest of being a piece that could as easily be found in the middle of the *Consolation of Philosophy* as in the *Arithmetic*.

Boethius' second book is longer than the first and continues to follow Nicomachus' second book closely. It begins by picking up a theme ending the previous book, that inequality is secondary to a logically prior equality. All things in the world spring from the four elements of earth, air, water and fire (illustrated by a line from Lucretius i, 715 'Ex imbri terra atque anima gignuntur et igni'), and will eventually dissolve into them again. Speech is made up of syllables, syllables of letters, and it all ultimately comes back to the constituent letters and sounds (from Nicomachus ii, 1). Analogously the sound of music. In each case all inequality is reducible to equality, as if it were something being resolved into an element of its proper genus. Three terms in proportion, of multiple, superparticular or superpartient form, can be reduced to three equal terms, by reversing the conversion process described at the end of book i. This interdependence of the three types of ratio is 'a profound and wonderful speculation', which fills Nicomachus with excitement (ii, 2, 3), because it illuminates the harmonic intervals according to which, in Plato's *Timaeus* (35–6), the world-soul is generated. More than any other part of the *Arithmetica* this chapter attracted scholiasts, especially an exposition by Gerbert of Aurillac which in the twelfth century became famous as the 'saltus Gerberti'.

Chapter 4 of book ii (= Nicomachus ii, 6) brings Boethius to the theory of polygonal numbers, illustrating how arithmetic is the 'mother and root' of geometry. Numbers can be represented by dots, a lot of adjacent dots produce a line, and lines can be made to form plane figures—triangles, squares, pentagons 'as the Greeks call them', etc.

The method of working out triangular or square or other such numbers is explained (ii, 9 ff.), and the development of squares from triangles, pentagons from squares, until we reach the pyramid (ii, 21) which may have a triangular, square, or any other polygonal base as long as it has its apex in a single point. Tetrahedral numbers are shown to be simply the sum of triangular numbers; pyramidal numbers in turn depend on tetrahedral numbers (ii, 23). Cube numbers are the product of three equal numbers, in contrast to 'scalene' numbers which are the product of unequal numbers (25). Other solid numbers, and their fanciful Greek names, are successively reviewed (26 ff.).

Chapter 27 contains a characteristic digression on the Pythagorean principle that duality is the principle of alterity, but is of a nature all of its own akin to no number other than the original ingenerate unity. For odd numbers in principle stem from 1 and even from 2; so any odd number 'participates in the nature of immutable substance'. Everything in the world is constituted of odd and even, unity and duality, and everything is either of immutable substance, such as God or the soul or mind or whatever is blessed with an incorporeal nature, or is mutable and corporeal (ii, 31, p. 123, 25 ff; *PL* 63, 1138C). Unity and duality are the very principles of immutability and mutability, being and becoming. Although contrary to one another, they are mingled in friendship and kinship to make 'one body of number', as is taught by Plato in the *Timaeus* (35a) and by the Pythagorean Philolaus (B2 Diels) with his teaching that everything is either finite or infinite, limited or unlimited. The two quotations are drawn directly from Nicomachus ii, 18, 4,[8] to make the point that 'harmony' is the making one of multiplicity and the consent of dissident elements. The argument heads back to a discussion of numerical ratios and their relation to plane figures.

The last fifteen chapters of the Arithmetic (ii, 40–54 = Nicomachus ii, 22–29) are devoted to proportionality, an arithmetical subject fundamental 'to musical speculations, astronomical subtleties and the force of geometrical argument'.

The ancients distinguished arithmetic, geometric and harmonic proportionality. To these three later students added a fourth, fifth, and sixth, and even later still the numbers were brought up to ten, a number held in deep regard by Pythagoras. Respect for this number as the very symbol of perfection explains why Aristotle, anticipated by Archytas the Pythagorean, decided to have ten logical categories (ii, 41). It is conceded by Boethius (adding a point not in Nicomachus) that the 'Archytas' who wrote on the categories in a highly Aristotelian manner is thought by some to be later than Aristotle. Boethius also alludes to this same dispute about the authorship and date of the 'Archytas' texts in the first book of his commentary on Aristotle's *Categories*,[9] where he reports on the disagreement between Iamblichus, who upheld pre-Aristotelian authenticity, and the modernist Themistius who denied them to Archytas of Tarentum and attributed them to a later Aristotelian who used the same name to give authenticity to his new work. Iamblichus' conservative views on the subject are freely reproduced in Simplicius' commentary on the *Categories*.

Boethius' account of means briefly surveys all ten types of proportionality, following Nicomachus, but gives special attention to the arithmetic, geometric, and harmonic, which play an important role in the structure of the world according to Plato's *Timaeus* (35 ff.) in a passage which Boethius concedes to be uncommonly obscure (ii, 46).

Porphyry's commentary on the *Harmonics* of Ptolemy presents a fragment of Archytas on Music, carefully defining the three main types of mean:

(a) arithmetic, when a exceeds b by the amount that b exceeds c;
(b) geometric, when a is to b as b is to c;
(c) harmonic, when 'by whatever part of itself a exceeds b, b exceeds c by the same part of c' e.g. 12 exceeds 8 by a third of 12, 8 exceeds 6 by a third of 6.

The harmonic mean is akin to the geometric (Boethius observes, ii, 49),[10] because a cube has twelve edges or 'angles', 8 sides, 6 faces, and is so named from its importance in music. A fourth is the ratio 8:6, a fifth 12:8, an octave 12:6.

So at the end Boethius concludes by anticipating his Introduction to Music with the observation that the ratio of 9:8 is that of the whole tone 'which is the common measure of all musical sounds' (ii, 54), and is constituted by the difference between a fifth and a fourth.

Music

The Pythagoreans had a high reputation for their researches in number-theory and music.[11] They first discovered that the relative pitch of musical sounds depends on the lengths of string or pipe. They discovered that the ratio for the octave is 2:1, for the fifth 3:2, for the fourth 4:3. In Plato's *Timaeus*, ratios are the basic principle by which the world soul is immanent in the cosmos and gives it its ordered structure (35b, 36a). In *Republic* 546bc skill in understanding ratios can disclose the perfect 'nuptial number' determining the times when good or bad offspring are conceived. In the *Timaeus* the world-soul rolls on its everlasting way without emitting any sound (37b). But according to the myth of Er at the end of the *Republic* each of the planets gives out a sound together with the fixed stars beyond them, so that their total harmony of eight notes constitutes a vast concord (617ab). In the *Cratylus* (405cd) Apollo as god of concord presides over the cosmic harmony of the heavenly bodies as well as earthly music.

Aristotle (*De caelo* ii, 9, 290b 12 ff.) reviews the arguments for holding that the planets emit sound. The Pythagoreans held that bodies of such a size must emit a considerable volume of sound. Moreover, they even claimed to observe that their speeds in relation to measured distances are in the same ratios as musical concords. Aristotle thinks the idea beautiful and poetical but absurd, since a principal feature of the heavenly bodies is their silence. It is ridiculous to argue that we do not hear music of the spheres only because we are used to it from the moment of our birth, and therefore hear it no more than blacksmiths hear the noise of the smithy to which their ears are accustomed.

The Pythagoreans were unmoved by such sceptics. According to Nicomachus of Gerasa as reported in Porphyry's *Life of Pythagoras*, 30, Pythagoras himself had the inspired gift of being able to hear the music of the spheres; that is, the capacity to hear the music is given only to unique individuals.

The poetic qualities of the idea, added to the reassurance it offered to humanity that the universe has principles of order, ensured a long career for the notion of planetary music. Philo of Alexandria explains that providentially we cannot hear it since, like the song of the Sirens, it would induce frenzied longings; but he is sure that Moses heard it on Sinai.[12]

In the sixth century the Alexandrian Neoplatonist Simplicius, a junior contemporary of Boethius, sought to reconcile Aristotle's negative position on the harmony of the spheres with the affirmative Platonic/Pythagorean tradition. He suggests that Pythagoras' 'hearing' of the music of the stars should be understood not as a physical disturbance of the air striking his ears but as an act of intellectual discernment of the harmonic ratios governing all cosmic order.[13]

Among the Christians Basil echoes Aristotle's criticisms,[14] but in the Latin West Ambrose (who had Basil's text before him) succeeded in combining the sceptical Aristotelian view with Philo's notion that providentially we are deaf to the music of heaven because, could we hear it, it would drive us to frenzy.[15] Augustine is as nearly silent on the subject as Aristotle believed the stars to be. But in his homily on Psalm 42 he declares that, when a man comes to the very point of death, the mind becomes detached from this world and hears an 'intellectual music'. 'A sound from above so strikes in silence, not on the ears but on the mind, that whoever hears that melody is filled with loathing of corporeal sounds, and all human life becomes in comparison a din interrupting the incomparable, ineffable song from heaven.'[16] In his tract on *Christian Instruction* Augustine is certain that 'music and number' are keys to unlock the exegesis of scripture. Moreover, numbers are governed by immutable rules and are a signpost to the unchanging Creator.[17] So the Augustinian tradition of Christian Platonism domesticated within the Church a substantial part of the old Platonic language about numbers and harmony as roads to the truth of the God who is.

Macrobius, following his model in Cicero, has also much to say on the cosmic principles of number and ratio, and especially on the music of the spheres.[18] It would have seemed natural and congenial for Boethius, who admired both Augustine and Macrobius, to accept the belief, thereby assisting Macrobius to ensure it a vast future in western literature.

> Sit, Jessica. Look how the floor of heaven
> Is thick inlaid with patines of bright gold:
> There's not the smallest orb which thou behold'st
> But in his motion like an angel sings,
> Still quiring to the young-eyed cherubins;
> Such harmony is in immortal souls;
> But whilst this muddy vesture of decay
> Doth grossly close it in, we cannot hear it.[19]

Outside the *Consolation of Philosophy* no passage of Boethius has had a more potent literary influence than the second chapter of the first book of the *De institutione musica*, where he distinguishes three kinds of music: cosmic, human, and instrumental. Instrumental music includes not only cithara and reed-pipe (*tibia*) but also the human voice in song. This third kind of music, the lowest in the hierarchy, is that with which he will begin his exposition; and it is the subject that occupies the entire extant text. But the Latin text transmitted by the manuscripts is incomplete. It breaks off in the middle of a sentence in chapter 19 of the fifth book with a report on Ptolemy's view of the proper division of the tetrachord. At the beginning of Book V the chapter headings show that this book went on to fill 30 chapters, all on subjects treated in the first book of Ptolemy's *Harmonica*. The temptation is virtually irresistible to suppose that Boethius' complete work ran to six or seven books, and that the lost parts of the work contained the discussion of cosmic and human music which we are promised at the beginning of the work. Ptolemy goes on to write of these matters in the third book of his *Harmonica*.

Cosmic music is a leading Platonic/Pythagorean theme, that is, the fitting together of the heavens, the harmonic ratios and intervals being the principle controlling the distances between the planets. For this doctrine the *Timaeus* offered classical authority. According to Porphyry's *Commentary on the Timaeus* (a book exploited by Macrobius and probably known to Boethius), the Platonists hold that the physical universe is constructed on the model of musical concords in harmonic ratios which are part of the fabric of the world-soul. This doctrine is expressly set out in Calcidius' *Commentary on the Timaeus*, 96.

In his commentary on the first book of Aristotle's *Metaphysics*, Alexander of Aphrodisias uses a detailed exposition of Pythagorean number theory, which may be drawn from a lost work by Aristotle himself, in which the Pythagoreans are credited with computing the distances between earth or moon and the sun as being in duple proportionality, Venus triple, Mercury quadruple, and so on. Alexander's exposition explains that they think numbers the very principle of nature and of all things that naturally exist, on the ground that nothing can exist or be known without numbers, whereas numbers can exist apart from anything else.[20]

So in the poem at the literary climax of the *Consolation of Philosophy*, 'O qui perpetua' (iii m. 9), Boethius will speak of the world-soul and its 'consona membra'.

Cosmic harmony also means the holding together in consonance and equilibrium of the four elements of earth, air, fire, and water; or the cycle of the four seasons. 'Harmonia' in Greek never loses its root meaning of the fitting together of disparate, potentially conflicting elements. In the third book of Ptolemy's *Harmonica*, however, cosmic harmony is seen above all in the zodiac. Movements of the stars correspond to musical intervals; configurations in relation to the sun answer to the tetrachords; the notes from Nete to Hypate are sounded by the conjunctions of the planets. The threefold division of theoretical philosophy into natural science, mathematics, and theology (below, p. 109) corresponds to the three genera of enharmonic, chromatic, and diatonic respectively. This harmonic structure of the celestial world is worked out in astonishing and far-reaching detail.[21] Macrobius felt embarrassed when cosmic harmony was taken so far as to be traced into the smaller details. He was also aware of the need to reconcile Platonic principles laid down in the *Timaeus* with the calculations of the mathematicians, especially Archimedes.[22] The text of Hippolytus' *Elenchos* (iv, 8–10), severely corrupted in the manuscript tradition, gives figures for Archimedes' calculations of the distances between the planets, intended to illustrate Archimedes' contradiction of the Platonic dogma, and also cites a Ptolemaic attempt to reconcile them (iv, 11–12).

To Boethius 'human music' means the blending of incorporeal soul and the physical body. It is grasped by introspection through which we are aware of being compounded of rationality and irrationality. Moreover, the different parts of the body form a harmonious structure. What Boethius is likely to have said in the lost ending of the *Institutio musica* may be seen in Ptolemy's third book on *Harmonica*. The primary concords of octave, fifth and fourth correspond to the soul's threefold power to think, to perceive, and to acquire a skill or habit; or to kinds of virtue in moderating sensual desires, e.g. discretion (*sophrosyne*), self-control (*enkrateia*), and modesty (*aidōs*). Seven varieties of rational virtue can be distinguished answering to the seven modes or *tonoi* admitted to Ptolemy's list. Changes in modulation are linked with changes in manner of life. That music is directly bound up with the moral and spiritual life is proved by Ptolemy from Pythagoras' prescription to begin each day with prayer sung to a chant.[23] This kinship of music and worship is included by Boethius in his prefatory matter, except that he refers to Pythagorean vespers rather than mattins.

Ptolemy, then, was probably followed in the missing sections of Boethius which dealt with cosmic and human music.[24] The subject, however, is a regular theme in several other writers. A substantial fragment of Aristotle on music, quoted in the treatise on music transmitted among the works of Plutarch, explains that the discernment of the divine harmony by the bodily senses of sight and hearing is possible because this harmony enters into the very constitution of the human body.[25]

An elaborate Neoplatonic treatise on the philosophy of instrumental, cosmic, and human harmony is preserved in Greek from the pen of Aristides Quintilianus, written for his friends Eusebius and Florentius. The date of this author is hard to determine with confidence. He shows some affinities in terminology and viewpoint with the school of Iamblichus, and may well belong to the middle years of the fourth century. But no weight can be placed on the mention of two mid-fourth-century men named Eusebius and Florentius in the history of Ammianus Marcellinus, since the names are both common in late antiquity. Like Boethius Aristides includes diagrams with the names and notation of musical notes. But unlike Boethius he omits almost all the complicated mathematical calculations of Pythagorean harmonic theory. The three basic intervals of octave, fifth, and fourth, and the three genera of enharmonic, chromatic, and diatonic, correspond for Aristides to the triadic structure of the Platonic cosmos which is divided into incorporeal or divine, psychic, and corporeal (iii, 11 p. 110, 10 ff. Winnington-Ingram). The soul is constituted by numbers (iii, 24, p. 125, 29 ff.), as taught in Plato's *Timaeus*. Aristides' treatise well illustrates the late Platonic interest in musical theory as a vital clue to the meaning and structure of the cosmos, of which man is in himself a representation.[26] The work was much drawn upon by Martianus Capella for his account of harmony, and therefore could easily have been known to Boethius. But there is nothing in the extant text of *De institutione musica* which is directly borrowed from it.

Boethius' Treatise on Music and its sources

Boethius had few Latin predecessors in expounding the theory of music. A treatise on the subject, known to Cassiodorus and also mentioned by Boethius, had been composed probably late in the fourth century by Albinus. Albinus also wrote a 'Geometry' known to Boethius, and was reputed to have written something 'on dialectic' which Boethius confesses he has been unable to trace (*Perih.* i 4 Meiser = *PL* 64, 393). Cassiodorus admired the extant Greek treatise by Gaudentius, and persuaded his friend Mutianus, to whom he had also entrusted a Latin version of some John Chrysostom, to make a version of Gaudentius for the library at Vivarium. Cassiodorus also knew Boethius' work, and must therefore have thought that Gaudentius would still add something to Latin knowledge of the subject.

Apart from these monographs the main sources of information about Latin musical education are the occasional digressions in Vitruvius' work on architecture, and an essay written by Censorinus in AD 238 on the significance of birthdays, *De die natali*. It is no doubt incorrect to speak of Vitruvius' discussions of music as digressions. He helped to transmit the idea that the proportions of a building or of a room would look right to the eye if the dimensions were to be based on the proportions that rule the art of music, and so set (for example) Palladio on to the idea that his villas should be designed with harmonic ratios built into their structure.

Augustine's treatise on music is principally concerned with rhythm and metre, turning in the sixth book to a general Platonic discussion of the principles of harmony in the cosmos.

There is less concern with sound than we find even in the pages of Boethius.

Boethius could reasonably hold that the Latin world possessed nothing from which one could learn of the finer points of Platonic/Pythagorean musical theory as set out by the principal masters acknowledged in the contemporary Neoplatonic schools, above all Nicomachus and Ptolemy.

Nicomachus' full treatment of harmony is lost except for fragments. But from these excerpts and from his extant *Enchiridion* it is easy to demonstrate that Boethius' *Institutio musica* begins by following Nicomachus very carefully and exactly.[27] The first two books have almost no other source, and are closely interconnected with the *Institutio arithmetica*, the argument of which is recapitulated in the first seventeen chapters of book ii. There are, however, some minor touches which look like borrowings from Iamblichus' commentary on Nicomachus' *Arithmetica*.[28] And he is already looking forward to the material he will incorporate from Ptolemy later in the work, so that there are references to the doctrines of the Ptolemaic harmonic system. It is far from impossible that these stood before Boethius in his text of Nicomachus, who could easily have read Ptolemy's work. To Nicomachus Ptolemy might well have seemed to make too many concessions to the critics of Pythagorean musical theory.

The mutilation of the fifth book is likely to have been accidental rather than the deliberate tearing away of the highly Platonizing sections on cosmic and human music. The extant text breaks off in the middle of a sentence with the words 'nusquam una . . .', to which a few manuscripts try to apply some remedy.[29] One thirteenth-century manuscript claims that he was unable to complete the work 'because of the envy of the Italians' bringing about his death.[30] Several manuscripts give only the first two books, these containing the heart of the Pythagorean theory.

The modern reader of Boethius' *Institutio musica* is often surprised to discover that the work is militantly theoretical. Like Plato and Augustine, Boethius regards practical music-making as none of his concern, though the fourth book includes several matters that bear on practice. It is characteristic that the practical material is confused and less easy to follow than the chapters containing the more abstract mathematical matter in the first three books. Both Augustine and Boethius are known to have had a strong love for the physical sound of music. Augustine's *Confessions* record the profound emotional effect on him of the psalm-chants at Milan (ix, 6, 14); and, while he came to feel guilty if church music became more significant to him than the words and truths thereby conveyed, he will have none of puritans wishing to exclude all music from worship, insisting that words can find their way to the heart and mind more effectively when sung than when said; for there is 'hidden kinship' (*occulta familiaritas*) between music and the soul (*Conf.* x, 33, 49–50). A certain ironic reserve can be felt when Augustine comments on 'the many for whom *beata vita* consists in the music of voices and strings, and who count themselves miserable when music is lacking to their lives' (*de Libero Arbitrio* ii, 13, 35). The nine Muses, he feels, ultimately offer no more than theatrical, frivolous entertainment (*De Doctrina Christiana* ii, 18, 28). Boethius, too, in the *Consolation of Philosophy* mentions how much he loves the sound of music (*Cons.* iv, 6, 6); but the Muses receive a sharp rebuff when they offer help to the distressed prisoner, dismissed as theatrical harlots (*Cons.* i, 2) in language which could be an echo of Augustine.

The disparagement of actual music-making is more than a social attitude conventional in an aristocratic élite towards the low standing of professional musicians in ancient society where, after the classical period, most professional pipe-players were negligibly clad girls brought in at dinner parties to entertain the guests with music and dancing. Aristotle (*Politics* 1339a–41b10) says professional musicians belong to the lower orders, and gentlemen only play instruments when drunk or for a joke. Even the Epicureans, who liked music at feasts, did not think gentlemen should be performers; so expressly Philodemus. But for Plato it was a matter of principle that music be studied as an abstract and pure science. If the Pythagoreans of his time were not seen by him as properly setting about the escape from the flux of time and sense, later Pythagoreans like Nicomachus clearly regard music as lacking disciplinary value in higher education unless its study is as remote from actual sounds heard by the ear as possible.[31] As

Augustine puts it, the proper object of intellectual inquiry is 'not the art but the science' of music. For Boethius the true *musicus* is not the executant but the one who understands the theory, as superior to practice as soul is to body (*Mus.* i, 34). In the *Life of Plotinus* 14, Porphyry claims that his master had an extensive knowledge of the theory of geometry, mechanics, optics, and music, but no practical interest. In consequence, the late writers do not pursue the fascinating questions raised in the (pseudo-) Aristotelian *Problemata* xix, e.g. why people especially like pipe(*aulos*)-playing when feeling either sad or glad; why some notes are harder for a singer to pitch than others; why familiar music gives more pleasure than unfamiliar; why a solo singer gives more pleasure when accompanied, whereas a voice singing wordlessly is less agreeable than a pipe; why sound is felt to have a moral character when colour, odour, and taste have none.[32] There is little inquiry among late writers on music into its capacity for emotional diversity. Though they cannot but be aware of music's extraordinary power to penetrate the inmost feelings, that power is somehow regarded with fear and reserve. Boethius, accordingly, is writing on musical theory without the least likelihood that he knows much of the practice of the art. He may be an unusual man but he would not have defied all social conventions.

Pythagorean turning away from the soiling of one's mind by contact with the actual practice of the art came under robust criticism in the fourth century BC from Aristoxenus' of Tarentum.[33] Although no scientist (indeed he writes with deliberate defiance of the profession), Aristoxenus stands out in the history of this subject as one of the greater figures in Greek intellectual achievement, even if the technical difficulty of comprehending ancient Greek musical writers (when we can have so little knowledge of what sounds were heard when musicians sang and played) may have limited the recognition of his stature and originality. He writes also with a delightful and urbane irony (e.g. ii, 31 of the illusion of those who think harmony so sublime a science that its study will improve their moral character). Aristoxenus tells us that at Tarentum his father had personally known the Pythagorean theoretician of music Archytas; and he felt himself to be well acquainted with the Pythagorean mathematics and harmonics of his own time. The more he knew about it the less plausible he thought it to be.

Pythagorean musicology was based on a fundamental and wholly correct observation that intervals can be precisely expressed as numerical ratios—a fifth 3:2, a fourth 4:3, an octave 2:1. If a string is stopped at two-thirds of its length, the pitch of the note sounded will be a perfect fifth higher than the open string. If stopped at a quarter of its length, a perfect fourth is heard. To play an octave higher, one must stop the string at halfway point. A fifth and a fourth together add up to an octave, which in mathematical terms is found by multiplying the ratios, $3/2 \cdot 4/3 = 2/1$. A whole tone can be expressed as the ratio 9:8, that is, the difference between the fourth and the fifth: $3/2 \div 4/3 = 9/8$. The Pythagoreans calculated that neither the concordant ratios nor the ratio for a whole tone can be equally divided without an irrational number, which is ruled out as inadmissible and 'ludicrous'; a view already known to Plato (*Republic* 525e). It is therefore axiomatic that the figure must be expressed in a whole number. The ratio 9:8 has the same proportionality as 18:16. But in geometric or harmonic proportion 17 is not the halfway point between 18 and 16, since 17/16 is greater than 18/17. In short, by however much the basic ratio of 9:8 is multiplied, there will be no way of expressing the precise mean in terms of a whole number. It also follows that six whole tones in the proportion of 9:8 cannot, when added together, give an interval that is precisely in the ratio of 2:1. They have a slight overplus. By this small but mathematically and aurally significant amount, which Boethius (ii, 31) and the Neoplatonists call a 'comma', the sum of six whole tones exceeds the octave concord. Furthermore, the Pythagoreans argued, a 'semitone' is not in reality half a tone. The diatonic tetrachord contains in descending order two whole tones plus a fraction of a tone which is conventionally called a semitone but, in 'natural' as opposed to 'tempered' tuning, is rather less than half a whole tone. If the proportion of a fourth (4:3) is given in figures multiplied by 64, the ratio appears as 256:192. If 192 is the *mese* or middle note taken as the base of calculations, a fifth below it is a relative string length of 288 ($192 \cdot 3/2 = 288$). The numbers of the intervals are therefore in descending pitch 192, 216, 243, 256, and 288. 288:256 = 9:8 (32), a whole tone. Again it is demonstrated that the small semitone contained within the fifth cannot represent a proportionality that is precisely half a tone.[34] A tempered half of a 'natural' whole tone would be the square root of (9:8), and that is an irrational number.

The Pythagorean argument is mathematically set out in the 'Sectio Canonis', or division of the Monochord, transmitted, perhaps rightly, under Euclid's name, though the argument is no doubt older than his time. If there are six intervals in the ratio 9:8, one can set out their numerical relation in tabular form by beginning with the figure $(8^3)^2$, that is 262144. If each descending interval is a whole tone, the series of numbers in 9:8 proportion is: 262144 294912 331776 373248 419904 472392 531441. But 262144 . 2 = 524288 which is less than 531441. Therefore six whole tones exceed the octave.[35]

Although the Pythagorean calculations are correct, it should not be deduced that the calculators were consistent or that they understood much about the physics of sound. Boethius (Mus. iii, 5) preserves a fragment of Philolaus (A 26 Diels) which assumes that because in the ratio 256:243 the *diesis* or quarter-tone is 13, this 13 is also the difference for other figures. That is, he takes 27, cube of 3, the first odd number and held in awe in Pythagorean reckoning, and also the difference between 216 and 243;[36] he rightly declares that 27:24 is the 9:8 ratio of a whole tone; but then he splits 27 into 13 and 14 to give 2 *dieses* differing by a significant unity which Philolaus calls a *comma*.

In a related fragment of Philolaus (B 6) quoted by Boethius (iii, 8) the Pythagorean defines the *diesis* as the difference between two whole tones and a perfect fourth (4:3), a *comma* as the difference between a whole tone and two *dieses* (13 + 13 + 1). He then proceeds to talk as if both *dieses* and *comma* can be bisected, apparently forgetful of the central Pythagorean doctrine that such intervals cannot be precisely split into halves.

Archytas of Tarentum is reported by Boethius (Mus. iii, 11; A 19 Diels) to have devised a simple but subtle calculation to underpin Pythagorean doctrine that an octave, fifth, fourth, and whole tone cannot be divided into precisely equal parts expressible in terms of a whole number. It is characteristic of the ratios of all these intervals in superparticular proportion that the numbers being compared differ by a fraction whose numerator is 1; when the ratios are expressed in their minimal and most elemental form, the numbers must be prime to one another. There is no whole number which is the mean proportional of any ratio whose smallest compared quantities differ by no more than the smallest of whole numbers (a proposition also laid down by Euclid, *Elementa* vii, 22).

Boethius notes that the observation is correct but the definition given is too fluid (*nimium fluxa est*) to satisfy a logician. Boethius concedes to Archytas that in the case of 'superparticular' proportions i.e. where the compared quantities differ only as n + 1:n, then the division into half of the fraction must produce an irrational number. But Archytas' argument does not hold good for 'multiple' ratios, in which the smallest possible integers may also differ by 1.

The original discovery that the consonances of fourth, fifth and octave are the result of simple numerical ratios was attributed in the Pythagorean tradition to the master Pythagoras himself. The legend is told by Boethius, in common with Nicomachus, Iamblichus, Macrobius, and other ancient writers, that 'by divine providence' (Boethius takes the phrase directly from Nicomachus) Pythagoras passed a smithy when five hammers of different weights of 12, 9, 8 and 6, were producing sounds, four being consonant in the ratio 2:1, 3:2, 4:3, 9:8, and the fifth dissonant. On reaching home he verified the observation with strings and other instruments.[37] It is a pity that so picturesque a story cannot be true.

Whatever may lie behind the legends, there is no doubt of the great antiquity of two elements in Pythagorean theory: the concept of a cosmic musical harmony and the veneration for the triangular number 10.

The group of numbers 1, 2, 3, 4, whose sum is 10, give a perfect triangle (according to the modern algebraic formula for triangular numbers ½n(n+1)).

For Pythagoreanism it is no mere social convention or the fact that we count on our fingers that leads all people to divide numbers into tens, but a profound insight into the very structure of reality.[38] From the fact that 10 is produced by a triangle on a base of 4, Pythagoreans drew large inferences about the importance of the musical tetrachord, the fundamental interval of the fourth on which the tuning of the lyre or cithara is based.

Aristoxenus took no notice of theoretical ratios, and preferred to express differences of pitch in terms of quality rather than of quantity.[39] He understood intervals of pitch as analogous to segments of a line, a view encouraged by the 'geometrical' view of number as linear. Experiments with the 'canon' or monochord supported him.[40] From these it was easy to see that the differences between notes are like the differences between colours on a rainbow,[41] a continuum where one note gradually merges into the next. He took not the fourth but the octave as the basic unit, divided it into twelve equal semitones, and maintained that a semitone is exactly half a whole tone. Accordingly a progression of six tones gives an octave interval if the string is divided on the system which today we would call 'equal temperament'. Aristoxenus had no interest of course in making it easy to modulate into a different tonality.

To Aristoxenus it was a matter of indifference that the resulting numerical ratios cannot be expressed except in 'irrational' numbers. In his view the ear is the sovereign judge, not the mathematical reason with its doctrinaire imposition of abstract theory.

The Pythagoreans replied by expatiating on the general deceptiveness of sense-perception and on the non-controversial superiority of mind to body. If musical harmonies are providence's gift to point our minds up to discern hidden harmonies in our human constitution and, higher still, in the harmonic structure of the very cosmos itself,[42] then that eternal harmony which is represented by immutable truth in numerical ratios overrides any mere observation by our animal, bodily sense of hearing. The ear hears sounds, but only mind can interpret them and grasp their harmony.[43]

The Platonic tradition (*Republic* 398–400) was nevertheless not only aware but insistent that music, despite its detachment from anything touched or seen, has curious links with practical moral action; that some 'modes', or ways of tuning the lyre, are suitable for austere or funerary or noble music, other 'modes' for drinking songs and more light-hearted stuff. According to *Laches* (188d) a truly patriotic Greek should prefer the authentically Hellenic Dorian mode to the effeminate and foreign Lydian or Phrygian. In the *Laws* (669cd) Plato deplores modes associated with eroticism and the mixing of modes.[44] The authentic old tradition is against both change and complexity, as Boethius can show by quoting in archaic Greek the text of a Spartan decree of censure upon Timothy of Miletus for dangerous innovation. Boethius no doubt follows Nicomachus when in his preface he explains that different modes get their names from the races or tribes whose national characteristics show affinity with the music associated with them, like Lydian or Phrygian. It is noticeable, he pointedly remarks, that the harsher modes make music congenial to tough Gothic ears, but gentler modes would be liked by moderate Goths 'though at the present time there are virtually none of these'. Boethius recounts the legend of Pythagoras sobering up a dangerously intoxicated young man at Tauromenium (Taormina, founded in 408 BC well after Pythagoras' time) by singing him a melody in the Phrygian mode[45]—a Ciceronian story which Boethius may have borrowed either from Augustine's polemic against Julian of Eclanum (*C. Jul.* v, 5, 23), or directly from Cicero's book *De consiliis suis*. Boethius does not use the variant of the story told by Quintilian (i, 10, 32).

Boethius likewise enjoys anecdotes of music therapy, of Terpander and Arion delivering Lesbians and Ionians from plague by their songs, or of Empedocles calming an angry armed man by music. Martianus Capella (ix, 926) similarly stresses its curative effects on the sick in mind and body. Among the mathematical sciences, declares the sixth-century commentator on Aristotle Elias, music alone has the capacity to bring therapy to both body and soul.[46]

In book iv he gives a translation of the *Sectio canonis* ascribed to Euclid which gives a crucial statement of the Pythagorean/Platonic theory and which is also cited in full by Porphyry in his commentary on Ptolemy's *Harmonica* (pp. 99–103 Düring). Boethius then embarks on an endeavour to relate theory to practice by determining the relative pitch of different notes on the scale. It is hard to use the word 'scale' without immediately suggesting the familiar diatonic scale of modern western music. This would be misleading. Ancient Greek music had no note corresponding to our tonic, a fact that profoundly affects one's understanding of the term 'mode'. At first the standard interval round which everything is constructed is the perfect fourth, and the middle string or Mese is the note to which the other strings of the cithara are tuned.[47] The chant moves up and down within a fourth either side of a middle note (the nearest modern analogy might be ecclesiastical chanting e.g. in the eucharistic Preface). A fourth below the Mese is the Hypate ('highest'), a fourth above it is the Nete ('lowest'). These derive their names from their position on the instrument: the 'lowest' string was tuned to the highest pitch, the 'highest' to the lowest. These three notes are constant in their relative intervals. Between them two intervals were played with a tuning that could vary widely. Three types of tuning were recognized:

1. *Diatonic*, in which the first two intervals of the descending tetrachord normally proceed by whole tones (hence the name of this method of tuning), leaving a narrow semitone as a remainder before reaching the Hypate.
2. *Chromatic*, i.e. coloured or shaded, in which the first descending interval is more than a whole tone (nearer to a minor third), leaving two semitones to reach Hypate.
3. *Enharmonic*, in which the first descending interval approximates to our major third, say A to G double flat, with two quarter tones to Hypate.

Aristoxenus (i, 19 and 23) explains that the diatonic is the oldest of the three genera; the enharmonic the most recondite, learnt with difficulty and hardest for the ear to assimilate; while the sweet chromatic is the most popular.

The subtle intonations of the chromatic and enharmonic genera were evidently valued because they gave more variety and possibility of expression. Ancient music is melodic, and has no reliance on counterpoint or harmony. (*Harmonia* in Greek does not correspond to our word 'harmony', but means 'fitting together', and often can mean a 'scale' or the pattern of a tetrachord.) The absence of what modern westerners would think harmonic feeling is shown by the declaration of Aristoxenus that an interval of less than a fourth is discordant on the ear; whereas a major or minor third would not be regarded as dissonant by a European ear at any time after the high middle ages. On the other hand, many testimonies, such as that of Aristoxenus just quoted, treat the enharmonic genus as a piece of pedagogic pedantry which no practical musician ever uses. Commenting on Aristotle's *Categories*, Porphyry illustrates the point that something can be knowable without anyone actually knowing it with the observation that 'in antiquity musicians could hear the quartertone (*diesis*), but later as enharmonic melody passed out of use, the ear has lost its sensitivity to this interval.'[48] Macrobius says of his own time in the fifth century that the enharmonic genus is never used because of its difficulty, while the chromatic is disapproved of because of its erotic associations.[49] Boethius notes that diatonic tuning, to which Plato's *Timaeus* had imparted a superior authority, lacked some quality of 'softness', characteristic of the subtler, narrower intervals of chromatic and enharmonic.[50] The account of the modes in *Mus.* iv, 8 takes the diatonic genus as the norm, and this preference is evidently grounded on Plato's *Timaeus* 35b. Proclus' exposition of this passage observes that Plato's diatonic scale is 'simpler and nobler', though the enharmonic scale has educational value; the chromatic Proclus sets aside as weak and ignoble.

Accordingly, while the top and bottom notes of a tetrachord are fixed and stable, the names of the intervening notes in the middle of the tetrachord (viz. Lichanos or 'index finger' and Parhypate if descending; Paramese and Paranete if ascending) give no indication of relative pitch, within a defined locus, unless one also knows in which of these three *genera* of tuning the melody is set.

To read Boethius' explanation of these matters is to be aware of an immense mathematical refinement being brought to bear upon a popular music originally rooted in the lost folk-songs of archaic Greece. Like Ptolemy and Greek models, Boethius tries to bring order and simplification to an intricate matter by assigning a letter of the alphabet to each variation of pitch, beginning with A as the label of the lowest note playable on a cithara. But his alphabetical series is not that of our modern nomenclature. He has not seen the advantage of giving the label A both to the lowest note and to the note an octave above it. The alphabetical series is a convenient form of reference for his theoretical operation of giving a description and a label to every successive note, be it tone, semitone, or quartertone, in each of the genera taken all together. He therefore needs to extend the alphabet beyond A–Z to include AA–LL. Boethius' use of the Latin alphabet marks a noteworthy step on the way towards the western nomenclature that is now universal convention. Moreover in chapter 4 of book iv he is sufficiently interested in practicalities to provide a detailed list of the notational signs for each note within the double octave in all three genera. (Similar lists occur in other ancient writers on music.) Nevertheless, the ensuing discussion of the division of the monochord (iv, 5 f.) reverts to being quite severely theoretical. Boethius computes in numerical terms the notes within the double octave in the Lydian mode, calculating on the principle that in the several genera the middle intervals within each tetrachord are strictly regular and constant; that is, the mathematical proportions for the diatonic intervals (two tones plus a small semitone) in the lower tetrachord ('hypaton') will be in the same mutual relation as those for the diatonic intervals in any higher tetrachord.

The way in which Boethius here distinguishes the 'inconstant' intervals in each genus within the constant fourths is of some interest. In the highest tetrachord ('hyperboleon') the top note is computed at 2304. The octave below this is then 4608, the fourth below 3072. Accordingly in all three genera the highest pitch, the Nete hyperboleon, is constant at 2304, and the fourth below this (Nete diezeugmenon) constant at 3072. Boethius' calculations thus give the following figures:

	diatonic	chromatic	enharmonic
Nete hyperboleon	2304	2304	2304
Paranete hyperboleon	2592	2736	2916
Trite hyperbolcon	2916	2916	2994
Nete diezeugmenon	3072	3072	3072

The figures for the internal intervals are computed first for the diatonic genus by calculating the two descending whole tones in 9:8 proportion. Nine-eighths of 2304 is 2592, and nine-eighths of 2592 is 2916. Boethius decides, not unreasonably, to assign this last figure not only to the Trite in the chromatic genus but also to the Paranete in the enharmonic. However, when he has to compute the remaining two 'internal' intervals, the chromatic Paranete and the enharmonic Trite, he resorts to the arithmetic mean.[51] He assigns to the chromatic Paranete a figure which is the diatonic Nete hyperboleon (2304) *plus* half the difference between this and the diatonic Paranete (2592); i.e. 2592 + ½ (2592–2304) = 2736.

To reach the enharmonic Trite he simply adds to 2916 (enharmonic Paranete) half the difference between this and the Nete diezeugmenon (3072); i.e. 2916 + ½ (3072–2916) = 2994.

In addition to the surprising resort to arithmetic rather than geometric or harmonic proportionality, Boethius also gives cause for remark by taking the Lydian mode to be the standard 'because it is simpler and the first' (iv, 6 p. 318, 5). One would expect a Platonist, who is so manifestly working here primarily on the basis of Platonic or Pythagorean sources, to prefer the Dorian. At least that would be the expectation if Boethius were seriously influenced in this part of his treatise by Ptolemy's *Harmonics* in which it is taken for granted, apparently without polemics, that the Dorian mode stands midway in a list of seven modes, with three modes above it and three below. On the other hand, in the Third Anonymous tract on Music, first edited by F. Bellermann (1841) and recently re-edited by D. Najock (1975), the author gives the notational signs only for the Lydian mode which he ranks as the 'first'.[52] The Third Anonymous stands in the tradition of Aristoxenus, and perhaps the Lydian mode was preferred by the Aristoxenians in conscious dissent from Plato's explicit preference for the Dorian. The date of this anonymous author is difficult to determine except within the wide choice of being later than Nicomachus (used in sections 48–9) and prior to the sixth century (since the manuscripts, though of the twelfth and later centuries, preserve some words written in uncial script, which is unlikely if the archetype was written later than this time). In choosing the Lydian mode Boethius or his source may therefore have been making some minor concession to the

Aristoxenian tradition. (Pseudo-)Plutarch's tract on *Music* (15, 1136bc) remarks on Plato's disapproval and Aristoxenus' acceptance of the Lydian mode, but does not take sides.

Ancient Greek music found that the two overlapping tetrachords available on a seven-stringed lyre could receive extension upwards and downwards. Below the Hypate there was added an 'extra' note, 'proslambanomenos' meaning additional or supernumerary. It was soon found that by beginning the tetrachord a tone above the Mese, the range could be extended upwards by one tone to produce a perfect fifth from the pitch of the Mese. The two tetrachords do not then overlap, sharing the Mese, but are disjunct (i.e. if the Mese is tuned to a, the 'Nete' or top note is moved up one tone from d to e). The range of the instrument could be extended upwards to enable the performer to play notes covering the normal range of the human voice, viz. two octaves. Boethius twice (i, 20 p. 212 and iv, 15 p. 241 = *PL* 63, 1188 and 1279) catalogues the resulting range of notes with their Greek names transliterated, on the second occasion omitting the Proslambanomenos but prefixing alphabetical labels running from A to O, as follows:

(Proslambanomenos, in i, 20 only)
A   Hypate hypatōn (i.e. of the lowest tetrachord)
B   Parhypate hypatōn
C   Lichanos hypatōn
D   Hypate mesōn (the middle tetrachord)
E   Parhypate mesōn
F   Lichanos mesōn
G   Mese
H   Paramese
I   Trite diezeugmenōn (the disjunct tetrachord)
K   Paranete diezeugmenōn
L   Nete diezeugmenōn
M   Trite hyperboleōn (the extended tetrachord)
N   Paranete hyperboleōn
O   Nete hyperboleōn

From Hypate (A) to Paramese (H) and from Mese (G) to Nete hyperboleon (O) are octaves, Boethius notes. He carelessly asserts that a fifth lies between H–D, G–C, F–B, E–A, which confuses the perfect fifth with the tritone, an error for which a Reichenau monk of the eleventh century, Hermannus Contractus, justly reprehended Boethius.[53] The sounds are evidently still mentally grouped in tetrachords as is shown by the keeping of the names of the tetrachords—hypatōn, mesōn, diezeugmenōn (disjunct, i.e. ascending from the tone above the Mese, not from the Mese itself), hyperboleōn (the highest in pitch). Nevertheless, the significance of the octave is not to be underestimated. Boethius and his Greek sources are well aware that they have a coherent scale, in which the lowest note sounds to the highest note as a double octave in a ratio of 4:1, and that a double octave is the normal range of a singer.

Boethius proceeds to explain: the octave scale is the basis of the varying 'ways' of tuning the cithara which the Greeks call *tropoi* or *tonoi* and which in Latin may be called *modi* (modes). These *tropoi* are in Boethius' view systems of tuning in which the pitch of the different fingerings of the instrument varies. In the diatonic genus, the two octaves run up from Proslambanomenos to Nete hyperboleōn; and the lowest *tropos* in pitch is the *Hypodorian* 'mode'. According to Boethius' account, if the string of the Proslambanomenos is stretched so as to raise it by a tone, then the Hypate hypatōn immediately above it is also raised by a tone; and all the other tones are sharpened to the same degree relative to one another, to produce the *Hypophrygian* mode. A similar transposition of a tone gives the *Hypolydian*, a further semitone the *Dorian*; a tone up again the *Phrygian*, a further tone the *Lydian*, a final semitone to the seventh, the *Mixolydian* (i.e. half-Lydian). In iv, 17 Boethius adds, with acknowledgements to Ptolemy, an eighth mode, *Hypermixolydian*, but Ptolemy is making the point, omitted by Boethius perhaps following his source, that the Hypermixolydian is a superfluity since in its order of tones and semitones it is identical with the Hypodorian, only being pitched an octave higher.[54]

Boethius confesses to finding his authority's account of the *tropoi* or *tonoi* hard to follow, and therefore supplies a visual aid in the form of a table. Unfortunately the manuscripts reproduce the diagram in corrupt and varied forms. In the Teubner edition, mainly based on a few manuscripts at

Bamberg and Munich, Friedlein despaired of a solution and frankly adopted the labour-saving course of reprinting Westphal's hypothetical reconstruction rather than telling the reader what he had found in such few manuscripts as he had consulted(!). This diagram,[55] however, turns out to be hardly more than a transposition table. Boethius' account of the 'modes' suggests to the unwary reader that he supposed them all to preserve identical relative intervals, only at successively rising pitches. If so, that could explain his incomprehension of Ptolemy's observation that, if the Hypermixolydian mode is identical with the Hyperdorian, it is a superfluity.

It is no doubt certain that the ancient 'modes' of Boethius and Ptolemy were not, as old textbooks of musical history used to assert, simply octave scales beginning on successive notes of the familiar, modern, diatonic (or piano) scale. On the other hand, it would defy reason to think they can be only transpositions of a scale in which the sequence of tones and semitones is unvaried between the different modes. The simplest interpretation is to suppose that the 'modes' are seven divergent ways of apportioning the sequence of tones and semitones within an octave whether of constant pitch or transposed up in series with the order of modes, and that the sequence of tones and semitones therefore includes many notes that, in relation to the modern diatonic scale, we should think of as 'accidentals', i.e. 'sharps' and 'flats'.

Ptolemy's account of 'modes' or *tonoi* (the term *tropoi*, which evidently stood in Boethius' source, is not used by him) is in some ways similar to that in Boethius, but has a number of differences. Ptolemy is interested in the tetrachordal structure of the nomenclature, e.g. Hypodorian a fourth below Dorian, Hypophrygian a fourth below Phrygian, Hypolydian a fourth below Lydian, Mixolydian a fourth above Dorian. Accordingly the Dorian 'mode' is the middle or standard tuning for Ptolemy, in contrast to Boethius' admission of the Lydian as principal norm.

Ptolemy (ii, 10) also draws up a diagrammatic scale to illustrate the intervals between his seven modes:

Mixolydian
   Leimma ('called a semitone' by Aristoxenians)

Lydian
   Tonos
Phrygian
   Tonos
Dorian
   Leimma
Hypolydian
   Tonos
Hypophrygian
   Tonos
Hypodorian

Ptolemy seeks to show how the Mese changes position as it moves up this octave scale to remain the 'middle' note of each successive mode. This diagram and the discussion of the movement of the Mese are closely akin to the text of Boethius.

It may seem surprising that Boethius, who claims firmly to stand in the Pythagorean/Platonic tradition of strict theory, should include not only the Pythagorean mathematical theory from Nicomachus (and in part Iamblichus), but also details directly bearing on musical practice such as notation. The explanation may lie in the direct or indirect influence of Ptolemy's *Harmonics* on him. Ptolemy in the main agrees with the Pythagoreans against Aristoxenus that the numerical ratios take precedence over the tempered scale calculated as if the interval of the octave were a spatial line that can be divided into twelve equal semitones without distortion of intonation. But Ptolemy concedes to the Aristoxenians that the verdicts of the ear have a right to assert themselves in company with, if not over against, the abstract mathematical reason. He aims to pursue a *via media* between Pythagoreans and Aristoxenians: 'nothing in reason can be in contradiction to the ears', and vice versa (Ptolemy i, 2 = Boethius v, 3). At iv, 18 Boethius must surely be following Ptolemy in admitting the very Aristoxenian dictum that the ear is able to judge of consonances without the least hesitation. The theme appears as early as iii, 10, immediately preceding the critique of the Pythagorean Archytas, where Boethius says that all concords should be right to both mind and ear, and mere theory is vain. Moreover Ptolemy argues at length against the Pythagorean dogma that the eleventh (octave plus fourth) is no concord since its ratio is 8:3. Aristoxenus lays down as a self-evident truth that if any concord is added to the octave, the sum is a concord.[56] According to undeviating Pythagorean principle, concords fall exclusively within the 'superparticular' category of ratios. If they fall within the 'superpartient' category, then they are disbarred from being considered as consonances. For Ptolemy the octave rather than the tetrachord has become a natural unit, and to him it seems bizarre to affirm the Pythagorean dogma that a fourth is a concord while an eleventh is not.[57] Some departure from strict Pythagorean orthodoxy seems clear here. Accordingly, Ptolemy's maintenance of Pythagorean harmonic principles undergoes modifications and makes concessions to the opposition, in principle granting the point that the ear may also judge as well as the mathematical reason, and that actual sounds are not a matter that the theoretician of music can afford to scorn.

Boethius' introduction to musical theory is much more Pythagorean than Aristoxenian, and is accordingly a remove distant from the actual art on which he is not utterly clear, and of whose practice he is surely ignorant. Like Augustine he sets out to describe the science, not the art. The Pythagorean doctrine of cosmic harmony lies at its heart, and this came to him with the high authority of Plato's *Timaeus*. It is not surprising that *De institutione musica* anticipates many themes which are restated in the *Consolation of Philosophy*: the harmony of the heavens and the seasons,[58] the 'love' that produces concord out of the warring elements in the world,[59] the binding of the elements by numbers, and the 'consonant members' of the world-soul.[60] Arithmetic directs the mind towards immutable truths unaffected by the contingencies of time and space. But music advances even further towards that 'summit of perfection' for which the *quadrivium* is a prerequisite.[61] The theory of music is a penetration of the very heart of providence's ordering of things. It is not a matter of cheerful entertainment or superficial consolation for sad moods, but a central clue to the interpretation of the hidden harmony of God and nature in which the only discordant element is evil in the heart of man.[62]

Geometry and Astronomy

The preface to Boethius' *Institutio arithmetica* implies an intention to write introductions to all four mathematical disciplines. Declarations of intent are not always fulfilled. At one time Augustine intended to write treatises on all seven liberal arts, but he completed only his projects on grammar, rhetoric, dialectic, something on geometry, and the six well-known books on music. His Grammar was already lost from his own library at Hippo before he came to write his *Retractations* (i, 6) near the end of his life. A comparable misfortune seems early to have struck Boethius' writings on geometry and, especially, astronomy.

Nothing by Boethius on astronomy has been transmitted by the medieval manuscript tradition, nor is any such work mentioned by Cassiodorus in his *Institutiones*. In the tenth century Gerbert of Aurillac, to be Pope Sylvester II from 999 to his death in 1003, speaks of Boethius as author of eight books on astronomy (*astrologia*) which he had seen in a manuscript at Bobbio. But the work (if really that by Boethius) failed to find copyists. Students preferred to find their astronomy in Macrobius' commentary on Cicero's *Dream of Scipio* or from Martianus Capella or from Cassiodorus. However, one likely model for Boethius' treatise is the summary of Ptolemy's *Mathematike Syntaxis* (the 'Almagest') composed by Proclus, a work which is still extant, though not edited since L. Allatius' edition (Leyden, 1635). If Boethius' work followed this precedent, he will have taken the earth as the static centre of a spherical cosmos, the Ptolemaic system assumed in his commentary on the *Categories* (212BC), and will have explained how the heavenly bodies move in relation to it; the solar year and its relation to the lunar months; the design and use of the astrolabe (an instrument in whose use Ammonius' high skill is reported by Simplicius, *In de Caelo*, p. 462, 20); eclipses, fixed stars, the precession of the equinoxes; finally the courses of the planets. How far he comprehended Ptolemy's trigonometry we cannot guess, and it is idle to speculate further. The allusion to Ptolemy's astronomical geography in the *Consolation of Philosophy* (ii, 7, 4) as a work specially studied by Boethius is no doubt to be interpreted as an allusion to Boethius' treatise on the subject.

Geometry and Astronomy 103

Gerbert also saw at Bobbio a Geometry ascribed to Boethius adorned with finely drawn diagrams. The medieval manuscript tradition has transmitted two short Geometries under Boethius' name, but both are disappointing works. Neither can be the Geometry that Gerbert saw. It is certain that in their extant form they cannot represent an original text from Boethius' pen, since they use Arabic numerals, a feature which must be later than Boethius' time. Moreover, in general they represent a more modest intellectual achievement than we expect from his mind. It is a delicate, perhaps unimportant, matter to determine how much genuine text from Boethius' original may lie behind these productions. A dedication to Patricius is likely to be genuine, as we meet this name in the dedication of his commentary on Cicero's *Topics*; he was an orator and advocate in Rome. But an eleventh-century gloss, printed by Usener from Vatic. lat. 3123, fo. 54v, says that Boethius' Geometry was, like his Arithmetic, dedicated to his father-in-law Symmachus. The glossator adds that to his version of Euclid Boethius added explanations of the more difficult chapters; in a noteworthy conclusion he remarks that the work as transmitted seems to offer no more than excerpts from Boethius, not his full original text.

The translated excerpts from Euclid preserved in the medieval manuscripts probably go back to Boethius. These offer the definitions of the first book of the *Elements*, five postulates, three axioms; the enunciations of book i; ten propositions of book ii, and some pieces from iii and iv. But the demonstrations are almost entirely lacking. It has been suggested that the proofs were somehow conceived of as a commentary on Euclid's primary text consisting of the definitions, postulates, axioms, and enunciations.

Cassiodorus certainly suggests that Boethius completed his quadrivium. 'By your translations Latin readers now have Pythagoras' music, Ptolemy's astronomy, Nicomachus' arithmetic, Plato's theology, Aristotle's logic, and Archimedes' mechanics' (*Variae* i, 45, 4 of 507). In the *Institutiones*, written decades later after the destruction of the Gothic kingdom, Cassiodorus again mentions that Boethius has adapted Euclid for Latin readers; and some manuscripts of the *Institutiones* include excerpts from a Latin version of Euclid which may well be that by Boethius. A palimpsest in Verona Cathedral

Library, written in a script which E. A. Lowe was reluctant to date after 500, contains excerpts from a Latin version of Euclid's *Elements*, books xii and xiii (but numbered xiv and xv). If this contains Boethius' version, the manuscript could be from his personal library, close to the autograph. But this cannot be established with certainty. Boethius is not the only person in fifth- or sixth-century Italy to think Euclid a desirable author for the study of Latin readers who would need excerpts for educational purposes. In his first commentary on Aristotle's *Interpretation* Boethius speaks of his predecessor Albinus, to whose work on logic he has not gained access, but whose work on geometry is known to him. Albinus' Geometry evidently enjoyed some circulation. (Boethius' *Institutio musica* mentions Albinus on music.)

If Boethius' Geometry consisted in the main of excerpts from Euclid, he is likely to have prefixed to these a preface seeking to place the subject in two basic respects: first in relation to Roman practical interests in the utility of geometry for calculating areas of land; secondly, in relation to his Neoplatonic interests in the position of geometry on his map of human knowledge and in the hierarchy of the sciences.

Naturally the latter interest is that about which Boethius cares most. Ancient Platonists felt geometry to be a central intellectual discipline. Even if it has less obvious practical usefulness than astronomy, its principles are more precise. It teaches the mind to think logically and to see how an inferential argument can proceed to an irresistible conclusion. In Plato's *Republic* (526c) geometry's educational merit is to compel the soul to contemplate unchangeable being rather than the uncertain flux of becoming. In Plato's century geometrical method was beginning to make striking progress, and both he and Aristotle wished to treat geometrical argument as an ideal model for all departments of human knowledge where certainty is desired. Its method was (and it still is) to lay down the initial definitions and axioms, to grant certain postulates, and then to ask what must necessarily be the consequence following from whatever is initially given, so that the final conclusion will be one that no rational mind has any choice but to accept. Unless one can dispute the initial premisses, there will be no stopping short of the conclusion. In the *Posterior Analytics* Aristotle experiments with the assumption that the demonstrative method proper to the mathematical sciences and especially to geometry provides a method of inference that can be applied to other sciences, indeed universally. In the generation after Aristotle the procedures of geometry were set out in ordered fashion by the Alexandrian systematizer Eukleides or Euclid in his *Elements*. Proclus wrote a commentary on the first book of the *Elements* with a long and important preface, which Boethius may well have known. Proclus says that Euclid was a Platonic philosopher of the time of king Ptolemy I (306–283 BC), evidently one of the scholars whom Ptolemy brought to Alexandria and encouraged to pursue scientific and literary studies. Proclus is the authority for the anecdote that after looking through the *Elements* Ptolemy asked Euclid if there was a shorter way to the study of this subject, and received the reply, 'Sire, there is no royal road to geometry' (p. 68 Friedlein). The *Elements* became a justly famous book in Greek education. From Archimedes onwards Euclid is often called simply the 'Stoicheiotes', the 'elements-man'. In the Latin West his name was known if only through Cicero, *De oratore* iii, 33, 132. But the characteristic Roman attitude to advanced geometry perhaps retained a secret sympathy with the soldier who killed Archimedes.

The fascination that geometrical method exercised over Boethius' mind is particularly evident in his third theological tractate, where he begins his argument in solution of his problem by laying down axioms and postulates which have the status either of geometrical axioms, such as that of Euclid 'If you take equals from two equals, the remainders are equal' (a familiar and much-quoted tag from the first book of Euclid's *Elements*—it was already an axiom for Aristotle), or of such principles as are self-evident to all educated minds, based on the universally accepted Common Notions, e.g. that 'incorporeal entities do not occupy space'. Everything here is conventional school doctrine. Alexander of Aphrodisias (*Metaph.* 256, 10; 267–8) remarks that each science has procedures that can be taken back to certain axiomatic foundations. Ammonius of Alexandria observes that the first principles in any discourse are like geometrical definitions and

Common Notions (*Perih.* 7, 19–20). Philoponus (*In Anal. Post.* i, 1 CAG XIII, 3 p. 10, 32) treats Euclid's axiom quoted above as one that applies to several departments of human inquiry, especially arithmetic and music as well as geometry.

To Proclus and the Neoplatonic schools geometry presented a puzzle in comparison with arithmetic. Number theory seemed the most abstract, pure and certain of all mental activities. Yet geometry could lead one to conclusions with a degree of certainty that made it a path towards immutable reality, surprising when geometers use figures: triangles, squares and other polygons have physical shapes. The geometer knows that a triangle is a concept rather than a concrete shape; but he needs the figure to help his imagination. Mathematics in general and geometry in particular therefore occupy a half-way house between the material world and the purely abstract world of concepts. At one point in his preface (p. 49 Friedlein) Proclus asks himself if it can be true that geometry accustoms the mind to immaterial realities when it depends on the use of figures in the imagination. Mathematics is a bridge between physics and metaphysics. The very name, he says (p. 45), was invented by the Pythagoreans because they saw that learning (*mathesis*) is remembering. Mathematics is not a subject learnt by rote on authority from a teacher; its principles already correspond to the structure of the soul, which therefore learns from its innate resources, assisted by props such as figures, which are needed as an inferior stage on the ascent to abstract truth. Boethius' first theological tractate addressed to Symmachus contains ideas that belong with these Neoplatonic themes about the cartography of mathematics, and especially of geometry, in the map of human knowledge. Even Augustine follows Plato's *Meno* in holding that the doctrine of reminiscence, anamnesis, is proved by a slave's mastery of geometry (*De trin.* xii, 15, 24). The same principle no doubt underlies Boethius' care with his many diagrams.

The pervasive influence of Neoplatonist discussion of geometrical arguments on the mind of Boethius is illustrated by a passage in the third book of the *Consolation of Philosophy* (iii, 10, 22–6). The lady Philosophy has argued that both God and happiness (*beatitudo*) are the highest good and therefore are identical. From this conclusion there is a corollary which geometers call a *porisma*, namely that human beings are made happy by a process of deification.

Euclid wrote a book entitled *Porismata*, on which Proclus comments that he used this Greek word in a sense other than corollary. Proclus uses the word *porisma*, exactly as in Boethius, to mean an 'incidental gain arising out of the demonstration of the main proposition' (*In Eucl. Elem.* I, 212, 16; 301, 22 Friedlein). In Hierocles' commentary on the *Golden Verses* of Pythagoras the term *porisma* is used in a moral context similar to that in the *Consolation* (*In Carmen Aureum* 23, p. 96, 14 ff. Koehler). Accordingly, Boethius is here making use of Neoplatonic convention derived from studies in geometry.

One cannot conclude without asking why Boethius' Geometry and Astronomy, if he wrote one, failed to survive. In the case of astronomy, it is very possible that he prejudiced readers against him by dark hints about horoscopes, a study which, as may be illustrated by Sidonius Apollinaris' correspondence with Lupus bishop of Troyes (*ep.* viii, 11, 9–10), was not necessarily a matter of which a Christian was expected to be ignorant, but was certainly regarded as dangerous. Moreover, the astronomical geography set out at length in Macrobius' *Commentary on Scipio's Dream* probably made Boethius' book superfluous. In the age between Boethius and Alcuin little of Boethius' work on the quadrivium was of interest to anybody. Only the *Arithmetica*, of which John the Scot makes plentiful use, survives complete. A general verdict must be that Boethius' labours on the four mathematical subjects, even though he believes them to be the fourfold road up to sublime wisdom, failed to achieve any large part of their purpose. They stand in strong contrast to the remarkable success which attended his sweat and toil with logic.

III

LOGIC

Part of philosophy or a tool of all philosophy?

THE place of logic in the hierarchy of knowledge was one of the many matters long in dispute between the Aristotelians and the Stoics. To the Stoics 'logic' meant something wide, an independent branch of philosophy, the other two contrasted branches being ethics and 'physics' (the scientific study of nature). The Stoics could point out that this threefold classification had a basis in the *Topics* (A, 14) of Aristotle himself. The Aristotelians, on the other hand, treated logic almost in our modern sense as a practical instrument for the discovery of fallacies in argument on any subject, an indispensable tool for every department of human inquiry. This Peripatetic attitude, from which the title Organon derives, presupposes a narrow understanding of the discipline as concerned with propositions and syllogisms and terms.

The Platonic tradition originally preferred to speak of 'dialectic', according to Boethius because it is a power of dividing (*In Cic. Top.* i, 1045B following Plato, *Sophist* 253d). Through its distinctions we learn to divide genera into species, and classify different things under their proper genus. But neither the Neoplatonists of Athens and Alexandria nor Boethius mark a significant difference in force between 'logical' and 'dialectical' reasoning.[1] Until the twelfth century, when an attempt was made to classify dialectic with grammar as two branches of *Logica*, the terms were to be used more or less interchangeably.

The Peripatetic case for their estimate of logic is most eloquently put by Alexander of Aphrodisias in his commentary on the *Prior Analytics* (CAG II, 1) in a way that makes minor concessions to the Platonic tradition. We have a number of late Platonist accounts of this dispute, e.g. the commentaries on the *Prior Analytics* by Ammonius (CAG IV, 6 pp. 8–11) and Philoponus (CAG XIII, 2 pp. 6–9). It is incautious to assume with Courcelle that Boethius had Ammonius before him when writing his second commentary on Porphyry in which the dispute is discussed.[2] One major element in Boethius' argument there, that logic is not confined by the limits and aims of other parts of philosophy, and is not restricted to a particular set of questions, stands without parallel in Ammonius. It is difficult to affirm a literary relation when one is dealing with a convention of the schools which every Neoplatonic teacher will think it his duty to expound.

In the *Enneads* (i, 3) Plotinus explains the place of logic in the gradual process of advance to metaphysics and theology. The first stage of education will be in music and the mathematical disciplines. These train the mind up to abstract thought, and teach the musician that the beauty of ordered sound belongs to the very harmony of the intellectual world. After mathematics the mind must acquire skill in dialectical method. Plotinus rejects the view that dialectic is merely a tool of metaphysics. The Stoics are right, he declares, that it is the most valuable part of philosophy aspiring to ascend to reality and truth. Here Plotinus is influenced by Plato's *Republic* (532a ff.) and *Theaetetus* (189e–190a) where Plato speaks of thinking as an inward dialogue within the soul, 'asking questions and giving answers, affirming and denying', in the silence of one's own self. *Sophist* 263e is also close to this notion. Dialectic is inherent in the process of introspection, in the zigzag of contemplative ascent to the divine realm.

Plotinus' view is echoed in Proclus' commentary on the *Parmenides* (1015, 38 Cousin) where dialectic is an exercising of the mind to train it for the vision of transcendent truth. It is the purest part of philosophy (986, 29). It discovers the universal.

Most of the Platonists upheld the truth contained in both the Stoic and the Aristotelian positions; and this is Boethius' verdict in the second commentary on Porphyry. There (as at the beginning of the *Consolatio*) philosophy is divided into two broad divisions: speculative and practical. Practical philosophy is concerned with ethics, politics, and economics; speculative with the natural sciences, with mathematics, and with theology or metaphysics. This three-tiered hierarchy of speculative philosophy is set out by Aristotle himself in a number of places, in the *Physics*, *Metaphysics* (especially E 1, 1026a

13–16), and *Ethics*. It is evidently related to the tripartite division of being in the Platonic tradition, viz. things of sense, mathematics, and the Forms or Ideas. This division was understood to go back to Plato himself. Proclus attributes its scholastic development to the school of Aristander and Numenius in the second century (*In Tim.* ii, 153, 18).

This tripartite division of theoretical philosophy is a commonplace very frequently repeated by Boethius' Neoplatonic masters. In Boethius it receives its most striking statement in the second section of his first theological tractate, *De trinitate*, where he is seeking to place theology in relation to other human knowledge. To the scheme he there presents, a virtually precise verbal parallel occurs in a commentary on *Metaphysics* E 1 transmitted under the name of Alexander of Aphrodisias, but agreed to be properly attributable to another ancient hand. The physical sciences are defined as concerning objects that move; here the form cannot be abstracted from the matter without the subject ceasing to exist. Secondly there are the mathematical sciences concerned with things that do not move (Boethius and pseudo-Alexander forget the special position of astronomy) and with geometrical figures that have shape in our imaginations but no actual matter in reality; for the triangle drawn on the paper is not the real triangle of geometry but a lowly visual aid to the human imagination assisting the mind towards the comprehension of an abstract concept. Finally there are the transcendent objects of theological science which do not move, have no matter, and cannot be understood unless the concept of form is purged of all images so as to leave the mind in contemplation of pure being.[3]

Boethius adds the characteristic Aristotelian point that each discipline has its own method and logic; and in theology purely intellectual concepts control the inquiry: 'in divinis intellectualiter versari oportebit.' It is the nearest that Boethius comes to the notion of analogy, a subject on which he has much less to say than Proclus and other late Platonists. Proportionality can apply outside mathematics (below, p. 154); but not to the infinite (*Cons.* ii, 7, 17).

The term 'intellectualis' of theology appears also early on in the first commentary on Porphyry, where Boethius is distinguishing the three objects of knowledge in speculative theology with the labels 'intellectual, intelligible, and natural', evidently corresponding to a Greek original *noeta, noera, physika*. This vocabulary is not found in Ammonius at any point. But it is well attested in Proclus or in Syrianus' commentary on the *Metaphysics*, and can be shown to be older. In his *Literal Commentary on Genesis* (xii, 10, 21) Augustine rejects a distinction certain unnamed persons make between 'intellectual' and 'intelligible'. It is natural to think of Porphyry (cf. *City of God* x, 9). The distinction has its roots in Plotinus.

In the first commentary on the *Isagoge* Boethius describes the midway 'intelligibles' as including (a) the study of astronomy ('all the celestial works of the highest divinity'), (b) the higher regions of the sublunary realm, and (c) human souls 'which once were of that prior intellectual substance, but by contact with bodies degenerated to the level of intelligibles'. Good sense is made of this obscure passage as soon as one recalls the intimate link in the Platonic tradition between the structure of the soul and mathematics. Therefore the earlier version of the three divisions of theoretical philosophy found in the first commentary on Porphyry ought not to be presented as standing in contradiction or sharp antithesis to his later statement in the *De trinitate*.

The hierarchical ordering of the sciences is established doctrine for the Neoplatonic schools. Simplicius in the sixth century sums it up with the beginning of his commentary on the *Physics*: the mind has the power (a) to examine nature where the forms are inseparable from matter, (b) to consider forms wholly separable from matter as in theology and metaphysics, (c) to inquire into forms partly separable, partly inseparable, viz. doctrines concerning mathematics and the soul. Boethius simply takes over this map of knowledge from his Neoplatonic masters, and it is already a ladder at whose top stand the mysterious tasks of theology. In the *Republic* (534e) Plato declares dialectic to be the intellectual discipline standing over all the mathematical sciences like the coping-stone of a building. For Boethius, therefore, the studies of mathematics and of logic are foothills of a massif whose summit is in heaven.

Logic and rhetoric
In the study of logic the combination of apparent simplicity

with a mathematical complexity accessible only to the specially gifted, the remoteness of large parts of the subject from practical living, and the contrast between its technical precision and everyday usage, helped to make the subject not immediately attractive to the beginner. Aristotle and after him the Stoics wrote major treatises about their discoveries in logic, but the most important pieces are formulated in a style that ordinary mortals find rebarbative. In Boethius' time Ammonius of Alexandria observes that his young students were finding it hard to read both the medical authority Galen because of his longwindedness, and Aristotle because he is so concise, 'a lover of brevity'. In the next century a similar observation is found in the Alexandrian exegete Elias: students dislike Galen and Proclus for being so wordy, Hippocrates and Aristotle for being terse to the point of oracular obscurity.[4] In the Latin world there was less predisposition than in the Greek to expect logicians to teach one something of value. Boethius, however, was convinced that if human minds have any capacity to discern truth from falsity, an ignorance of logic will have disastrous consequences. He therefore dedicates himself to urging that the subject be taken seriously. Not that he is quite without sympathy for the critics. A passage in the *Consolation of Philosophy* (iii, 12, 30) shows that he knows what it is to suspect logicians of being clever people playing verbal games. On more than one occasion he writes of the tension, to become of special interest to Anselm five centuries later, between the usage of everyday speech (*usus loquendi*) and the technical accuracy required by philosophers.[5] Once he even describes Aristotle himself as a man who 'disturbed' the normal use of nouns and verbs, and declares that he has attempted to translate him into a more palatable style.[6] Boethius is also aware that inferences valid under the rules of pure logic can be quite false when asserted of the real world.[7]

The Roman cultural tradition was largely dominated by the needs of law and government. Rhetoric was the principal thing. The good orator needed a smattering of logic to find persuasive arguments or to convict opponents of sophistry and fallacies. Aristotle wrote his 'Topics' (the word means general types of argument with many possible detailed applications) partly to offer the weapons of logic to aspiring orators. The

Platonists of Boethius' time know that in Aristotle's mind rhetoric and logic are linked, and classify the rhetorical works as a constituent part of the Organon. They called the logical and rhetorical works 'the instrumental works', or the 'tools', *organika*. (The singular Organon appears to arrive about 1502 with early printed editions of the Renaissance.[8]) Cicero's brief *Topics*, hastily composed for a legal friend in seven days, tried to do something of the sort for Latin oratory and advocacy, but the logical content is less than in Aristotle' *Topics*. In *De inventione* Cicero sought to harness the discoveries of the logicians to the purposes of persuasive rhetoric. In the West an interest in the more difficult areas of Aristotelian, to say nothing of Stoic, logic was only a dimly flickering flame. In the second century AD Apuleius of Madaura, much admired for a best-selling novel spiced with magic, religion and sex, wrote a brief exposition of Aristotle on *Interpretation*, which Boethius never mentions. But the similarity of its general structure to his own longer exposition suggests either a common source or, more probably, a direct use by Boethius of Apuleius' work.[9] Apuleius' authorship of this piece has often been denied, but without cogent reason, and the work is in any event evidence of the rising concern for Aristotelian logic emerging in the Middle Platonic school of the second century AD. Apuleius' tract was to be freely exploited in the section on Dialectic in 'The Marriage of Philology and Mercury' by Martianus Capella in the fifth century, probably of the generation immediately preceding Boethius' lifetime, whose work may well have been known to Boethius. (Both authors employ the form of alternative prose and verse. The *Consolation* has phrases in the verse sections that could be reminiscences of Martianus Capella.[10]) Specifically commended by Cassiodorus (*Inst.* ii, 3, 12 and 18), Apuleius was eventually but very gradually replaced by Boethius' longer and more ambitious expositions; but this first becomes evident from the mid-eleventh century.

In his second commentary on Perihermeneias Boethius writes of Albinus, whose Geometry he knows, but whose Dialectic he has not been able to find. Lorenzo Minio-Paluello has conjectured that Albinus' lost work on Dialectic may conceivably be identical with the extant Latin adaptation of

Themistius' paraphrase of the *Categories* transmitted under the name of St. Augustine. This work, *Decem Categoriae*, was known to Isidore of Seville, John Scotus (Eriugena),[11] and Alcuin who ascribed it to Augustine. It is printed among Augustine's works, e.g. in Migne, *PL* 32, 1419–40, and has now been critically edited by Minio-Paluello in *Aristoteles Latinus* i, 1–5 (1961). At one point (*AL* i 162, 21; *PL* 32, 1434) the author goes out of his way to praise the view of Agorius 'whom I hold to be among the most learned'(ut Agorius, quem ego inter doctissimos habeo, voluit). Unless one resorts to the desperate expedient of seeing this remark as an interpolation from a marginal note by an early reader, this text must decisively disprove the old opinion[12] that the pseudo-Augustinian text can be confidently ascribed to Vettius Agorius Praetextatus, the distinguished pagan aristocrat at Rome in the time of Pope Damasus (366–84). Boethius expressly says of him that he adapted for Latin readers Themistius' epitome of Aristotle's *Prior* and *Posterior Analytics*. He may have performed a similar task for the *Categories*. The author of *Decem Categoriae* treats Themistius as his contemporary ('nostrae aetatis', *PL* 32, 1422 cf. 1440). Three members of the family of Albini appear in Macrobius' *Saturnalia* as members of the circle close to Vettius Agorius Praetextatus.[13] One of them may be the Albinus mentioned by Boethius as author of works on geometry and on music, perhaps also on logic. Minio-Paluello's hypothesis remains an attractive and open possibility.

In several works Augustine discusses the liberal arts, notably in his *De doctrina christiana*. The brief tract on logic, *Principia Dialecticae* (*PL* 32), long dismissed as inauthentic (though of Augustine's age), is now generally thought a treatise to be restored to the list of his authentic writings.[14] However, it cannot be reckoned a source for Boethius. The work leaves no discernible echo in Boethius' writings, and there is no reason to suppose that either he or Cassiodorus had seen or heard of the treatise.

Cassiodorus mentions a textbook of dialectic by Tullius Marcellus of Carthage, in which he explained the various types of syllogism, and commends its study to his pupils at Vivarium where he has deposited a copy in the library.[15] But of this work

Boethius betrays no knowledge.

Among Boethius' Latin predecessors the most considerable and weighty place is occupied by Marius Victorinus, the African who taught in Rome in the middle of the fourth century. Victorinus had a lively interest in the application of dialectical skills to rhetorical purposes and, after his conversion to Christianity about 355, to the service of polemical divinity, maintaining Nicene orthodoxy against Arianism of various shades. His standing at Rome rose so high that a statue in his honour was erected in Trajan's Forum, and he was long remembered. On his granddaughter's epitaph it is declared that 'Rome had the glory of having him as rhetor'.[16] Jerome studied under him for a time. In Augustine's account of his conversion, Victorinus is spoken of as 'most expert in all the liberal arts', including philosophy.[17] Boethius would have thought this last addition excessive, but concedes that he was 'perhaps the most learned orator of his time'.[18]

A hardly concealed professional rivalry makes Boethius reluctant to recognize the achievements of Marius Victorinus. In fact Victorinus' work as translator is not inconsiderable in making Neoplatonism accessible to the Latin world. His versions of pieces by Plotinus and Porphyry played a material part in Augustine's conversion. He made a Latin adaptation of Porphyry's *Isagoge*, much being a verbatim translation, but parts being a summary or précis in Victorinus' own words. He replaced the name of Porphyry's friend Chrysaorios by that of Menantius; and in a reference to the work in his tract *On Definition* he speaks about it blandly as if it were entirely his own unaided effort, which perhaps he hoped uninformed Romans might take it to be.[19] ('Not a translation, only taken from the French', says a character in Sheridan's *Critic*.) Early in his first commentary on the *Isagoge* Boethius pointedly says of a certain phrase that this is 'Porphyry, not Victorinus'.[20] Although Boethius bases this commentary on Victorinus' translation, he also kept Porphyry's original Greek text before him for comparison and correction.

Victorinus' tract *On Definition* has survived among Boethius' works and is printed under his name in Migne (*PL* 64) which is ironical since Boethius is frankly critical of its dialectical capacity and gives the impression that he would prefer to see his own works ascribed to Victorinus than Victorinus' works to himself. The tract shows considerable interest in logic as a method of classification, and again there is probably a substantial debt to a monograph by Porphyry. Boethius several times stresses that Victorinus was not seriously committed to logic as an inquiry for its own sake. His concern was essentially for its utility to the orator and advocate in court seeking to make his arguments persuasive. At one point in the first *Isagoge* commentary Boethius makes a legitimate comment that by interpreting the word 'genus' according to its usage in Latin rhetoric Victorinus has confused the interpretation of Porphyry's text. Boethius self-consciously designates his own work as the pursuit of truth rather than fine prose, 'non luculentae orationis lepos, sed incorrupta veritas'.[21] Not that Boethius or his circle is disrespectful towards grammarians and rhetoricians. Donatus he acknowledges to be a great name in Latin grammar. Boethius has some interest in grammatical points; in his second commentary on Porphyry he draws attention to Porphyry's use of hyperbaton and zeugma.[22] The contacts between Priscian and Symmachus show that the Symmachus circle was not scornful of such elementary things. A passage, however, in Boethius' monograph on the categorical syllogism (i, 796C–797A), paralleled in *Perihermeneias* ii, 14–15, contrasts the philosophers' view that of the parts of speech noun and verb are primary, the other six merely supplementary, with that of the grammarians that there are simply eight parts of speech. The grammarians' side of this story is in Priscian (Keil ii, 551, 18–552, 14).

Victorinus was a prolific polymath. He wrote a commentary on Cicero, *De inventione*, and another on the *Topica*, the latter in four books (it lay before Boethius and is a traceable influence in Martianus Capella and Cassiodorus).[23] He wrote an *Ars grammatica*, part of which survives. His adaptations of Aristotelian and Porphyrian logic for Latin readers strikingly anticipate the areas in which Boethius was later to work: the *Isagoge*, the *Categories*, *Perihermeneias*, and monographs on Definition, apparently also on Categorical and Hypothetical Syllogisms. These, with Cicero's *Topics*, provided the structure for the school course in dialectic for orators both in Cassiodorus and in Martianus Capella. It is likely to be no accident that Boethius' translations of other parts of the Organon, falling outside this school curriculum, came to have a very precarious transmission. Victorinus seems to have set a teaching pattern with limits that even Boethius found it hard to break out of.[24] Jerome (*ep.* 50, 1) writes of a course in logic as covering *Categories, Perihermeneias, Analytica,* and Cicero's *Topics.*

Apart from the rhetorical works of Victorinus, Boethius twice mentions with respect a commentary on Cicero's *Topics* by the fifth-century soldier-orator from Baetica in Spain, Merobaudes, of whose prose and poetry some minor pieces survive.[25]

Boethius' own commentary on Cicero's *Topics* he feels to be justified by the incompleteness of Victorinus' treatment. The work is dedicated to a close friend Patricius, 'most expert of contemporary orators', described as 'presiding over the Muses' (1063D). Cassiodorus (*Variae* x, 6–7) says he worked as an advocate in Rome and became Quaestor of the Palace in 534. Patricius' friendship has moved Boethius 'to set down what I have gathered by much labour and study, not merely with rhetorical skill but also with dialectical subtlety'. Against Victorinus' four books of incomplete and intellectually inadequate commentary, Boethius sets an exposition in seven books. Unhappily much of the sixth book and the whole of the seventh book are lacking in the manuscript tradition, so that the work has suffered much the same fate as *Institutio musica.* One manuscript of the twelfth century (Paris. lat. 7711, fo. 47b–49b) attaches to the truncated sixth book an attempt to supply matter for the missing exposition by transcribing pieces from Augustine's *City of God*; but it has no credibility as genuine Boethius.[26]

Even though the commentary on the *Topics* of Cicero shows Boethius unbending from the strict rigour of his logical studies and seeking to offer something useful for orators, he expects his commentary to be resented by those who think logic has nothing to teach oratory (1153C). The work was written at a fairly late stage in Boethius' career, and he has had time to gather critics ready to find fault with anything he does.

Boethius' sensitivity to criticism does not prevent him from disparaging Victorinus on almost every occasion that he refers to him, whether on the ground of his mistranslations of Porphyry or for his limited dialectical capacities.[27] At one point (1100A) he bluntly describes Victorinus' procedure in *De definitionibus* as 'quod maxime ratione caret', wholly irrational. At another he observes that he is omitting 'places which Victorinus pointlessly and inappropriately inserts' (1156C). On the *Topics* he comments on Victorinus' inability to distinguish between a question and an argument, which has led him off into lengthy expositions of matter 'which I do not think worthy of mention'. The book *On Definition* is vitiated by a faulty understanding of what an Aristotelian logician means by this word. Some of this criticism no doubt simply continues a long-standing tension, apparent both in the Latin and in the Greek worlds, between the philosopher and the rhetor. Victorinus himself is aware of this ancient tension, remarking once that he is glad to use philosophical terms to enrich his vocabulary, even though the philosopher characteristically condemns all the arts of rhetoric.[28] Ammonius of Alexandria puts it succinctly: philosophers do not guess, rhetors do.[29]

Victorinus himself would clearly have labelled himself a rhetor rather than a philosopher. Yet it is not self-evident that Boethius is fair to his rival's achievement quā philosopher. Cassiodorus (*Inst.* ii, 3, 18 p. 128) reports that this achievement included a translation, with commentary in eight books, of Aristotle's *Categories*, a translation of his *Interpretation*, and a tract on the seven moods of the Hypothetical Syllogism. This last work must have overlapped with, if it is distinct from, the section of Victorinus' commentary on Cicero's *Topics* dealing with this subject. Moreover, despite Boethius' contempt for Victorinus' catalogue of the fifteen types of definition, he himself feels somehow bound to include the same list of fifteen types, and indeed to repeat the list twice,[30] except that on both occasions he expresses it in so laconic a form that these sections in Boethius can be fully understood only with the help of the fuller statement in Victorinus' treatise *On Definition*, for which he has reserved special scorn. In his second commentary on Porphyry Boethius borrows from Victorinus' *On Definition* a quotation of Cicero to illustrate the ambiguity of the term 'necessary'.[31]

With his friend Patricius and his fellow advocates in mind Boethius decorates his commentary on Cicero with legal examples, and includes important quotations from the jurists, Ulpian (1071B) and the *Institutes* of Gaius (1093AB). The constitutional changes of 476 had not made such matters merely of antiquarian interest. Roman law remained in force in Theoderic's Italy where the Romans continued to be governed under the old imperial system. Gothic soldiers were answerable in Gothic military courts. Nevertheless, Boethius' passionate personal interest in questions of logic with wider ramifications emerges even in the commentary on Cicero. Cicero's text gives him a peg on which to hang not only a discussion of the propositional logic of hypothetical syllogisms but also to discuss Aristotle's view of chance, with a passing reference to his own annotations on the *Physics* for further elucidation (1152C). Cicero defines chance as an event with unseen causes. Yet we do not know the cause of eclipses, and they do not occur by chance. Therefore one must be so bold ('some will call me arrogant') as to say Cicero is wrong. Aristotle is wiser in saying that a 'chance' event is one which is unintended, rare, not part of the recurrent, everlasting order of nature ('quid ex fortuna sit, in sempiternis non est'), and an accidental consequence of other things.

Boethius' sixth book, of which the end is lost, embarks on a reply to those orators who think philosophical logic irrelevant to their skills. It is not necessary, he concludes, to be a philosopher in the sense that it is necessary to live. But the alternative to living philosophically is a merely animal existence (1161C). For to be a philosopher is to study virtue, those moral actions which are on a higher plane than behaviour in which personal choice plays no part (1162A). Philosophy can teach us that virtue is always in our power, and that riches are at the whim of the capricious mistress Fortune. Those stable possessions of a good character which none can take away are better than the uncertain things of which our tenure is precarious. We know which are which by an intellectual process of comparison, just as we also judge that the interest of princes properly takes precedence over that of a private individual (1162CD). Here themes prominent in the *Consolation of Philosophy* are already being anticipated.

Boethius' commentary on Cicero was probably written as late as 520–2, well after the completion of his commentaries on Porphyry and Aristotle. At the time of writing it he was already planning in draft his last extant work on logic, the four books *De topicis differentiis*;[32] that is, on the different senses of the term 'topic' in logic and in rhetoric. This is a work in which he brings together and compares Cicero's *Topics* with a study of the rhetorical value of Aristotle's *Topics* taken from the fourth-century Greek orator Themistius. These last studies show Boethius under some pressure to convince his Italian contemporaries of the utility and necessity of his dialectical inquiries.

The commentary on Cicero's *Topics* contains an exceptional number of references to Boethius' hostile critics. 'Savage minds' accuse him of arrogance (1152AB). He is 'attacked by the rash criticisms of insolent men' (1157A). Similar sensitivity to unkind reviewers appears in *De topicis differentiis* and *De divisione*.[33] At the beginning of the sixth and last book of his expansive second commentary on *Interpretation* (ii, 421; *PL* 64, 601B), he rebuts charges that from motives of vainglory and ostentation he has composed a prolix book on a subject that could have been treated much more shortly. A propensity to be long-winded, and to express regrets for it, is a trait Boethius shares with his admired master Proclus. The commentary on the *Categories* twice seeks the reader's benevolence by saying the discussion is being cut short to avoid prolixity (250C, 274B). The second commentary on *Interpretation* five times expresses a wish not to go on too long. The intention to avoid repetitiousness appears also in the second commentary on Porphyry (*CSEL* 48 p. 340, 14), which must be admitted to be on the whole a verbose piece. Boethius' adaptation of Nicomachus' *Arithmetic* manifests the same tendency, by being almost always longer than the Greek original, even though he is aware that excessive exposition can end by leaving the reader confused. This undoubted fault in Boethius' writing might have been less prominent had he been more attentive to the precepts of the masters of oratory.

Porphyry

Aristotle's logic was notorious in antiquity for its difficulty to readers with no exceptional intellectual endowments. Cicero remarks that even among professional philosophers few read him (*Topica* i, 1). In the *Confessions* (iv, 16, 28–9) Augustine recalls the ridiculous vanity of his African teacher when initiating his pupils into the mystery of the Categories, which a clever youth like Augustine, then in his twenties, could master without difficulty. In Martianus Capella (iv, 329) the lady Dialectic says things that 'the majority cannot understand'. According to his friend and biographer Marinus, the high ability of Proclus as a young man was demonstrated by the ease with which he grasped Aristotelian logic, 'a subject which most people find unreadable' (*V. Procli* 9).

Marinus adds that the youthful Proclus studied Aristotle initially at Alexandria under a Peripatetic philosopher named Olympiodorus (distinct from the later Neoplatonist of the same name who was a pupil of Ammonius). But dissatisfaction with the Alexandrian interpretation of Aristotle led him to move to Athens to study under Syrianus, whom he later succeeded as head of the Platonic Academy. In other words, Proclus wished his Aristotle to be interpreted within an explicitly Platonic framework. He feared 'Peripatetic heresy' (*Th. Plat.* ii, 4 p. 90P).

Aristotle was read and studied in the school of Plotinus (Porphyry, *Life* 14) together with the great Peripatetic commentators, Andronicus, Aspasius, Adrastus and Alexander of Aphrodisias. The reconciliation of Plato with Aristotle, keenly debated during the second century AD, became accepted wisdom after the work of Porphyry towards the end of the third century. Porphyry set out to make the Platonic schools safe for the study of Aristotle, whose logic deeply impressed him. The opportunity came when a distinguished friend named Chrysaorios found the *Categories* hard to understand and requested an explanation. For him Porphyry wrote his terse and astonishingly influential introduction, *Isagoge*,[34] setting out in a few lapidary pages that, underlying Aristotle's distinction between substance and accidents, there are five predicables: genus, species, differentia (or distinctive characteristic), property (peculiar and permanent attribute), and accident, which can be present or absent without the basic substance being essentially altered or destroyed. These five predicables are an exhaustive list of the elements in any philosophical definition.

So, for example, man (*homo*) is a species within the genus animal, whose distinctive characteristic is to be rational and mortal, whose permanent peculiar attribute is the capacity to laugh, but to whom literacy or musical skill or being white or black is a mere 'accident', not a mark of a separate species. (Colour becomes a genus when considered as a term inclusive of particular colours.) Accordingly, a correct definition should be so exactly worded as to be reversible or 'convertible'. Man is a laughing animal. If someone points out a laughing animal, you may be sure it is human.

Porphyry's analysis adapts a text from Aristotle's *Topics*, adding species to the list there given of the constituent elements in the problem of logical definition. Modern complaints that he was at fault in so doing seem to be misconceived. Porphyry thereby provided a vocabulary and a system of classification which is still in use today in everyday speech whenever we distinguish the specific from the general, or the substance of a thing from whatever is accidental to it. In his first commentary on the *Isagoge* Boethius affirms that 'all beginners in logic since Porphyry have started by studying this little book' (*CSEL* 48 p. 12, 20). Through Boethius' commentaries the *Isagoge* became a basic textbook for the medieval West. At about the same period as Boethius, a learned Syrian, perhaps Sergius of Reshaina, was translating Porphyry's work into Syriac. Another Syriac version was made in AD 644–5 by Athanasius of Balead. An Armenian translation followed in the eighth century, an Arabic version in the tenth.[35]

Porphyry taught his readers to distinguish between the predicables which answer the 'substance' question 'What is it?' (genus, species, property) and differentia which answers the 'quality' question, 'What kind of a thing is it?' He also taught that some accidents can be in practice inseparable, e.g. all known crows and Ethiopians are black; nevertheless colour is an accident and the mind can abstractly think of white crows or Ethiopians. Porphyry writes as if, with the aid of his rules, there is no difficulty about defining, which is to specify the essence of a thing. Nevertheless he concedes that in most cases the distinction between genus and species is relative rather than absolute. A genus exists as such in relation to the various species falling under it. Genera and species are 'names of names', Boethius says in his commentary on the *Categories* (176D) echoing Plato's *Sophist* (244d); a formula that medieval thinkers took to be the epitome of nominalism. A bird is a species of the genus animal, but a genus to the many species of bird. However, there are 'very special species' and 'very generic genera' (like the ten categories), the latter being describable but not definable since there is no higher genus for them to belong to, in terms of which they are defined. Definition can never be sought for a single individual thing. A classification system is not interested in features that may be unique, since its purpose is to bring order to a bewildering multiplicity.

The analysis of differentia also reveals many problems. Not much light is thrown by saying that a distinctive characteristic is what makes something different or other. Socrates differs from Plato by being other than Plato; he also differs from himself as a boy or as a man or in his various actions. He also differs from someone else with different inseparable accidents, e.g. a curved nose, blind eyes, and a scar. The differentia that Porphyry's classification is concerned with is that of species. Separable differentiae are matters of accident; but then there are also inseparable accidents, which is tiresome for the classification system. Differentiae in substance either divide the genus into its species or are so shared by all members of the species that they are constitutive and unitive.

Property, or permanent peculiar attribute, similarly requires care in handling. Porphyry offers a fourfold division: (a) an attribute applicable only to one species but not to every member of it (*soli non omni*), e.g. physician or geometer in the case of man; (b) an attribute applicable to every member of the species but not exclusive to the species (*omni non soli*), e.g. man being a biped; (c) an attribute applicable only to one species and to every member, but not invariable (*soli et omni et aliquando*), e.g. white hair in old age; (d) an attribute applicable only to the species, to every member of it, and invariably so (*soli et omni et semper*), e.g. that man is risible or that a horse can neigh. The last category is the ideal case for logical clarity, but Porphyry has to allow that 'property' can be used in the first three cases.

The goal of the classification is to reach a definition which is exact. A definition must not be too wide, greater than its object so as to include other things; or it will fail to manifest the substance of the object. Nor should it be less than the object, failing to bring out what it really is and what its qualities are. Of the adequacy of a definition, 'convertibility' (or reversibility) is a good test.

One difficulty that Porphyry mentions as a problem which he will not stop to examine concerns a grand question in the debate between Plato and Aristotle, namely whether genus and species quā 'universals' are rooted in the matter of the sensible things that constitute them; or perhaps a mixture of mind and sense; or rather solely intellectual and immaterial entities, as on the Platonic view where the species humanity is prior to any individual instance of the species and is a purely mental concept, even if knowledge of it is derived by a process of abstraction from concrete instances. In *Metaphysics* Λ Aristotle denies that universals are things with an existence and reality independent of constituent individuals (1071a 19 ff.; 1078b 30–2). There are only particular specimens of the human race. Our mental construct of a universal 'humanity' in which all individuals share has no separate reality. The universal exists only in the particular thing. Here Aristotle's view appeared so opposed to Plato's that it needed very careful massage to adapt it to Porphyry's Neoplatonism.

A point made by Porphyry and taken over by Boethius stresses that in reducing all discourse to ten manageable divisions, no more and no less, in the *Categories*, Aristotle does not thereby admit that 'being' is some kind of supreme and ultimate genus in which the ten categories participate. This proposition, explicitly rejected by Aristotle in the *Metaphysics* (B 3, 998b 22) and *Topics* (iv, 6, 127a 28–9), is disowned by Boethius in both his expositions of the *Isagoge* (p. 73, 22; 144, 6). We are not to think of the categories as if they are entities that participate in some higher condition of pure being. The verb 'to be', he remarks in the second commentary on *Interpretation* (ii, 51 and 77), may signify Being, as of God; or Existence, as of particular facts true at a certain time in a certain place; and these are distinct senses of the word. As for the precise number of categories, this is Aristotle's exhaustive list, and implies that because their number is finite, they fall under human knowledge. Boethius liked to repeat the axiom that the infinite is unknowable.[36]

For his friend Chrysaorios, Porphyry also wrote a treatise 'Concerning the disagreement between Plato and Aristotle'. So at least it is entitled by the sixth-century commentator on Porphyry, Elias. In the Byzantine encyclopaedia called 'Suda' the book's title is given in the positive form 'Concerning the agreement between Plato and Aristotle', which is presumably the same work.[37] Lost in Greek its principal matter has survived in Arabic through the tenth-century treatise by Al-'Amirî (first printed by M. Minovi, Wiesbaden 1957) which collects citations from Plato and Aristotle to show their essential agreement.[38] This theme of concordance is assumed in virtually all the Neoplatonists after Porphyry, and prominent in Syrianus, Proclus, Hierocles, Ammonius, and Simplicius. Porphyry sees Aristotle's logic and metaphysics as providing criteria of meaning only for the sublunary world of concrete things, not applicable to the higher realms of ideas and those abstractions which in Neoplatonism are so much more potent than any particular and individual manifestation of their reality. At Athens early in the fifth century Syrianus read with his brilliant pupil Proclus the whole of Aristotle as 'small mysteries' in preparation for the greater mysteries of Plato. (The verbal allusion is a reminiscence of *Gorgias* 497c.) Boethius sees his translations of Aristotle and then Plato as 'steps' on a ladder (*Perih.* ii, 79). Syrianus' commentary on the *Metaphysics* makes the detailed reconciliation of the two authoritative philosophers a central concern.

Porphyry went on to compose two commentaries on Aristotle's *Categories*. The first is a simple dialogue in the form of question and answer. The Greek text is preserved through a damaged thirteenth-century codex at Modena which, even when undamaged, may have contained no exegesis of the so-called Postpraedicamenta of chapters 10–15 (11b 15–15b 32). However, it is as good as certain that Porphyry covered this appendix to the main text of the *Categories*. Boethius' commentary on the *Categories* is heavily dependent on Porphyry's Question and Answer commentary, and the debt explicitly continues in the fourth book where he is expounding these appended chapters, twice acknowledging his following of Porphyry by name (263B, 284A).

Porphyry's second commentary on the *Categories* is never mentioned by Boethius. Simplicius cites from it, and says it was a lengthy treatise in seven books dedicated to Gedaleios. There is nothing in Boethius' exposition of the *Categories* that looks as if it must be directly drawn from this longer exegesis. One citation from Porphyry to which the Question and Answer commentary offers no parallel, is likely to have been quoted from the commentary by Iamblichus.

In addition Porphyry wrote a detailed commentary on Aristotle's obscure tract on the simple, unconditional (or categorical) proposition, *De interpretatione*, which deals also with modal statements containing the words 'necessary' or 'possible'.

His commentary passed over the last chapter which perhaps he thought Aristotle's work but wrongly added here. The Greek text of Porphyry's commentary is lost, but it was gratefully used by Ammonius, author of the one surviving Neoplatonic commentary on this text preserved in Greek. Boethius acknowledges a large debt to Porphyry's exposition in his own double commentary on the treatise. In addition to Ammonius and Boethius, there are echoes of Porphyry's commentary in the Arabic of Al-Farabi of Baghdad (c.870–950), to whom Porphyrian exegesis was transmitted by Nestorian Christians.

Through Porphyry's encyclopaedic, tidy, and essentially pedagogic mind Boethius had access to some ideas of the pre-Porphyrian commentators, e.g. to Theophrastus, Eudemus, Andronicus (1st century BC); Aspasius (1st century AD), Herminus (2nd century), and especially Alexander of Aphrodisias (c.200). Some part of Alexander's voluminous writings may easily have been on the shelves of Boethius' own library. Porphyry's commentary on *Perihermeneias* also included extended discussions of Stoic propositional logic, especially concerning conditional statements. But, to the great regret of historians of logic, Boethius thinks his readers will be grateful if he omits these. Other works of Porphyry known to Boethius include a commentary on Theophrastus' treatise 'Concerning affirmation and negation', a commentary on Plato's *Sophist* (the dialectic of which had an importance for the Neoplatonists which is easily seen in Proclus' commentary on the *Parmenides* and in his *Platonic Theology* i, 4; ii, 4; iii, 20), and also an introduction to the categorical syllogism.

Neoplatonists after Porphyry: Iamblichus, Syrianus, Proclus, Ammonius

A more complex question is the route or routes by which Boethius had access to the writings of philosophers after Porphyry's time, nearer to his own generation. He knows about, and may directly know, the Paraphrases of Aristotle produced in the fourth century by the orator-statesman Themistius, a writer to be classified more as a Peripatetic than as a Neoplatonist, though in some places he shows traces of Neoplatonic influences.[39] Themistius had read Iamblichus' commentary on the *Categories*, a substantial part of the purpose of which is to demonstrate how profoundly Aristotle depends on unacknowledged borrowings from a Pythagorean text by Archytas of Tarentum. This argument carried the congenial implication that in a fundamental treatise of his Organon Aristotle was so far from being at variance with the Platonic–Pythagorean tradition that he actually derived one of his most important notions from a major figure within this school. Among Pythagoreans Archytas held an honoured name; his musical theory we have already considered in the second chapter. Themistius, however, expresses the judicious opinion that, in the case of the text much quoted by Iamblichus, 'Archytas' is the pseudonym or perhaps homonym of a writer after Aristotle's time, who was anxious to cover his work with the authority of a venerated name. In his commentary on the *Categories* (i, 162A) Boethius takes note of the disagreement between Iamblichus and Themistius concerning the authenticity of the Archytas text. In his *Institutio arithmetica* (ii, 41) he inserts a similar note on the same subject, aware that not everything current under Archytas' name is authentic. It is noteworthy that Simplicius, Boethius' militantly pagan contemporary who held Iamblichus' commentary in profound awe, cannot bring himself to make any reference to Themistius' critical doubt about this text. Boethius need not have had Themistius directly before him, since the same information about Themistius' scepticism of 'Archytas' appears in the tenth-century Arabic tradition in Al-Farabi; this suggests that Boethius had a scholion by some fifth-century Neoplatonic exegete, perhaps Syrianus.

The complete Greek text of the pseudo-Archytas was first printed from a Milan manuscript in 1914.[40]

Boethius' commentary on the *Categories* (224D) has a second reference to Iamblichus' commentary. It could be of interest if the evidence sufficed to establish the probability of Boethius having had direct rather than indirect access to this work. The task is made difficult by the loss of Iamblichus' text except in so far as it can be reconstructed from the numerous borrowings in the pages of Simplicius.

Is Boethius' knowledge of Iamblichus acquired by direct reading of a copy on the shelves of his own library, whose treasures appear in the nostalgic sadness of the *Consolation of Philosophy* as a source of the deepest humane pleasure and pride to him? Or is it indirect, through some later commentator citing Iamblichus?

On five occasions in the second commentary on *Interpretation* Boethius mentions Syrianus, the Athenian master of Proclus. Two of the five references are adverse, on rather technical points, and the question arises whether Boethius has had direct access to Syrianus' commentary or, perhaps more probably, has used some exegetical notes by a Neoplatonist later than Syrianus, inclined to feel critical towards some of his detailed exegeses. Proclus always speaks of Syrianus in terms of such filial veneration that the critical comments are unlikely to stem from anything by him.

Proclus' pupil Ammonius offers many parallels in detail to pieces of Boethius' commentary on *Interpretation*. Since both exegetes are drawing on Porphyry, this is not surprising, and one cannot therefore be confident that Boethius directly used Ammonius' commentary on the same text. But he may easily have had access to scholia or to lecture notes taken in Ammonius' classes. Ammonius himself remarks that Aristotle's logical writings have received a library of commentaries, and frequently refers to 'the exegetes' whose labours have been available to him. Ammonius puts it beyond doubt that among this corpus of exposition he possessed scholia on Aristotle by Proclus and by Syrianus. He begins his commentary with an acknowledgement that whatever is distinctive in his contribution he owes to the exegesis of Proclus.

That Boethius had actually read works by Proclus is not difficult to show. In the *Consolation of Philosophy* the parallels in argument are frequent with Proclus' tracts on providence and the problem of evil, or with parts of his massive commentaries on the *Timaeus*, *Parmenides*, and *Republic*. In the first book of the *Consolation* (i, 4, 30) Boethius quotes from an unnamed teacher of philosophy: 'If there is a god, whence comes evil? But if there is not, whence comes good?' Scholars have puzzled over the source of this quotation. It can be securely identified as a verbatim quotation from Proclus' commentary on the *Parmenides* (1056, 10–16 Cousin). The justly famed poem *O qui perpetua* (iii m. 9) which marks the literary and philosophical turning point of the *Consolation* has long been recognized to be intimately dependent for the detail of its ideas on passages not only in Plato's *Timaeus* but also in Proclus' *Timaeus* commentary.[41]

In his second commentary on *Interpretation* (421) Boethius writes of the great labour the work has cost him 'during almost two years of continuous sweat', because he has compressed into a single book the contents of very many books— 'plurimorum sunt in unum coacervatae sententiae'. James Shiel has given a radical interpretation to this sentence, viz. to make it say that in writing his commentaries on the *Isagoge*, on the *Categories* and on *Interpretation*, Boethius had before him not a large number of independent commentaries, but a single codex in which the Greek text of Aristotle was provided with wide margins filled with summaries of the exegeses of the principal expositors.[42] The sweat, then, consisted in the deciphering of the tiny handwriting. Otherwise the work had all been done for him already by a previous compressor.

It is certain that Boethius' summaries of the exegesis of commentaries before Porphyry follow a lead given by Porphyry himself. In almost every case Boethius follows a summary of the opinions of Aspasius, Herminus, or Alexander with a statement of the superior opinion of Porphyry on the controverted issue. But Shiel thinks that even Porphyry was available to Boethius in the form of a potted summary in the margins of his codex of the Organon. He is able to appeal to the fact that an early codex of the Organon, Urbinas 35, is an example of exactly such a manuscript as he postulates where the margins are packed with minuscule scholia. Moreover, we have similar matter (p. 138) in a Florence codex of the thirteenth century unearthed by Minio-Paluello which has marginal or interlinear notes intended to accompany Boethius' Latin translation of the *Prior Analytics*, and drawn from a Greek model.

Boethius may have had a codex of the Organon of the type that Shiel postulates; if so, this is the likely source from which he draws, e.g. his notes on Syrianus' exposition of *Interpretation*. But I have been unable to persuade myself that Boethius did not have, for *Categories* and for *Interpretation*, a complete text of Porphyry in front of him, and probably also for the *Categories* the exposition of Iamblichus. Did Boethius, of all people, need to say to anyone, 'Do not give me a book, I have one'?

In the case of Boethius' commentary on the *Categories*, Shiel's arguments for supposing that he did not have a complete copy of Porphyry's Question and Answer commentary come to look distinctly frail when inspected in detail. The minor differences of matter and order do not add up to such a conclusion; Boethius keeps to the order of Aristotle's text whenever he diverges from that of Porphyry. Where his text is not visibly dependent on Porphyry, then parallels in Simplicius often suggest that Iamblichus is the direct source being used. Unfortunately a detailed comparison is possible only for the *Categories*, since for *Interpretation* Porphyry's Greek text is lost.

In Boethius' commentary on the *Categories* there is nothing which looks inexplicable unless it is derived from the extant scholia by Ammonius. Their commentaries on the *Isagoge* and on *Interpretation* have a number of school clichés in common, but often show striking divergences. In the second commentary on Porphyry Boethius' discussion of universals owes an avowed debt to Alexander of Aphrodisias,[43] but nothing whatever to Ammonius' handling of the same subject.

The second commentary on Porphyry also has a long discussion of the question whether logic is an independent part of philosophy, or an instrument used in all parts of the subject, or both (above, p. 108). This discussion is closely paralleled in the extant introductory notes by Ammonius on the *Prior Analytics*. But the conclusion that Boethius simply attended Ammonius' lectures or had some lecture notes from his school in the margin of his codex or had even read his published commentary on the *Prior Analytics* is hasty. Striking features of Boethius' analysis of the various divisions of philosophy in his first commentary on Porphyry are absent from Ammonius' text.[44]

Boethius' commentaries on the Isagoge

At how early a stage of his pilgrimage Boethius' gaze is fixed upon the summit of philosophy can be seen even in so early a work as the first commentary on Porphyry's *Isagoge*. Here, at the beginning of his first writing on logic, Boethius sets out to explain that philosophy passes through *scientia*, in the knowledge of the various *artes*, to *sapientia* which is the knowledge of God, the living mind in need of nothing and the sole originating reason of things. From this source, he continues, our souls receive illumination which instils the desire and love for wisdom, so that the process is describable as mind withdrawing again into itself. For the divine wisdom leads every genus of soul back to its own purity, and thereby makes it possible for our minds to discern truth beyond the bounds of sense perception and to act in purity.

These evident echoes of Augustine and of the Neoplatonists are elaborated in the second commentary on Porphyry where Boethius begins with a statement of the soul's powers not only to give life to the body's animal existence or to empower us with capacity for feeling, but to set aside the senses to reach abstract concepts. Admittedly in this process of abstraction the mind remains confused by visual images (*imaginationes*). The upward ascent proceeds from the known to the unknown. Nevertheless the reasoning mind has not lost its power to know things as they really are, provided that in the active life there is a moral seriousness as a prerequisite. The mind has the capacity to put together things disjoined and to analyse things composite. By its *speculatio* (which Boethius establishes as the standard translation for the Greek *theoria*) incorporeal nature can be distinguished from bodies in which it exists in the concrete. By abstraction of physical matter we can reach the concept of pure form.

This doctrine of the second commentary on Porphyry has affinity with the scholion on *Prior Analytics* i, 25 (42b 24) printed by Minio-Paluello in *Aristoteles Latinus* iii (p. 310, 9 ff.): 'When the soul examines superior things true in themselves and eternal, it is called mind. When it considers universal conventions, it is called opinion. But when its objects of perception are individual things, it is called "sensus vel fantasia".'

Boethius' first commentary on Porphyry shows no sign of having been written with the intention already in view that one day it would be supplemented by a second. All we have is a declaration of intention to write 'in another work' about logic as an instrument rather than as part of philosophy (p. 10, 5); and this declaration is startlingly paralleled in Ammonius, *Isag.* 23, 23. But when writing the second commentary, evidently a few, perhaps five, years later than the first, Boethius conveys the impression that he had meant the first commentary to be only an elementary introduction for beginners, while the second is now intended for more advanced students, and adds verisimilitude to the claim by giving a backward reference, 'as was said in the first *editio*', when in fact nothing of the kind is to be found there (p. 154, 4). The second commentary does not in actuality make more serious demands on the reader than the earlier effort. Indeed at one point the first commentary becomes esoteric as the second never does, when, in the discussion whether universals may be incorporeal realities which nevertheless require bodies for their actualization, the reader is blandly told that there is such a thing as 'a first incorporeality after the limits' (*prima post terminos incorporalitas*) as if this were something every Roman schoolboy knows. Fabius, the faceless and no doubt fictitious interlocutor in the dialogue, protests that he does not understand this phrase, and is told that it would be a long explanation, not relevant to the matter in hand. He should be content to know that the *termini* are the extremities of geometrical figures; if he wishes to know more, then let him go to the first book of Macrobius' *Commentary on Scipio's Dream*. There (i, 5,

5–13) Macrobius explains that the first stage of ascent from corporeal to incorporeal is won by considering the *termini* of geometrical figures, even though they are indissolubly tied to bodies. The doctrine may be echoing Aristotle's *Metaphysics* (1020a 13): 'Limited plurality is number, limited length is line, breadth a surface, depth a solid.' (Likewise *Metaph.* 1028b 15 f.) But the point is more fully illustrated by a passage in Philoponus' commentary on *Categories* ch. vi (84, 10–85, 7), arguing that the limits of a finite body do not themselves fall within the body which they limit. The very act of considering the boundaries of a visible geometrical figure therefore becomes the first step towards the realization of what is meant by a concept.

Although much of the logic of Porphyry's *Isagoge* and of Boethius' commentaries is essentially Peripatetic, whenever metaphysical questions are touched upon then language is used that would be at home within the Platonic tradition. Substance may be either corporeal or incorporeal, body animate or inanimate; animal may be rational or irrational; the rational animal (i.e. being endowed with soul and reason) may be mortal or immortal. The disjunction of mind and matter is important in Boethius' discussion. He insists with all possible emphasis in the first commentary on Porphyry that nothing corporeal in genus can be placed under an incorporeal species (26, 24). The discussion of universals in the second commentary turns out to be, surprisingly, more Peripatetic than that in the first, conveying almost an impression of indecisiveness and incoherence. He restates Alexander of Aphrodisias' opinion that universals such as genera and species exist as mental constructs but only in so far as there are concrete particulars independent of our minds, which these universal terms serve to classify and hold together in a unity. But then follows a more Platonic statement that forming universals in the mind by putting things together (*per compositionem*) leads to error. The mind needs to proceed by the negative way, by abstraction, thinking away all corporeal nature until it reaches pure form alone (164–5).

Translator of Aristotle[45]
Boethius approached both Plato and Aristotle with deep rever-

ence. In his logical writings he expresses reserve towards the Stoics, following Porphyry. But Plato and Aristotle are wise men who represent the greatest philosophy of classical Greece and offer something more important than access to certain mental skills useful for social success. Their positions ought to be received with awe. In his commentaries Boethius more than once refers to Plato or Aristotle, or (on one occasion) Plotinus, as possessed of 'auctoritas'.[46] This veneration extends also to the master-commentator Porphyry, 'a man of the most weighty authority' (*Syll. cat.* 814C), and also to Iamblichus (*Cat.* 225B). Once in the second commentary on *Interpretation* (ii, 40) he remarks that 'here Porphyry agrees with the exegesis of Alexander of Aphrodisias, and I accept it either as Alexander's opinion or on Porphyry's authority'. The attitude that Plato and Aristotle ought to be read on one's knees in a spirit of devotion is all-pervasive among the Neoplatonists, and explains why Boethius finds so congenial the programme which he found in Porphyry, namely, of reconciling in fundamentals the doctrines of Plato and Aristotle (above p. 125). If these great figures are authorities, it is psychologically intolerable to find them in manifest discord with each other. Some Platonists before Porphyry, like Atticus, had insisted embarrassingly on the differences between Plato and Aristotle; so much so that Eusebius of Caesarea (*PE* xv, 4–9) cites Atticus to prove that wherever Aristotle and Plato disagree, Plato agrees with the Bible.

Boethius' first philosophical translation was the *Isagoge* or 'introduction' by Porphyry. The Latin adaptation by Victorinus irritated him by its mistakes and typical rhetor's misunderstandings, and even in the first commentary he had Porphyry's Greek before him to control Victorinus' Latin. In the second commentary a few years later he used a full translation of his own. About 300 manuscripts contain Boethius' version of the *Isagoge* without any commentary attached. This continuous text cannot have been assembled by an editor by piecing together the excerpts incorporated in the second commentary, since there Boethius omits the citation of sentences on which he thinks no explanation is necessary, and from this editorial method an incomplete text would result. Therefore the publication of a continuous and independent translation of Porphyry, without exegesis, must go back to Boethius himself. There is no manuscript of the second commentary containing the full text of the translation of Porphyry.

Victorinus' version of the *Isagoge* was known to Cassiodorus (*Inst.* ii, 3, 18, p. 128, 11–16 Mynors). But no manuscript has preserved it, and for our knowledge of it we depend on the fragments quoted in Boethius' first commentary, about a hundred in all, many being very short and hardly more than a few words torn from a sentence. Because Boethius simultaneously had Porphyry's Greek in front of him, it can be a delicate matter to determine exactly when he is quoting Victorinus and when he is directly translating the Greek. A noteworthy reconstruction of the remains has lately been printed by Minio-Paluello in *Aristoteles Latinus* i, 6–7 (1966), together with a critical text of Boethius' later version as a continuous text current apart from its exegesis in the second commentary. He expresses doubt whether or not Victorinus really translated every word of Porphyry (p. xiv n. 1). Brandt (*CSEL* 48, p. xv), with whom Pierre Hadot declares agreement, suggested that while much of Victorinus' text is a simple translation of the Greek, some sentences he tersely summarized or paraphrased in the interest of brevity. The difference between the two opinions cannot be called wide. Hadot has also printed a reconstruction (1971).

At the beginning of the second book of the second commentary on *Interpretation* written perhaps about 514–15, Boethius announces his purpose of translating and commenting on the whole of Aristotle, 'so far as accessible' to him (a qualification indicating awareness that there are writings of Aristotle not to be had in his library), and then the dialogues of Plato. By the beginning of the sixth book of this commentary his ambition appears restricted to an intention to complete at least the six treatises on logic in the Organon. Peculiar difficulties attach to attempts to determine precisely at what stage of his career Boethius made his translations and in what order. Some part of the task had evidently been completed before he announced the full scope of his scholarly and educational ambitions in the second book of the second commentary on *Interpretation*. The fundamental researches of Minio-Paluello in the manuscript tradition have shown, moreover, that Boethius produced revised forms of his versions, all of which amply attest the quasi-devotional fervour with which he approaches the text of Aristotle. He feels he has to translate 'word for word', as also for Porphyry (*CSEL* 48, p. 135, 7). The manuscripts of his translation and commentary on the *Categories* have revealed two types of text: one preserved in its pure state in an eleventh-century codex, Einsiedeln 324 (*a*), and another (*c*) contained in the great majority of manuscripts, the earliest of which, now at Karlsruhe (Augiensis CLXXII), was at the monastery of Reichenau on Lake Constance before the making of the extant Reichenau catalogue of 822. It emerges that *a* bears the marks of being the original version from Boethius' hand, and agreed with the text implied by the commentary. *c* shares with *a* about two-thirds of the wording, but for the remaining third draws on a different version *x*, which Minio-Paluello believes to have been a prior and inexpert translation also made by Boethius. *c* is therefore a conflation of two versions going back to Boethius himself. (Stylistic considerations tell against the hypothesis that *x* might be the lost version of Marius Victorinus.) *c* is the text of the manuscript tradition lying behind all the printed editions prior to 1961, which explains why, in the Migne edition, the exegesis often presupposes a version different from that printed in the successive excerpts from the Latin Aristotle. The Migne text reprinted the Basel edition of Henricus Loritus Glareanus (1546, 1570) which in turn drew upon the edition of the Venetian humanist Julianus Martianus Rota (Venice, 1543) for all Boethius' logical works except for the translations of the two *Analytics*, *Topics* and *Sophistic Refutations*; the Latin version of these was taken from the revised text of Lefèvre d'Etaples, Faber Stapulensis, who in 1502–3 produced a beautiful annotated edition of the Organon at Paris. (A copy of this very rare book is at Corpus Christi College, Oxford.)

The evidence accordingly points to the hypothesis that early in his career Boethius produced a provisional version of the *Categories*, and then revised and polished it at the time when he was writing his commentary in 510 during his year as consul. Probably at the time of the Carolingian renaissance, a scholarly editor (Alcuin being a possible candidate) produced a recension of the Latin Aristotle, in which Boethius' two versions are conflated to produce the 'vulgate' text underlying all printed editions before Minio-Paluello's 1961 edition of the text.

In the case of the treatise on *Interpretation* (*Aristoteles Latinus* ii, 1–2, 1965) the textual evidence of the manuscripts discloses that three forms of Boethius' version survive: one in the manuscripts offering a continuous text, a second in the excerpts given by Boethius' shorter commentary (which omit about a third of the whole), and a third, improved version in the more extensive excerpts accompanying the longer second commentary. The user of Mciscr's admirable Teubner edition of 1877–80 needs to be on his guard only against the editor's mistaken assumption that both commentaries presuppose a common and identical Latin translation without amendment by their author, and that all differences between them can be treated as scribal variants.

Similar phenomena appear in the Boethian version of the *Prior Analytics* and *Topics*, both of which show a double recension that is to be ascribed to Boethius himself. Only the *Sophistic Refutations* has come down in a single text-form; but perhaps that also passed through a revision at Boethius' hands, which has left no mark on our manuscript tradition.

The *Posterior Analytics* were probably included in Boethius' series of translations. His commentary on Cicero's *Topics* explicitly refers to his translations ('transtulimus') of both the *Prior* and the *Posterior Analytics*. The second book of his monograph 'on the Categorical Syllogism' has references to 'our Analytics', one of which uses the past tense as of work already achieved (822B), the other the future tense (830B). Since the monograph itself is almost wholly an exposition of the *Prior Analytics*, these references may reasonably be taken to mean that at the time of writing Boethius had completed his version of the *Prior Analytics* but not yet of the *Posterior*. Nevertheless, the inclusion of the *Posterior Analytics* (perhaps the hardest treatise in the Organon to interpret) is a declared intention announced already in the second commentary on Porphyry perhaps about 508–9 (*CSEL* 48, p. 158, 8), and he had evidently completed the task of the translation by the time of his commentary on Cicero's *Topics*. *De divisione* 885D passes by a complex question about definitions, referring the reader to the *Posterior Analytics* in a way that presupposes the book's availability to Latin students. Despite the inherently difficult content of the *Posterior Analytics*, which would militate against its preservation in times when education was not strong, a trace of the version made by Boethius survives. This is in a statement of the mid-twelfth-century translator John that 'Boethius' translation of the *Posterior Analytics* does not survive intact for us, and that part of it which is available is obscured by the fault of corruption' ('translatio Boethii apud nos integra non invenitur et id ipsum quo de ea reperitur vitio corruptionis obfuscatur', *Arist. Lat.* iv, 1–4, 1968, p. xliv). No manuscript containing the Boethian version has been found.

For the *Prior Analytics*, on the other hand, we now have not only two recensions that again seem to go back to Boethius himself, but also an important series of anonymous scholia contained in interlinear and marginal notes in a twelfth-century manuscript at Florence (Bibl. Naz., Conv. Soppr. J. 6.34) which Minio-Paluello has recognized as bearing characteristic marks of Boethius' style and interests.[47] The scholia have close affinity to some notes on Aristotle from the pen of Philoponus and a successor to him who added some exegesis of the second book of the *Prior Analytics* (*CAG* XIII, 2, ed. M. Wallies, 1905). Both Greek and Latin annotations draw on a common source, which does not correspond to the extant commentary of Ammonius. Naturally the Boethian authorship of the scholia is no more than conjecture.

The *Topics* of Aristotle was first translated into Latin by Boethius. Minio-Paluello's researches have again unearthed two recensions. Besides the normal Boethian version transmitted by the manuscripts, there is evidence of a second recension in a substantial fragment of the *Topics* which, perhaps by mere chance, was inserted into the middle of Boethius' tract *On Division* and has been there preserved in 12 manuscripts, the earliest (Orléans 267) being of the tenth or eleventh century. A couple of folios probably became misbound in a codex round about the sixth century. Boethius refers to his translation of the eight books of the *Topics* on three occasions: once in his commentary on Cicero's *Topics* (1052AB), and twice in *De differentiis topicis* (1173CD,

1216D). The early interpolated text of Cassiodorus' *Institutes* also knows of the existence of his work (Mynors, p. 129, apparatus). Although these references come from works written late in Boethius' life, nevertheless there is a clue to suggest that he had made a translation of the *Topics* even before his commentary on the Categories of 510. The translation of *Cat.* 1b 16 printed in the commentary on the *Categories* (*Arist. Lat.* i, 1–5, p. 6; *PL* 64, 177–8) is almost verbally identical with a translation of the same Greek sentence in the *Topics*, 107b 19 (*Arist. Lat.* v, 1–3, p. 26).

The *Sophistic Refutations* seems not to have been put into Latin by the time he wrote the second commentary on *Interpretation* where (ii, 132–4 Meiser) he discusses the work without the customary cross-reference to an available version. There is no other passage in his writings where Boethius alludes to the book. Nevertheless the version preserved in the manuscript tradition bears the print of his style and can be confidently accepted as his, even though we have no external testimony to the book's existence before Burgundio of Pisa about 1173 (*Arist. Lat.* vi, p. xii).

In addition to the logical writings of Aristotle, Boethius also worked on his *Physics*, a major essay on the philosophy of science containing discussions of motion, infinity, space, time, chance, ultimate being, the one, the prime mover. Two references in the second commentary on *Interpretation* (190, 13; 458, 27) and one in that on Cicero's *Topics* (1153B) make it certain that Boethius wrote some explanatory comments on the work, perhaps scholia (like those on the *Prior Analytics* in the Florence manuscript) rather than a full exposition of the long text, which would require a version to go with it. The *Physics* naturally attracted considerable attention from the Neoplatonic schools of Athens and Alexandria, an interest of which the most notable surviving monument is the immense commentary by Simplicius which runs to 1366 pages of print in Diels' edition (*CAG* IX–X, 1882–95). Simplicius himself had a substantial body of existing exegesis to draw upon. Both Alexander of Aphrodisias and Porphyry composed long commentaries on it, and Simplicius seems also to have had scholia by Syrianus and some lecture notes from the teaching of Ammonius. As in his commentary on Aristotle's *De caelo*,

Simplicius is here mobilizing his forces against the Christian Philoponus with his outrageous denial of a divine quality to the celestial frame of the sun and stars.

Boethius' discussions of time, eternity, and perpetuity in the last book of the *Consolation of Philosophy* show a number of close parallels to the language of Simplicius' commentary on the *Physics*, and Courcelle has suggested that both writers drew on a lost commentary by Ammonius. This is a speculation that may turn out to have substance to it, but is not required by the evidence. Themistius' paraphrase of the *Physics* (ed. Spengel, 1866) may have been before him. Whatever the form of the exegetical notes on the *Physics* compiled by Boethius, there is no evidence that they were copied. The medieval West first learnt about Aristotle's work from a new translation by James of Venice made from a Greek copy which he found probably at Constantinople on a visit about 1136 (attested in the *Dialogues* of Anselm of Havelberg).[48]

Boethius' achievement as a translator of the Organon was only partly successful. His mastery of Greek was never complete. His version of Porphyry's *Isagoge*, of the *Categories* and of *Interpretation* did well; and he had provided in each case substantial expositions to make them intelligible. But the translations of the two *Analytics*, of the *Topics*, and the *Sophistic Refutations* did not win a sufficiently general diffusion to become known. So Porphyry's *Isagoge*, and the first two of the six treatises of the Organon became for the medieval West 'the Old Logic', *Logica Vetus*, as contrasted with the exciting new translations of the remaining treatises of Aristotle which began to emerge in the West during the twelfth century. Boethius had indeed put these into Latin, but not enough people knew about it for this to make a difference.

Of Boethius' method as a translator it is enough to say that it shows him to be a man of meticulous care, with the utmost anxiety to convey the true 'word for word' sense of the quasi-sacred text of the great philosopher. Hence his revisions of his early versions which have complicated the manuscript tradition. His driving motive is to enable his Latin contemporaries and successors to have access to 'Aristotelica auctoritas'.

The plan to translate Plato's Dialogues as well was never realized. The Latin West in Boethius' time and until the twelfth century possessed only about half a single dialogue by Plato, Cicero's version of the *Timaeus* (which Boethius, like Augustine, knew well).[49] In addition Boethius proposes a book showing the fundamental harmony between Plato and Aristotle. Though he does not mention that Porphyry had done the work for him, it would evidently have been an adaptation of Porphyry's work on the consensus of these contrasting philosophers (above, p. 125), the conclusions of which provide a basic assumption for the Neoplatonic schools of Boethius' time. Augustine (*Contra Academicos* iii, 19, 42) takes Porphyry's position for granted.

The Ten Categories

Near the end of the second commentary on the *Isagoge* Boethius refers the reader to his forthcoming exposition of the *Categories* (he translates the Greek word as *praedicamenta*). The date of the commentary on the *Categories* is securely fixed to 510 by the preface to book ii explaining how his consular duties have been a distraction from this public educational task. Therefore the second commentary probably belongs to 508–9; and since the first commentary on the *Isagoge* shows no sign of having been written with any intention that it be supplemented, this probably falls four or five years earlier, after Boethius had completed his quadrivium, say about 505.[50]

In the commentary on the *Categories* Boethius allays western fears with the assurance that he is keeping everything simple and has avoided deeper questions. So at the beginning he lays down that the purpose of the categories is to examine words, not significations, and that he is proposing to follow Porphyry. 'It is in mind,' he says, 'to discuss the old questions, one of which is the intention of the *Categories*.' This is the form in which this sentence appears in the oldest manuscripts and in the earliest printed editions.[51] It would suggest that Boethius had in mind some brief prolegomena (of a type closely resembling the extant tract on this subject by Olympiodorus, *CAG* XII, 1). But in the sixteenth century it was amended to say that Boethius' intention is to discuss the questions of intention, utility and order 'in another commentary on the *Categories* addressed to the learned' (160A Migne). This is how the text reads in Rota's edition of 1543 copied by the Basel edition of 1546 and by subsequent printed editions including Migne.

The method of a double commentary was used by Boethius to justify his second exposition of Porphyry's *Isagoge*; and he also made use of it for the *Perihermeneias*, where the second exposition is two and a half times as long as the first. It may have been the same wish to go over the material twice which led him to write two closely similar treatises on the categorical syllogism, and twice, in effect, on Cicero's *Topics*. For an example of the method Boethius had Porphyry himself with his twin commentaries on the *Categories*, which would be a weighty precedent if there were evidence that Boethius knew Porphyry's second and longer commentary for Gedaleios.

A good number of manuscripts and the earliest printed editions (not Rota's) declare that their Boethian commentary on the *Categories* is the Prima Editio, even though they know nothing of a Secunda. Although the improved text as printed e.g. in Migne is false and misleading, it remains possible that this inspired guess might be correct. The authentic text tells us that his future plan is to compose another treatise treating in depth the special question of the intention of the *Categories* and the other 'introductory' matters required by scholastic tradition, and that this will include profounder questions than those considered by Porphyry's Question and Answer commentary; they will pertain 'to Pythagorean knowledge and perfect teaching' (160B). Later (180C) he excuses himself from explaining why Aristotle is right in fixing on ten as the number of the categories, on the ground that this needs to be done in another work. In the second commentary on the *Isagoge* (224, 24) Porphyry is cited for the view that the number ten depends on Aristotle's authority rather than on reason. The Pythagorean numerologists had their own views on why Aristotle chose this number, as one reads in the *Theologoumena Arithmeticae*. At 252BC Boethius indicates that in comparison with the *Metaphysics* the *Categories* are an elementary introduction to greater things. If, therefore, Boethius wrote a second commentary on the *Categories*, it is likely to have made much more use of Iamblichus. In a ninth-century Berne manuscript Pierre Hadot has found a Latin fragment of a commentary on the *Categories* which shows close affinity with Simplicius, i.e.

with Iamblichus, and he may therefore be right that it comes from the mysterious second commentary of Boethius.[52]

Detailed scrutiny and comparison of the two texts shows at once how closely Boethius' commentary follows Porphyry's Question and Answer exposition. From this source he takes his allusion (212B) to the second-century exegete Herminus. On the other hand one cannot be sure that he draws from Porphyry his information at the beginning of the fourth book (263B) as Porphyry's exposition after chapter 9 is lost. Boethius reports that Andronicus of Rhodes, the Peripatetic philosopher of the first century BC, regarded chapters 10 to the end, the Postpraedicamenta, as a misplaced appendage attached by an early editor who thought it would help to make the work a suitable introduction to the *Topics*, and even gave the work the title 'Before the Topics', Antetopica. This last title is attested for the *Categories* by a number of ancient writers sometimes apart from any question of the connection between chapters 1–9 and 10 to the end. It may reasonably be held to be a very early title for the treatise before 'Categories' became established. A scholiast transmits the information that the man who put the 'Categories' before the *Topics* and called the book 'Before the Topics' was Adrastus of Aphrodisias.

Boethius reports Porphyry as agreeing with Andronicus that the 'Postpraedicamenta' are an editorial addition, but as dissenting from the opinion that the editor who added them here made a mistake in thinking these chapters closely connected with what has preceded. Porphyry sees these last chapters as a necessary complement. Neither Andronicus nor Porphyry is reported as denying Aristotle to be the author of the Postpraedicamenta.[53]

It is impossible to be clear from what source Boethius drew this information about Porphyry's view, whether directly from the Question and Answer commentary or from a later user of Porphyry's longer commentary for Gedaleios, such as Iamblichus. Perhaps something was said about it in Themistius' paraphrase.

Iamblichus' exposition of the *Categories* is described by Simplicius as long, as following Porphyry in essentials, but distinctive in making much use of 'Archytas' the Pythagorean whose work, Iamblichus thought, Aristotle had happily plagiarized to the great benefit of his own treatise. Simplicius adds that Iamblichus offers the best commentary for bringing out the metaphysical significance of the book. This explains Boethius' reference to a Pythagorean doctrine of the *Categories* deeper than Porphyry's (160B). This must surely be an allusion to Iamblichus' work, though Boethius' compassionate determination to preserve simplicity for his Latin beginners encouraged the greatest restraint in his use of Iamblichus. Simplicius is avowedly a grateful follower of Iamblichus, whose actual words he confesses himself frequently to have transcribed (3, 3). If Iamblichus' work lay also before Boethius, that immediately explains why in a number of places where his exposition is not parallel to Porphyry's Question and Answer commentary, he is paralleled by matter in Simplicius. In the fourth book of Boethius' commentary, where the parallel text of Porphyry has not survived, several correspondences with Simplicius occur, in one of which Simplicius names Porphyry as his model (414, 34 ff. = Boethius 283B–D). Yet probably Boethius' recourse to Iamblichus in this section was again restricted. One cannot confidently affirm that none of Simplicius' Iamblichan matter appears in it if only for the reason that Simplicius can be demonstrated to be capable of reproducing Iamblichus verbatim without actually saying so. In the second book of his *Categories* commentary (224D–225B) Boethius quotes two observations from Iamblichus. Without the least mention of Iamblichus' name in the context both points reappear in Simplicius (184, 4–21), meeting a criticism that Aristotle's definition of relatives as mutually entailing one another is too wide since the same can also be true of some non-relatives. Iamblichus' first observation, that Aristotle's text does not say precisely and in set terms just what the critics attribute to him, is set aside by Boethius as negligible nit-picking. It is accordingly certain that Simplicius drew more matter from Iamblichus than merely those passages where he tells us that this is what he has done.

Boethius could easily have taken from Iamblichus the quotation from Porphyry in book ii (233B–D) illustrating the idealist view that the knowing mind and the object of knowledge are relatives which mutually imply each other. This quotation is not taken from Porphyry's Question and Answer commentary, though that exposition offers a terse summary of his opinion. It may therefore be an excerpt from the second, longer commentary of Porphyry on the *Categories*, dedicated to Gedaleios, which Boethius found in his text of Iamblichus.

Boethius' close attachment to Porphyry's simpler commentary can be demonstrated from book i, 172B–D, where he follows Porphyry's Question and Answer in declaring 'in something' to have nine possible meanings. (Aristotle, *Physics* iv, 3, is the unnamed source for eight of them.) Both Ammonius (*Cat.* 26, 34; 29, 5) and Simplicius (*Cat.* 46) as also Philoponus (*Cat.* 32, 7) claim that there are 11 meanings. In other words, post-Porphyrian exegesis in Iamblichus had elaborated on his ninefold list. Boethius abides by Porphyry's original position, but then inserts a substantial discussion of accidents as being *in* a subject, and this has no correspondence in Porphyry but some parallel matter in the Iamblichan texts reproduced by Simplicius (46–7) and especially by Elias (*CAG* XVIII, 151, 25 ff., parallel to Boethius, 173C).

Alexander of Aphrodisias' commentary on the *Categories* does not survive except for a few fragments. Boethius has one direct parallel to one of these pieces of Alexander in a passage where Porphyry's Question and Answer commentary is not his model. (196A 3–4 = Alexander cited by Elias, *Cat.* 180, 1–3.) This can have reached Boethius by direct reading of Alexander, but may equally well have come via Iamblichus or some later Platonic exegete.

Boethius begins both his first commentary on Porphyry and his exposition of the *Categories* by answering six initial questions which were conventional in the Neoplatonic schools, viz. intention, utility, order, to which part of philosophy, authenticity, title.[54] Ammonius' commentary on Porphyry gives the same list plus a seventh, the chapter divisions (*Isag.* 21, 8–10). In his commentaries on the *Categories* (7, 15–8, 10) and on *Interpretation* (1, 12–20 and 4, 25) Ammonius has only six headings; he keeps the chapter divisions, and omits 'to what part of philosophy'. The full list of seven after Ammonius' model is given by his pupil Philoponus (*CAG* XIII, 2, p. 1, 7–10).

Later in the sixth century Elias' commentary on the *Categories* explains that Proclus was responsible for a special treatise prescribing ten subjects that every commentator ought to include in his introduction, ending with the evidently already conventional six questions, which are listed as intention, utility, title, authenticity, order, and the division of Aristotle's works. That is, 'to what part of philosophy' and 'the divisions into chapters' are replaced by a heading 'to which section of the Aristotelian corpus' (CAG XVIII, 1, p. 127, 3–129, 3).

Simplicius' commentary on the Physics (CAG IX) begins with the work's intention, the section of Aristotle's philosophy, title, utility, order, and authenticity.

Evidently this scholastic list suffered some variation not merely in its order but in the interpretation of particular items. It is noteworthy that Boethius stands more immediately in line with Proclus than any of the three versions of the list in Ammonius. The parallel between Boethius, *Isag.* 4, 17–5, 10 (Brandt), with six items, and Ammonius *Isag.* 21, 8–10, with seven items, is not so exact as to fortify the case for a demonstrated literary dependence,[55] and the evidence given above proves that we are dealing with a conventional cliché known to everyone.

From Boethius' commentary on the *Categories* the Latin reader would gain a reasonably discerning account of the book's structure and meaning. The ten categories (substance, quantity, quality, relation, active, passive, when, where, having, position) are explained as concerned not merely with verbal distinctions; nor are they merely mental concepts. They are significant of things that actually are the case. Aristotle and Boethius share a confidence that words generally correspond to things; but caution is always necessary, and in his *De Interpretatione* Aristotle shows many qualifications to this confidence. The exegetes of Aristotle disagreed among themselves on the placing of the categories on the map of his logic and of human knowledge. To Alexander of Aphrodisias they concern exclusively verbal distinctions. To Porphyry they express ideas and intellectual concepts; for they are the ultimate genera. Iamblichus adopts a mediating position: the categories are significant sounds signifying things that are in so far as thoughts act as a mediator. The Iamblichan position is adopted by Boethius in his second commentary on *Interpre-*

tation.[56] In the commentary on the *Categories* he keeps close to Porphyry.

Things-that-are are classified in two pairs: universal (genera or species), particular (individuals), substantial, accidental. Boethius illustrates this fourfold classification with a diagram (175B) which appears in identical form in Ammonius' commentary on the *Categories* (25, 12). Boethius' use of a Greek source is so undisguised that he keeps the Greek word *asystaton* in transliteration (though since we have no critical edition of the work as yet it is premature to assume that the printed texts faithfully reproduce what is in the manuscripts). There was no Latin word available to him for saying that there can be no such thing as a substantial accident or a universal particular.

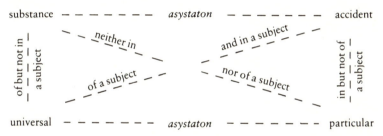

That is to say, four links are possible: substance (which is of but not in a subject) and accident (in but not of a subject) can either be universal or be individual and particular.

Porphyry's Question and Answer commentary remarks that Aristotle's division is 'chiastic' (78, 36) which suggests that a diagram could originally have been attached to this text to illustrate the point. The diagram is a regular part of the school convention. It reappears in Philoponus' commentary on the *Categories* (28, 25). A development of a similar diagrammatic scheme was developed to become the Pons Asinorum of the medieval logicians.

With chapter 5 Aristotle reaches the concept of substance: 'primary' substance for individuals, 'secondary' substance when referring to the species and genera which contain the individuals. For Aristotle the particular is prior to the universal. We infer the species man and the genus animal only from our knowledge of those particular instances that share common characteristics. The doctrine is identical here with that which Boethius has set out in the second commentary on the *Isagoge*; it reappears in the fifth theological tractate (*Contra Eutychen* iii, 25). This explains (Boethius continues) why Aristotle does not call by the name 'primary substances' the naturally first intellectible substances such as God and mind (183D).

Boethius proceeds to a résumé of the distinctions drawn in Porphyry's *Isagoge* between genus, species, differentia, property and accident. There can be more or less in qualities but not in substances; nor, as Boethius adds to Porphyry, in circles where no circle is more or less a circle than any other (197D; the point is in Aristotle, *Cat.* 11a 5–14).

After the preface explaining delay in completion because of consular duties with some suitable echoes of Cicero, his great consular predecessor in studying Greek philosophy, Boethius' second book embarks on Quantity, again closely following Porphyry (100, 12 ff.), but does not succeed in bringing tidiness to a category that includes a huge variety of topics, such as number, language, lines, surfaces, bodies, time, and place. The order in which things happen is vital to their meaning. The syllables of the name Cicero (Socrates in Porphyry) would not refer to the Latin orator if pronounced in a different order. In that event the word would be as meaningless as the Greek nonsense word 'scindapsus' (a conventional instance e.g. in Ammonius' school, *Isag.* 59, 1; 60, 7; *Perih.* 17, 22; not in Porphyry's Question and Answer, whose instance of meaningless sound is the equally conventional *blityri*, 102, 5).

A minor ray of light on the rural population of Italy in the sixth century may conceivably be thrown by Boethius' comments on Aristotle's observation that large and small are not true contraries. Porphyry had said (109, 17) that in Athens 3000 are few, in a village 300 are many. In Boethius (214A) a village population of only 100 is large. But in this context Porphyry is not Boethius' sole source. When he adds that any hill looks small compared with the Atlas, comparison with Simplicius (150, 34) and Philoponus (*Cat.* 95, 31) proves that this addition to Porphyry was based on some other Greek commentator using the illustration of Hymettos and Mount Olympos.

A long discussion of relation follows: father and son, master and servant, mutually imply one another, and a true relation is 'convertible'. One cannot say a wing always implies a bird, for insects have wings; nor that anything with a head is an animal, for there are headless sea creatures. Here Boethius is adding to Porphyry's original a point that can be seen to be a school commonplace from his first commentary on the *Isagoge* (70, 22) or from Ammonius, *Isag.* 79, 7. Knowledge is relative. There can be no knowledge unless there is something to be known, e.g. that the sum of the three angles of a triangle is two right angles (229B; cf. Aristotle, *Top.* B 3, 110b 6), which is everlastingly true even if somebody does not actually know it to be so. But the temporal priority of the object of knowledge and its capacity to persist apart from the knower provide criteria for deciding the non-existence of imaginary entities such as a chimaera or centaur. On the other hand, the method of squaring the circle, which had not been discovered in Aristotle's times, has since been found (231B). In this assertion Boethius is simply following Porphyry (120, 10); not Iamblichus' more elaborate discussion claiming that the method for squaring the circle had been found by Pythagoreans as appears from the proofs of 'Sextus the Pythagorean' (Simplicius, *Cat.* 192); nor the comment of Ammonius (*Cat.* 75, 11–19) reproduced in Philoponus (121, 2) that after many efforts by geometers Archimedes alone succeeded with an approximate answer, and even now a method of getting an exact answer has not yet been found.

Book iii is devoted to chapters 8 and 9 on quality, with brief notes on active and passive. Quality is a term of so many meanings that Boethius reports some critics as suspecting Aristotle of equivocation (241A; cf. Simplicius 270, 15). Quality or differentia added to the genus gives the species. Socrates and Plato do not differ in the species of humanity, but are distinct only by the quality of their proper *persona*. (The sentence is important for the later interpretation by Boethius of this momentous word, below, p. 193.) Among qualities Aristotle distinguished transitory conditions (cold or hot) from lasting states such as knowledge. But he has to allow that severe illness may bring a diminution of mental powers. According to Proclus' commentary on the *Republic* (ii, 349

Kroll) Aristotle somewhere told of a distinguished orator who in a raging fever lost all knowledge of letters while retaining his other faculties. Boethius borrows the illustration (did he find it in Proclus?)[57] to explain the allusion in the text of Aristotle. But only the force of some greater passion could drive out of one's head the knowledge that the three interior angles of a triangle are equal in sum to two right angles.

Virtues are placed by Aristotle under the category of quality. For moral character is changed only with difficulty. One does not call just a man who has acted justly only once, nor an adulterer a man who has slipped once but is not in mind and intention persistently unfaithful. 'Aristotle declares virtues to be not knowledge, as Socrates, but habits of character' (242C).

The remainder of the exposition is hardly more than the slightest expansion of Porphyry's paraphrase of the text. The mention of form and shape (10a 11) leads Boethius to discourse of the geometrical definition of a figure as contained by its limits. Aristotle's observation that his list of qualities is incomplete (10a 25) calls Boethius to remark that the master wrote the *Categories* as a beginners' 'entrance and bridge' to deeper questions of philosophy, and that what he omits here he put into the *Metaphysics*, a work not composed for beginners. Aristotle deliberately left something for others to find out, providing a stimulus to teachers 'not only of his own school but also of ours' (252BC).

In the exegesis of Aristotle's antithesis between justice and its contrary injustice (10b 13) Boethius follows Porphyry in taking note of some who say injustice is the lack of justice rather than its contrary. He restates Porphyry's exposition of the doctrine that not only substances but some qualities are incapable of degree, such as health, justice, literacy, though we may say of a grammarian as a man that Donatus knew more grammar in old age than when he first embarked on these studies (257D). The remainder of the book keeps close to Porphyry, including the explanation of Aristotle's brevity here on active and passive and other categories, viz. that he deals with active and passive at length in his works *On coming to be and passing away*, and in the *Physics* with where and when; and with all the categories with deep subtlety in the *Metaphysics* (262A = Porph. 141, 11–17).

The fourth and last book (which is not in all manuscripts marked as such) deals with the 'Postpraedicamenta', contraries, time and simultaneity, change, and having; a section which Andronicus of Rhodes justly thought attached by an editor other than Aristotle. Porphyry's Greek text is lost, but Boethius explicitly acknowledges his continuing debt to him. And Porphyry's answer to Andronicus is given, namely that it is an essential supplement to the *Categories*. On contraries Porphyry discussed not only the debate between the Stoics and the Aristotelians but the disagreements among the Peripatetics themselves. Boethius does not wish to trouble his readers with Stoic logic, and omits this discussion.

Boethius carefully explains Aristotle's analysis of contraries, some of which are contradictory, others not; some of which allow medial positions, others not. Between odd and even, there is no mean. But grey stands between white and black, and 'we see red, as in the rose and many other flowers, brought to birth by the mercy of spring' (267D). Between good and bad Aristotle places the neither bad nor good (12a 19), and later philosophers like the Stoics have assigned the term 'indifferent' to riches and beauty. Boethius here runs parallel to Simplicius (386, 26), who in this section also has many other correspondences which show Boethius to be following either Porphyry or school convention. The commentary on chap. 11 (281B ff.) includes a definition of induction as 'a collection of individual instances and through them a reduction to universal knowledge and conclusion'. Simplicius (409, 23) shows that something on induction was traditional at this point in school exegesis. Simplicius expressly refers to Porphyry (Simplic. 414, 34) for the treatment of good and evil as genera that includes such species as justice and injustice (= Boethius 283 B–D); and in the next chapter (14a 26) on priority and simultaneity Boethius himself names Porphyry as writing of the verbal distinction between *antiquius* as a term for 'older' in reference to inanimate things, *senius* for animate and especially human beings (284A = Simplic. 419, 1 ff. with slightly different illustrations). Aristotle's remark that 'prior' is often a value word he illustrates by the sun's superiority to the moon, the soul's to the body, the mind's to the soul (this last instance having a strongly Neoplatonizing flavour). Simplicius' parallel passage is content to name the priority of gods to mortals.

Boethius' exegesis of chapter 14 is on species of motion. He refers the reader, in the manner used by Simplicius (427, 20; 428, 3 ff.), to Aristotle's differing treatment in his *Physics*, where he differentiates between change and motion and treats coming to be and passing away as two of the species of change (E 1, 224b 35 ff.; 225a 25 ff.). Finally we have Aristotle's square which remains square if a gnomon is added. This is provided with an illustrative diagram diverging from that in Ammonius or Simplicius, not in its mathematics but in the point at which the square is divided. It coincides exactly with the form of diagram given by Philoponus, and also has the merit of corresponding precisely to what Boethius' Latin text says. It is a mistake to suppose that because the form of diagram in e.g. Migne differs from Ammonius and Simplicius, it has been incorrectly transcribed by medieval scribes or modern printers.[58]

On interpretation

The most extended single work from Boethius' pen is his double exposition of Aristotle's difficult treatise 'On Interpretation', which the early editors of the Peripatetic school placed second in the Organon after the *Categories*. Aristotle's study of the logic of the simple proposition and of modal sentences containing the words 'necessary' and 'possible' was famous in antiquity and later for causing headaches in its interpreters. The commentaries by Boethius and Ammonius are the principal ancient survivors of a rich exegetical mine. The commentaries by Stephanus (*CAG* XVIII, 3) and Proba (extant only in Syriac) depend on Ammonius and have no independent value. A little light, however, to illuminate Boethius' relation to his sources can occasionally be derived from the tenth-century commentary and treatise by the Arab philosopher of Baghdad, Al-Farabi. His work is now translated into English by F. W. Zimmermann (1981).

About AD 200 Alexander of Aphrodisias felt the impulse to write a commentary on the problematic work in consequence, he says (Boethius ii, 3), of the bewildering disagreements of the exegetes. Porphyry (Boethius ii, 293, 27) declares that in his time some philosophers simply despaired, throwing in their hand because they found its darkness inspissated to the point of impenetrability. Porphyry's commentary, evidently a substantial work, is known largely through its adaptation to the purposes of Boethius and Ammonius. Ammonius wittily reports that when exegetes reached the tenth chapter, on contradictory opposites, even the most scholarly commentators thought the only alternative to the simplest exegesis a frank resort to mantic clairvoyance (*CAG* IV, 5, p. 167, 15–18). Cassiodorus cites the maxim 'When Aristotle wrote Perihermeneias, he dipped his pen in his mind' (*Inst.* ii, 3, 11, p. 114, 21 Mynors).

Because Boethius and Ammonius have a number of points in common, it does not follow that Boethius used a copy of Ammonius' commentary directly. No parallel occurs not readily explicable as the result of both men using Porphyry or the school tradition. Courcelle, the advocate of direct dependence, at one point weakens his case by importing the name of Ammonius into a corrupt text in Boethius. In a passage on the classification of dialectical and non-dialectical questions (Boethius ii, 361), the manuscripts unanimously read 'sicut audivimus docet'. Meiser emends 'audivimus' to Eudemus, Courcelle to Ammonius. But that Eudemus is the right correction is certain from a passage in Alexander of Aphrodisias' commentary on the *Topics* (69, 13–23), to which James Shiel draws attention. Alexander there attributes to Eudemus the exact classification that we have in the text of Boethius.[59]

That many of the common features are school convention is briefly shown. Two allusions in Aristotle's *De anima* iii, 8 (432a 12) occur in Boethius (ii, 11, 23 and 43, 17). Ammonius uses the same quotation to make the identical point (25, 31) in refutation of Andronicus' arguments against the authenticity of the treatise. But it seems as good as certain that this citation from *De anima* has long been a regular constituent of exegetical arguments over the question.

Between Boethius and Ammonius there are striking differences. At chapter 14 Ammonius records serious doubt about the chapter's authenticity. He mentions Syrianus' observations on the incompatibility of this chapter on contraries with Aristotle's views earlier in the treatise, and suggests that, if the chapter is an authentic piece of Aristotle, his intention must have been to provide his readers with a test to see if they could detect the falsity in plausible arguments. He adds that Porphyry composed no commentary on the chapter. Of these weighty matters Boethius says not a word except obliquely in so far as his exegesis seeks to harmonize the chapter with the doctrine of *Categories* x–xi (e.g. Boethius ii, 465, 22; 466, 14 f.), and stresses its consistency with the rest of the treatise *On Interpretation* (500, 17 ff.). This at least proves that at this point Boethius is not following Syrianus, and he may have had little to help him except a few scholia. The lack of Porphyry to guide him explains why in general his treatment of the chapter is jejune. But it was not to Ammonius that he turned to fill the gap. Ammonius, for example, provides no model for Boethius' endeavour to explain *Perih.* 23b 33 by considering proportionality. The true beliefs that the good is good and the bad is bad, or the false beliefs that the good is not good and not good is good, are compared by Boethius with the numerical relations of the ratio 2:4 = 6:12, where it is also true that 2:6 = 4:12. That is, if A:B = C:D, it will also be true that A:C = B:D, and this will hold good for any term or proposition substituted for these variables. A comparable resort to the principles of mathematical proportionality also appears in the Florence scholia on the *Prior Analytics* (*AL* iii, 1, 4, p. 328, 27 ff.).

Ammonius' commentary is carefully signposted with emphatically marked chapter divisions (which also appear in Stephanus' commentary epitomizing Ammonius and in Al-Farabi). None of these is reproduced by Boethius. Ammonius' work is therefore not likely to have been open before him or, if it was so, treated as enjoying high authority. Syrianus is followed for an absurd count of the number of possible propositions totalling 144 (ii, 321–4); by Ammonius' time the calculation has increased to 3024 (*CAG* IV, 5, p. 219, 21). Boethius' adds some critical comment on Syrianus' confusion of affirmations and negations. He has surely got some Neoplatonic exegetical notes to be dated between Syrianus (d. 437) and Ammonius fifty or sixty years later.

Boethius' two commentaries appear not to have been composed simultaneously, which one would suppose an easier course, but one after the other. Hence the revisions of the translations of Aristotle presupposed in the second commentary.

The second commentary begins with the customary notes on intention, title, authenticity, utility and, by implication, its place in the order of Aristotle's writings. The examination of the simple or unconditional proposition is prerequisite to a discussion of the simple syllogism in the *Prior Analytics*. Points in the earlier parts of the commentary are closely paralleled in Boethius' two monographs on the categorical syllogism; i.e. (a) the short treatise on one book entitled in the manuscripts 'Antepraedicamenta' and in the printed editions *Introductio ad syllogismos categoricos* (*PL* 64, 761C–794B); (b) the first of the two books *De syllogismo categorico* (PL 64, 793C–832 A), the second book of which is a summary of the *Prior Analytics*. Of these two treatises, which overlap in subject matter, it is more the content than the wording that is shared; both bear marks of being adaptations of a Greek original. This puzzle of two different adaptations of a single model has an analogy in his different attempts to translate the Organon. In his first commentary on the *Isagoge* he mentions a treatise by Porphyry 'on categorical syllogisms' (15, 10 Brandt; *PL* 64, 14 D1), which is the likely model. In the second commentary on *Interpretation* Boethius declares his intention to write a short summary (*breviarium*) largely in the very words of Aristotle himself but with expansions for clarity. It is hard to decide whether for help he turned to Porphyry's monograph or to Themistius' paraphrase. The two studies on the categorical syllogism contain much that is close to Aristotle's text. The *breviarium* could well be the *Introductio ad syllogismos categoricos*.[60] At ii, 172 Boethius refers his reader to the two-volume work on the categorical syllogism as already completed.

The Peripatetic commentators disagreed among themselves whether different societies which use different words mean the same thing and whether individuals have identical mental experiences. Aspasius held that just as moral codes are valid for their own communities but not for others, so thoughts in the mind vary from individual to individual. Against him Alexander of Aphrodisias felt such relativistic doctrines to threaten the possibility of rational communication. He asserted that, though our languages may differ and speech conventions vary, nevertheless all minds find identical rational considerations valid. On this issue Boethius gratefully follows Alexander. Goodness and justice are, he feels, identical among all nations. The concept of a supreme Being is a universal phenomenon. If there is disagreement on religion or morals, this is because we make errors, not because there is no such thing as truth to aim at (ii, 41–2).

After a catalogue of types of fallacy (ii, 129) slightly differing from Ammonius' list (84–5),[61] Boethius expounds the categorical or unconditional proposition which has subject (noun) and predicate (verb) and therefore affirms or denies something (ii, 136 ff.). He explains the fourfold pattern of quantifiers with a diagram (ii, 152) which is also that given in both the *Introductio ad syllogismos categoricos* 775A and in *De syllogismo categorico* i, 800A. The original Greek pattern, using a different sentence however, is reproduced in Ammonius' commentary (*Perih.* 93, 15–18). A similar diagram may be found in Apuleius, *Perih.* p. 180 Thomas.

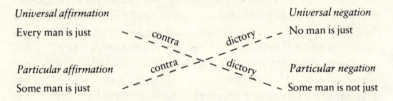

The purpose of the diagram is to illustrate where contradictions lie. A particular negation is contradictory of a universal affirmation, a universal negative of a particular affirmative.

Concerning the indefinite proposition 'A man is (or is not) white', where there is no quantifier, Boethius reports Alexander's opinion that since it is reducible either to a particular or to a universal, it can carry opposite meanings. But he then prefers Porphyry's subtle analysis of negative indefinite propositions which include the contrary of the affirmation which they deny, e.g. 'a man is not white' may mean 'a man is black' (Boethius ii, 159). Boethius concludes that the indefinite has the force of the particular (ii, 172 cf. *Syll. Cat.* i, 802D). He rejects Syrianus' opinion, which he supported by texts from both Plato and Aristotle, that an indefinite negative has the force of a universal negative, i.e. 'Not: a man is just', is equivalent to 'no man is just'. Boethius refers the reader to his first book on the categorical syllogism (802CD, parallel to *Introd.* 776C–778A). In any event according to *An. Pr.* i, 4, two indefinite propositions cannot yield a syllogism, whereas a particular negative can be inferred from a particular affirmative and a universal negative.

Since Ammonius' exegesis follows Syrianus, whom Boethius is rejecting, he is evidently not the inspirer of Boethius' criticism of Proclus' master. Boethius may have had some scholia on the work composed by a Neoplatonic teacher inclined to be a little critical of Syrianus and Proclus. Damascius will not have been the first Neoplatonic philosopher to think Syrianus and Proclus capable of correction and improvement. Admirers of Iamblichus were critical of Proclus and his doctrines (Simplicius, *In Phys.* 795, 15 ff. Diels).

Future contingents

The famous ninth chapter of Aristotle, *De interpretatione*, provokes from Boethius the observation that it touches on matters too deep for a textbook of mere logic. Many questions in it converge with the treatment of possibility in the *Prior Analytics*.[62]

Events of the past or present cannot be reversed and so are 'necessary'. There are also constants about the physical world which are 'necessary' because they are always the case, even if we cannot always know about them, as, for example, whether the number of the stars is even or odd; they must be one or the other, but which we cannot know. (Boethius confuses 'they must be either one or the other' with 'whichever they are is subject to necessity'.) There are other constants such as the rising and setting of the sun, the property of fire to give heat as long as it burns, the indelible rationality of humanity. Other things are 'contingent'; that is, they need not necessarily be as they are but could be otherwise. 'Contingent' Boethius explains as meaning that the likelihood of a thing being one thing rather than another is equal, and here wants to distinguish it from what is possible but very unusual and from what is usual but not invariable, e.g. if a man's hair fails to whiten in old age (an example drawn from Aristotle's *Prior Analytics* i, 13; 32b, 6–7).

If we say a thing is 'contingent' (a word in the coinage of which Boethius was anticipated by Marius Victorinus),[63] the uncertainty whether or not something will occur is not ascribable to our ignorance. We mean, Boethius explains, that in nature itself, in the process of causation, there is an uncertainty or 'instability' that is like a coincidence or a chance meeting of friends. The world does not have to be exactly as it now is; for providence controls the heavenly bodies, but in the sublunary realms things are not so inflexibly ordered.

This is the Peripatetic position over against the Stoics, for whom chance is only another name for human ignorance, and everything in nature really happens by necessity and destiny or 'providence'. The Stoics grant that human beings possess some freedom of choice, but it is in principle the same as animal instinct. Our will is constrained by the necessities imposed by providence, and the antithesis between will and nature is therefore unreal. The Aristotelian reply to this is that the Stoics ignore powers of rational deliberation and decision. Freedom is in the judgement, not in the will impelled by the 'imagination', and in our actions we are often active initiators, not passive followers being dragged along.

Mingled with the arguments about the chain of causation is Aristotle's logical point that a proposition about the future, if a proposition at all, will be either true or false, just as one about past or present; and if true, then large questions may be raised about determinism. Boethius warns against exegetes who take Aristotle to be indifferent to the truth or falsity of future contingent propositions. A man predicts: 'There will be a seafight tomorrow.' 10,000 years previously the same prediction could have been truly made, i.e. before the present chain of events producing the conflict could be visible to the onlooker. According to the determinist, if the prediction is true, the event predicted must be necessary. Aristotle denies neither that there are human causes which make a seafight imminent, nor that there is a logical necessity inherent in a true prediction that one will occur which entails that, because it is true, it must occur. He seems content to observe that necessity is a term inappropriate for statements true of individual events in time and is appropriate only for statements of what is always true.[64]

The ancient exegetes of Aristotle, Boethius prominent among them, saw this problem as having large theological implications. Predictions are made by divine oracles. Does divine omniscience mean that because of God's foreknowledge events predicted occur by necessity? If so, does this abolish human freedom and/or chance? The Stoics supported their determinism by appealing to oracles and divination.

Boethius observes that ancient oracles often take the form of predicting that X will happen unless Y occurs in which case it will not. The prediction concerns a world in which uncertainty is a natural constituent. Nor is there an argument from omniscient foreknowledge as being essential to a true concept of God. If not all events happen by necessity, God would be holding mistaken beliefs if he were to suppose that everything is by necessity. It inheres in the contrast between necessary and contingent that contingents are by definition non-necessary and therefore cannot be known, even by God, to be necessary. So God truly knows the future as a future of open possibilities, and this is compatible with full knowledge of the outcome of human deliberation and action (ii, 225–6).

In saying this Boethius occupies Peripatetic ground. Alexander of Aphrodisias (*De fato* 31) declares that oracles, to which the Stoic fatalists especially appealed, are like advice on action to avoid. Apollo's prediction is therefore not the cause of Oedipus' parricide and incest. Had he taken the oracle more seriously, he could have avoided these polluting crimes.

Boethius now turns to consider various definitions of the possible (ii, 234). The logicians of Megara gave special thought to this concept. The determinist Diodorus Cronus (whose views appear in Cicero, *De fato* ix, 17, so that Boethius is not bringing on to the stage a character unfamiliar to the Latin world) saw in Aristotle's ninth chapter some vacillation. The only thing, he said, that is possible is that which either is or will be true. He defines the possible as only theoretically distinct from the necessary, for in a world of strict cause and effect only the necessary occurs. Whatever is non-necessary is impossible.

Philo of Megara defines the necessary proposition as that which is true and incapable of being false; the non-necessary proposition is that which is inherently susceptible of being untrue; the impossible is that which is inherently incapable of being true; the possible is inherently capable of being true, as for example, that today I shall re-read Theocritus if nothing external intervenes to stop me. This last formulation, however, covers both situations where external interference is unlikely and those where it is very likely indeed. So Simplicius (*Cat.* 195–6) and Philoponus (*An. Pr.* 169, 19 ff.) say that Philo defined the possible as merely remote and theoretical; e.g. a piece of timber at the bottom of the sea is in principle combustible but in practice its burning is unlikely to occur.

Boethius' account of the Stoic position (ii, 234, 27 ff.) corresponds to what we are also told by Diogenes Laertius (vii, 74). Boethius portrays it as distinct from Philo's. The Stoics stressed the absence of external obstacles as a necessary condition of possibility. Boethius then criticizes the Stoics (no doubt after Porphyry) for a division of propositions into possible and impossible; dividing possible propositions into necessary and non-necessary; and non-necessary into possible and impossible, thereby completing the circle. Boethius remarks that the Stoics here cause confusion by treating 'possible' as both a wide genus and a narrow species, a remark which seems uncomprehending. He assumes the Stoics to work with a pattern of this shape:[65]

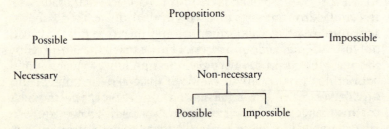

But the Stoics correctly regarded a proposition as possible if and only if its negation is non-necessary, and impossible if and only if its negation is necessary. The scheme is therefore a square of opposition:

In the *Prior Analytics* (32a 18–20) Aristotle explains the admissible (*endechomenon*) as either the non-necessary or the not-impossible. But the notion remains a slippery one to handle. Boethius we have seen to be aware of various meanings that the term 'contingent' may have: (a) an 'outside chance', as we might say '99 to 1 against', but still in theory possible; (b) an equal chance, as we might say 'fifty-fifty'; (c) a very high probability, '99 to 1 in favour', but not utterly certain. (He has the embryo of post-Renaissance probability theory.) At ii, 423, 26 he takes 'contingent' to mean not-impossible. Once (392) he hovers on the edge of a distinction between possible and contingent.

John of Salisbury (*Metalogicon* iii, 4) 600 years later reflects medieval consideration of Boethius' doctrine when he marks a distinction between something that happens only rarely (for John 'contingent') and something that does not necessarily exist but, if it were to exist, would result in no impossibility. Boethius is not interested in anything as purely hypothetical as the latter.

For Aristotle the necessary is a concept bound up with the constants of nature. Constants are what they are because they are not vulnerable to contraries (Boethius ii, 236). Snow remains cold until warmed up. Non-necessary things are those which admit contraries and do not therefore continue permanently in one stay. The 'divine bodies' in the heavens (238, 22; 244, 26) undergo no modification. They do not pass from potentiality to actuality, and are so constituted by reason and nature that whatever they are, they are by necessity. The sun cannot stand still but moves necessarily (243, 8; 407, 22). In the lower sublunary order things come to be and pass away (247, 10 ff.), and in this inferior realm not everything is determined.

In Alexander of Aphrodisias the Peripatetic tradition modified its customary denial of providential activity in the sublunary realm. Alexander taught that through the heavenly bodies providence exercises a general care for the sublunary world (*Quaestiones* i, 25, p. 41 Bruns). The Platonist in Boethius finds this congenial: nature controls trees and irrational animals, but cattle are also subject to the decrees of the stars. Men are subject partly to nature and partly to the stars, but are for the rest self-determining. Men are limited by necessity so that free will does not mean the ability to do anything one wishes. The soul is bound to the body and suffers passions of desire and anger. Moreover, we are all subject to divine providence and depend on the will of divine powers. Therefore to affirm free will eliminates neither that destiny which the stars control nor the element of unpredictable chance (ii, 231, 1 ff.). We live in a complex tangle of causes intermingling together. In rejecting both the Epicurean view that everything happens by random chance and the Stoic view that everything happens by necessity, we should not go to the opposite extreme of supposing that everything results from our free choices (223, 239). But the importance that we attach to the area in which free will operates is shown by the way we treat antisocial delinquents whose punishment takes into account their intentions more than their acts (223 f.—a position similar to Alexander, *De fato* 19).

In an important further point Boethius transmits an Aristotelian distinction in the concept of necessity. Aristotle (*Physics* B, 9) distinguishes two modes of necessity: unconditional necessity as in the case of the sun's movement, and time-conditioned necessity, as when we say that when Socrates sits, provided that we speak truth, he must then be (sitting and) not standing (ii, 241-2). This distinction was noticed in the Neoplatonic schools (Ammonius, *Perih.* 153, 13). To Boethius it seemed sufficiently important to be reaffirmed in his discussion of free will and necessity in the last book of the *Consolation of Philosophy* (v, 6, 27). For that discussion many of the themes and arguments are given as it were a dress rehearsal in the commentary on *Interpretation*.

In the commentary the discourse moves wholly within the framework of the Peripatetic exegetical tradition, as is shown by the evident contacts and parallels between Boethius and Alexander's treatise on destiny whenever they deal with chance, necessity, and the force of nature. Probably Boethius had read Alexander. Alexander holds that if the gods have perfect knowledge, they foreknow possible events as what they truly are, namely open possibilities (*De fato* 30). How conventional this anti-Stoic argument was can be seen in Origen, *Contra Celsum* ii, 20 (Jesus' prediction of his own betrayal does not make him the cause of the event). That foreknowledge does nothing to make an event necessary is an opinion which Proclus (*De providentia et fato* xii, 63) contrasts with the Platonic view. The Peripatetic position suffers from the difficulty that it is impossible to prove that future events cannot be known in advance.

Through Porphyry, Boethius has received the exegetical Peripatetic tradition within a Platonic metaphysical framework. The Porphyrian doctrine of the essential harmony of Plato and Aristotle begins to be seen in operation in the combining together of the Platonic conception of providence seen at work in immutable patterns of causation, especially in the heavenly bodies, with an Aristotelian assertion that in this inferior order of things, where the forces of nature determine much but not everything, there remains an openness to future contingencies, partly because of human capacity for deliberative choice, partly because even in the natural order itself there is an element of indeterminacy. But of the higher order, Aristotle (*De caelo* i, 12) holds that whatever is *always* true of an indestructible object is also *necessarily* the case. Neoplatonic reflection on these problems suggested that in the celestial sphere everything is undeviatingly ordered under providence, but that here below things are controlled by destiny; moreover, that while we understand ourselves to be in some measure acting freely, divine foreknowledge knows just how we shall act, and what is uncertain to us can be clear to divine time-transcending mind. In the *Consolation of Philosophy* the same themes recur as we have met in the commentary on *Interpretation* but reformulated in the light of the late Platonic tradition and the treatises of Proclus. This is carried through mainly with the help of Iamblichus' thesis (reported in Ammonius' Commentary) that although future contingents are in themselves indefinite, to God they are definite, but with the further suggestion that, since God transcends time, he knows all past, present, and future in an eternal now. The commentary on *Interpretation* has not progressed so far.

The monographs on logic

Boethius' commentaries on Porphyry, on the *Categories*, and on *Interpretation*, are supplemented by a series of short monographs. The exposition of the *Isagoge* is completed by the short treatise 'On division' (*PL* 64, 875D–892A). The tract concerns linguistic tools for drawing distinctions and explains the right way to divide a genus into its species, a whole into its parts, a word into its various meanings;[66] then how to divide by accidents, e.g. according to colours; how to use the four antitheses Good/Evil; Possession/Privation; Affirming/Denying; and Relation. Lastly there is the distinction between division and accurate definition which is its goal. Although Boethius regards this subject as 'very easy' (877A), he also says that he is addressing readers who have passed the elementary stage (882D). The discussion moves entirely within a Peripatetic framework. Except for the initial references to Porphyry and Plotinus as authorities for commending the Peripatetic discussions of the subject, the Platonists put in no appearance. At one point (883A) he says that the nature of privation has already been explained by the *Categories*. It is tempting to conclude that the monograph is later than 510. But there are also references to Aristotle's *Physics* (833A), *Posterior Analytics* (885D), and *Topics* (889D); probably all these references come from Porphyry.

To show what weight attaches to division within the later Aristotelian school (which at the end Boethius contrasts with the earlier school said to be careless of such matters), Boethius begins by referring to a treatise on division by the Peripatetic master, Andronicus of Rhodes, of the first century BC. He has found in Porphyry's commentary on Plato's *Sophist* a report that Plotinus warmly approved of Andronicus' work. Plotinus (i, 3, 4, 3 f.) associates skill in division with questions about being and non-being such as are raised in Plato's *Sophist*. Unfortunately Boethius' reference to Porphyry's commentary is our sole evidence about the book's existence and content. But prima facie the reference suggests that Boethius' source is an essay by Porphyry designed to introduce the Platonic dialectic of the *Sophist* by linking it to the work of Andronicus on division.

The various types of classification and division examined by Boethius in the monograph turn up in a number of other writers, including Albinus the second-century Platonist, Sextus Empiricus, and Clement of Alexandria. Some very close parallels are also to be found in the *Dialectic* of John of Damascus, probably from Porphyry. Albinus, Sextus, and

Clement will have depended on Andronicus.[67]

The twin monographs 'On the Categorical Syllogism' supplement, and in part offer an epitome of, the long commentary on *Interpretation* to which both monographs refer (764A, 795B). One cannot simply deduce from these two references that the commentary's date precedes that of the monographs, for two reasons. The second commentary on *Interpretation* refers to the two-volume monograph on the categorical syllogism as a completed study. Further, the two allusions appear in almost but not quite identical wording, and look uncomfortably like variant translations of a sentence in his Greek model, probably Porphyry again. The *Introductio* covers much the same matter as the first volume *De syllogismo categorico*, but has passages of some weight without parallel in the twin work, e.g. when he investigates the consequence of attaching a negative to a proposition. Boethius classifies predicates under five heads (779C–781A) (i) inseparable from the subject, as rationality from man; (ii) inseparable from the subject but not on the same level with it, as literacy from man; (iii) incompatible with the subject, as stone with man; (iv) distinct from a subject but greater and wider, as justice from man (Boethius stops to note that in the case of 'divine substances' there is no distinction to be drawn); (v) always joined with the subject but never greater than it, as risibility in man. The convertibility of propositions is treated in both monographs, but more briefly in the *Introductio*.

It is not easy to determine which of the two monographs Boethius wrote first. De Rijk has observed that in the wording of its version of Aristotle's definitions of noun and verb the *Introductio* coincides with *Perihermeneias* whereas *De syllogismo catgorico* does not, which may be plausibly taken to suggest that the latter, two-volume monograph is earlier in date.

The second volume *De syllogismo categorico* offers a succinct summary of the *Prior Analytics*, and shows how well Boethius comprehended Aristotle's use of letters as variables in the construction of his logic. In formal logic, he explains, we use letters to represent terms, partly for brevity but mainly to show that the syllogisms apply universally, whatever matter is substituted for the form. Apart from Aristotle himself, a main source is explicitly named as Porphyry, through whom he can report about work done in this field by Aristotle's immediate pupils Theophrastus and Eudemus (813C; 814C; 829D). Where Aristotle gave four moods for syllogisms in the first figure, Theophrastus added five more. In this Porphyry concurred, and Boethius simply follows his list. On the other hand, Boethius later says that, since all syllogisms of the second and third figure are dependent for their cogency on the first four syllogisms of the first figure which are perfect and indemonstrable (i.e. self-evident), they must be classified as 'imperfect', that is not immediately self-evident (817B; 823A). This doctrine is expressly discussed by Ammonius in his commentary on the *Prior Analytics* (CAG IV, 6, p. 31, 15 ff.), where it is said to have been upheld in Themistius' paraphrase but not in Porphyry. The suggestion is therefore hard to resist that Boethius' second volume on the categorical syllogism is making silent use of Themistius on the *Prior Analytics*. The main body of the second volume consists of a dry catalogue of unconditional syllogisms, but without the complication of modal syllogisms containing the words 'necessary' or 'possible'.

Propositional logic and the hypothetical syllogism

Aristotle's logic is concerned with terms and their relation in the simple syllogism or discourse in which, certain things being granted, something other than what is granted necessarily follows. The move towards an examination of the logic of propositions was tentatively initiated by Theophrastus and Eudemus, but its full development first came with the Stoics.

Boethius derived from Porphyry an adverse picture of Stoic logic which is unlikely to have been fair to acute logicians. The Stoics held, for instance, that the only unambiguous way of indicating the negative of a proposition is to place the negative particle at the beginning. Otherwise it can be unclear to which term the negative applies. Their position is clearly expounded by Sextus Empiricus (*Adv. math.* viii, 89–90): the negative should be so prefixed as to control the entire proposition. This doctrine is also taught in Apuleius, *Perihermeneias* (177, 26; 191, 21). But Boethius, surely echoing Porphyry, criticizes

Propositional logic and the hypothetical syllogism

them for an ambiguity in that if the negative is thus prefixed it may be easily read as applying to the opening subject of the sentence. 'Non homo ambulat' may mean 'a non-man walks'. The Stoics intended 'It is not the case that a man walks'. (Boethius, *Perih*. ii, 261, 27). Porphyry and Boethius did not appreciate the Stoic point about the complexities of the negative of a proposition, which is suprising in view of Aristotle's clear grasp of this point (e.g. *Anal. Pr.* i, 46).

The Stoic logicians followed Aristotle's example in using letters of the alphabet to stand for variables, but with a difference that in their logic the letters represent ordinal numbers and stand for propositions, not for terms.[68] They identified five basic types of inference scheme:

1. If the first, then the second; but the first, therefore the second.
2. If the first, then the second; but not the second, therefore not the first.
3. Not both the first and the second; but the first, therefore not the second.
4. Either the first or the second; but the first, therefore not the second.
5. Either the first or the second; but not the second, therefore the first.

The Stoics believed these five self-evidently valid schemes to constitute a complete list, and to be the groundwork of all inference whatsoever.

The Peripatetic school observed that this notion was a development of something that Theophrastus and Eudemus had worked on, and incorporated the Stoic logic within their own under the title 'the hypothetical syllogism', in the characteristic form 'if . . . , then . . . ' From there the study passed into the Neoplatonic schools, and became a regular part of the logic taught by the masters of Athens and Alexandria in the fifth century. In Galen's *Institutio logica* 'hypothetical' is generic for complex statements, conditional, disjunctive, or conjunctive.

A tenth-century Paris manuscript preserves a summary of an otherwise lost monograph 'on hypothetical syllogisms' by Ammonius, in which he compared the structure of categorical and hypothetical syllogisms, briefly cataloguing the five Indemonstrables of the Stoics, and tried to explain why it had been left to the Stoics rather than to Aristotle to develop this branch of logic (*CAG* IV, vi, 67–9).

Boethius' monograph on the hypothetical syllogism (*PL* 64, 831–876C) appears in the old printed editions, including Migne, as divided into two volumes. But the majority of the manuscripts, followed by the critical edition of Luca Obertello (1969), divide into three. (The second book begins with the sentence 'Hypotheticos syllogismos...', Migne 843D 11.) The monograph is dedicated to an unnamed friend with whom he shares a love for philosophical study as 'the supreme consolation in life' (*summum vitae solamen*); a phrase which tells why he chose his title for his prison masterpiece. There is none of the language of deep veneration which Boethius seems to reserve for Symmachus, or one would be tempted to think the work could be dedicated to him. On the other hand, he is unlikely to be the distinguished orator and advocate Patricius[69] for whom he wrote on Cicero's *Topics* since, except for one passage where Cicero's *De inventione* is quoted on whether the number of parts in a syllogism is three or four or five (884B), his concerns are technical. Even where Cicero is quoted, the purpose is not to show the utility or relevance of these studies to practice at the Roman bar or to public speaking. Although the third theological tractate shows John the Roman deacon to have considerable interest in the finer points of Platonic logic as bearing on theology, this monograph contains no sentence that suggests a theological (or any other) bearing for its content. We should conclude that Boethius possessed a trusted friend in the senatorial circle who shared his enthusiasms, and who may perhaps have been absent in Constantinople at the hour of Boethius' crisis in 524–5. Renatus, who will appear later in this story, is a possibility.

Boethius claims that no Latin writers have said anything about hypothetical syllogisms. The claim is surprising when one recalls that Cassiodorus attributes to Marius Victorinus a monograph or at least some specialized treatment of this subject, which any reader of Cicero's *Topics* could hardly fail to be aware of.[70] Cicero (*Topics* 54–7) includes the five Stoic Indemonstrables given above, and extends the list to seven, his sixth being a reduplication of the third and a seventh ('Not both this and that; but not this, therefore that') which is invalid.[71] Cicero's list of seven, however, was evidently current independently of him. A version of the longer list appears not only in Latin in Cassiodorus' summary based on Victorinus' monograph (*Inst.* ii, 3, 13) and in Martianus Capella (iv, 414–21), but also in Greek in a note contained in a tenth-century Paris manuscript (gr. 2064) together with dialectical material from Ammonius (printed in *CAG* IV, vi, p. xi).

In the fifth of his seven books of commentary on Cicero's *Topics* Boethius juxtaposes Cicero's list of seven inference schemes with a reference to his fuller discussion in his monograph on hypothetical syllogisms (1135D). His seven rules of inference are identical with those in Martianus Capella (iv, 420) going back to Cicero. On the other hand, a scholion on *Prior Analytics* 40b 26 (*Aristoteles Latinus* iii, 1–4, p. 304, 5–22) records the standard five moods of Stoic propositional logic without any regard to Cicero's longer list of seven. He is no doubt simply translating his Greek source.

Boethius' monograph has a very different structure from that of Ammonius.[72] He begins by defining his terms. A proposition which the Greeks called hypothetical we Latins may call conditional, and has the form (1) *if A, then B*. Its characteristic nature is revealed when we ask how it can be refuted and how its contradictory may be correctly stated. It is not refuted by a demonstration that (2) *either A or B is untrue*, but by showing that (3) *if A is true, B does not necessarily follow, for A can be true even if B is not*. The negation of (1), however, is stated by Boethius, not in the Stoic form above, viz. (4) *It is not the case that (if A then B)* but simply in the form (5) *if A, not B*.

To refute this negative, he continued, we need to prove not that A is not, or that B is, but that if A, B remains possible and is alone possible. So to see whether a proposition is affirmative or negative, one must look to the consequent, not to the antecedent. (6) *If not A, then B*, is affirmative. But negative are (7) *If A, not B*, and (8) *if not A, not B*.

The second book begins with a digression whether the constituents of a syllogism include the supporting arguments to establish the truth of the major and the minor premiss. Cicero's

De inventione i, 57–71 already considers this question, and Boethius naturally feels it necessary to take account of his view familiar to all his serious readers. Moreover, Victorinus would be sure to have said something about this passage. To a strict logician a syllogism has only three constituent parts, whereas in rhetoric four or five appear possible because one may have to go about establishing the truth of the premisses.

Boethius explains that his principal concern is to elucidate those conditional syllogisms which carry necessary consequences. Conclusions can be drawn from conditionals just as coercive in every respect as those drawn from categoricals. He begins with the four 'perfect', i.e. self-evident, inferences:

1. If A, then B; but A, therefore B. (But if B, no conclusion about A or not A follows.)
2. If A, then not B; but A, therefore not B. (But if B, no conclusion follows about A or not A.)
3. If not A, then B; but not A, therefore B. (But if B, no conclusion follows about A or not A.)
4. If not A, not B; but not A, therefore not B. (But from not B, not A does not follow.)

Boethius next lists eight syllogisms where the first premiss is categorical, the second hypothetical, and shows how necessary conclusions follow:

1. Given B, if A, then C. (Then, given B, if not C, not A follows.)
2. Given B, if A, then not C. (So when B and C, then not A.)
3. Given not B, if A, then C. (So when not B and not C, then not A.)
4. Given not B, if A, not C. (So when not B but C, then not A.)
5. Given B, if not A, then C. (So when B but not C, then A.)
6. Given B, if not A, then not C. (So given C, if B, then A.)
7. When not B, if not A, then C. (So when not B but A, not C; *or* when not B and not C, then A; *or* when not B but C, then not A.)
8. Given not B, if not A, then not C. (So given not B, if C, then A.)

Boethius' next list is of syllogisms where the first premiss is

Propositional logic and the hypothetical syllogism 171

hypothetical, the second categorical (853), e.g. 'Given A, if B, then C.' This is followed by the more complex 'three-termed propositions', Theophrastus' account of which is reported with some care by Alexander of Aphrodisias in his commentary on the *Prior Analytics* i, 29 (*CAG* II, i, p. 326). Here there are two conditionals interlinked, and like categorical syllogisms they can be classified under three figures. So in the first figure we have

1. If A, then B, and if B, then C. This allows the conclusion 'If A then C', which in turn allows 'If not C, then not A'.
2. If A, then B and if B, then not C. So if A, then not C.
3. If A, then not B, and if not B, then C. So if A, then C.
4. If A, then not B and if not B, then not C. So if A, not C.
5. If not A, then B and if B, then C. So if not A, then C.
6. If not A, then B and if B, not C. So if not A, not C.
7. If not A, then not B and if not B, then C. So if not A, then C.
8. If not A, then not B and if not B, then not C. So if not A, then not C.

Only these eight inferences possess cogency.

Boethius' third and last book begins with three-termed propositions of the second figure. He warns that no deduction is possible from propositions equal either way, i.e. of the form *If A, then B and if A, then not C*. Inference becomes possible if we have the form

1. If A, then B and if not A, then C. Inference: if not B, then not A; if not A, then C; so if not B, then C.
2. If A then B, and if not A, then not C. Inference: if not B, then not C. But if B, then no inference about C is possible.
3. If A, then not B; if not A, then not C. Inference: if B, then C. But if not B, no inference follows.
4. If A, then not B; if not A, then not C. Inference: if not C, the not B. But if C, no inference is possible.

Hypothetical syllogisms of the third figure are next listed (863 D ff.), all 'three-termed', of the type

1. If B, then A and if C, then not A. So if B, not C.
2. If B, then A; if not C, then not A. So if B, then C.

3. If not B, then A; if C, then not A. So if not B, then not C.
4. If not B, then A; if not C, then not A. So if not B, then C. (But if B, no inference follows.)
5. If B, then not A; if C, then A. So if B, then not C. (If not B, no inference.)
6. If B, then not A; if not C, then A. So if B, then C. (If not B, no inference.)
7. If not B, then not A; if C, then A. So if not B, then not C.
8. If not B, then not A; if not C, then A. So if not B, then C. (Migne mistakenly inserts a *non* too many, for which there is no ms. authority.)

Sixteen inferences can be shown where two conditionals are conjoined, of the form (1) If, when A, B, and when C, D; then it follows that if, when C, but not D, then if A, not B. (2) If, when A, B and when C, not D; then it follows that if, when C, D, then when A, not B.

And so on. Enough has been given to show the nature of Boethius' analysis. He concludes with three important observations. The first concerns disjunctive propositions, distinguished from connective or conjunctive of the form 'If A, B; if not A, not B'; *or* 'if A, not B; if not A, B'. Disjunctives are in the form 'either/or but not both'. Either A or B, either not A or not B, etc.

But disjunctives can present alternatives of two kinds, exclusive and non-exclusive. Exclusives are of the type: *If not A, then B, and if not B, then A.* (But it is either one or the other.) Non-exclusives are of the type: *Either not A or not B.* It may be neither A nor B. But if A, not B and if B, not A. If not A, no inference about B; and if not B, no inference about A.

Throughout this examination of conditionals, the reader will have had an uneasy feeling that the words 'if' and 'when' are slippery to handle.[73] Boethius was not wholly unaware of the difficulties that may attend the apparently innocuous formula 'if . . ., then . . .' At 835B he tries to distinguish accidental conditionals ('when fire is hot, the sky is round') from those where there is a necessary connection, i.e. the consequent is implicit in the antecedent. It is a passage out of which the logic of medieval times developed its doctrine of implication. Boethius intends simply to say: If the antecedent is true, the consequent, being implicit in the antecedent, must also be true. To interpret 'if' invariably of material implication can produce difficulties in the understanding of Boethius' monograph. In one or two places *si* and *cum* are no more than conjunctions, replaceable by the word 'et' (cf. 1140D). But sometimes he uses *si* or *cum* to indicate mutual implication or equivalence, linking two propositions by 'if' in the sense of 'if and only if', where each of the two sentences represents a necessary and sufficient condition for the other.

In short there is a layer of imprecision in the language of Greek logic which Boethius took from the contemporary Neoplatonic schools and transmitted to the Latin West. No one before him had clarified these questions. Nevertheless his monograph on the hypothetical syllogism remains a modest landmark in the history of logical analysis. Through its mediation a great part of the propositional logic of the Stoics, as developed by the Peripatetic school and then taken over by the late Platonists, was passed down to the western philosophical tradition. I have not thought it rash to assume that the monograph does not represent independent thinking on his part. We may naturally suppose that he will have had before him either a tract by Porphyry or something by a Peripatetic logician that may have enjoyed some currency in the Platonic schools. It is enough to claim that if Boethius had never written on this subject, our modern knowledge of ancient propositional logic would be meagre.

Boethius' writings on logic are wholly deficient in literary grace. One cannot enjoy them for the prose. There is no pause for light refreshment with verse and song as there is in the *Consolation of Philosophy*. He asks a rigorous attention of his readers as he relentlessly catalogues every valid syllogism under each successive figure. What cannot be missed is the intense seriousness with which he writes about dialectical matters: western education could run no greater danger than to continue its neglect of logic. In the second commentary of Porphyry the monitory note is sounded: 'Those who reject logic are bound to make mistakes. Unless reason shows the right path, the incorrupt truth of reality cannot be found' (*CSEL* 48, p. 139, 1 ff.; *PL* 64, 73A).

Among those for whom neglect of logic is dangerous Boethius thought theologians had a special place.

IV
CHRISTIAN THEOLOGY AND THE PHILOSOPHERS

FIVE tractates of varying length dealing with questions of theology are transmitted by the manuscripts, often in association with the *Consolation of Philosophy*, but in many cases independently. The first three and fifth of these pieces attempt tersely to disentangle some of the central logical problems besetting the traditional language of the Latin churches. These tractates attracted great interest from medieval commentators from the ninth century onwards, culminating in masterful discussions of the first and third from the pen of St. Thomas Aquinas. Although the third contains nothing specifically Christian, the remainder discuss fundamental questions of Church Dogmatics—the Trinity and the Person of Christ— and can only have been written by a Christian thinker with a special interest in logical questions. At one time it was customary to contrast the Christian opuscula with the pagan *Consolation*, and to propose the hypothesis of two different authors, perhaps of the same name. In the tenth century Bovo of Corvey considered this possibility, but rightly rejected it on stylistic grounds. In the modern period the hypothesis was favoured in the eighteenth and especially the nineteenth centuries, going back to Gottfried Arnold's highly prejudiced 'Impartial Church History to the Year 1688' (1700), I, vi, 3, 7. The most elaborate statement advocating this hypothesis was advanced by Nitzsch in 1860, but has long been seen to rest on radical misunderstandings. Today it is accepted by all scholars who have given attention to the subject that the careful Neoplatonic logician who, in the first three and fifth tractates, seeks to unravel logical tangles in the usage of the Church, is none other than the author of the *Consolation* and of the commentaries on Aristotle, with which they manifest numerous parallels in thought and diction. It has come to be acknowledged, and will be made clear beyond a peradventure in the present chapter, that the tractates, other than the fourth, contain even more Neoplatonism than the *Consolation of Philosophy* itself. If there remains a problem in the reticence of Boethius' masterpiece about his relation to Christianity at the time of writing, whatever solution commends itself must take a less naive form than the abandoned notion that we have to deal with two distinct authors.

Faith and history: De fide catholica

Among the five tractates of the opuscula sacra the fourth stands apart. In the manuscripts it normally appears without a title either in superscription or in subscription. In the majority of manuscripts it follows on after the third tractate but marked as a new beginning, e.g. by rubrication of the initial capital. In a few codices it receives the prefix *sermo* or *epistola*. Vallinus' princeps (Leiden, 1656) entitled it 'Brevis fidei christianae conplexio'; so also Migne, *PL* 63, 1333. An early Einsiedeln manuscript has *De fide catholica*. The style and content of the work set it on its own among the opuscula, in that it is not concerned with dialectical problems (though its author has a very tidy mind), but is a vibrant confession of faith in the biblical story of redemption as interpreted by Augustine. Augustine is not mentioned by name, but sentence after sentence echoes his various writings, especially the *City of God*, the *Enchiridion*, and some of the letters. In 1877 Usener accepted the authenticity of the first three and fifth tractates, fortified by the new text of the *Anecdoton Holderi* (above, p. 7) with its excerpt from Cassiodorus to the effect that Boethius 'wrote a book on the Holy Spirit and some dogmatic chapters and a book against Nestorius'—where *capita quaedam dogmatica* would be a likely description of *De fide catholica*. Usener, however, rejected the fourth tractate as a Carolingian addition to the corpus, drawing attention to the fact that a ninth-century manuscript written by Reginbert of Reichenau (Karlsruhe, Augiensis XVIII) has, at the end of the third tractate and before the fourth, the words 'Thus far Boethius' (ACTENVS BOETIVS), in red capitals. Reginbert evidently felt that this tractate, with its different style, belonged to some other author, and the impression has persisted with many modern scholars. In fact, it is not difficult to establish the authenticity of the fourth tractate.

There is no reason to accord authority to Reginbert's rubric, as if he settles the question and saves scholars the trouble of thinking further. The researches of the Harvard scholar E. K. Rand at the beginning of this century demonstrated that *De fide catholica* was not an addition to the original corpus, but formed part of the group of five opuscula from the earliest period in the sixth century. The dogmatic statements contained in the tractate diverge in no way from those in the first, second, and fifth tractates, i.e. on the Trinity and against Eutyches and Nestorius on the Person of Christ. Finally, it is easy to show that the non-theological diction of the fourth tractate, its vocabulary and turns of phrase, are all in the closest accord with his other certainly authentic writings. Even the logician in Boethius cannot be suppressed, e.g. in line 90 (Loeb, 2nd edition, 1973) with *omnis* followed by a threefold definition in a manner exactly paralleled in the first commentary on *Interpretation* (i, 82, 15), or line 259 where the universal claim of the Catholic Church is established in three ways, *tribus modis probatur exsistere*. Boethius loves to explain that something can be shown *tribus modis*. He includes an allusion to Horace in line 143 'numerosam annorum seriem', and an occasional Virgilian phrase as in line 78 'ima petierat' (of the fall of man).[1] The prose-poem of the ending resembles the end of O *qui perpetua* (*Cons.* iii m. 9).

The content of the work is a statement of what is to be believed on authority in contrast with what may be understood and elucidated by the reason. Christian faith rests on the New and Old Testaments, and does not begin from the reasoning processes of the natural mind. Its basic affirmations see humanity as part of an enfolding divine development. Before the creation of the world and so before time, God exists: the Trinity of the Father, Son, and Spirit who is one God, not three. The Son is eternal, begotten of the Father's substance. To use the title 'Son' is to indicate that he is distinct from the Father. But this language should not make us imagine that there is a kind of heavenly genealogy: the Father has never been a Son himself. The Holy Spirit is neither Son nor Father, but 'proceeds from the Father and the Son'. (The *Filioque* recurs in the first tractate.) About the mystery of the procession of the Spirit we cannot speak any more than of the generation of the Son. Christians accept the terms because they come with biblical authority.

Boethius is succinctly summarizing Augustinian teaching.[2] For Augustine it is important that the world and time were created together (e.g. *City of God* xi, 6). He is emphatic in his repeated insistence that the Holy Trinity is one God, not three (*De trinitate* v, 9; vii, 8); that 'the Father has no father from whom he has his being' (vi, 11); that the unity of God may be best safeguarded against Arian division by saying that the Spirit proceeds from both Father and Son, though the distinction between 'generation' and 'procession' is one of which in this life we can say nothing clearly (v, 15; ix, 17, xv, 45).

Boethius marks this doctrine as 'Catholic' in contrast to three deviationist positions which he rejects: Arius who gives the Son the title God but teaches that he is another, inferior substance; the Sabellians who hold that Father, Son and Spirit are not three 'distinct persons' (*exsistentes personae*) but one person with three different names; and the Manichees who think it unworthy of God to have a Son, such language having too earthly and carnal a force, and accordingly deny the Son's Virgin Birth to avoid defiling God by contact with a human body (see Augustine's *Confessions* v, 10, 20, for an account of his Manichee rejection of the Virgin Birth as a pollution).

Boethius continues that the Divine Nature, immutable from all eternity, by act of will formed a world when it did not exist at all (cf. Augustine *City of God* xii, 17). He did not make it of his own substance, so that it is not divine (cf. Aug. *De Gen. ad Litt. impf.* 2; *Op. impf. adv. Julianum* v, 42; *c. Secundinum Manich.* 7). Nor did he create it out of any existing material. Nothing not made by him exists (cf. Augustine, *Enchiridion* 9: 'nullam esse naturam quae non aut ipse sit aut ab ipso').

But although in heaven there was order, one part of the created angels was expelled. God did not wish the number of angels to be diminished, and therefore formed man, endowed with the breath of life, reason, and freedom of choice, and placed him in Paradise. Had man remained sinless, he would have been able to replace the fallen angels. (This doctrine appears in Augustine in the widely read *Enchiridion*, 28–9 and 62; cf. *City of God* xiv, 26. It is worth observing Boethius' implication, with which Augustine would not have disagreed, that the creation of man followed *after* the pre-cosmic fall of the angels.) But Adam and his consort were tempted by 'the father of envy'.

Augustine knew of some theologians who thought the devil's fall came when he envied the glorious creation of man, but insisted that Satan fell by pride rather than by envy which is a consequence of pride and not its cause (*Gen. ad Litt.* xi, 18–21).[3] Boethius is assured of the truth of all this by the books of Moses; for the biblical books bear a divine authority. For their interpretation one must bear in mind that they sometimes relate historical facts, sometimes use allegory, sometimes combine the two. (Augustine's hermeneutic rule is similar in *City of God* xvii, 3; cf. *Contra Faustum* xii, 7.) Boethius leaves it open in which of his three categories we ought to place the narrative of Adam and Eve.

The punishment of Adam's sin was death which he transmitted to his posterity; its awfulness was brought home to him by his surviving to witness the murder of Abel.[4] The heresiarch Pelagius has given his name to the denial that posterity has inherited the transmitted curse of Adam's sin.

Out of this ruin God's grace set aside a few who obeyed his will. Although they were deservedly condemned, yet God made them partakers of the secret mystery. He sent chosen men to help in the recovery of lost humanity—Noah, Abraham, the twelve patriarchs, Moses, Joshua, David, and then, through the Ever-Virgin Mary, Christ. Just as Christ corresponds to Adam, so Mary corresponds to Eve, so that the incarnation resumes the plan of creation.

The incarnation of the Son is impugned by the rival heretics, Nestorius and Eutyches (to whose opinions Boethius devoted his fifth tract). But it is the focal point and climax of redemption. Christ was baptised, chose twelve apostles, was crucified, dead and buried. He rose again and ascended to heaven whence as Son of God he had never been absent.[5] He gave his disciples baptism, teaching, and miraculous powers that they should go and tell all nations. So the gospel extends to all the world, and the Church is a single body.

Lastly, the faith upholds the resurrection of the body and the final destiny of man in either heaven or hell. Boethius does not touch on the charitable explorations of the idea of purgatory which Augustine tentatively bases on the universal liturgical custom of prayer for the departed, and which he thought virtually essential if men were not simply to reject Christianity in revulsion from the cruelty of hell (*Enchiridion* 109–10; cf. *Conf.* ix, 13, 35; *Sermo* 172, 2, 2, and elsewhere). Boethius may have regarded the idea as a legitimate personal speculation on Augustine's part, but less than a constituent part of the authoritatively given faith he sets out to expound here.

This is the faith proposed to us by the universal Church diffused throughout the world, and it rests upon either scriptural authority or universal tradition. In addition, there is catechetical instruction handed down in each local church, which is free to make its own rules and customs. In this monolithic picture of a single authoritative faith presented by a single authoritative society, modified to the extent that it allows for regional diversities in minor detail, both the terminology and the ecclesiology are again Augustinian (*ep.* 54, 1–2). But Boethius' language has a very close contemporary parallel in the letter to Senarius by John the Roman deacon,[6] whose spiritual son Boethius feels himself to be. It is evidently from John that Boethius has received instruction.

On the surface, except in so far as the tract briefly sets aside the Arian doctrines favoured by his master Theoderic, Boethius' outline of the Catholic faith cannot be seen to have an obvious purpose other than that of offering an accurate description of what he believes authentic Christianity to be. But the entire absence of allusion to the philosophical and logical problems that we know to have fascinated him cannot be accidental. The tone of the tract is strikingly free of apologetic: he is not interested in stressing the rational character of the Catholic faith, its roots in human need, its capacity to answer to the highest aspirations of the human spirit, its ability to take into its bosom the logic of Aristotle, the ethics of the Stoa, and the metaphysics of Plato. The Augustine of whom Boethius is making a précis is not the young philosophical inquirer of the Cassiciacum dialogues. The tract reads almost like a gage of challenge to the educated, late Roman, aristocratic reader, emphatically, even defiantly insisting on the supernatural and distinctive elements in orthodox Christianity. Four heretical positions are mentioned, Arianism, Sabellianism, Manicheism and Pelagianism, with neat summaries of the alternatives they propounded. But these heretics were not the only people to find difficulty in the Catholic doctrine of the Trinity, or in the story of the Virgin Birth, or in the concept of original sin transmitted from Adam to involve the entire race in death. Boethius seems carefully to have picked out those features in their heresies which would strike a chord of sympathy in a philosophical humanist, who on reading his summary of their positions would immediately feel himself more in rapport with them than with Catholic orthodoxy.

The point may be an important clue to Boethius' purposes in the composition of the tract on the faith, which looks far too carefully composed a piece to be regarded as a private essay not intended for publication.[7] W. Bark has suggested that it was a guide for bewildered laymen confused by theological intricacies.[8] If so, Boethius wrote it for himself. Be that as it may, the considerations above suggest that Boethius' intentions included a conscious design to bring out in sharp relief the disjunction rather than the harmony of faith and reason. The central point of the tractate is accordingly that the Christian confession is given in, with, and under the form of a saving history, thereby creating both its distinctiveness and, for the philosopher, its problematic character. Probably *De fide catholica* is the earliest of the tractates and was written by Boethius to crystallize in his own mind what John has taught him in catechesis. It has about it the air of someone trying to get the main points clear in a course of instruction which he has recently assimilated and very much wants to imprint upon his own mind.

The Person of Christ

The tractate 'Against Eutyches and Nestorius' stands fifth in the manuscripts and printed editions, but is probably earlier than at least the first and second. Dedicated to John the deacon this essay is among the most original pieces to come from Boethius' pen. Its force is not clear without an awareness of the background in contemporary theological debates.

The tractate begins by explaining its genesis in an embarrassing past occasion (perhaps six years rather than six weeks previously) when Boethius and John had been present at a council of high clergy and Roman senators. At this meeting a letter was read from an eastern bishop which affirmed Christ to be both of and in two natures, a position which the Greek bishop distinguishes from the Monophysite formula, here described as 'Eutychian', which accepts 'of' but not 'in'. This distinction of prepositions in a Christological context was unfamiliar to Boethius, and he asked for explanation.[9] During the ensuing babel of debate he kept his peace. From his seat he could not see the expression on the face of the man whose opinion most counted (presumably either his father-in-law Symmachus or, more probably the Pope, Symmachus or Hormisdas), so that he felt left without trustworthy guidance from authority. Appalled at the ignorance and arrogance manifested by some of the speakers in the debate, he went away to give the matter prolonged consideration. Now he is setting down tentative reflections on the Christological controversy, and asks John to place this essay in his collection of Boethius' writings if he judges it satisfactory. Any corrections John sends he will incorporate in a revised version which he intends to submit to his father-in-law.

The letter from the Greek bishop which precipitated the acrimonious Roman argument survives. It is preserved in an awkward, sometimes baffling, probably sixth-century Latin translation printed in T. Herold's *Orthodoxographia* (Basel, 1555), pp. 906–9, which is the sole authority for the text. The document is reprinted in the standard collection of papal letters for this period, made by Thiel, as Symmachus' *ep.* 12 (pp. 709–17), but is not found in Migne. The letter is undated but, since it is addressed to Pope Symmachus, it was probably written about 513, perhaps first considered under Symmachus' successor Hormisdas. The writer makes an impassioned plea that Roman policy towards separated brethren in the Greek churches become more constructive and positive. The Pope is asked to use his authority to loose and not merely, as hitherto, to bind. The author writes in the manner of an ecclesiastic who cares greatly for church unity and who has, or at least has had, considerable authority. He is probably of not less than metropolitan status, and could be writing from the northern Balkans; probably not from Thessalonica, however, whose bishop Dorotheus, under Pope Hormisdas, was very unamenable to western policy. Since the author refers to Acacius as 'our father' he could conceivably be the gentle disillusioned ex-patriarch of Constantinople Macedonius. He had refused to see Chalcedon and the Henoticon as alternative choices at a time when the emperor Anastasius was inclined to listen to Severus of Antioch and hard-line Monophysite voices. Macedonius' sympathies led the emperor to send him into exile at Euchaita (Avkhat) in 511.

This anonymous writer complains that, on account of Acacius' error, Rome has cut off all the Greek churches even including those which are happy to accept Chalcedon and the Tome of Leo. The bishop of Rome may grumble at the reluctance of loyal Chalcedonian bishops to break off communion with those bishops who have accepted the Henoticon. (Gelasius, *ep.* 27, 11 does just that, and in 519 this question of any touch of compromise with the Henoticon became a weighty issue for Hormisdas.) But the Pope seems to have failed to appreciate that highminded rejection of such economy towards colleagues is easier at a safe distance. In the East the price of refusal of communion is abdicating one's office and so surrendering one's flock to the wolves. Under the régime of the emperor Anastasius, to reject the Henoticon is to be immediately suspected of Nestorianism. Force is being used against any bishops whose diphysite convictions have led them to withdraw from eucharistic communion with those content to accept the Henoticon, and have thereby polarized their local communities. The Greek bishop then concludes by asking Rome for a positive lead in unravelling the tangle of Christological terms. Could the Pope please show us the middle way between Nestorius and Eutyches? This way, he adds, is one the very possibility of which is now being denied by some (a group of which we would like to know more). The sceptics evidently think the logic of any form of two-nature Christology excludes a real unity in the person of Christ, whereas the logic of any form of one-nature doctrine entails the ultimate loss of the humanity of the incarnate Lord; that is to say, Nestorius and Eutyches at least share the capacity to offer a coherent and intelligible account of the person of Christ. Orthodoxy in its *via media* havers and hedges, with a position whose sole identity is found in a series of vacillating affirmations, firm only in negation. The Greek bishop does not know how to answer those who urge that no middle position is logically coherent or consistent. But he offers some exploratory feelers towards the desired middle way of orthodoxy. For example, one must not say with the anti-Chalcedonians 'one nature after the union'. Nor can one admit that unity is impossible if we affirm that in the incarnate Lord the two natures remain two. We affirm Christ, he declares, to be both in and of two natures, and this marks us off from the anti-Chalcedonians whose identity-card is their intolerance of the preposition 'in' as opening the door to a Nestorian flood.

This approach from the Greek bishop, which caused such a storm in the Roman council, is in effect inviting Symmachus to reoccupy some of the ground cautiously explored by Gelasius, more incautiously by his successor Anastasius, in the 490s. The Greek author implicitly asks for Acacius' name alone to be dropped from the diptychs. He sees that some sacrifice is needed both for the sake of Roman dignity and face-saving and for a sufficient outward sign of Byzantine adherence to Chalcedonian doctrine. All this is coherent with the 'softly softly' policy of Pope Anastasius II which most people thought Symmachus had been elected to reverse. In proposing to accept both in and of two natures, the Greek letter is in line with the pioneer move towards this conciliatory formula advanced by Pope Gelasius in his treatise 'On the two natures', a tractate which anticipates some of Boethius' work.[10]

Gelasius' tract 'On the two natures' accepts the orthodoxy of the formula 'one person of both natures' (p. 93, 15 f. Schwartz), and even the formula beloved by Monophysites and inherited from Cyril of Alexandria 'one nature incarnate' (p. 92, 16). Admittedly the Pope is sadly ill-informed about Nestorius' doctrine which he tries to distinguish from his own 'two nature' Christology by claiming that, according to Nestorius, there is in Christ only one nature, the humanity. This absurd misrepresentation of Nestorius is no doubt motivated by Gelasius' desperate need to open up a gulf between Chalcedon and Nestorianism. Gelasius equally succeeds, however, in misrepresenting his Monophysite opponents, partly by treating any and all signatories to the Henoticon as necessarily hostile to Chalcedon; partly by refusing to distinguish between them and Eutyches whom, as the Severans vainly sought to explain in this ecumenical dialogue of the deaf, they in fact disowned as a heretic, partly by treating their vulnerable formula 'one nature after the union' as presupposing a time before the union when in Christ both natures were independent, in short implying an adoptionist and indeed extremely Nestorian Christology (p. 88, 22 ff.).

To the Monophysite appeal to the analogy of the one nature of man, though consisting of body and soul, Gelasius replies with a momentous eucharistic analogy. In the mass, the Pope teaches, we verily receive the body and blood of Christ, a divine thing (*res*) by which we are made partakers of the divine nature; 'yet the substance or nature of bread and wine does not cease to be' (p. 94, 28). So also in the case of Christ the humanity is not so swallowed up by the divinity as to cease to remain itself.

Gelasius' objective is to construct a doctrine of personal unity on a Chalcedonian foundation of two natures. Insofar as his purpose is to build a bridge to the more rational critics of Chalcedon, his disastrous misrepresentations of his opponents' position must have doomed the success of his enterprise and thereby encouraged his successor Anastasius II to listen to the East more attentively. A diphysite florilegium appended to Gelasius' tractate makes it probable that he had been briefed by zealous Chalcedonians from the Greek East who had a nest on the Asiatic shore of the Bosphorus in the monastery of the Sleepless monks or Akoimetae. At least he wrote with better information at his disposal than Avitus of Vienne, whose treatise explaining the Christological controversy for the Burgundian king ascribes Nestorius' doctrines to Eutyches and vice versa.

At the council of Chalcedon in 451 Dioscorus of Alexandria, courageous but at all times politically imprudent, had ensured that the final definition of the council would contain the formula 'in' rather than 'of two natures', by resolutely declaring that to him 'of' was acceptable, 'in' never. Thereafter the rejection of 'in' was the non-negotiable demand from the

Monophysite camp. But it did not follow that all Chalcedonians must reject 'of'. About 507 an Alexandrian named Nephalius, a convert from the so-called Acephali (a splinter group of ultra-Monophysites in Egypt who broke with Peter Mongos after his signature to the Henoticon in 482 because that formula did not explicitly censure Chalcedon), advocated the maintenance of Chalcedon balanced by the equal affirmation of the twelve anathemas or 'chapters' of Cyril of Alexandria.[11] Nephalius supported the legitimacy of both 'of' and 'in' two natures, but allowed 'one nature' when understood as an expression of the unity of Christ's person. He also proposed that the formula 'one of the Trinity suffered in the flesh' be affirmed by Chalcedonians since it was well known to be highly objectionable to Nestorians. 'One of the Trinity' was a slogan first made current coin in 434 by Proclus of Constantinople's 'Tome to the Armenians', then incorporated into the Henoticon.[12] The liturgical acclamation of 'Holy God, holy mighty, holy immortal, have mercy upon us' was being chanted in Syria even before 431 with the words 'crucified for us' inserted after the word 'immortal'.[13] This addition became one to which the Monophysites became attached. But whereas at Antioch in Syria the Trishagion was understood to be addressed to Christ, at Constantinople it was taken to refer to the Trinity.[14] The Syrian Monophysites enforced their interpretation by inserting the phrase 'one of the Trinity' into the doxology of the prayer immediately preceding the expanded Trishagion. In November 512 the emperor Anastasius, at that time pursuing an explicitly anti-Chalcedonian policy, ordered the Trishagion to be chanted at Constantinople with the addition customary in Syria. He immediately found that he had on his hands a major riot in the city with much bloodshed, and the order had to be countermanded. In July 518, when Chalcedonian orthodoxy was formally proclaimed at Sancta Sophia at Constantinople, the Trishagion was solemnly chanted without the addition.[15]

The Scythian Monks

From 507 to 512 the Monophysite influence on Anastasius reached its high-water mark. But as the emperor discovered that the current ecclesiastical policy failed to bring peace to the divided churches, least of all in the capital where store was set by the Chalcedonian resolution, so hated by Rome, asserting Constantinople to be the second see of Christendom after old Rome, this tide receded. From 512 at least until 515 the Gothic army commander Vitalian, who came from the Danube delta in the Dobrudja, was putting pressure on Anastasius in the Chalcedonian interest. Checked in 515, he returned to power with the accession of Justin in 518. Among Vitalian's associates there was a group of zealous monks called 'Scythians', i.e. Goths from the Dobrudja, one of whom, Leontius, was a blood-relative of Vitalian himself. They included Dionysius Exiguus ('Tiny' is at this time a common sobriquet of monks, in a paradoxical assertion of humility), who moved to Rome there to play a notable role as translator into Latin of a body of Greek theology and canon law, and as the chronographer who first established the calculation of all dates on the basis of his estimate of Christ's birth. (Once the consulship came to an end, because the office was too costly for anyone to meet the charges, Dionysius' 'Anno Domini' system gradually prevailed.) At Constantinople the theological leader of this group of monks was Maxentius, from whose pen a ninth-century Bodleian manuscript has preserved Latin treatises designed to refute and to reconcile Monophysite critics of Chalcedon. Maxentius, a fervent admirer of Augustine, also feared the continuing influence of the British theologian, Faustus of Riez in Provence, who wrote on grace and free will about 473 to the distress of rigorous Augustinians; exiled by the Gothic king Euric in 477, Faustus died soon after 480, but his writings continued to be circulated. Maxentius' fear was also shared by African bishops, some of whom had taken refuge from Vandal persecution by going to Constantinople hoping to enlist Byzantine support for their cause. Maxentius' influence in the capital remained potent at least until July 520 when Vitalian was murdered in the palace. In terms of power Vitalian was a major rival to Justinian, and had to be eliminated.[16]

    Maxentius had a worked-out theological programme. First of all, one must accept the 'in two natures' of Chalcedon, but then qualify this by four further propositions taken from the critics of Chalcedon's inadequacy as a wall against Nestorianism, viz. (i) there is one nature of the incarnate Word; a formula, said Maxentius, which some mistakenly think contrary to Chalcedon (ii) after the incarnation Christ is 'of two natures' (iii) the incarnate Lord is 'one of the Trinity' (iv) Mary is Theotokos, Mother of God.

In addition, however, it is necessary to reject two Monophysite assertions: (a) there is one nature after the union; (b) 'nature' and 'person' are interchangeable synonyms, so that if there is one person, as agreed by all parties, there must be one nature. For Maxentius the treatment of nature and person as synonyms is the cardinal error which Nestorius and Eutyches share in common. God and man, he says, are both natures and persons. In the Holy Trinity each Person is 'ex trinitate', a phrase Maxentius gratefully quotes from Augustine (*De Trin.* ii, 9, 16). 'Man' can mean either human nature or the individual person. Nature is therefore the substrate of the person. A human embryo is perfect in nature, but develops into a 'persona' as it grows in the womb. 'Persona' is defined as 'una res individuae naturae', a single thing of individual nature.

Maxentius attacks some Chalcedonian exegetes of the conciliar definition who see a disjunction in the formula 'one person, one hypostasis' and who take 'person' of the human nature of Christ, 'hypostasis' of the divine.

A subsidiary point in Maxentius' polemic turns against a Nestorian doctrine that, since everything composite is passible, i.e. dissoluble into its constituent elements, we may say that Christ is composite in respect of his human nature, but not of his divine.

Convinced that in all this they had an ecumenical formula of affirmation to solve the impasse dividing the churches of East and West, Maxentius and the 'Scythian' monks came to Constantinople. They sought to enlist the support of Justinian, who cannily sent some of them on to Rome in 519 to see if their formula could win the approbation of Pope Hormisdas. At a time when normal relations of communion were nervously being restored in an atmosphere of less than total trust, Justinian was not going to sponsor a complicated theological programme of ecumenical significance without first inquiring what the Roman reaction would be. At Rome the Scythian monks gave the impression of being a noisy and conceited bunch who alone knew what was good for the Church. The Pope and his advisers, friendly at first, cooled. Senators on whom the monks called were likewise reserved. To the senator Faustus who asked whether these ecclesiastically militant Goths deserved support, a Roman presbyter Trifolius expressed grave apprehension. Researches in the archives showed that 'one of the Trinity suffered' is first found on the lips of a Eutychian archimandrite in the Acts of Chalcedon. The Tome of Proclus, to which Maxentius appealed, turns out on investigation to have been the private opinion of a patriarch and to possess no synodical status. Above all, Trifolius advised against making the least hint of concession that Chalcedon and Leo stand in need of any supplement of explanatory nuance.[17]

Congruent advice was simultaneously being offered to Pope Hormisdas by one of his most experienced legates at Constantinople, the toughly right-wing Chalcedonian deacon Dioscorus (above, p. 65), who frankly regarded Maxentius and his colleagues with unqualified suspicion. The Pope must not smile on the Scythian formulas: 'Nothing can be added to the decrees of the four councils and the letter of Pope Leo.'[18]

Maxentius, however, enjoyed more success in his correspondence with the leading theologian among the African bishops, Fulgentius of Ruspe (above, p. 15). Under the Vandal persecution of the Catholic churches Fulgentius was from 503 in exile in Sardinia, whence a stream of polemical divinity poured from his pen. Like Maxentius he deeply admired Augustine, and was alarmed by Faustus of Riez who interpreted predestination wholly in terms of a divine foreknowing which is in no sense causative. If Maxentius could quote Augustine in defence of his propositions, that was enough for Fulgentius. He exchanged letters with the Scythian monks in Rome (*epp.* 15–17), accepting on Augustinian authority the proposition that 'Christ is one of the Trinity who suffered in the flesh' (*ep.* 15, 10, 18 *bis*). But the controversy over grace and original sin concerns Fulgentius most. He expressly denies that the Virgin Mary was born without original sin.[19] In all these propositions Fulgentius is closely followed by his junior contemporary and biographer, Ferrandus deacon of Carthage. Ferrandus also affirms both 'of' and 'in' two natures.[20]

Ferrandus, on the other hand, differs from Maxentius a little over the formula 'one of the Trinity suffered'. After the time of Pope Hormisdas Roman theologians came to think better of the Scythian monks and their theopaschite formula, and this shift is probably to be attributed to the influence of Boethius' fifth tractate. To Justinian their programme offered high possibilities for that reconciliation of the churches which was close to the emperor's heart. By 534 John II would write a formal letter to a group of Roman senators (among whom we find Boethius' old enemy Opilio) explaining that Rome now accepts the orthodoxy of 'one of the Trinity suffered in the flesh', and likewise admits 'of' as well as 'in' two natures.[21] Nevertheless, it looks as if a number of Latin theologians continued to feel misgivings about it. This would explain why Ferrandus, and also the sharp African critic of Justinian's church policy, Facundus of Hermiane, regard the dispute among Chalcedonians about the propriety of saying 'one of the Trinity suffered' as a merely verbal matter, requiring mutual toleration between those who like it and those who do not, without leading to breach of communion.[22] Maxentius' position is more dedicated than this. The formula was felt to be a necessary part of the programme for meeting reasonable criticisms of Chalcedon by moderate Monophysites. The Greek evidence shows that Maxentius was, in political terms, right in his assessment. Severus of Antioch reports his theological discussion at Constantinople with two western senators on embassy, one being Renatus (above, p. 27), that their reluctance to concede the formula 'one of the Trinity suffered' betrayed their Nestorian sympathies.[23] Cyril of Scythopolis, to whose biographies of Palestinian saints of the sixth century we owe much of our knowledge of Justinian's ecclesiastical policies and who was a true-blue Chalcedonian, once remarks that a refusal of the formula is a sure sign of Nestorianism.[24] In Palestine where the Chalcedonian Christology had been accepted only after acute conflicts, the Monophysite pressure was still strong enough to make the Scythian formula a most welcome defence.

One of Severus of Antioch's letters written about this time includes the comment: 'I hear that the Romans are saying, We are afraid to call him who suffered for us in the flesh "one of the Trinity" lest we subject the Trinity to numeration.' Severus is sad to learn of such western ignorance. 'The Trinity is numbered as three hypostases, but as one essence the Trinity transcends number.'[25] This last dictum is very close to Boethius' position as we shall see it in the first tractate.

Severus wrote a lost treatise to prove the equivalence of nature (*physis*) and hypostasis, and therefore to establish that two natures must also be two hypostases, in contradiction to the Chalcedonian formula.[26] Such criticisms show that the Scythian theological programme was well conceived as a reply to the weightiest critics of the diphysite Christology. After Hormisdas' initial reserve the popes became more friendly towards Maxentius' work, as we saw in the case of John II's letter of 534. Justinian himself became convinced that Maxentius' Neochalcedonianism offered real hope of success, and the crucial formulas are incorporated in the documents of the Council of Constantinople of 553.

By the end of the century, in Gregory the Great's *Homilies on the Gospels* (38, 3), the bishop of Rome can say, without trace of anxiety, that Christ is both of and in two natures.

The West's ability to change its mind owed much to Boethius' fifth tractate. As with Pope Gelasius' treatise on the two natures its prime objective is to reconcile the critics of Chalcedon by assuring the hesitant that Chalcedon's 'two natures' is both necessary to avert Eutychianism and altogether distinct from Nestorianism. Gelasius' stance in the Acacian schism requires him to present his cautious conciliatory moves in the form of rough polemic. Boethius' attitude of philosophical detachment conceals the degree of his engagement with the issues. He is convinced that a number of divisive problems in ecclesiastical communion are created simply by a fog of linguistic confusions. Among logicians he is one of that rare species who hopes, by drawing distinctions and looking for clear classification, to reconcile rather than to separate.

Nature and person

Boethius begins by setting out to define his terms. Nature is a word with various senses. It may mean everything that exists; or physical objects only; or incorporeal substances only. In the first case we may say that 'nature is a term for those things which, insofar as they exist, can in some way be apprehended by the intellect'. Here Boethius' formula is adapting one ascribed to the Pythagorean tradition, viz. that philosophy is 'the knowledge of things that are, insofar as they exist'. This definition appears in several Neoplatonists, including Syrianus (*In Metaph.* 63, 34–35) and Ammonius (*In Isag.* 2, 22). Boethius explains that 'in some way' must be added because it is an axiom that God and matter lie beyond the grasp of the intellect, both being defined negatively. This observation also has many Neoplatonic parallels as in Calcidius' commentary on the *Timaeus* (319, p. 315, 20 W.), or Proclus (*In Tim.* I 256, 9; 391, 13), or Philoponus (*In Categ.* 52, 2–8). Augustine (*Principia dialectica* 5) remarks 'bodily objects are known, spiritual entities are mentally understood; but God himself and unformed matter lie beyond our grasp'.

In Boethius' definition of nature the words 'insofar as they exist' have to be added, he observes, for the reason that 'nothing' signifies something, but not nature. The Platonic attribution of value to being carries a corresponding attribution of disvalue to non-being. 'Nothing' is a concept containing a metaphysical problem. Augustine (*De ordine* ii 6, 44) inquires 'quid sit nihil, quid informis materia', characteristically linking Nothing with unformed matter, and in several passages adopts the Plotinian doctrine of degrees of being, with evil as a defection from being towards nothingness.[27]

In the second place, where 'nature' is defined in terms of substances alone, whether physical or incorporeal, Boethius adopts Plato's formula that 'nature is that which can either act or be acted upon', a definition taken from *Phaedrus* 270d (cf. *Sophist* 247de) whose school status is clear from Aristotle's *Topics* (148a 18). This definition reveals that the terms nature and substance are synonymous.

In the third place, Aristotle and his school restrict the term nature to physical substances. Accordingly in his *Physics* (192b 20) Aristotle defines nature as 'the principle of movement *per se* and not as accident'; that is, every body has its own proper movement—fire upwards, earth downwards. Hence a wooden bed falls not because it has the shape of a bed but because it is made of wood. (Cf. Aristotle, *Physics* 255a 32 ff.).

Fourthly, nature is also defined in Aristotle's *Physics* (193a 28–31) as 'the specific difference which gives form to each thing'. On this last interpretation of the word, Catholics and Nestorius are agreed in affirming that there are two natures in Christ. But the same distinctive characteristics cannot hold good for both God and man.

Boethius does not put it beyond doubt which of his school definitions of nature stands nearest to the usage in a Christological context; the third and fourth clearly bring him close to his target. Behind this discussion there stands a sentence in the Tome of Leo which caused particular anger and distress to Monophysite theologians, where he declares that each of the two natures in Christ does, in common with the other, what is proper to its nature: 'agit enim utraque forma cum alterius communione quod proprium est', the Word doing what is the Word's, the flesh what is the flesh's. Leo is repeating an axiom. 'Agit enim cuiusque rei natura quod proprium est' (*Cons. Phil.* ii, 6, 17 (53)). But Boethius' objective is to establish that nature is a wide term in contrast to 'person' which is individual and particular. A difference of some importance between these two terms is that nature may include both substance and accidents, whereas one cannot think of person as consisting in accidents such as colour or size. 'Person' must refer exclusively to substance.

Boethius then proceeds to go through the so-called Porphyrian Tree illustrating the distinctions between substances. He expounded this in both his commentaries on Porphyry's *Isagoge*. Substance divides into corporeal and incorporeal. Corporeal divides into animate and inanimate; animate into sensible and insensible; sensible into rational and irrational. Incorporeal divides into rational and irrational (e.g. the life-principle of animals); rational into that which is impassible and immutable by nature, viz. God, and that which is so by grace and transformation, viz. angels and the soul. Within this general scheme 'person' cannot be applied to inanimate objects or to irrational animals. The term applies only to rational beings, that is to man, God, and angels. Moreover, 'person' is a term of substance, not accidents, and is individual, not universal. Its location is therefore established in relation to the grid set out early in Boethius' commentary on the *Cate-*

gories (above, p. 149). Person is a term of individual rather than universal substance. Therefore the correct definition of person is 'the individual substance of a rational nature': *naturae rationabilis individua substantia*. It corresponds to the Greek word 'hypostasis'.

Boethius is aware that he needs the Greek background to explain his meaning. In everyday Latin usage 'persona' does not carry the same overtones and harmonics. Its Latin etymology is found in the usage of the drama: the masks worn in comedy or tragedy give the term the sense of the character an actor plays—*dramatis personae*. Here Boethius uses much material borrowed from Aulus Gellius' *Attic Nights* (v, 7). Greek usage and vocabulary, as Boethius observes on more than one occasion, are clearer and richer than Latin.[28] Hypostasis carries the sense of the individual instance of something universal, such as rational nature. Boethius goes on to quote a terse sentence in Greek that 'substances (*ousiai*) can fall under the class of universals, but subsist (*hyphistantai*) only in individuals and particulars'. His source is not named and has not hitherto been traced; but its milieu can hardly be in doubt. The question being raised here concerns whether universals, like genus and species, can be properly called substances. This is discussed in the Peripatetic tradition, e.g. in the commentary transmitted under Alexander's name on *Metaphysics* Z 13 (CAG I 523 f.), and is then taken on by the Neoplatonic exegetes of Aristotle's distinction between primary (i.e. particular) substance and secondary (i.e. universal) substance. In the second commentary on Porphyry Boethius specifically names Alexander as the model he is following for his exposition of the problem of universals. The Peripatetic doctrine there stated (*CSEL* 48, 166 f.) is identical with that contained in the anonymous Greek sentence cited in *Contra Eutychen*. Alexander of Aphrodisias wrote a (lost) commentary on the *Categories*. The sentence Boethius quotes could easily have been taken from this or some such source in the Peripatetic tradition.

Boethius next explains the technical distinctions. What the Greeks call *ousiosis*, we Latins call *subsistentia*. What they call *hypostasis*, we call *substantia*. A thing subsists when it does not need accidents to be. A thing is substance when it provides a substrate for accidents. Accordingly, genera and species, which are universals without accidents, subsist but do not have substance. Individuals have both subsistence and substance, but not even they depend on accidents for their being, since their form is given to them by their specific characteristics and distinctive differentia. Accidents, on the contrary, depend on them as a foundation for their being. This doctrine of the individual's priority to accidents also appears in the second commentary on Porphyry (316, 2–4).

The Greeks use not only the term *hypostasis* but also *prosopon* as a synonym, and *prosopon* corresponds to the Latin *persona*. There is a difference between Latin and Greek however, in that Greek never applies *hypostasis* to irrational animals. Latin can use *substantia*, but not *persona*, with reference to the beasts.

Man has *essentia* or *ousia* because he is *subsistentia* or *ousiosis* (because he is not an accident in a subject) and is also *substantia* or *hypostasis* (because he is a substrate to other things that are not *subsistentiae* or *ousioseis*); and he is *persona* or *prosopon* because a rational individual.

A comparison of the fifth tractate with Boethius' other writings shows that his treatment of 'person' varies according to the degree to which Aristotelian language about primary or individual substance is enfolded within a Platonic metaphysic of universals. In the second commentary on *Interpretation* (ii, 136–7) 'person' is the incommunicable quality of the individual within the human species. Plato has a *Platonitas* in which Socrates cannot share. In the commentary on the *Categories* (241D) again, Socrates and Plato differ not in species, but in the quality of their own persona. Here Boethius' Greek source in Porphyry's Question and Answer commentary is available, and shows that Porphyry has no distinctive Greek word to correspond to *persona* but speaks of the difference as 'a peculiar combination of qualities' (*CAG* IV, 1, p. 129, 9–10). But set within the Platonic framework, as is the case in Boethius' *De trinitate* 2, the species humanity is a universal, and individual men differ only in accidents, as inferior to the universal as multiplicity must be inferior to unity. The priority of an individual to his accidents is forgotten. On the other hand, Platonism is also a help to Boethius since, in stressing rationality as a cardinal constituent of personality, he makes it possible to see 'person' as a word linking God and man together. Boethius' definition of 'persona' achieved classical status, but troubled some readers even in his own century and later, because of his bold application of the term to God. One could hardly object to it on the ground of its anthropomorphism, since in Boethius the distinctive substance of humanity is far removed from any corporeality. A generation after Boethius' time, the Roman deacon Rusticus, nephew of Pope Vigilius, hammer of both Justinian and the Monophysites, wrote a Latin tract expressly disowning the applicability of the term 'person' to God if the term is defined, nearly with Boethius (who is not mentioned by name), as 'individual rational nature' shared by God, angels, and man. Rusticus felt that this left Catholic orthodoxy defenceless against a charge of Nestorianism since in this version of the definition nature and person are equivalent terms. Rusticus therefore agreed with the Boethian thesis that a sharp distinction between nature and person is necessary for the coherent statement of Chalcedonian orthodoxy (*PL* 67, 1196).

In the twelfth century Richard of St. Victor, who warmly shared Boethius' view that Christian talk about the Holy Trinity cannot take refuge in a fog of confused terminology, nevertheless attacks Boethius' definition of person if it is applied to God, on the ground that God's 'persona' is not an *individual* substance (*De trinitate* iv, 21 f., *PL* 196, 944 f.). Similarly reservations appear in Peter Abelard's *Christian Theology* (3, *PL* 178, 1258). Peter of Poitiers' commentary on the Sentences (I 32, *PL* 211, 1258) observes that on this subject Boethius has been felt by many theologians to write more as a philosopher than as a theologian and therefore to speak more to probability than to truth. Thomas Aquinas (*ST* i, 29) reviews objections made by schoolmen to Boethius' classic definition, e.g. that the unique is inherently indefinable; it is unclear whether 'substance' is particular or universal, first or second; Boethius' definition omits a man's physical features which we cannot divorce from what we understand by his *persona*. But in general Thomas defends Boethius as a writer on the subject who is received with the veneration due to authority.

It is noteworthy that Boethius regards both angels and souls as sharing in impassibility. But he then remembers his Augustine and qualifies this initial Platonism by adding that the rational soul needs grace.

The application of the word 'persona' to God was given by the tradition of the Latin Church, but only in the special context of the 'persons' of the Trinity. Boethius has behind him Augustine's unconcealed dislike of the formula 'three persons', language that had been established western usage since theology first spoke Latin in the pages of Tertullian. In his *De trinitate* Augustine concedes that the word 'person' has some utility in safeguarding the Christian confession from the obliteration of all differentiation within the being of God. God is one. Yet a purely unitarian or monarchian account of his nature is inadequate to express the love of God in Christ through the Holy Spirit.

The term 'substance' is hardly less difficult. The Peripatetic tradition in the background has often given to the word 'substance' an inescapably physical connotation. Clearly that is not at all the sense intended. It is closer to the philosophical use when we speak of e.g. 'the substance of the matter' in contrast to its discardable or variable or 'accidental' features, which can be mentally subtracted without the essentials ceasing to be.

Augustine insists repeatedly that in God to be, and to be good, great, and omnipotent, are one and the same. To subtract from God the divine attributes of goodness and power is the death of the concept. In fact Augustine dislikes talk of 'one substance' almost as much as 'three persons'. What he wants to say is that God is *essentia*, being. And, of being, 'good' is not a transitory epithet because God is all that we mean by goodness itself. To Augustine the plurality of Father, Son, and Holy Spirit is not a differentiation of being or substance, but of relation; a relation of equals and identicals for which no earthly analogy can really be found. All that is certain is that Father, Son, and Spirit are not words separately expressive of substance, and that in the Holy Trinity relation is eternal, and not an accident (*De trinitate* v, 5, 6).

Much of this sets the stage for Boethius' discussions. To him God is essence or *ousia*, the very source of all being; subsistence, since he subsists and that is to say he is self-sufficient; he needs nothing to subsist; he is also *hypostasis* since he exists (*substat*). So we may say there is one *ousia*, i.e. essence or subsistence, of Deity, but three hypostases, that is 'substantiae'. If this scheme of terminology were followed, we would say that the Trinity is one essence, three 'substances' or persons. However, the usage of the Church (*ecclesiasticus loquendi usus*, cf. above, p. 112) excludes 'three substances'. The Church says that God is one substance. Here one must be careful to remember that substance is being predicated of God not in the sense that he is substrate to other things such as attributes or qualities, but rather that he is the origin and source of all being.

This last observation coincides with Augustine who says (*De trin*, v, 5, 10) that God subsists and is a substance but not a substrate. The Neoplatonists maintain the same, as for example Syrianus (*In Metaph.* 171, 27 f.) and Ammonius (*In Cat.* 37, 1 ff.). In his first tractate on the Trinity (*Opusc.* I 2) Boethius will expressly hold the same position.

In the fourth section of the fifth tractate Boethius explains that his objective is to mark out the difference between nature and person. How the terms are applied is a matter for decision by the usage of the Church. What is certain is that Nestorius indefensibly treats the words as interchangeable, so that for him two natures become two persons, neither being deprived of independent rationality (and therefore freedom). Nestorius leaves one with a juxtaposition or, as the Greeks say, *parathesis*. (In fact Nestorius' term for preference is *synapheia*, conjunction, and in this choice uses a technical term of Neoplatonic usage, since Proclus contrasts 'union', which Nous can have with Nous, with *synapheia* or 'conjunction' which Psyche can have with Nous, and 'participation' which is all that bodies are capable of: *In Tim.* ii, 102, 24–6.) Against Nestorian dualism Boethius first argues from the proposition that the very name Christ implies singularity, to which Nestorius does not do justice. According to the axiom of Plato's *Sophist* (245), beloved of the Neoplatonists from Plotinus on (*Enn.* vi 9, 1), especially of Augustine (*De ordine* ii, 18, 48; *Vera relig.* 36, 66; *De musica* vi, 17, 56 etc.), whatever has being is a unity, even if constituted of parts. For Proclus (*Theol. Plat.* ii, 1, p. 73 P) every existent is one. Boethius has repeated the axiom in his second commentary on Porphyry (*CSEL* 48, 162, 2–3) and in his commentary on Cicero's *Topics* (1057D). It is noteworthy that the Monophysite John Philoponus also deploys this argument against Nestorianism (*PG* 94, 745 f.).

This last argument Boethius reinforces by the logical observation that if the name Christ applies to two disparate entities, it becomes equivocal and therefore defies precise definition. Theological arguments follow: Nestorianism makes the miracle of the virgin birth and Old Testament prophecy superfluous, and prejudices the possibility of salvation—*quod credi nefas est*, a conclusion irreconcilable with the faith. Here again it is evident that certain positions are simply given as inhering in the very nature of Catholic faith.

From Nestorius Boethius passes in his fifth section to Eutyches, whose basic error, as Maxentius also said, springs from the same root, namely the assumption that nature and person are synonyms. From the true doctrine that Christ is one person, he deduces that he is also one nature. Eutyches' favourite formula 'one nature after the union' (it is in fact common to all Monophysite critics of Chalcedon) is beset by ambiguity. It could be taken to imply that the flesh of Christ was not derived from Mary. It might also mean that the union to form a single nature took place at the time of his birth or even as late as the resurrection, either of which ends in an adoptionist Christology. (Boethius' argument here coincides with that used by Pope Gelasius.)

Moreover, if Christ did not derive his human body from Mary, Eutyches needs to be asked if the humanity he assumed is 'fallen' or not; i.e. did he assume a humanity one with that of Abraham and David (and Mary) of whose seed God's prophets were inspired to say that this person would bring salvation to the world? If not, then one must deduce not only that no man could ever be born free of original sin, but that the humanity he assumed was unreal. If so, the birth and passion of Christ are evacuated of redemptive significance, the incarnation becomes mendacious play-acting by God, and nothing useful is achieved. 'I feel bound to think that even in the case of man a useless action is foolish' (Boethius allows himself an allusion to Aristotle's well known dictum that 'nature does nothing use-

Nature and person 199

lessly'). So Eutyches is refuted by a *reductio ad absurdum*.

The theology defended by Boethius can be plentifully illustrated from Augustine (e.g. *ep.* 164, 7, 19; 190, 25; *Pecc. merit.* ii, 24, 38) and also from Ferrandus of Carthage (*ep.* 3, 3–4, *PL* 67, 891–93).

Boethius dismisses Eutyches with the remark that, in supposing Christ to have brought his body with him from heaven, he has misunderstood the text of John iii.13 'No one has ascended to heaven but he who descended from heaven, the Son of man'.

In the sixth section of the fifth tractate, having discarded both Nestorius and Eutyches, Boethius asks how the unity of divine and human in Christ can be understood. It is impious (again *quod credi nefas est*) and irrational to think immutable divinity can be transformed into humanity. (So also Augustine, *S.* 186, 2; *De trin.* vi, 8, 9; Ferrandus, *ep.* 3, 8–9, *PL* 67, 987–8.) On the other hand, to think that humanity can be changed into God defies the philosophical axiom that a corporeal substance cannot be changed into an incorporeal, or vice versa. Not even the forms of incorporeal entities can be changed about. Change is possible only to entities that share a common substrate of the same matter, a proposition Boethius has learnt from Aristotle's treatise 'On coming to be and on passing away' (226a 10). Even among material things bronze objects cannot be transmuted into stone or vice versa. Matter is the very basis and presupposition of all change. Incorporeal substances possess no material substrate to make transformation possible. God and the soul are therefore immutable (as Boethius the Platonist has already expounded in discussing *persona*). The human soul of Christ is not changed into the divinity by which it has been assumed. Neither body nor soul are capable of being transmuted into divinity, and so humanity cannot become God.

Here Boethius' argument that incorporeal things cannot interchange among themselves because they have no matter presupposes that in matter lies the root of all mutation, an opinion which Augustine once records as maintained by 'some' (*City of God* viii, 5). Among late Neoplatonists it is the general view, as, for example, in Simplicius' commentary on Epictetus (p. 176 Dübner). The axiom, however, contains potential difficulties for Boethius if it is applied to the visible heaven which, unlike Augustine, he regards as everlasting and part of the immutable (but not 'eternal') order.

Boethius' sharp disjunction between corporeal and incorporeal echoes a dictum to which he draws emphatic attention in his first commentary on Porphyry's *Isagoge* (*CSEL* 48, 26, 19 ff.), viz. that nothing corporeal in genus can fall under an incorporeal species.

It follows that in Eutyches' Christology there is an inherent defiance not only of authority but also of reason. He loses both of the two elements united in Christ, just as a mixture of honey and water produces a compound being neither honey nor water, 'of' both but not 'in' both. Catholics, on the other hand, are in harmony with philosophical reason when they affirm Christ to be both of and in two natures.

The seventh section of the fifth tractate expounds more closely the meaning of the Catholic Christology. The constituent elements continue as in the case of a crown composed of gold and of gems, where both retain their own form. Nevertheless there is a true union of the two natures, on the ground of which one and the same Christ is both perfect man and perfect God, one of the Trinity, not an addition thereto so as to make a quaternity (so already Augustine, *S.* 130, 3; 261, 7; *De dono pers.* 24, 67). Therefore in him God may be said to have suffered, not because humanity became deity but because it was assumed by deity. The God-Man, *homo deus*, is a single *persona*.

Along this path we may find the middle way, *media via*, between heresies, just as, in ethics (according to Aristotle) virtue is the mean between vices.

Augustine had already described orthodoxy as the middle channel between the Scylla of Arianism and the Charybdis of Sabellianism (*Tr. Joh.* 36, 9; 71, 2). He also allows theopaschite language such as 'the crucified God' (*ep.* 169, 2, 8). Moreover, he deduces from the unity of both natures that we may say 'the Son of man descended from heaven', or that 'the Son of God was crucified' though he suffered this not in his divinity by which the Only-begotten Son is coeternal with the Father, but in the weakness of his human nature (*c. serm. Arianorum* 6, 8—one of the obvious sources of Leo's Tome).

Boethius is now facing the climax of his investigation: how can two natures be understood to be united in one substance? At this point he evidently thinks the logician can hardly help, for the eighth and last section of the fifth tractate turns away towards a very different problem bound up with the speculations of Augustine about the fall of Adam, namely, how Christ could have had a human nature in true solidarity with ours and yet have had no will to sin. May we say that he assumed from Mary humanity such as Adam had before the Fall, neither open to sin nor vulnerable to death, so that his human nature stood in no need of healing medicine? Such questions were still buzzing, especially after Faustus of Riez, and particularly concerned African theologians such as Fulgentius of Ruspe with whom Boethius is almost certainly in contact.

Boethius answers the question with an Augustinian analysis of three possible states of man: Adam before the Fall had within his free being the possibility of the will to sin. Had he chosen to abide in God's precepts, an additional gift would have been granted, removing not only the will to sin but the capacity for sinning or of feeling any impulse to sin. But the fact of the Fall entails the consequence of death and sin and man's sinful will. The antithetical parallel between Fall and Redemption means that in different modes all three possible states are found in Christ.

1. Christ's human nature assumed our mortal body to overcome death, the punishment for the sin of Adam.

2. Christ had in himself no impulse to sin; that is, the state to which Adam would have attained had he obeyed God's commands.

3. Christ shared in the middle or ethically indifferent physical state which Adam had before the Fall in respect of eating, drinking, digesting, sleeping—all the natural human physical features and necessary functions.

Boethius is touching on an acute difficulty perennially besetting the Pauline doctrine that physical death is a consequence of man's sinful rebellion. Adam is provided by God with the fruit of the Garden of Eden. Whether or not he had sinned, he would have died of simple starvation if he had failed to eat sufficiently. Because Christ voluntarily assumed a human body, he shared the need for food, but (Boethius thinks) by choice, not by necessity. After his resurrection his human body was transformed, in the way that Adam's body could have been changed had he kept the divine commands. The resurrection of believers will bring them to this state, and it was for this that Christ taught us to pray in the Paternoster, asking that his will be done as in heaven so on earth, that his kingdom come, and that he may deliver us from evil.

Throughout this discussion the terms of reference are drawn from Augustine, but the discussion is being taken further and presented in scholastic order, not as a series of obiter dicta. Augustine taught that Adam would not have died had he not sinned. His body needed food and drink for sustenance; but the fruits of the tree of life kept him deathless and ever-young (*City of God* xiii, 23). Augustine does not consider, however, what would have befallen Adam had he stopped eating and drinking in Paradise. He is content simply to affirm that Adam's body suffered no ageing or decrepitude, and had he not fallen he would have passed into the incorruptible state of immortality, like Enoch and Elijah, without passing through death (*Pecc. merit.* i, 2–3). Augustine holds that before the resurrection Christ's body needed food and drink, but after the resurrection he ate 'by power, not by necessity' (*S.* 116, 3; 297, 2). The *City of God* (xiv, 12–15) suggests that Adam's free will left him by nature able not to sin, and the extra help (*adiutorium*) of divine grace would easily have enabled Adam to achieve the higher state of losing even the capacity to sin.

A tidy mind putting all these scattered observations together could easily deduce from Augustine that unfallen Adam was able not to sin, and could by grace have risen to incapacity for sin, but in sad fact fell to corruption and death.

Boethius concludes the tractate by asking John the deacon if he will signify his approval. 'I am not such a lover of myself as to contend for whatever I have once poured out in preference to wiser judgement.' If there is no source of goodness in ourselves, we have no right to be attached to our own opinions. All things are good that come from him who alone is good.

Absolute and relative goodness

The third tractate, dedicated to John the deacon, is the most technical and obviously Neoplatonic of the five opuscula. Boethius wrote it apparently to answer a question put by John arising out of another work of his entitled 'Hebdomads', groups of seven. In the middle ages 'De Hebdomadibus' was mistakenly taken to be the title of the third tractate itself, and commentators offered fanciful explanations of the mysterious word. The ninth-century commentary ascribed to Remigius of Auxerre (long recension) derived 'Ebdomas' from a fictitious Greek word *ebdo* meaning 'conceive'. Thierry of Chartres and Gilbert of Poitiers treat the noun as meaning 'mental concepts'. Thomas Aquinas, who is well aware of the 'concept' exegesis, interprets Hebdomad as a Greek equivalent of 'edere', to publish. Modern scholars have replaced these medieval fancies by equally improbable suggestions, e.g. that Boethius wrote a diary of philosophical reflection once a week, or enjoyed a weekly Platonic reading party with a circle of friends of whom John the deacon was one.

A work entitled Hebdomads survives among the corpus of writings ascribed to Hippocrates. This was known in the Latin West in late antiquity since it is cited by Calcidius in his commentary on the *Timaeus* (203, p. 86, 7–8 W.). The Hippocratean work has lately been reedited by C. I. Toul for the Athens Academy (1975). But this text contains nothing remotely resembling Boethius' subject in the third tractate. The learned Roman Varro wrote a book entitled Hebdomads. A summary fragment in the *Attic Nights* of Aulus Gellius (iii, 10) shows that Varro expounded the mysteries of the number seven after the manner of the Pythagoreans. The Neopythagoreans and Neoplatonists were fascinated by the cosmic mystery of seven, and liked to classify things in sevens. For Syrianus seven is the number of created things under the care of providence (*In Metaph.* 146, 1–2). In the fifth book of his *Platonic Theology* Proclus lengthily expatiates on the sevenness which pervades the continuous evolving of the great chain of being (v, 2. 4. 37). This last theme has clear affinities with Boethius' theme. A simpler suggestion would be that the axioms set out in the tractate, and in the printed editions numbering nine, were really intended by Boethius to number seven, the first being merely an illustration of the principle, the seventh and eighth being wrongly divided into two.

In some manuscripts (e.g. Bodleian, misc. 457) the third tractate has no title. But most manuscripts give a neat summary of its argument: 'How substances are good in that they exist, yet are not substantial goods'. The central contention of the treatise is more obviously conventional than its dialectical method. Boethius is setting out to vindicate two basic principles of Platonism:

1. To exist as such has moral value and is a good.
2. All particular goods are 'good' insofar as they participate in the ultimate, universal source of goodness, the Idea of the Good, which for Plato is the source of all being.

These truths are treated by Boethius as esoteric truths safe only in the hands of an intellectual élite, and therefore requiring to be expressed with laconic terseness, unsuitable for those who scorn all literature not intended to offer entertainment. Boethius' master Proclus, though hardly a practitioner of brevity in normal circumstances, certainly regarded many of his doctrines as intended only for a narrow circle of elect persons. Proclus has strong convictions about the revealed character of the truths disclosed by Plato (*In Parm.* 991), and deep fears as to what may become of these truths in the hands of the unworthy (*ibid.* 1024). He goes so far as to wish for a kind of pagan Holy Office to control the reading of his fellow-citizens. His biographer Marinus records the dictum 'If it were in my power, I would suppress all ancient books except the *Chaldean Oracles* and the *Timaeus*. The rest I would have destroyed, because some suffer injury by reading without critical guidance' (*Vita Procli* 38). If the world is to be made really safe for pagan Neoplatonism in an unappreciative society, some control is desirable. Proclus evidently felt that Christian Neoplatonism was dangerous.

In the sixth and seventh books of the *Republic* Plato teaches that the Idea of the Good stands at the summit of the intelligible world. Particular things in this world are good by participation in this Idea, which is the reality giving truth to objects of knowledge and the power of knowing to the mind, as sunlight does in the realm of physical vision. Indeed, the Idea of the Good confers on objects not merely their power to be known but also their very being (509b). The mind's dialectic is able to attain to these abstractions by a method similar to that used in geometry where the figure or image is the starting-point but is then set aside (511). It is therefore a question whether one may be able to deduce the entire cosmos from a single principle or cause. In the *Philebus* (27a) Plato affirms the superiority of cause to effect, a principle which the Neoplatonists took to imply metaphysical superiority in the hierarchy of being and a potentiality in each entity to produce what is immediately inferior to it in the continuum. (See Proclus' *Elements of Theology*, 7.) Aristotle explains that in causation eternal principles are more powerful and important than particular manifestations of them. In each science demonstration begins from axioms and common beliefs (*Metaphysics* A 1, 993a 23–30; B 2, 997a 2 ff.). Aristotle criticizes a lecture of notorious obscurity which he had heard Plato give on the Good, where Plato sought to give a grand synthesis of the foundations of mathematics as a logical road ascending to the Idea of the Good, the initiating first cause of all that is inferior to it (fragments of Aristotle's critique in W. D. Ross, *Aristotelis Fragmenta selecta*, pp. 111–20). In his commentary on the *Metaphysics* Alexander of Aphrodisias explains that whatever is the cause of being to other things is also the cause of truth in them; so that each being, insofar as it participates in being, to that degree participates in truth. Eternal things have being, and therefore *a fortiori* the things that are cause of their eternity. Against those who think the ultimate principle of things is matter Alexander protests that being is incorporeal and immovable. Being as such stands at the apex of things (Alexander, *In Metaph.* 147, 8 ff.; 239, 6 ff.; 265, 33 ff.; 240, 24).

Plotinus (v, 5, 13) sharply separates the transcendent primal Good from all particular things to which goodness is adjectival. He even says that of the primal Good the term 'good' is used in a sense differing from that when it is applied to inferior things (vi, 2, 17). There is therefore a basic distinction between goodness as the first hypostasis and goodness as an accidental possession of a given entity (vi, 6, 10, 27–33). This distinction is paralleled for Plotinus by a like antithesis between *ousia*, being, and *ta onta*, actual existents (vi, 6, 10, 44–5). Simplicius (*In Categ.* 45, 24 ff.) shows that this becomes standard school doctrine. Plotinus answers a worldly objector who claims that in mere existence as such there is nothing good, and that life is made good by its pleasures, including no doubt that of philosophical contemplation.

Proclus (*In Tim.* i, 363, 11–18) follows through the antithesis between the Good in itself and things which are good by acquisition or participation. In the *Elements of Theology* (8) he lays down that all that participates in the Good is subordinate to the primal Good which lies beyond any actual existents. In his commentary on the *Parmenides* (1033, 26 ff. Cousin) he holds that at the apex is the One beyond being, then the One-Being, which by diminution comes forth into actual being. The One in itself is superior to the One which is being, while below abstract being is actual existence. This for Proclus makes possible his distinction between the imparticipated One and the participated One (1034, 34; 1066, 34). To lie even beyond the possibility of participation by inferior entities in the scale of things is the ultimate in transcendence.

The orthodox Platonists, following *Republic* 509b, hold that the Good or One is 'beyond being'. This transcendence was linked in the Neoplatonic schools with the language of Plato's *Sophist* about 'non-being'. If the One transcends being, it may be described as Non-being in the sense that it is not 'yet' being. Proclus explains this in *Elements of Theology* 138, and in the fragment of the seventh book of his commentary on the *Parmenides* preserved in the Latin version of William of Moerbeke and discovered by R. Klibansky (*Plato Latinus* iii, 1952, pp. 44–5). According to Parmenides' argument in Plato's dialogue, the tenses of the verb 'to be' are so bound up with time, past, present, and future, that it is inappropriate to affirm that the One is or has being (141e, 162a).

Augustine echoes the general Platonic view in his *Literal commentary on Genesis* (xi, 13 f., 17–18): 'All that is, so far as it is substance, is good and comes necessarily from the true God from whom all good is. Even the devil is good insofar as he exists.' 'A nature with no good in it cannot exist' (*City of God* xix, 13). On the other hand, for Augustine God is goodness and being, not beyond being. He is *ipsum esse*, and this is the meaning of eternity and its associated notion of immutability. He is Good, whereas to all other things in the universe 'good' is only adjectival (*En. ps.* 134, 4). In God being and existence are one and the same, *esse* is also *subsistere* (*De trin.* vii, 4, 9). There is no antithesis of act and potentiality.

In the third tractate Boethius is clearly influenced by Proclus and his school. Pierre Hadot has suggested that he is actually translating a Neoplatonic piece.[29] The diction is so Boethian that there may be exaggeration in this view, but if so of a very mild nature. Possibly we should attribute it to Augustinian influence that Boethius says nothing of Non-being or of the One as transcending being, a proposition of which Proclus frequently likes to write (e.g. *In Parm.* 1073, 2 ff.). Instead of speaking of Non-being Boethius suggests the antithesis of abstract and actual, a move which has the merit of escaping Aristotle's onslaught on obfuscating talk about 'non-being' (*Metaphysics* N 2).

Boethius lays down the axiom that everything existent is good, since everything tends to what is its good and to what is its like, (this form of argument is found closely paralleled in a number of passages in Proclus, e.g. *Elements of Theology* 8; *In Parm.* 1199, 20 ff.; *Plat. Theol.* ii, 2 p. 80 P; 6 p. 95 P). But is this goodness so essential to all these good entities that it cannot be mentally abstracted, i.e. so that without goodness they would cease to be? The consensus of all men, of whatever race or education or culture, affirms that there is a primal Good. (Proclus, *In Tim.* i, 228, 12, makes the same confident asseveration concerning the notion of eternal being.) From this primal Good it is impossible mentally to substract the notion of goodness. But in the case of all things which derive their existence from it, it is one thing to be, another to be good. Their goodness is received by participation in the primal Good. To say that all things are God would be blasphemous (*dictu nefas*). So the goodness in creatures is neither substance nor mere accident, but attaches to their *esse* which tends to God who is their good. Remove their relation to God, and the goodness then becomes accidental.

Boethius ends the tractate by some incomplete, exploratory aphorisms about the relation of created existences to their divine Creator. If all things are good because the good God willed their existence, it does not follow that all things are just because the just God willed them to be. To be just requires activity, justice being an active thing. In God being and acting are identical because he is 'simple'; in us they are not identical because we are not 'simple', but composed of disparate elements. Moreover, 'good' is a universal genus. Justice is a species of goodness inapplicable to all good actions (so already Aristotle, *Topics* 116a 24 *An. Pr.* 43b 20–1). There are three other cardinal virtues in addition to justice (Boethius, *Top. diff.* ii, 1188D). So goodness is a more all-embracing term than justice. Everything just is good (*Cons. Phil.* iv, 4, 19(64)), but not everything good is just.

The argument is in part a Neoplatonic reply to Aristotle's insistence (*Metaphysics* Z 6, 103b 11–12) that the good, wherever found, must be identical with goodness. The notion of metaphysical degrees of goodness is dangerous if 'good' then comes to be used in a Pickwickian sense.

Boethius, however, does not simply restate the Platonic position. Above all, he tries to make its truth a matter of mathematical demonstration by prefixing nine definitions and axioms from which the conclusion is deduced with irresistible force. It is a self-evident commonplace of geometry that if you take equals from two equals, the remainders are equal. Euclid lays this down at the beginning of his *Elements*. In the time of Plato and Aristotle, it was already a standard example of an axiom needing no argument to establish its truth. Boethius elsewhere cites it in his commentary on Cicero's *Topics* (1176C). In attempting to work out in detail Plato's programme of deriving everything from the Idea of the Good, the Neoplatonists constantly hold the geometrical model before themselves. Euclid, at the beginning of the Elements, had linked geometrical definitions with the 'common notions' on which all men of reason are in agreement. So to Ammonius 'the first principles of discourse are like the definitions of geometry and the common notions'. In Proclus very frequent appeals are made to the 'common notions' in physics, ethics, logic, mathematics, and theology.[30]

Boethius' axioms are in matter and manner often reminiscent of the theses set out by Proclus in the *Elements of*

Theology. He begins from the distinction between simple being (*esse*) and existence (*id quod est*). Being in itself, as an abstract concept, is prior to existence. Existence (*quod est*) is and exists as soon as it has received the form of being, *forma essendi*. Naturally for a Platonist the implicit temporality of 'as soon as' or 'prior to' is only a figurative way of speaking. The priority is logical and metaphysical, not temporal. Simple being (for the Platonic tradition the simple is always prior to and superior to the composite) cannot participate in anything higher than itself. But granted existence, then participation is possible. Again, simple being can have nothing added to it. Plotinus, whom Proclus follows, says that any addition to the Good would be a diminution (iii, 8, 11; 9, 3; v, 5, 13; Proclus, *El. Th.* 8, p. 10, 10 Dodds). It would add accidents to the original essence or substance, and no accidents can be predicated of supreme being. In the *Consolation of Philosophy* Boethius makes deductions from this base (iii, 10).

Everything that is participates in being (*in eo quod est esse*) in order to be, but in something other than being in order to be a particular thing. In whatever is simple, being and existence are a unity, whereas in whatever is composite, being and existence are distinct from one another.

The concluding axiom runs that like is attracted to like, so that whatever is drawn to the good, must itself in some sort be good. The presupposition is common in Proclus; e.g. in his commentary on the *Parmenides* (1081, 5), the affinity of like to like is the basis of knowledge of the One.

It is easier for the exegete of Boethius to find parallels to illuminate him in the Neoplatonic commentators than to be perfectly certain what he and they mean. He and Proclus would obviously have agreed that in this world to be is impossible without being something. Existence in this world of experience requires the possession of some quality, some accidental features Boethius would have said, without which distinctness is lost to sight. In a Neoplatonic world the abstract has far greater power than the actual and concrete.

Boethius' argument brought to the Latin West a conceptual framework and a terminology which is present only partially and incompletely in Marius Victorinus and Augustine, and it fascinated his mediaeval successors, especially by the distinction between being and existence. The momentous implication that there is some element of 'fall', some metaphysical inferiority inherent in the process of transition from abstract possibility to concrete actuality, has enjoyed a long history in western thinking, lasting into the twentieth century and no doubt beyond. It is common human experience that into any actualization of an ideal there enters some element of imperfection and disappointment, as if a musical score were never so beautiful as when being read by an experienced musician's eye while actual performance in real sound is in some degree inferior. In philosophical theology the notion arises easily from formulating the concept of God as wholly self-sufficient and yet as simultaneously the grand cause of all that is, which is his creation and yet is other than himself. That is to imply that he is not a concrete existent which, in order to be something, has to be distinct from other things and therefore is limited. So it comes about that he is spoken of as either being itself or even as 'beyond being'.

Boethius' third tractate taught the Latin West, above all else, the method of axiomatization, that is, of analysing an argument and making explicit the fundamental presuppositions and definitions on which its cogency rests. He taught his successors how to try to state truths in terms of first principles and then to trace how particular conclusions follow therefrom. The West learnt from him demonstrative method.

The parallel argument in the *Consolation of Philosophy* runs to the effect that the goodness of the first principle of all things is simply a universal notion of all mankind. By the word 'God' we mean the best we can think (*nihil melius cogitari*),[31] and that best must be goodness to a supreme and ideal degree. All that is perfect is prior to whatever is imperfect, since it is by comparison with the perfect that the imperfect is known to be what it is. Boethius argues from degrees of perfection, much as Augustine, *De trinitate* viii, 3, 4 (cf. *De doctr. christiana* i, 102, 7). It is an accepted truth of philosophy that an infinite regress is impossible, or knowledge of causes, which in practice means all real knowledge, would become impossible. This proposition is incisively stated by Proclus (*El. Th.* 11; *Th. Plat.* ii, 3) and appears in Boethius' first commentary on Porphyry (*CSEL* 48, 66, 21). Moreover, in God happiness or *beatitudo* is not something received or acquired from some external source. That nothing can be superior to its own cause is again for Neoplatonists an axiom of cosmic range; see Plotinus, v, 4, 1; Porphyry, *Sententiae* 13; Proclus, *El. Th.* 7. The supreme beatitude and the highest good are identical, because the very notion of perfection excludes two or more competitors for this position at the apex of the hierarchy of being. In the *Consolation* Boethius expressly compares his method of inference to that of the geometers by adding that there is a pleasing 'corollary' called in Greek *porisma*, viz. that as man is made happy by happiness, which is shown to be divinity, so the acquisition of happiness may be called deification (*deos fieri*). By nature God is one only. But there is no limit to the possible number by participation.

Neoplatonists also liked to draw attention to corollaries, using the technical term of geometry in non-geometrical contexts. A strikingly similar passage occurs in Hierocles' *Commentary on the Golden Verses of the Pythagoreans* (23, p. 96, 14 Köhler). We can see from Ammonius' commentary on *Interpretation* (248, 2) that the pupils of Proclus had learnt this from their master (cf. Proclus, *In Eucl.* i p. 212 Friedlein).

In accepting the language of deification, Boethius is no pagan but is in line with Augustine in a series of well-known and much discussed passages (*En. ps.* 49, 2; 52, 6; *City of God* ix, 23; *Tr. Joh.* 48, 9). It is quite mistaken to see Boethius' admission of the language of deification as marking abandonment of Augustine in favour of pagan philosophical tradition. In fact Proclus actually rejects the language of deification as too misleading to be allowed (*In Tim.* iii, 231, 5–27; 245, 20), though he allows mystical union with the One (i, 211, 24 ff.).

God the Trinity

The first two tractates in the collection of opuscula are probably the latest of the five to be composed. Both concern the doctrine of the Trinity, discussion of which had been sharpened at Rome by the activities of the Scythian monks armed with the writings of Maxentius. The second tractate is theologically and philosophically less technical than the first and does not take the argument so far. It may well have been written while the first tractate was in gestation in his mind. John the deacon, to whom the second tractate is dedicated, may have put a question to him. In some early manuscripts the first word is not *quaero*, I ask, but *quaeris*, you ask. The issue under examination is whether the words Father, Son and Holy Spirit are predicated of God substantially or otherwise. In this argument the foundations of Catholic faith must be deemed the presupposition of the discussion. Ask a Catholic believer if the Father is a substance, and he will say Yes; likewise if you ask him of the Son and the Spirit. Yet he will say there are not three substances, but one substance. Everything predicated of the divine substance must be common to Father, to Son, and to Spirit, so that, for example, each of the three is God, truth, goodness, immutability, justice, omnipotence. All terms which are true not only of each individually but of all three together are predicated substantially. All terms which are true of each separately and not of all together are predicated not substantially but otherwise. Accordingly the name Father does not apply to the Son or to the Holy Spirit, and vice versa. Therefore these terms are not substantial, but relative. By the same rule of method even the term Trinity itself is not predicated substantially of God. The Trinity consists in the plurality of the Persons, the Unity in simplicity of substance.

Boethius' conclusion begs John to advise him whether or not he has this right. If not, he is please to offer a better way of conjoining faith and reason. This last phrase reflects Boethius' awareness, which surfaces at several points in his writings, that faith and reason operate in different spheres and from divergent premises.

Apart from the conclusion, the second tractate is in almost all its particular detail a mosaic of phrases from Augustine, especially *De trinitate* v and *City of God* xi, 24. Its central thesis is in line with *De trinitate* v, 6, 7; not, however, with vii, 6, 11 where Augustine writes 'substantia patris'. Augustine cannot say that 'persona' simply means relation, and the idea for him remains confused and imprecise, so that it is unclear whether we are being told that the three Persons exist in relation to one another, or whether relation is integral to the notion of Person. Boethius' verdict is identical with that of the Scythian monk Dionysius Exiguus in his covering letter to his translation of Proclus' Tome, addressed to Felicianus and Pastor; and the parallel reinforces the evidence of the fifth tractate that Boethius supports Maxentius.[32] Questions about the Trinity arose directly out of the Christological debate, especially because of the anti-Nestorian slogan 'one of the Trinity suffered in the flesh'. The Scythian monks' theology sounded dangerously close to making an intimate link between Monophysite Christology and a strongly pluralistic doctrine of God, in antithesis to Nestorius' tendency to link a diphysite Christology with an exclusively unitary doctrine of God.

Boethius tells us that he spent a long time reflecting on the problem of the Trinity being one God, and devoted much study to Augustine. The dedication of the first tractate asked his father-in-law Symmachus to judge whether or not his Augustinian studies have borne fruit. The subject is wrapped in mystery, so that Boethius is again writing for an esoteric circle. He disavows any confidence that he has an all-sufficient answer for the difficulties. Theology, like all other subjects, has limitations. Medicine does not always succeed in curing the patient. Talk about God is beset by the weak eyes of human reason. Nevertheless Boethius is confident that the philosopher can help a little, especially by recourse to the classic commentaries on Plato's *Parmenides* for a disentangling of the logical problems of identity and difference. But Boethius begins by taking his stand resolutely within the Catholic tradition of authority. Christians have received a revelation of the word of God, and his concern is solely with the exposition of Catholic orthodoxy. Among the many claimants for the name Christian the greatest, indeed exclusive authority attaches to that form whose prescribed doctrines are universal and whose geographical extension is almost universal. Hence the title 'catholica'. He is not entering into debate with alternative doctrines which the Church has rejected, and Catholic dogma is the starting-point of the inquiry. This is the agreed truth of this society.

Accordingly, in contrast to the graduated Trinity of the Arians, Catholic faith holds that Father, Son, and Holy Spirit are one God without difference. Now if one says something is either the same or other, that identity or otherness must be located either in genus or in species or in number. (This is laid down by Aristotle in the *Topics*, A 7, 102b 6 ff.) In the case of number, individual difference within a shared species is caused by accidents. Thus three men share humanity but differ in their accidents, if only in the irreducible sense that, even in the case of wholly indistinguishable triplets, each body occupies a different space (Boethius makes the same point in his commentary on the *Categories*, 173A, 202B); and position 'where' is defined as among accidents; that is, one can mentally subtract the notion of being in this place rather than that without destroying the substantial notion of humanity. (Admittedly, one cannot subtract the notion of being three-dimensional: *In Cat.* 202B.) But when we speak about God, how can one talk of a difference of number? That neither genus nor species comes into the discussion is self-evident.

At this point Boethius makes a fresh start in his argument by restating the conventional Platonic scheme for the classification of the sciences (above, p. 110). He remarks that this accords with a wise precept (to be found at the beginning of Aristotle's Ethics, *E.N.* i, 1) that a learned man's task is to state his belief about each thing corresponding to its being. Classification is a primary task if clarity is to be achieved. Physics, mathematics, and theology are the triad constituting the speculative branch of philosophy, and this scheme is taken to provide a basic map of human knowledge in Boethius' first commentary on Porphyry. In many passages of Syrianus, Proclus, Ammonius, and Simplicius the same map is presupposed. Boethius is the first writer to put it down succinctly in Latin.

The subject matter of theology is abstract, separable from matter, and dealing with immutables. The mind therefore has to pass beyond the images or shapes with which a geometer begins his work, even though soon he too kicks away the ladder that has enabled him to get off the ground. Theology has not only to set aside material shapes (*imaginationes*) but also to think wholly in intellectual concepts (*in divinis intellectualiter versari oportebit*), since its ultimate object is that form which is Being itself (*ipsum esse*) and the source of being (*ex qua esse est*).

All being depends on form. A statue is what it is not because of the bronze material, but because of the form into which it is made. Bronze itself is a form of earth as one of the four elements of the cosmos, and earth in turn is not formless matter, but matter to which the forms dryness and weight give particularity and distinctiveness. (The general argument here is borrowed from Plotinus v, 9, 3; cf. ii, 5, 1 ff.) So without form nothing can be said to be. In the case of divine substance, we speak of form without any matter, and because there is no composition of separate elements in combination, the divine substance is one and is what it is (*est id quod est*). Its unity and its being coincide; it is itself. Earthly man, however, is composite, consisting of body and soul, and is neither body nor soul in separation from each other. Earthly man is therefore not what he truly is, *id quod est*.

Here Boethius' phrase *id quod est* is used not, as in the third tractate, to express existence in antithesis to essence. The fluctuation in terminology, however, may reflect a certain lack of clarity in the argument as a whole. Boethius does not show how God as pure form is distinguished from other forms in which there is no material element. As in Augustine's arguments for the existence of God, the thrust is towards the establishment of an immaterial or 'spiritual' world of concepts. But among these concepts is there something special about the idea of God? In a Platonic scheme all forms have being apart from matter. In an Aristotelian framework, on the other hand, universals have being solely as instantiated in the particulars that compose them, which is the position Boethius has occupied both in his second commentary on Porphyry and in the fifth tractate. There is a certain hesitancy and mistiness in the argument which is related to the ambiguity of Boethius' relationship to Plato and Aristotle.

Boethius continues his argument by denying that in the supreme One there is number. This is Plotinus' doctrine (vi, 6, 9; echoed in Ambrose, *De fide* i, 2, 19). God is not the first in a series of numbers. Number belongs to the particular, says Plotinus (vi, 9, 2). Moreover, the divine substance cannot be substrate of anything, as Boethius has already observed in the fifth tractate. Humanity, though an immaterial form, is a substrate for accidents but that is because matter is attached to it. No form without matter can be a substrate. If there is form 'in matter', it is an image, not form (cf. Plotinus, ii, 6, 3, 18).

Accordingly, Boethius concludes that in God there is no

difference, no plurality, no multiplicity (because in God there are no accidents) and therefore no number. Number rests on a diversity of substrates, whereas in God there is unity alone. 'Number has two distinct senses, that by which we count, and the objects which we count.' The identical distinction occurs in Proclus' commentary on the *Parmenides*, 1188, 5–7.

From Aristotle it is familiar doctrine that if we use three synonyms for the same object, we speak of one object, not three; e.g. a sword remains one entity even if it is referred to as a blade or brand. Boethius has used the same illustration to make the same point in his first commentary on Porphyry (92, 13) and in his second commentary on *Interpretation* (ii, 56). That this is a school convention is clear from Simplicius on the *Categories* (38, 26) or Philoponus (CAG XIII, 1, 15, 2; *PG* 94, 753B).

Accordingly, to say God the Father, God the Son, and God the Holy Spirit does not for Catholics result in a plural number; only for Arians. Father, Son, and Spirit are the same (*idem*), yet not individually identical (*ipse*). At least Catholics will not concede that the Father is one and the same (*ipse*) with the Son. This formula *et ipse et idem*, or *idem non ipse*, is already anticipated by Marius Victorinus in his anti-Arian work (i, 41, 20 ff.; 54, 14; 59, 7; ii, 3, 42–4; iii, 17, 19–22; iv, 32, 4 ed. Henry and Hadot). Boethius' task is to discover a possible way to interpret it.

First of all he sets down a principle familiar from the pages of Plotinus (v, 5, 10; vi, 2, 3, 7) that the ten categories apply to the realm of sensible things, not the supra-sensible realm of Forms. Plotinus' proposition is regarded as a basic datum by Augustine in the *Confessions* (vi, 16, 28–9) and *De trinitate* (v, 8, 9); and it is also found in Proclus (*In Parm.* 1192, 1 ff.). The ten categories cannot, then, provide a system of classification of pigeon-holing statements about God. For instance, relation cannot be predicated of God, as Proclus also holds (*In Parm.* book vii, p. 45 Klibansky). Can even substance itself be predicated of him? God transcends substance. Moreover in God there are no accidents. In him to be and to be just or great are one and the same. Categories which apply in a divided way to things in this world of sense appear united in God. This principle is familiar to Iamblichus (*De myst.* i, 3) and to

Proclus (*In Tim.* i, 352, 17; *Decem Dub.* i, 3–4). Man is what he happens to be because of accidents, and therefore is not substance as such. This last remark echoes Aristotle's *Metaphysics* (H 3, 1043b 2–4) where he says that, because man is a composite being, 'to be man' and 'man' are distinct things. For Boethius the categories are delicate tools to handle, even when restricted to discourse of things in the world of sense-experience. In particular it is necessary to distinguish between those categories which show what a thing (*res*) is and those which indicate the external circumstances; that is, one must distinguish predications *secundum rem* and accidents *secundum rem*.

This last distinction is explained in the first book of Boethius' commentary on the *Categories* (i, 175D ff.), where he observes that it is one thing to say of a man that he is animal, another to say he is white.

But when talking of God, there are no accidents, and all predication concerns substance.

Boethius anticipates a theme of the *Consolation of Philosophy* (ii, 7, 17 (60)) that between infinite and finite there can never be any comparison.

To predicate place (*ubi*) of man is not to speak of a property he permanently possesses, but to relate him to other sources of information. To say God is everywhere does not mean that he is in every place you care to specify. God cannot be localized at all. We mean rather that every place is present for him to contain, even though he himself cannot be contained in any place. This is fully shared Neoplatonic and Christian doctrine which can be seen in Plotinus (i, 11, 9–10; iii, 9, 3; v, 5, 9; vi, 4, 3), Porphyry (*Sent.* 31), Augustine (*Conf.* i, 3, 3; etc.), and Fulgentius (*De incarn.* 8, PL 65, 577D).

Similarly with time, to say of a man that he came yesterday does not tell one anything essential about him. But to say of God that he always is means that he is present alike to past, present, and future; to him all is now. The philosophers affirm the everlastingness of the visible heaven and of other deathless bodies. But this implies the unceasing successiveness of time, perpetuity, or 'sempiternity'. The Now of God signifies eternity, which is other than everlastingness.

This distinction reappears to play a crucial role in the argument of the last book of the *Consolation* (v, 6). It is frequently found in Proclus (e.g. *In Tim.* i, 238, 15 ff.; 277, 30 ff.) and his school (e.g. Simplicius, *In Phys.* 1154–5 Diels). Boethius has already used the vocabulary of sempiternity in his second commentary on *Interpretation* (ii, 412, 414). Proclus (*In Parm.* 1213, 17 ff.) scathingly criticizes natural philosophers who take it for granted that eternity must mean endless time and imagine that all things are in time and space; which the One altogether transcends.

It is the same with 'having' (or condition) and 'doing' (activity). When we say of a man, 'He is running clothed', or of God that 'Possessing all things he rules', we are not referring to anything essential (*quod est esse*). Moreover, to God the categories of situation and passivity cannot apply.

Relation, however, occupies a distinctive place in Aristotle's list, since it can say something of ontological significance. The colour of a thing is an accident, i.e. to change or suppress the colour is not to destroy the thing. But in a master-slave relationship, take away the slave, and the master ceases to be *dominus*. Predication of relationship neither adds to nor subtracts from the essential object. It implies some comparison, which may, however, be not only with something other than the object but also with itself. 'Right' and 'left' depend on the side of a man to which you stand; you make no change in the man's essence by variation.

Father and Son are relational terms. ('God', as Boethius has already said, is not.) When speaking of the Holy Trinity, if there were no distinction other than that of relation, the predication of relation would not itself imply otherness as an objective fact (*alteritas rerum*). Yet it can imply an otherness of 'persons' (*alteritas personarum*) if in some way this language is permissible to interpret terms which we can hardly understand. It is an axiomatic rule that distinctions between incorporeal entities are not differences of space. (This has already been said in the third tractate, and may be found in e.g. Plotinus, vi, 9, 8; Augustine, *City of God* ix, 17; or Proclus, *El. Th.* 176.) Nor may we say that an accident is added to God to enable him to become 'Father', since to him the generation of the Son is substantial, even though the term 'Father' is only relative. The unity of the Trinity is expressed by the Church in the proposition that God the Son proceeded from God the Father, and the Holy Spirit from both. (Boethius has the *Filioque*, as in the fourth tractate.) There is no spatial separation to put one here, one there, and one somewhere else. There are no differentiae to distinguish God from God. Nothing but God can be begotten of God.

Boethius' reserve towards the ecclesiastical usage of the term 'Person' is very Augustinian (as in *De trin.* v, 9, 10 etc.). Here and in the fifth tractate he accepts the word as the traditional way in which orthodox Christians talk. But the word's precise meaning is hard to elucidate. The term originally entered theology through Tertullian's attempt to explain the distinctions in God signified by the words Father, Son, and Holy Spirit. Now this word has itself become a problem that needs to be explained. Western theology would one day find itself treating the word 'transubstantiation' in a similar way; that is, a word introduced to diminish a difficulty becomes in time the independent source of other problems. For Boethius the word 'Persons' may cast little light. But the relational terms express the 'numerositas trinitatis'. As Augustine once expresses it (*De trin.* vii, 6, 12), all plural verbs are used of the Trinity only of relatives, not of the divine substance. The unity is above all secured by the absence of any difference of substance or operation. (*Operatio* has been an established word in the discussion of Trinitarian theology since Hilary of Poitiers.) That which makes the Trinity plural is relation; but this has to be formulated in each case singly and separately, e.g. 'the Father is not the same as the Son', 'neither of them is the same as the Holy Spirit', 'yet they are one and the same God'.

With this problem of identity and difference Boethius comes back to Plato's *Parmenides* as the classic discussion of the problem. To say x and y are 'the same' may mean x and y have every property in common, but are distinguishable entities. In the Holy Trinity Boethius suggests that we have something 'like a relation of an identical to an identical'. In this transitory flux of earthly experience a comparison for this cannot be found. Our difficulty is that we are tied down by our pictorializing tendency, and what we grasp in this field can be approached only by 'simple intellect', by which Boethius means pure mind emancipated from body entirely.

Augustine, who can be a little kinder to 'imagination' than Boethius (e.g. *De trin.* viii, 4, 7), also utters similar warnings: one must purge the mind of size, space, and all bodily images (vii, 6, 12), which for us is extremely difficult to achieve (viii, 2, 3; 4, 7; ix, 6, 10–7, 12; especially x, 8, 11).

Boethius concludes his tractate by asking for Symmachus' authoritative verdict on his efforts. The doctrine of the Holy Trinity stands on the wholly firm judgement of faith without need of any help (*sponte*), but this does not mean that suitable arguments can offer no help to the understanding.

Boethius' main arguments concerning identity and difference find parallels in Proclus' commentary on the *Parmenides* (e.g. 1172, 39–1173, 7; 1193, 26 ff.) and other late Platonists. In his commentary on the *Categories* (169) Simplicius inquires what relation we may have to God. It is relation, not unity, since we are not of one *ousia* with him. But the relation is a reality, a *hypostasis*. Some logicians deny that relation is a hypostasis, but they forget that identity and difference in entities that transcend our capacity of utterance are matters of relation. To speak of relation is not, however, to lapse into relativism. The school of Proclus as represented by Ammonius (*In Categ.* 66, 21 ff.) denies the contention of Protagoras that in such matters everyone is right, just as some like honey and some do not. The late Platonists show themselves anxious to see relation as affirming something objective, and never more so than when they write of the development of the very first entities of the hierarchy of being. Proclus (*In Parm.* 937, 10) writes that 'what is relation in the case of earthly entities, is identity in the transcendent realm.'

Boethius' juxtaposition of Neoplatonic logic and Christian theology rests on a two-source view of truth. Revelation and reason are seen as parallel ways of discerning reality, and in this respect Boethius diverges in some degree from Augustine for whom Christ is the highest reason of all things, and all knowledge is illumination from God. Boethius is less sanguine than Augustine (or at least than the young Augustine) about the capacity of the divinely illuminated reason to attain to adequate statements about God. In the *Consolation of Philosophy* (v m. 3) he is ready to envisage the parallel affirmation of two truths which reason cannot reconcile.

It will have become evident that Boethius passes the more easily into a two-source view of truth because, although a Platonist and a pupil of Proclus, his central philosophical concern remains in the field of logic, of which Aristotle is his supreme master—the Organon, the *Physics*, the *Metaphysics* are all-pervasive influences on his mind and method. Whether intentionally or not, Proclus' vast Platonic scheme of metaphysical speculation in effect provides a competing alternative to Christian theology, offering a rival account of nature, man, and the gods, which is intended to be exhaustive and to leave no gap through which supplements and correctives can be infiltrated. Proclus' achievement certainly seemed massive to his contemporaries, whether Christian or not: to his pupils Ammonius and Marinus; to the masterful Greek of unknown name and elusive milieu who incorporated much of Proclus' speculative theology within a Christian scheme and published it under the name of Dionysius the Areopagite; to Boethius in the West, who, like his contemporary Dionysius, sifts his material and does not take over everything Proclus has to say. The mythological jungle of pagan gnosticism that characterises the later books of Proclus' *Platonic Theology* is discarded by both Dionysius and Boethius. It was not easy to see there usable techniques of logic and rationality, and Boethius does not reproduce it. He is soaked in Neoplatonism, but does not incorporate into his writings those features of Platonism which Proclus fills out with aggressively polytheistic symbols.

What Boethius most likes in Proclus seems to be the domestication of Aristotelian logic within the Platonic framework. The commentaries on the *Timaeus* and *Parmenides* contained much that Boethius felt to be true, and therefore essential to his scheme of thinking. Neoplatonic logic, especially in the discussion of the categories, of equality, identity, and difference, is turned to serve the cause of Christian reflection on the being of God. Moreover, the Christian parabola of creation, fall, redemption, and ultimate restoration is in principle capable of being reconciled with a theme dear to the heart of Proclus, namely, that of the emergence from the One of that which, having become other than its source, then returns to whence it came. This cycle of original being, emergence to otherness, and then reversion to identity, is latent in the structure of the

Consolation itself. Hence it is no accident that in the *Consolation* he can state an exclusively Neoplatonic doctrine of redemption, which is nevertheless capable of being read in a Christian sense with the minimum of force to the text. Boethius is unlikely to have achieved this by chance or without careful thought. The Christianising reading of the *Consolation* is one that Boethius himself makes possible by the way in which he writes the book.

V
EVIL, FREEDOM, AND PROVIDENCE

SINCE the Renaissance, and especially since the scientific revolution of the seventeenth century altered our understanding of the nature and structure of our environment, Boethius has come to seem a rather lonely and forgotten foreigner in a world grown strange. Yet something of that isolation belongs to him even during his lifetime, and never more so than in the near dereliction of the imprisonment during which he wrote the *Consolation of Philosophy*.[1] By common consent this remains one of the high masterpieces of European literature, translated since early mediaeval times into many languages; a work whose English translators alone include King Alfred, Geoffrey Chaucer, and Queen Elizabeth I; a dominant force (with Thomas Aquinas) in the making of Dante's mind. The *Consolation* is the work of a refined humanist scholar with a richly stocked memory, delighting in lyrical poetry and elegant prose, fascinated by logical problems almost to the point of obsession. In Theoderic's prison at Pavia he knew that his time was limited (iv, 6, 5), but he evidently had more than sufficient leisure to produce polished composition and a sophisticated structure. The work has a Virgilian quality in being almost a mosaic of subtle literary allusions. Joachim Gruber's commentary (1978) marks a signal advance in the identification of his literary echoes, but also makes it clear that he is not transcribing sources. This is not a man composing with a library of books open before him, but a very well-read mind which can recall a phrase from here or from there at will. His Latin is densely packed with concentrated argument; and the argument is carried on from the prose sections into the poems which he inserts, he says (iv, 6, 57), with the intention of lightening the reader's task with a difficult subject. The poems normally have subtle links with the prose sections that precede or follow them.

The method of mixing prose and verse had been practised by

Martianus Capella and by Ennodius. The style was associated with the Greek, Menippos of Gadara in the third century BC, whose work is lost. But something of its nature can be deduced from Lucian of Samosata and from remnants of Varro's 'Menippean Satires'. A light touch is deliberately employed with a deeply serious purpose. Jerome (*Vir. ill.* 111) mentions an otherwise unknown Christian named Acilius Severus who composed an autobiography, with the Greek title *hodoiporikon* or 'travel-book', cast in both prose and verse. Ausonius and Sidonius Apollinaris composed letters in the prosimetric form. It is probable that on Boethius the greatest influence is that of Martianus Capella, since his work also decribes a kind of intellectual pilgrimage ending in heaven.

Among the writings that have been produced by men and women in prison awaiting the execution of a death sentence under tyranny, the *Consolation* holds a place of lasting preeminence, partly because of the two grand problems of innocent suffering and the reconciliation of divine providence with human freedom with which it deals, and partly because in this profoundly religious book there is an evidently conscious refusal to say anything distinctively Christian. The book is a work of natural, not of revealed, theology, and strives after a universal appeal to every man. Boethius' subject is the consolation not of theology but of philosophy. Throughout his life philosophy, and especially dialectic, has been the ruling passion of his mind. Now at the supreme crisis he asks what it may have to say to him, especially concerning providence and evil. The question of providence was a topic much discussed in the late Platonic schools. Boethius declares that he had studied the subject deeply (v, 4, 1), a statement which answers the query of many rapid readers who wonder whether so elaborate and sophisticated a book could really have been composed in custody. We have already seen that his family had the resources to persuade his guardians to allow him a few books and papers should he have needed anything. The ground for his labours had already been prepared. The Alexandrian Platonist Hierocles had written at some length on the subject, while Proclus addresses himself to the issue both in his commentary on the *Republic* and in his three opuscula concerning providence. There is good reason to think these works familiar

The lady Philosophy

The *Consolation of Philosophy* begins in a low minor key with a sad poem echoing Ovid's *Tristia* and *Letters from Pontus*. A writer who recalls having once written cheerful verses (an allusion perhaps to the bucolic poem recorded among Boethius' works by Cassiodorus in the Anecdoton Holderi) is now compelled at the bidding of the Muses to embark on tearful songs of self-pity. But then a dreamlike vision follows in the ensuing prose section (a dream which is the ancestor of many mediaeval dream-poems). The lady Philosophy appears to comfort him. She has burning eyes; a face old yet fresh and young; her height, too, varying in appearance, at one moment of normal human size, but then reaching up to and passing through the very heavens. Moreover, her dress woven with her own hands (like Athene's *peplos* in *Iliad* 5, 734, a text on whose symbolism late Platonists liked to meditate)[2] is of fine thread and decorated with two Greek letters, Pi below, Theta above, linked by ascending steps. This dress has been roughly torn by violent hands.

The Theta on Philosophy's dress may have been suggested to Boethius by a Theta on his own.[3] The Carolingian theologian Prudentius of Troyes, in an attack on John the Scot's dangerous treatise on divine predestination, prefixes to each censured excerpt from John a Greek Theta 'because some have used this letter to mark those condemned to death' (*PL* 115, 1012AB). Accordingly a prisoner on whom the death sentence had been decreed was required to wear regulation prison clothing marked with the initial letter of *thanatos*, intended either to increase his sense of humiliation or to safeguard the executioners from mistaken identity in their victim. An early allusion to the practice occurs in one of the epigrams of Martial (vii, 37, 2) which establishes the certainty that this was Roman custom with condemned criminals. It seems to follow, then, that if Boethius was in the 'condemned cell' and wearing some old torn sacking inscribed with a fateful Theta, he is likely to have been enduring more severe custody than the mild house arrest sometimes claimed for him on the presupposition that so elegant and urbane a work as the *Consolation* can hardly have emerged from a dank subterranean gaol. Certainly Boethius' freedom to write shows that he was not (or not yet) consigned to the worst of dungeons at Pavia. A text in Augustine's *Tractates on St. John's Gospel* (49, 9) attests the variety of treatment accorded to prisoners, not all being confined in rat-infested cellars. (For a modern analogy one might think of the gradually deteriorating conditions, through many months of imprisonment, inflicted by the Pakistan government on Zulfikar Ali Bhutto, culminating in his execution under sordid circumstances.) Boethius' father-in-law Symmachus was still *caput senatus*, though no doubt treading delicately, and had more than enough resources to provide the prison officers with douceurs to persuade them to allow the poor convict a few books and writing materials. The mere survival of the text of the *Consolation* (where the embittered scorn for Theoderic's government is unconcealed) proves that members of Boethius' family were allowed some access to him, or the work would no doubt have perished in the gruesome fires of the torture-chamber to which Boethius was to be compelled to make his way. The impression which the text is intended to convey is that he is writing under physical conditions of some discomfort. He is far from his beautifully furnished library with its ivory and glass décor, but his mind is filled with its contents (i, 5, 6, cf. i, 4, 3). He is encumbered with a heavy chain round his neck (i m. 2, 24–7). This, however, is primarily a symbol of his earth-bound condition. It may be literal as well as symbolic; one cannot be sure, for his physical prison is simultaneously the counterpart of the Platonic prison of his soul from which he seeks liberation.

Philosophy's alphabetical symbols would be no mystery to an ancient reader. They represent practical and theoretical studies, that is the hierarchy of sciences already set out in Boethius' exegesis of Porphyry and again in scholastic form in his *De trinitate*, ascending through the inferior disciplines of moral philosophy, politics, and economics, up to the less practical, purer disciplines of natural sciences, mathematics, and theology. In a gesture strikingly paralleled in Augustine (above, p. 86) the lady Philosophy dismisses the Muses as lighthearted meretricious entertainers whose song and dance, as it were of the *commedia dell'arte*, are wholly lacking in sufficient seriousness to speak to the sick patient's condition. Let him look to Philosophy who has been his gentle nurse since his youth and who, through the books in his library, has taught him both human and divine things, the mysteries of the stars and the secrets of nature. With her he suffers in good company. For Philosophy has had its martyrs: Socrates, Anaxagoras, and Zeno of Elea among the Greeks; Canius, Seneca, and Soranus among the Latins. Indeed Boethius' philosophical studies have been made the ground for the accusation against him of *maleficium*, sorcery, or *sacrilegium*, in the pursuit of his ambitions.

Most of the first book consists of Boethius' political apologia; a long protestation of innocence written with contempt both for Theoderic's barbarism and for the cowardice of his fellow senators. But once he has all that off his chest, the lady Philosophy has stern rebuke to offer him. He has forgotten his true self altogether. His citizenship is not in the realm of the many, subject to the changes and chances of political life, but in that of the One, the single ruler and king of a famous Homeric line which Aristotle cites in a theological context in the *Metaphysics*. Obedience to his justice is liberty. (Seneca says that 'obeying God is liberty', *Beata vita* 15, 7; and Augustine coins the phrase 'in his service is perfect freedom', *Quant. An.* 34, 78.) Nothing can exile Boethius from the kingdom of God except his own choice. But the emotional misery he is enduring suggests to Philosophy that his physical exile mirrors his spiritual exile. He has forgotten the nature and destiny of man. Merely to answer the question 'What is man?' with the Aristotelian definition 'a rational, mortal animal', is to disclose a loss of awareness of one's higher self and of the guiding hand of providence in ordering the world. To know oneself in this sense is to be free from all the peaks and troughs of emotion, to drive out both joy and fear, hope and grief, and to see the path of truth in a clear light. Philosophy wants to recall him to what he has learnt from Plato's *Parmenides* about abstract being (i, 1, 10), to liberate him from his attachment to this world, and to make possible his return to God who is true being and goodness. But his present 'lethargic' condition means that the healing drugs have to be applied gradually. He cannot take too much medication all at once; a principle familiar to ancient medicine (as in Galen XII, 590 Kühn) which had long been applied by moralists to the therapy of the soul, as in Seneca, *Consolatio ad Helviam* 1, 2, or in the excerpt from Origen's Exodus commentary in *Philocalia* 27, 4–5.

The first book of the *Consolation* is limited, then, to diagnosis by his gentle physician. Consolation proper begins with the second book. The argument, however, stands less in the tradition of ancient consolation literature than in that of the *Protrepticus* or exhortation to philosophical conversion. It gradually ascends from a Stoic moralism to a Platonic metaphysical vision of the divine ordering of an apparently chaotic world. Book ii is almost wholly Stoic in its inspiration, with many parallels in Seneca and in the *Consolation to Apollonius* among the works of Plutarch. Cicero's *Tusculans* are also much used.

From Stoic moralism to Platonic transcendence

The Platonists and the Stoics were the two philosophical schools of ancient Greece in which there was a serious defence of belief in providence, though the two schools undertook their defences from very different premises. For the Stoics there is no real distinction between providence and fate and the inexorable chain of causation. The cosmos rolls on its everlasting way as an interlocking, ineluctable pattern of cause and effect. Human freedom is largely an illusion of grandeur, for in principle it is scarcely distinguishable from animal instinct, though the Stoics vigorously (and to their critics unconvincingly) protested their belief in the freedom of the will. What they meant by this is an inward process of personal psychotherapy, in which each individual's task is to learn to bear himself nobly before the blows of outrageous fortune, to conduct himself with a strong sense of public duty however adverse the circumstances, and to accept the benefits of nature with gratitude. In a world of complex diversity everything has its place. Even bedbugs may have the beneficial effect of preventing one from the enervating effects of oversleeping.

The Platonists, on the other hand, began quite at the

opposite end of the cosmic scale, namely with the transcendence of the divine realm. God must be exempted from the least responsibility for evil. Since the cosmos is held to mirror the ideal noetic realm above, some explanation is required for the fact that human experience of this cosmos produces pain and dissatisfaction. The Platonists offered a series of explanations: (a) evil is rooted in a misuse of free choice; (b) 'evil' is merely a relative term for a defect of goodness, for as one descends the hierarchy of being, one also descends in degrees of the good; (c) evil inheres in matter, the very principle of multiplicity and so also of flux and change. Under different forms and variations Platonic philosophers expanded on these themes, and all three explanations find a place somewhere in Boethius' theodicy.

Accordingly, the second book and the first sections of the third operate with Stoic themes in which comfort is discovered by reconciling onself to a world of determined inevitability 'Do not try to change things, but adapt yourself to the way things are', said the moralist Teles (p. 9, 8 f. Hense). 'If our free wills could change the world, each of us would need his own private world; we all desire different things, so the only power we possess is to adapt ourselves', says the Platonist Hierocles (*de Providentia*, in Photius, *Bibliotheca* 251, 465a 4 ff.). We have to take the rough with the smooth. Farmers have bad as well as good years, sailors stormy as well as calm seas. One cannot reasonably complain if that deceitful and fickle lady Fortune turns her wheel with her well-known caprice, and suddenly removes power and affluence (a reflection much like Seneca, *ep.* 107, 7 f.).

In the past Boethius has done pretty well with Fortune: taken into Symmachus' household when he lost his father, married to a chaste wife, nobly honoured by the nomination of his young sons to be consuls, able to display his munificence to the populace at the circus. He has been a remarkably lucky man. And is he not tempted to exaggerate the awfulness of his situation? Hitherto his family remains untouched. Symmachus himself, most precious glory of the human race, is unmolested so far. (Boethius is evidently aware that a threat is very possible.) Inverting a damnatory Ciceronian phrase from *Pro Cluentio* 72, Boethius praises his father-in-law as 'a man wholly made of wisdom and virtue'. He has been taken far from home, but his place of exile is home to those who normally live there (perhaps echoing Seneca, *ep.* 24, 17). But then Boethius turns upon himself with the realization that there is no crumb of comfort in looking back on a distinguished past that is now for ever lost. Echoing a phrase from Augustine's *Confessions* (x, 21, 30 'tristis gaudium pristinum recolo'), he laments that the worst of all miseries is to remember past happiness now irrecoverable (ii, 4, 1). Alas, the human condition is that all such benefits hang by a thin thread. The very best of good fortune cannot be free of anxiety. No man is so content as to be without some cause of irritation or worry. Those who have most end up by desiring the satisfaction of ever more insatiable needs. The truth is that nothing is miserable unless thinking makes it so. Happiness should not be sought in any external circumstances. One must learn to be self-possessed ('sui iuris', i m. 4, 16 from Cicero, *ep. ad Brut.* 24, 4), self-contained ('sui compos', ii, 4, 23; used of God in v, 6, 8). The comfort of one's body is a gift of chance. Only the soul is immortal, as those have known who have sought their happiness through sufferings and pain (ii, 4, 29; possibly but in no way necessarily, a reference to Christian martyrs). One has to build one's house upon the rock (ii, m. 4). This world's values are merely relative. What is prized by one nation is censured by others. Life is brief but dignity is even more shortlived. High office confers no moral virtue on the holder and is extremely dangerous to society when united with vice. The praetorship was once an office of high standing, but is now empty and is felt to be a heavy burden by the senators who have to hold it, while the 'prefect of the annona', once of supreme distinction but now fallen to be a mere distributor of food in the capital (Cassiodorus, *Variae* vi, 18, 1), has become the lowest form of senatorial life. Nothing is more precarious than posts of high honour. To hold them is like living under the suspended sword of Damocles (so already Cicero, *Tusc.* v, 21, 61–2). Remember Seneca offered a choice of suicides by Nero; or Papinian, prince of jurists, butchered by Caracalla (iii, 5). When the time comes for you to fall they cannot even allow you quietly to resign and retire and to surrender your wealth. Both past and very recent history offer many instances of kings whose felicity has changed to calamity (iii, 5, 2 'plena exemplorum vetustas' echoing Cicero, *Pro Archia* 14).

Moreover, honour's relative status is proved by its local character. A grandee of one place is a nobody somewhere else. Boethius refers to his study in Ptolemy and the astronomical geography of Macrobius' commentary on *Scipio's Dream*, which has taught him what diversity there is in the regions of the inhabited world. Great officers of state are of no account at all once they step outside the Roman world.

And what appalling indignities have to be endured by the seeker after office! If he is to gain support, he must cultivate people he dislikes or even despises, knowing they will be ready to betray him whenever it suits them. None can hurt more than someone who was once your familiar friend. At least by falling into serious trouble Boethius has the advantage of having quickly discovered who his real friends are. They are remarkably few.

When one is suffering innocently, it is a discipline teaching one how independent one has to be of the opinion of the multitude. If one's praise is merited, popular estimation is no true guide to one's value and adds nothing to a wise man who is a better judge of his own merits. (The remark recalls Aristotle's dry observation that the pleasure given to a wise man by an honour is to see that others have reached a conclusion long apparent to himself.) The moral virtue in innocent suffering is even greater if other people do not realize one is innocent (i, 4, 33). Under insults a true philosopher should remain silent. He may even forfeit his title to be a true philosopher if he speaks about his patience under abuse (ii, 7, 20); a Boethian dictum whence has sprung the proverbial saying 'had you kept silent, you would have remained a philosopher', *si tacuisses, philosophus mansisses*. Boethius' words may call to mind not only a saying of Epictetus (iv, 8, 15 ff.) but also the preface to the *Contra Celsum* where Origen thinks the silence of Jesus before mocking accusers a model for wise Christians to follow.

In any event the frailties of life apply to all. Rich men too feel the cold and will bleed if pricked. Death is the great equalizer (ii m. 7).

Adversity is paradoxically better for one's character than prosperity (ii, 8, 3). The supreme duty is to keep a clear conscience. That is to be liberated from the bonds of this earthly prison. The sentiment strikingly combines Stoic and Platonic themes (ii, 7, 23).

The concluding poem of the second book (ii m. 8) is a fine hymn of praise to the love that binds together the cosmos to prevent its disintegration. The various races, married couples, all manner of incompatibilities are held together by this cosmic force. How happy men would be if only the love by which the stars are ruled could reign in their hearts:

> O felix hominum genus
> Si vestros animos amor
> Quo caelum regitur regat.

The providential equilibrium of the diverse elements of the world, the *pugnantia semina* (which Boethius probably borrows from Martianus Capella i, 1, 3), is a characteristic Stoic theme which recurs elsewhere in other verse sections of the *Consolation* (iii, m. 2, 1–5; iv m. 6, 4–5).[4] Latin poets before Boethius had rhapsodized on the subject of the love manifest in the bonds averting cosmic catastrophe (Lucan iv, 191 'sacer orbis amor'). In Paulinus of Nola (poem 27) the ties of intimate friendship reflect those which cement the entire universe together. From Posidonius onwards in the first century BC, this defence of providential order had ceased to be distinctively Stoic property, and was absorbed by Platonists. It can be seen in Apuleius. Accordingly the concluding poem of the second book is initiating the 'change of gear' which in the third book begins to move outside the Stoic conventions into the sketching of a Platonic metaphysic.

The first prose section of book iii announces Boethius' readiness for stronger medicines, bitter to taste, sweet once swallowed. But the shift is not explicit until the poem O *qui perpetua* (iii m. 9) which is both the literary climax of the *Consolation* and a major turning point in its argument. The first sections of the third book recapitulate Stoic arguments of the type predominant in the second book. Men seek happiness in external things: in riches, power, fame, pleasure, family ties, above all in friendship, which is a matter not of luck but of moral virtue. In this variety of goals all men agree in seeking what they believe to be their good. Even though we human beings are so earthbound, we nevertheless have some dim vision of our origin and therefore of our true end. But we mistake where happiness lies. Riches can never satisfy the avaricious; and the wealthy are miserable surrounded by envious people wishing to relieve them of their money so that they are less, not more independent. He who needs a bodyguard is hardly a free man (iii, 5). 'Nobility' means being praised not for your own merits but for those of your ancestors. Its one moral value is to impress you with a sense of obligation to live up to their ancient virtue (iii, 6, 9, echoing Aristotle, *Rhet.* ii, 15, 1390b 16 ff., and frg. 92 Rose, p. 58 Ross, Stobaeus iv, 29, 25). There is a proper pleasure in family life. But children can inflict such torment as to rob you of all happiness. It is impossible to locate the good in physical pleasures or in athleticism or in a beautiful body. Boethius cites a saying of Aristotle that to one gifted with second sight like Lynceus the beauty of Alcibiades would only contrast with the vileness within. A close parallel in Iamblichus' *Protrepticus* (p. 47 Pistelli) proves that directly or indirectly Boethius is drawing on Aristotle's *Protrepticus*, an exhortation to the study of philosophy extant only in fragmentary quotations. The correspondence between Boethius and Iamblichus does not extend further, and therefore can be no basis for flimsy hypotheses about a wider indebtedness to Aristotle's lost work.

Boethius now begins to perceive 'through a narrow crack' (cf. iv, 4, 40) where the lady Philosophy is leading him. 'But I would prefer to learn more plainly from you' (reminiscent of *Phaedrus* 263a). In seeking happiness man wants sufficiency, power, fame, respect, pleasure; he discovers that these goods cannot be had separately, but only as a single package, as one substance (cf. Plato, *Protagoras* 329cd) which is extremely rare. The actual happiness men know is marked by acute imperfections and beset by transitoriness and mortality. The prose section (iii, 9) concludes with a direct reference to Plato's *Timaeus* which teaches (27c) that in even the least matter we do well to ask for God's help. This explicit mention of the *Timaeus* prepares the way for the masterly poem summarizing the doctrines of the first part of this Platonic dialogue. Nothing in it has a correspondence with the second half, but that was not available to the West in Latin. Proclus' commentary on the

O qui perpetua

In the 38 hexameters of *O qui perpetua* Boethius fashioned an exquisite poem of petition to the Creator. It is a nodal point in the work as a whole, and Boethius knew it. An acute observation in the recent commentary by Joachim Gruber (1978) has noted that the various metres of the poems in the *Consolation* are grouped in an ordered and symmetrical structure round *O qui perpetua* which occupies a central position. This shows, in passing, that there is no good reason to embrace speculations that something is likely to have been lost at the end of the last book.

Boethius' ecstatic hymn is reminiscent of the Neoplatonic hymns on cosmic theology characteristic of Synesius and Proclus. The ideas of the hymn are derived both from Plato and from Proclus' commentary. This was established by Klingner (1921). The Creator, himself at rest, is cause of motion to everything (Proclus, *In Tim.* i, 396, 24 f., a theme going back to Aristotle's *Metaphysics*). Boethius will repeat this in prose at iii, 12, 37. God is moved to create by his own goodness (*Tim.* 29e), not by any external cause. In creating he realized a heavenly pattern, forming the cosmos in beauty and perfection (30b). Taking a theme also expounded in his *Institutio musica* (i, 2) Boethius says that God binds the world's elements together on mathematical principles, 'by numbers' (*Tim.* 31c 'analogia', or proportion). Thus he keeps the equilibrium of cold and hot, dry and wet (31bc). So also he binds the world-soul in its harmonious parts (*per consona membra*) and gives it a threefold structure (35ab; 37a), set in the middle of the cosmos (36e) to move all things (as Plato's *Laws* 896e, *Phaedrus* 245c). Proclus (*In Tim.* ii, 197, 16) says that the Creator 'divides the Soul among the various parts, fits together the diverse elements and makes them consonant with one another'.

This divided Soul is split into two, each part to move in a circle (*Tim.* 36bc) so as to return upon itself—a theme very dear to Proclus (e.g. *In Tim.* ii, 247–9). The Soul encircles a yet deeper mind (much as Proclus, *In Tim.* i, 403, 3 'soul dances round mind'), and so moves the heaven in a similar circle. From the mixture of the world-soul Plato's Creator brings forth (human) souls and inferior living beings (*Tim.* 41d expounded by Proclus iii, 246, 29 ff.). These souls are provided with 'light chariots' (41e), i.e. the astral vehicles of Neoplatonic speculation as stimulated by the Chaldean Oracles and perhaps also by Aristotle, *Gen. anim.* 736b 27 ff., which linked soul and body through a semi-material, semi-immaterial, starry pneuma.

Distributed like seed in heaven and earth (42d), the souls are then turned back by God towards himself (Proclus iii, 289, 29 ff.), like creatures attracted by fire.

The last seven lines of the poem sum up Boethius' petition.

Da pater augustam menti conscendere sedem. His language echoes the fourth-century poet Tiberianus (*da pater augustas ut possim noscere causas*, iv, 28) and perhaps Martianus Capella ii, 193 (*da pater aetherios mentis conscendere coetus*), but modified by a Vergilian reminiscence from *Georgic* iv, 228, 'sedem augustam'.

So he may discern the source of the Good if he now fixes his gaze on God and if the heavy cloudiness of the earthly body is dispelled. God is the clear heaven, a haven of rest to the devout. 'To see you is our end. You are our beginning, charioteer, leader, pathway, goal' (*Principium, vector, dux, semita, terminus idem*). The accumulation of substantives, which recalls the closing lines of *De fide catholica* (*delectatio, cibus, opus, laus*), is a characteristic mark of ancient hymns of praise, which finds echoes in the New Testament itself (e.g. John xiv, 6; xiii, 13). 'Deus unus et idem' is Augustinian (*City of God* vii, 9). Tiberianus iv, 7 f. has 'tu primus et idem postremus mediusque simul.'

Degrees of perfection: the quest for the One

A fragment of Aristotle's lost work 'On Philosophy' quoted by Simplicius (*In de Caelo* 288, 28–289, 15 = frg. 16 Rose = pp. 84–5 Ross) argues from the degrees of perfection in things up to God as the highest being we can think. A similar 'Anselmian' argument was deployed by Platonists known to Augustine (*City of God* viii, 6). So Boethius goes on to argue that the awareness of imperfection demonstrates the existence of an absolute perfection in comparison with which it is seen to be imperfect. The imperfections of the world can be arranged in a graded hierarchy of goodness and power, and this ascent presupposes an ultimate goal. All men share the notion that the first principle of all things is good (so Boethius, *Perih.* ii, 42, 3–6; *opusc.* iii, 93). Nothing better than God can be conceived (*nihil deo melius excogitari queat*), a definition going back ultimately to Aristotle in the piece cited by Simplicius, first found in Latin in Seneca, and common in Augustine (e.g. *De moribus* ii, 11, 24). Only the perfect good can be at the summit of the hierarchy of goods. By 'God', therefore, we mean the perfection of both goodness and happiness, and goodness is of the essence of happiness (iii, 10). The argument works with the same axioms as those of the third tractate (above p. 203).

For Boethius' Platonic ontology this is a demonstration with mathematical force, carrying a corollary that a perfectly happy man participates in the being of God and in this sense can be said to become a god. Augustine would not have regarded such language as intolerable (above, p. 211).

Plotinus (i, 4, 6) says that happiness is found not in a piecemeal amassing of individually desired ends but in a unity. Boethius lays down that individual goods confer happiness only when experienced as a unity (iii, 11): This points to the truth that the supreme God is also the One. Hence a principal good desired by humans, animals, and even plants (for they flourish in the right habitat) is a wish to avert destruction and disintegration, that is the loss of unity. The will to subsist is the desire not to fall apart but to remain one. The argument appears in Proclus' commentary on the *Parmenides* (1199, 20 f.): 'Everything has an instinctive urge towards the One, and everything is what it is by a desire for the One.' A comparable point has been made by Boethius in his *Arithmetica* (i, 7). Accordingly we look for an infinite first cause which is a simple undivided whole, free of the limitation resulting from division.

Reminiscence: natural theology and the Bible

The next poem (iii m. 11) is highly Platonic. The mind (*mens profunda* as in *O qui perpetua*) in its quest for truth has to turn back on itself. The doctrine appears in Augustine, *Conf.* vii, 10, 16. The body weighing down the mind does not altogether obliterate all light or the seed of the truth. Hence Plato's inspired Muse taught that knowing is recovering the memory of what was once known but has become forgotten because of the mists of corporeal existence. On passing into prose once more, Boethius emphatically endorses the doctrine of reminiscence, a belief accepted by the young Augustine (*Solil.* ii, 20, 35) also; for the lady Philosophy has been recalling him to truths that his mind once knew: 'Platoni vehementer assentior' (iii, 12, 1). But instead of a development of the Platonic doctrine of the soul, the argument turns away to the central problem of divine providence. The diversity of the different elements in the world threatens disintegration. Somehow providence checks the centrifugal forces of destruction. 'Whatever holds everything together is what I mean by God' (iii, 12, 25). Accordingly by 'God' we mean not only the supreme good but also the supreme power, a power so great that it is irresistible and yet is gently exercised by an infinitely good wisdom. With a turn of phrase Boethius thinks singularly felicitous, the lady Philosophy declares that 'There is a highest good which rules all things firmly and gently disposes them' (*est igitur summum, inquit, bonum, quod regit cuncta fortiter suaviterque disponit*). Boethius at once tells the lady how delighted he is not only by her conclusion but by the very words she has found to express it—'haec ipsa verba quibus uteris'. Now at long last he is ashamed of the folly that had so exquisitely tortured him.

Why should Boethius take such pleasure in 'haec ipsa verba'? The only natural answer is that the words come from the eighth chapter of the Wisdom of Solomon (*adtingit enim a fine usque ad finem fortiter et disponit omnia suaviter*), a text that Augustine had occasionally found congenial, and which was to mould the words of the great Advent Antiphon *O Sapientia*, of whose liturgical use our earliest evidence comes from Amalarius of Metz in the ninth century, but as a text taken for granted as long established in western churches.[5] In the context of the *Consolation* the effect of Boethius' cry of pleasure at the very words is as if he were saying to Philosophy: 'Fancy you, of all people, knowing the Bible'. The point has an evidently direct bearing on the interpretation of the religious standpoint of the *Consolation* and on Boethius' disposition towards the Christian faith at the time of its composition in prison.

There are a number of other places in the *Consolation* where an allusion to a biblical text is possible. Only in the case just considered does it seem the one natural interpretation of Boethius' prose. The others are curiously tantalising possibilities. The poem iii m. 10 begins 'Huc omnes pariter venite capti/Quos fallax ligat improbis catenis . . . (*libido*)'—'Come all you who are bound captive by the wicked chains of earthly desire . . . ' It is more than a little reminiscent of Matt. xi, 28 f. 'Come to me, all you who are heavy laden . . . ' At iv, 1, 6 Philosophy likens good and evil men to precious and worthless vessels in a great house; this is distantly reminiscent of Rom. iv, 21 ff. and 2 Tim. ii, 20. According to i, 1, 9 the meretricious Muses choke the good harvest of reason with the thorns of passion. A reference to the parable of the sower looks possible (Matt. xiii, 22). In v, 3, 34 Boethius writes of God as *inaccessa lux*. Is it recalling the 'inaccessible light' of 1 Tim. vi, 16? Other allusions could be catalogued, but are less likely than those here cited. It is no doubt the case that if one reference is virtually certain, the probability of other conscious or unconscious reminiscences is much enhanced. Nevertheless, even if these allusions are correctly identified as recalling his reading of the Bible, it is significant that each is presented in so ambiguous a way that the allusion could be picked up only by a reader well acquainted with the New Testament. Moreover, the reference to the Wisdom of Solomon enforces a doctrine of natural theology, not revealed. There is nothing specifically Christian about the content of what is being maintained, even at the point where a citation of the Bible seems as good as certain.

The problem of evil

The argument of Philosophy continues that if God is supremely good and powerful, he is the ultimate source of being. Indeed he is being (*esse*), and the imperfections of the graded hierarchy of being leading down from him are also, as one descends the continuum, the successive deprivation both of being and of goodness. Evil is deficiency of being, and therefore strictly nothingness. At this point Boethius betrays a little anxiety that the lady Philosophy begins to play a verbal game with him, when she says that 'Evil is nothing, since God cannot do it, and there is nothing he cannot do' (iii, 12, 29). The doctrine of the non-being of evil is language closer to Augustine (e.g. *Confessions* vii, 12, 18) than to Plotinus or Proclus, for whom evil has nothing absolute about it, yet has some relative existence. The lady Philosophy vigorously denies that she is playing a verbal game. Her argument appeals to no external authority, but is a deduction from positions which are granted. It rests on the affirmation of the perfect self-sufficiency of God, expressed in a quotation from Parmenides (8, 43 Diels), important to the Neoplatonists because of its citation in Plato's *Sophist* 244e. This self-sufficient perfection, like a sphere, turns the moving circle of things while remaining unmoved itself. Despite the lady Philosophy's overmuch protesting, the ordinary reader will sympathise with Boethius' feeling that the argument has suddenly begun to become a little esoteric. Philosophy, however, is here announcing for the first time a theme which will soon be orchestrated more richly and fully. And Boethius should not wonder that the argument rests not on authority but on reasoned inferences from the nature of divine perfection. Plato's *Timaeus* 29b teaches that words ought to have an affinity for the objects to which they refer; a Platonic text which played a prominent part in the discussions designed to reconcile Aristotle's opinion that names are a matter of convention with Plato's that there is that in them which corresponds to reality and is therefore 'nature'. Boethius' second commentary on *Interpretation* (ii, 246, 21 ff.) refers to this debate, and there is also an echo in Ammonius (*CAG* IV, 5 p. 154, 16 ff.).

Perhaps because he is conscious that the argument has grown heavy, Boethius lightens the reader's burden by a poem on

Orpheus and Eurydice (iii m. 12). Like Orpheus Boethius has found that sad songs fail to assuage his grief. But unlike Orpheus he is determined not to look back in his upward ascent towards the supreme good. The verses move lightly from a phrase of Vergil's to another of Horace's or Seneca's, and the unphilosophical reader is grateful for the relief of Boethius' touching *fabula*. At the end he finds that the underworld visited by Orpheus has become merged with the cave of Plato's myth in the *Republic*.

The fourth book opens with a very respectful protest by Boethius. This insubstantial evil may be demonstrated by pure intellect, but it is experienced as a painful actuality and outrage by the sufferings of humanity. If providence is good and powerful, how can evil go unchecked and unpunished?

The answer is a mixture of Aristotelian and Platonic themes. All men seek whatever they believe to be good. What evil men seek is what they imagine to be good. But it is the mark of evil men that they cannot succeed in their aim of achieving happiness for which true goodness is an indispensable constituent. They suffer a diminution of their humanity, and fall to the level of beasts (iv, 3). A poem on the tormented heart of a tyrant (iv m. 2) looks as if Theoderic is in mind. The passage developing the idea that evil men are like wild animals is as near as Boethius approaches to the Platonic notion of transmigration into animal bodies, a notion which was accepted by Plotinus, but rejected by Porphyry and Proclus. Proclus' commentary on the *Timaeus* (iii, 295, 30) has language close to that of Boethius here.

The poem iv m. 2 pictures a dreamlike flight of the soul, borne by Platonic wings, to a circuit of the heavens, from the height of which petty tyrants seem remarkably trivial.

Much of the philosophical argument in the first sections of the fourth book hangs on Plato's *Gorgias*, especially 466b ff. Plato reasoned that wicked men must be of all men most miserable if they succeed in their endeavours. For them punishment is a source of purgation and therefore of happiness (472e). The justice of their penalty confers a good upon them. So hereafter there will be a judgement of souls with harsh penalties for some, purifying mercy for others. The allusion could be Christian, but in the context is most unlikely to be looking beyond Plato's *Gorgias* 525b. Hierocles has an exposition of the doctrine in his commentary on the Golden Verses of the Pythagoreans (xi, 39–40 cf. xiv, 6; also Proclus, *In Tim.* iii, 236, 27; *In rem pub.* ii, 339–40).

So far as the moral problem of evil is concerned, the argument of the *Consolation* reaches its climax with the exegesis of the *Gorgias*. But from the poem of iv m. 4 onwards a subtle shift in the language takes place. Words like 'fate' and 'chance' begin to occur, and with the prose section iv, 6 there is an explicit switch from the moral scandal of apparently unpunished wickedness to the tangled problem of destiny and free will.

The shift is expressly and emphatically marked by Boethius as beginning a fresh approach to his problem. This is an echo of Cicero, *De divin.* ii, 101. (Hermann Usener, of all people, was responsible for the suggestion that at this point Boethius simply switches from one Neoplatonic source to copying out another.) Reflection shows that in altering his ground Boethius is not evading issues. He has first argued, with the Stoics, that we are given the opportunity of deriving profound moral benefit to ourselves and to society from having to live out our lives under adverse and precarious conditions. He has then argued that evil as such is a negative thing, a privation of perfection, a frustrating failure to fulfil powers; but evil can never exist on its own apart from the good, or the pain and the frustration could not be present. Boethius is in effect saying that many of the evils which hurt are unavoidable because the world in which we live, a world of natural incompatibilities and limitations and imperfections, could not be what it is without them. But is there even a small area where evils result from the misuse of free choice? He has followed the *Gorgias* in the paradox that evil men can find the happiness they too seek not by achieving their wicked ends but only by accepting just punishment which for some is purgation. The notion of an acceptance of responsibility is thereby inserted by implication. But there remains the burning question of misused freedom as a cause of evil, and therefore of the reconciliation of freedom with belief in an omnipotent providence. Boethius is surely right to see that unless he can disentangle the problems of freedom and determinism he will have left many loose ends in his argument.

Providence and fate

The Neoplatonists from Plotinus onwards (*Enn.* iii, 3, 5, 14) distinguish between providence, which concerns the higher realm, and fate which is another name for the unalterable chain of cause and effect in this inferior and determined world. The theme is prominent in Calcidius' commentary on the *Timaeus* and in several other late Platonic philosophers. Accordingly Boethius proposes to make this distinction: to our inferior mind 'fate' describes that nexus of causation in the cosmos which operates immutably in indifference to our wills. How it works we do not exactly know. Perhaps, as some think, it operates through ministering divine spirits i.e. Platonic daemons; but Boethius avoids the word which Christian ears found offensive. The ministrations of 'daemons or angels' (either word being equally acceptable to a Neoplatonist) are mentioned by Proclus in his Commentary on the *Republic* (ii, 255, 19 ff. Kroll) and in his 'Ten Doubts concerning Providence' x, 62. Boethius also thinks fate may perhaps be the action of the world-soul or of the entire natural order or the consequence of control by the stars, a possibility countenanced in his second commentary on *Interpretation* (above, p. 162). Augustine has comparable reviews of the possible ways in which the order of the world is maintained (*City of God* v, 9; *De trinitate* iii, 4, 9).

Fate, therefore, is subordinate to providence. But some things under providence are above fate. Boethius compares this to a number of spheres which move round the same centre, where the inmost sphere is most nearly stationary, the outermost fast moving. So also that which is closest to the first divinity (*primae propinqua divinitati*) is most free from fate. The further the distance from the first mind (*prima mens*), the tighter the grip of fate.

Augustine speaks of God as 'the supreme hub of causes' (*summus causarum cardo: De trin.* iii, 9, 16). The simile of the circle or sphere appears in several writers, e.g. Pseudo-Plutarch, *De fato* 569C, Plotinus (ii, 2, 1; iii, 2, 3; vi, 8, 18, 23), and Proclus, *Decem Dubit.* i, 5 (p. 60 Isaac; Greek in Isaac Sebastokrator, p. 158).

Boethius suggests, therefore, that as time is to eternity, so the circle is to its centre, and so is the moving inter-connection of events in fate in relation to the unmoving simplicity of providence. This chain of events controls the stars, the constant equilibrium of the elements, the birth and death of living things, and the acts and fortunes of men (cf. Boethius, *Perih.* ii, 231; above, p. 161). The constancy of causation depends on the immobility of the first cause. But from his high watchtower (*specula alta*, a Virgilian phrase for a Platonic idea) God looks out on the world and arranges what is best for each individual. Plotinus (iii, 2, 9) emphasises that great as the power of providence is, it is not so overwhelming that it reduces the individual to nothingness. Boethius' doctrine that there is a care even for the individual would be congenial to a Christian reader. But his sentence is set in a Platonic context.

To take providence seriously is to become aware that things do not happen as we expect or think right. 'Our Lucan' wrote that the conquering cause pleased the gods, the vanquished's cause pleased Cato (*Pharsalia* i, 128). So even things that seem perverse and wrong to us are nevertheless right. It seems monstrous to us when a man of holiness and virtue, *deo proximus*, is afflicted. In some cases providence protects such a person even from bodily sickness. Indeed, the lady Philosophy adds that 'someone more excellent than myself has said, 'The heavens built the body of a holy man'.' The hexameter is cited in Greek, and since Philosophy thinks its author superior even to herself, the conclusion that it is a quotation from the Chaldean Oracles, held in profound awe as the highest revelation by Proclus and other late Platonists, seems irresistible. (Thomas Taylor first made this observation as long ago as 1806 in his *Collectanea* p. 102, but his book has been disregarded by the learned. The line is accepted by Edouard des Places as fragment 98 in his recent edition of the Oracles.)

Often providence brings good men to the summit of power to beat back evil. But lest prosperity bring excess, felicity does not last long. Providence's most ingenious achievement is to use evil men to force other evil men to be good, if only from a desire to be unlike their vile oppressors. And God uses the natural course of events, or fate, to get rid of evil; a proposition which looks like a variant of 'while there is death, there is hope'.

The prose section iv, 6 is the longest in the work. It is followed by a poem of praise for the good order of the world in the heavenly bodies, the beauty of the ordered seasons, the love that holds everything together. Philosophy then teaches Boethius that all fortune is beneficent, whether pleasant or painful, either rewarding or exercising the good, punishing or correcting the bad. The correspondence between these words and Simplicius' commentary on the *Physics* ii, 6 (*CAG* IX, 361, 1 ff.) has been acutely noted by Courcelle. Similarly Hierocles, *In carmen aureum* 11. The book concludes with a poem, full of echoes of Seneca's tragedies, concerning the struggles of Agamemnon, Odysseus, and Hercules.

Divine foreknowledge and free will

The fifth and last book contains Boethius' most intricate discussion of the logic of divine foreknowledge and human freedom, in which he resumes many of the themes of his second commentary on *Interpretation* (above, p. 159). It is not certain that the book is constructed from Ammonius' commentaries on *Interpretation* and *Physics*. But it goes without saying that the exegetical tradition of the Peripatetic and then Neoplatonic schools in expounding these two books by Aristotle is lying behind Boethius throughout the book.

In the first prose section, there is an express reference by the lady Philosophy to the teachings on chance of 'my Aristotle'. Chance cannot mean a random event as opposed to a process of causation, or it becomes a meaningless word. It is axiomatic that 'nothing comes from nothing' (Aristotle, *Metaphysics* Z 7), though it applies not to the originating cause but to the material ordered by it. A causeless event is a nonsense and a nothing. Aristotle defines chance as a coincidence which happens without being intended; that is, because of the coincidence of different processes of causation. (Boethius has already mentioned this understanding of chance in his commentary on Cicero's *Topics*, above, p. 119.) Aristotle's views are expressed not only in the *Physics* (B 4–5) but also in the *Metaphysics* 1025a 14 ff. whence Boethius or the school tradition derived the illustration of a man digging in a field for another purpose and finding a treasure.

Both the Neoplatonists and the Christian Augustinian tradition treat freedom as a moral quality. No one is less free than the person dominated by vice. Freedom is attained by continual contemplation of the divine mind, lost when one slips down into the corporeal. The upward look is full of light, the downward of darkness. It follows that there are degrees of freedom (Proclus, *De providentia et fato* 48). Complete surrender to vice means a loss of capacity for rational deliberation (cf. Proclus, *In rem pub.* ii, 276, 8), lost in the fog of the cloud of unknowing (*inscitiae nubes*), alienated from God who is the true Sun (v, 2 and m. 2) who is, who has been, and who is to come (echoing Vergil, *Georgic* iv, 392 rather than Apoc. i, 8).

In the next section (v, 3) Boethius takes up the simple proposition of popular assumption: if God knows everything including all future events, then no human act is voluntary, and free will is an illusion. This proposition is rejected on the good ground that, from a doctrine of what God knows, nothing necessarily follows about the voluntariness of human action. What determines events is the nexus of cause and effect, not knowledge even in an omniscient power that can hold no mistaken beliefs without ceasing to be omniscient and therefore ceasing to be what we mean by God. The confusion here is seen by Boethius to lie in our all too human interpretation of divine foreknowledge as holding beliefs about acts in advance of their occurrence.

We think of the future as consisting of uncertain, contingent events: contingent in the sense that there are a number of possibilities, and for us they are open; it is not the case that any of them can be seen to be necessary. And 'necessary' itself is a slippery word; for some necessities are absolute, whereas others are conditional. That a man will die is absolutely necessary because man is a mortal animal. If you know someone is walking, then, if your belief is correct, it is necessary that he is walking; and if he is walking, he is going. Here necessity is conditional. We see how for Boethius necessity is being contrasted both with voluntary action and with the contingent event which happens but does not have to happen. Our wills are in the order of causes known to God.

The problem of God's foreknowledge of future contingents becomes criss-crossed with another difficulty; the relation of time to eternity. Boethius rejects the favoured solution of Alexander of Aphrodisias (*De fato* 30) and Calcidius (*In Tim.* 162) that God knows the uncertain future as uncertain, just as we do (cf. above, p. 162). He is not happy to think that temporal events can be the cause of an eternal knowledge. With Iamblichus and Proclus he affirms that the knowledge possessed by God operates on a different plane from human knowledge. For us events fall into past, present, and future time. God is outside time. For him the knowledge of temporal events is an eternal knowledge in the sense that all is a simultaneous present. Therefore to affirm God is omniscient does not entail that he holds beliefs about acts *in advance* of their being done; the temporality involved in the phrase 'in advance of' must be abstracted from the discussion. Without the abstraction of the temporality in saying 'in advance of', the logical circle leaves no escape. Eternity does not mean perpetuity (such as may be affirmed of the physical world), but the simultaneous and perfect possession of limitless life (v, 6, 4). Time, as Plato defined it (*Timaeus* 38a), is a moving image of eternity and because it is a moving image fails to attain to the nature of eternity; the present is a kind of likeness of the eternal, but differs in that it cannot be possessed permanently (v, 6, 12).[6]

The last book of the *Consolation* is a remarkable discussion of an intricate problem. The moral problem of innocent suffering is set aside in favour of the logical analysis of the difficulties inherent in any belief in providence and human freedom. The third verse section of the fifth book reflects on the necessity of holding together two truths that appear in tension with one another (v m. 3). The hierarchical Platonist theory of levels of knowledge and apprehension leads Boethius to suggest that some of the logical difficulty is caused by the limitation of our minds, bounded by the experiences of time and successiveness. In this life we can live only each passing moment, and cannot grasp past, present and future together (v, 6, 2).

But even in our minds there are four levels: (a) of sense which we share with animate creatures unable to move like limpets; (b) of *imaginatio*, the power to form corporeal images shared with animals that have powers of movement; (c) *ratio*, possessed by man alone on earth; (d) *intelligentia* which is God's (v,

5). An individual object taken by itself is singular; but reason has the power to discern the universal of which the particular object is a specimen (v, 6, 36).

The last sentences of the *Consolation* reaffirm that belief in free will is compatible with belief in providence and in a transcendent divine knowledge in which there is neither before nor after. Therefore prayers and the practice of virtue are not vain. To act out your life before a Judge who sees all things is to know that there lies upon you a great necessity of integrity (*magna necessitas probitatis*). There Boethius' pen fell from his hand. The rest is silence. The work shows no signs of being incomplete (above, p. 234). There is no discussion, admittedly, of the soul's immortality except for one observation (ii, 4, 28) that it is established by many proofs, and underlies the conviction of many whose happiness has been found through and in spite of pain and martyrdom. On the other hand, the theme of immortality is little discussed in the surviving Neoplatonic tracts on providence in Plotinus, Hierocles of Athens, and Proclus.

The religion of Boethius

From 900 to 916 the abbot of the Saxon monastery of Corvey (daughter house of Corbie near Amiens) was Bovo II, a man of wide culture. We have from his pen a commentary on the verse section 'O qui perpetua' (iii m. 9), and his prologue warns his monks against the dangers of Boethius. It is astonishing (he says) that a man who wrote such correct doctrine on the Trinity and on the person of Christ, works which Bovo studied in adolescence, should also have written the *Consolation of Philosophy* in which he is not only silent about the teaching of the Church but also wide open to philosophical and especially Platonic doctrines. That both the theological tractates and the *Consolation* come from the same pen Bovo regards as certain on ground of style.[7]

Bovo was evidently right in observing the unity of style shared by the opuscula and the *Consolation*. We have already seen the tractates other than the fourth to be even fuller of Neoplatonic logic than the last three books of the *Consolation*; because of their dry logical character they have less personal religious feeling than the later work. To this last description the fourth tractate *De fide catholica* is an exception, with its emotionally charged confession of faith cast in terms of high Augustinianism, offering neither logical elucidation nor apologetic defence, but simply setting down what Boethius believes the content of the revealed religion of Christ to be. But here as in the other opuscula Boethius shows the same sharp clarity and brevity, and the same eye for what is salient. The non-theological diction is very characteristic of Boethius. Moreover, the disjunction between faith and reason, revelation and natural religion, is presupposed by *De fide catholica*. It is sometimes suggested that there is anachronism in attributing such a notion to a man of the sixth century. In fact Boethius' master Proclus operates with much the same disjunction in treating the Chaldean Oracles as a transcendent source of divine revelation in verbally inspired form, towards which philosophy may aspire but which human reasoning could never have found unaided.

To affirm the authenticity of *De fide catholica* as the evidence of the language requires us to do is greatly to sharpen the question, Why does he exclude anything specifically Christian from the *Consolation of Philosophy*? Although the answer that the *Consolation* is an expression of deep inward disillusion with Christianity has been given by distinguished Boethian scholars, I think reflection shows the evidence is against this view. No doubt it is possible to speculate that at the crisis of his life Boethius may not have received from the higher clergy at Rome or northern Italy the support that he might have felt entitled to expect. Certainly there would have been great danger in submitting intercession to the angry Theoderic on behalf of a man against whom there was a political charge of treason. If Boethius' friend John the deacon is rightly identified with the John who became Pope in the summer of 523, his feelings would have been intelligible if this trusted friend, with whom (as the third tractate shows) he had enjoyed many metaphysical discussions in the more advanced flights of Neoplatonic philosophy, found it impracticable or for the sake of the good of the Church impolitic to offer any effective plea for Boethius. But the presence of subtle biblical and perhaps even liturgical allusions in the language of the *Consolation* makes the apostasy interpretation unlikely. If the *Consolation* contains nothing distinctively Christian, it is also relevant that it contains nothing specifically pagan either. Its character recalls Andromachus' defence of the Lupercalia before Pope Gelasius that its ceremonies are 'neither pagan nor Christian' (above, p. 13). Unlike Proclus whose *Platonic Theology* weaves an elaborate pattern to integrate the gods of polytheism into the structure of his metaphysical system, Boethius puts a distance between himself and polytheism. The sun, he says, gives light much inferior to the light of God's truth (iii m. 6, 3; cf. iii m. 10, 15 ff.; v m. 2, 1 ff.; iii m. 11, 8). To speak with Boethius of Socrates as having won a 'victory over unjust death' (i, 3, 6) evidently echoes Christian language, consciously or unconsciously. But the *Consolation* contains no sentence that looks like a confession of faith either in the gods of paganism or in Christian redemption. Not a word hints at the forgiveness of sins or the conquest of death through resurrection. Everything specific is absent, and probably consciously avoided. The ambiguity seems clearly to be deliberate. The work's intention is given by its title. Boethius is not in quest of consolation from divine grace in the remission of sins and the promise of eternal life to those redeemed through Christ. His doctrine of salvation is humanist, a soteriology of the inward purification of the soul. The *Consolation* is a work written by a Platonist who is also a Christian, but is not a Christian work.

Nevertheless, I think it a work written with the consciousness of Augustine standing behind the author's shoulder, so to speak. The argument that Boethius intended a Platonic confession of faith which he knew to be incompatible with Christianity fails against the observation that there is nothing in the Platonic themes admitted to the *Consolation* which one cannot also find accepted in the philosophical dialogues and the *Confessions* of the young Augustine. Even the mature works of Augustine, the *City of God*, the *Trinity*, and that neglected masterpiece the *Literal Commentary on Genesis*, offer many anticipations of Boethius' Platonism, especially as expounded in the last book of the *Consolation*.

For Augustine also God is absolute Being, from whom descends the great chain or continuum of derived entities, each grade having slightly less being and therefore less goodness than the grade above, until one finally reaches the absence of being which is the negativity of pure evil. To ask the cause of evil is for Augustine to ask to see darkness or to hear silence (*Confessions* iii, 7, 12; *City of God*, xi, 9; xii, 7). For him the good is unity, evil multiplicity and disruption (*Conf.* iv, 15, 24). Providence calls the rational creation to return to its true being and goodness which are one and the same (*City of God* xi, 28). Augustine confesses in the *City of God* (v, 5) that 'no philosophers are so close to us as the Platonists'. His discussion of divine foreknowledge and human free will (v, 9) begins with a reference to Cicero 'On divination', a reference which is evidently from memory since it is wrong, but which may well explain why in the *Consolation* Boethius also makes a similar reference in his own discussion of the subject (v, 4, 1). In what then follows Augustine mentions other matters familiar to the reader of Boethius: e.g. the interpretation of 'fate', *heimarmene*, as a name for the connected series of events that composes destiny outside the direction of human wills. Augustine differs from Boethius in thinking 'fate' a term with inappropriate associations. He knows about but is unsympathetic to the notion that fate rules lower things, providence higher. He is familiar with the Platonic view that our wills, to us creatures contingent and uncertain, are included among the causes whose outcome is certain to God; or with the view that chance is merely a name for an event whose causes are unknown.

Moreover, between the *Consolation* and Augustine's early philosophical dialogues there are a number of similarities: for example, the personification of philosophy (*Solil.* i, 1), though this is common enough and can also be found in Martianus Capella; the ejection of the Muses from a serious discussion (*C. Acad.* iii, 7; *De ordine* i, 24); the recognition that only a privileged few can attain the contemplative discernment of the divine order (*De ordine* ii, 24 f.; *C. Acad.* i, 1); the diagnosis of unphilosophical sensual life as a disease or a sleep (*De ordine* i, 24; *C. Acad.* ii, 16). All these points are no doubt common conventions, and do not add up to a demonstration of literary dependence. Nevertheless they help to show that in his Platonism Boethius is not necessarily turning away from Augustine.

Christine Mohrmann has drawn attention to the fact that

much of the vocabulary in Boethius' two passages about prayer in the *Consolation* (v, 3, 34; 6, 47–48), with 'commercium, deprecari, supplicandi ratione, praesidium, mereor, porrigere', can also be found in early Latin collects of the ancient sacramentaries. We have too little pagan Latin liturgy to be able to assert that such language is distinctively Christian. One would expect such vocabulary to be neutral in itself. Nevertheless, so far as it goes, her observation gives a marginal reinforcement to the view that there is a latent awareness of Christianity beneath the surface of Boethius' text. Boethius writes with such artistry and 'artificiality' that we may be confident he does nothing accidentally.

Between Boethius and Augustine there are also many notable differences. Most important of these is the difference in the ways in which the two men speak of the relation between faith and reason: for Augustine, parallel and reconcilable ways of knowing the truth; for Boethius parallel ways which only meet at certain points where logic may help to clarify the confusions of popular or common usage. Boethius' vision of the cosmos is of a single great whole kept from disintegration by the goodness and power of providence, and one might expect him to affirm an optimistic view of the concord of faith and reason. In actuality there is much more of this kind of optimism in Augustine than in Boethius.

Nevertheless it must be a correct conclusion which calls Boethius a humanist in the classical sense of that word: a man positive to the values of great literature and philosophy wherever found, and especially in the thought of Plato and Aristotle. There is a certain sadness in the fact that because his fascination with logical problems so gripped the mediaeval schoolmen, the reaction against the schoolmen at the time of the Renaissance ended by making him unfashionable as well. Moreover, his picture of the world belongs to that 'Discarded Image' of which C. S. Lewis wrote. Nevertheless, this last Roman, whose gaze is so profoundly retrospective, transmitted a whole cultural world to his mediaeval successors. The finesse with which he composed his *Consolation of Philosophy* made it possible for Alcuin and many others to read the book as a Christian work. The book is an essay in natural theology apart from revelation; and the very possibility of that rests on

Christian assumptions. The Christianizing readers have not been absolutely wrong.

Among all Boethius' writings the *Consolation of Philosophy* is rightly esteemed the climax of his achievement. The substructure that made it possible is seen in his other works on logic, mathematics, and theology, and it is only in relation to these other writings, and to his Neoplatonic masters, that the nature of his originality can be seen in clear outline. These other treatises came to be profoundly influential in mediaeval times. Alcuin and, after him, a thin line of Carolingian and later scholars found in Boethius' studies of the liberal arts and of dialectic a strength and resource which they badly needed. Without him their educational programme would not have made much headway. From the ninth-century commentaries were written to explain the obscurities of the theological tractates and of the *Consolation*. From his dialectical and mathematical treatises Boethius' readers learnt precision and order. He taught mediaeval thinkers to examine first principles, to be careful in the use of words, to try to trace an argument back to its basic axioms and presuppositions. The principles of axiomatization in the third of the opuscula sacra created a foundation on which in the twelfth-century Alan of Lille would set about the task of constructing the whole of theology as a deduction from a single self-evident truth. Although cut off in his prime so that his grand ambitions to translate all Aristotle and Plato were never realized, he nevertheless succeeded to a remarkable degree in his prime endeavour to salvage major parts of Greek philosophical learning for future generations.

In the twelfth-century schools his influence reached its peak. His works became central to the syllabus of instruction, and strongly stimulated that thoroughgoing study of logic for its own sake which becomes so prominent a hallmark of the mediaeval schools. The *opuscula sacra* taught the theologians that they did not necessarily need to fear the application of rigorous logic to the traditional language of the Church. He made his readers hungry for even more Aristotle, and prepared the welcome given to the new twelfth century translations of the *Analytics* and the *Topics*, although his own versions were scarcely known at all. From the first of the *opuscula sacra* mediaeval philosophers learnt how to draw up a hierarchy of the sciences and to see the different departments of knowledge, now being pursued together in community as the newly founded universities set themselves to their common task, as an organized and coherent scheme in which the various parts could be seen to be rationally related to each other.

But the humanists of the Renaissance found themselves constricted by the number-games of his *Arithmetic*, by the Pythagorean indifference to musical practice of his *Music*, above all by the obsessive concern with logical niceties which came to give the mediaeval schoolmen an unhappy reputation. As the reputation of Aristotle declined, so also that of Boethius was bound to fall with him.

Only the *Consolation of Philosophy* came through with remarkably little of its power diminished. The work of a layman, it remained the loved reading of laymen, especially if (like Thomas More) they held high office and suddenly found themselves deprived of their sovereign's protection and favour. The masterpiece of Boethius still speaks in the twentieth century to those who grapple with the perennial problems of evil, freedom, and providence. His solution to the problems of divine foreknowledge, exploiting Iamblichus' idea that divine knowledge wholly transcends the successiveness of the temporal process, though retaining its modern advocates, raises difficulties of its own. But no one can read the last book of the *Consolation* without having a clarified vision of the nature of the question needing to be answered. The ideas with which Boethius was working already lay to hand in the discussions of the Neoplatonists. To lay his work side by side with theirs is to realize the independence of his critical judgement as he formulates his personal synthesis. Boethius permanently marked the western philosophical tradition by his doctrine that 'personality' has something to do with the unique quality of the individual. In the *Consolation of Philosophy*, as in no other among his writings, his own individuality stands out for all to see.

PRESERVATION AND TRANSMISSION

THE copying and ordered preservation of his writings was a matter for which Boethius himself had some care. Manuscripts of his commentary on Cicero's *Topics* carry the author's note faithfully transcribed in later times: 'Conditor operis emendavi'—'I the author of the work have corrected the text.' A ninth-century manuscript of the *Institutio arithmetica* now at Florence (Laurent. plut. XXIX 20) contains the subscription: 'Severinus Boetius v.c. inl. ex cons. ord. patricius legi opusculum meum', a form of words which implies that he himself revised the text after his consular year of 510.[1]

The preservation of the *Consolation of Philosophy* can be due only to Symmachus and Boethius' widow Rusticiana. The manuscript could have been brought away from the prison by a member of his family allowed to visit him at Pavia; and Symmachus had plenty of resources for sweetening any reluctant prison warders. The bitterly hostile portrait of Theoderic in the first book would have made it dangerous literature during the brief remainder of his reign or during that of his grandson Athalaric. Rusticiana could hardly have released it for 'publication' until the Goths' withdrawal from Rome, at which time she could also go about smashing the likenesses of Theoderic still to be found in the city. Cassiodorus shows no knowledge of the *Consolation*, either in his *Institutes* (where he would hardly have had reason to mention it) or, more significantly, in the 'Anecdoton Holderi' where Boethius' works known to him are listed.

The earliest external evidence for the existence of the *Consolation* (and that evidence is vague and indecisive), is found in the *Elegies* of Maximian, a minor Latin poet on the subjects of love and old age. Maximian's date is uncertain; but since the earliest manuscript is of the ninth century, and since his work is imitated by Eugenius of Toledo in the mid-seventh century, his likely date is in or a little after the middle years of the sixth century. The third of Maximian's elegies refers to Boethius' high reputation as a scholar:

> Hic mihi magnarum scrutator maxime rerum
> solus, Boëti, fers miseratus opem.

The context makes these words less flattering to Boethius than they appear when quoted on their own, and the elegy has been interpreted by the American scholar Richard Webster as a malicious attack on Boethius, since its subject is the miseries of love which are approached with a world-weary disillusion. A frustrated lover's difficulties in attaining his desires send him for advice to the immense erudition of Boethius; but even that resource does not in the end solve his problems. Some lines in Maximian's verses read like echoes of the *Consolation of Philosophy*; if so, it is difficult to think of Maximian writing before Rusticiana could safely issue the work, which is after the fall of Rome to Belisarius in December 536.[2]

The transmission of the mathematical writings we no doubt owe in part to the family, but much to Cassiodorus' library at Vivarium; perhaps also to Eugippius' library at Lucullanum near Naples. Cassiodorus shows no knowledge of the *Astronomy*, and if in the tenth century that work came to be in the library at Bobbio available to Gerbert we can only guess how it got there.

The *opuscula sacra* were surely collected by John the deacon in Rome. The fifth tractate explicitly refers to John's existing collection of Boethius' writings. There seems no reason why the group of five should not have been available to a restricted circle in Rome by 523. The fourth tractate *De fide catholica*, we have seen to be written in a characteristically Boethian diction; its content is no doubt what he had learnt during the catechesis given him by John the deacon.

The dialectical writings, however, appear to depend for their transmission largely upon a friend an admirer named Martius Novatus Renatus, a senator (*vir clarissimus et spectabilis*) whose name appears in a series of scribal subscriptions in several manuscripts of the dialectical treatises. Among these notes pride of place is taken by one found in a manuscript of the tenth or eleventh century, once at Fleury, now divided between Orléans and Paris.[3] It contains the greater part of the corpus of logical works, omitting the first commentary on Porphyry and the two expositions of *Perihermeneias*. At the end of the monograph on hypothetical syllogisms, which is here divided into three books, not two as in the normal printed texts prior to Obertello's edition of 1969, there stands the notice: 'contra codicem Renati v(iri) s(pectabilis) correxi qui confectus ab eo est Theodoro antiquario qui nunc palatinus est'.[4]

'I have corrected (this) against the codex of Renatus, which was written by that Theodorus the librarian who is now an official in the palace bureaucracy' (evidently at either Ravenna or Constantinople).

After the title *De divisione* the scribe records: 'Martius Novatus Renatus v(ir) c(larissimus) et sp(ectabilis) relegi meum.'[5]

Theodorus the librarian turns up in two other manuscript subscriptions. In the one case the manuscript is lost. It was once at St. Germain, but disappeared in the troubles at the end of the eighteenth century, perhaps in the disastrous fire of 19 August 1794. But Montfaucon is witness that at St. Germain he had seen a codex containing Boethius' logical treatises together with a note to say that it was 'copied from a very ancient codex which Theodorus wrote with his own hand in the consulship of Mavortius, the fifth indiction [i.e. 527] from the autograph belonging to Flavian, who was Priscian's pupil'.[6]

In the second case the subscription occurs in manuscripts of Priscian's *Ars grammatica* at the end of books, v, viii, xii and xvii, each note recording the progress of the copying of the work by Theodorus. The manuscripts vary in their readings, and the form of the subscription is not identical (apart from the dates) in the four colophons. But the note at the end of book viii reads: 'Flavianus Theodorus Dionisii v(ir) d(evotus) memorialis sacri scrinii epistolarum et adiutor v(iri) m(agnifici) quaestoris sacri palatii scripsi artem Prisciani eloquentissimi grammatici doctoris mei manu mea in urbe Roma Constantinopoli die tertio iduum Januar̄ Mavortio v(iro) c(larissimo) consule indictione v.'

Theodorus reached the end of book vii early in February. Finally on 29 May 527 he ended the seventeenth book with:

'Fl(avianus) Theodorus Dionisii v(ir) d(evotus) memorialis sacri scrinii epistolarum et adiutor v(iri) m(agnifici) quaestoris sacri palatii scripsi manu mea in urbe Roma Constantinopoli tertio Kl. Junias Mavortio v(iro) c(larissimo) consule imperantibus Justino et Justiniano p(atribus) p(atriae) Augg.'[7]

Vir devotus is the normal rank of a 'scrinianus' and of a 'magister litterarum'.[8]

The Renatus for whom Theodorus wrote the codex of Boethius' dialectica is almost certainly identical with the Renatus mentioned in the letter of John the deacon to Senarius[9] (above, p. 27) and in Severus of Antioch's account of his meeting at Constantinople with the two western visitors, Petronius of Rome and Renatus of Ravenna, who both knew Greek and were therefore able to engage in dispute with Severus on the Christological debate, thereby convincing Severus of the essential Nestorianism of Latin doctrine.

EDITIONS

The most accessible edition of the collected writings of Boethius is in J. P. Migne's *Patrologia Latina* 63–4 (1847 and later reprints). Unfortunately it is not a good edition, but for a substantial proportion of the principal works better editions now exist. For the *Consolatio* Migne reprinted the 1679 edition of Petrus Callyus; for the opuscula sacra Vallinus' good edition (Leiden, 1656, 1671) which first printed *De fide catholica*, with a note to express unhesitating confidence in its authenticity on ground of style and content; for the remainder the text of Henricus Loritus Glareanus (Basel, 1546 and 1570), who had in turn reproduced the *Dialectica* from the edition of Julianus Martianus Rota (Venice, 1546) a Venetian humanist who also edited some Aristotle and Galen. In addition Migne reprinted two pieces, *De rhetorica cognatione* and *Locorum rhetoricorum distinctio*, which had been edited by Cardinal Angelo Mai (*Class. Auct*. iii, 315) as hitherto unpublished works by Boethius; but they are excerpts from *De differentiis topicis*. The treatise *De definitionibus* was shown by H. Usener (*Anecdoton Holderi*, 1877) to belong to Marius Victorinus. The tract *De unitate et uno* is a twelfth-century piece by Dominic Gonzalez (Gundissalinus). *De disciplina scholarium*, recently re-edited by O. Weijers (Leiden, 1976), is by an admirer of Boethius in early thirteenth-century Paris or Oxford.

Except for Vallinus, who published a good text of *Consolatio* and *Opuscula* with excellent notes, the sixteenth- and seventeenth-century editors of Boethius did not do their work well. In many places, especially in the *Dialectica*, an improved text can be obtained by consulting the princeps of the *Opera omnia* (Venice, 1492).

Although there is as yet no census of manuscripts available, it is certain that Boethius has a rich diversity of manuscript traditions for all his writings. The *Consolatio* alone is preserved in about 400 manuscripts; the number for the translations of Aristotle and for the opuscula sacra is not greatly inferior to this figure. The *Consolatio* was first critically edited by R. Peiper for the Teubner library (1871) from fourteen manuscripts. The work now has two good modern editions: that in the Vienna corpus (*CSEL* 67, 1934) by Wilhelm Weinberger on the basis of work by G. Schepss and A. Engelbrecht; and that in the Latin *Corpus Christianorum* 94 (1957) by Ludwig Bieler. Bieler's edition adds new manuscript material and, where he differs from Weinberger, in some cases improves the text.

The hand edition of K. Büchner (3rd edn. Heidelberg, 1977) is also marked by good judgement but much punctuation. The convenient edition in the Loeb Classical Library by E. K. Rand and H. F. Stewart (1918) has been bettered in the revision by S. J. Tester (1973). This volume fortunately includes the opuscula sacra.

Opuscula Sacra: it is still necessary to use R. Peiper's Teubner edition of 1871, based on a small handful of manuscripts accessible in south Germany. Rand prepared a critical edition for the Vienna corpus; it has never been published. For this text I have therefore collated early manuscripts accessible in British libraries to provide some control over the editions by Peiper and Rand, and have been led to think that Rand's Loeb text (Stewart contributed the translation) merits respect as usable, careful work. Further evidence for the text is also available in Gottschalk's quotations (edited by C. Lambot, 1945) and in the editions by N. M. Häring of commentaries on the opuscula by Thierry of Chartres, Clarembald of Arras, and Gilbert de la Porrée. The Marietti edition of Thomas Aquinas' commentary on *De trinitate* and *De hebdomadibus* (1954) is uncritical.

De Arithmetica and *De Musica*: G. Friedlein's Teubner text (1867) is ripe for replacement but must be used faute de mieux. The Geometria B ascribed to Boethius is edited by M. Folkerts (1970).

Dialectica: there are good critical editions of both commentaries on Porphyry by S. Brandt (*CSEL* 48, 1906) with an important introduction; of the two commentaries on *Interpretation* by C. Meiser (Teubner, 1877-80); and of *De syllogismis hypotheticis* by Luca Obertello (Brescia, 1969). There is no good edition of the other logical monographs nor, above all, of the commentary on the *Categories*, of which the Migne text is in some places lacunose, in others misleading. The text has to be checked against the often superior princeps of 1492. I have also consulted manuscripts accessible in British libraries, e.g. the Bodleian Laudianus 49.

Boethius' commentary on Cicero's *Topics* is edited by J. C. Orelli and J. G. Baiter in their *M. Tullii Ciceronis Opera Omnia* v, 1 (Zürich, 1833). His translations of Aristotle's Organon are edited by L. Minio-Paluello in *Aristoteles Latinus* (Leiden, 196 ff.), with important introductory matter: i (1961, 1966) *Categories* and *Isagoge*; ii (1965) *Interpretation*; iii (1962) *Prior Analytics*; v (1969) *Topics*; vi (1975, edited by B. G. Dod), *Sophistici Elenchi*.

English translations of Boethius: the *Consolatio* has often been translated. The Opuscula sacra are in the Loeb volume. Eleonore Stump has a good annotated translation of *De topicis differentiis* (Cornell, 1978). Porphyry's *Isagoge* is translated by E. W. Warren (Toronto, Pontifical Institute, 1975).

For editions of authors cited to illustrate Boethius I have used the best editions accessible, e.g. Teubner texts for Apuleius, Martianus Capella, Fulgentius (mythographus), Procopius, Theon of Smyrna, Iamblichus, Proclus' commentaries on *Timaeus* and *Republic* and on *Euclid;* Macrobius, Claudius Ptolemaeus, Galen's *Logic,* Aristides Quintilianus. Aristotle and Plato are cited from the Oxford Classical Texts, Plotinus from H. R. Schwyzer and P. Henry's edition. Proclus' commentary on the *Parmenides* is cited from V. Cousin's 1864 edition, reprinted 1980; his *Elements of Theology* from E. R. Dodds' Oxford edition (1933) with masterful commentary. His tracts on Providence from H. Boese, *Procli Diadochi tria opuscula* (Berlin, 1960); a Budé edition edited by D. Isaac is in 3 volumes, 1977–82. Proclus' *Platonic Theology* is cited from the Budé edition by L. G. Westerink and H. D. Saffrey. Calcidius is nobly edited by J. H. Waszink. Priscian: H. Keil, *Grammatici Latini* ii–iii (1855–9). The Anonymus Valesianus: ed. J. Moreau and V. Velkov (Teubner, 2nd edn. 1968) under the misleading title 'Excerpta Valesiana'.

Other Christian texts are cited from *Corpus Christianorum* or *Corpus Scriptorum Ecclesiasticorum Latinorum* wherever available; otherwise from Migne. The principal documents of the Acacian and Laurentian schisms are in E. Schwartz, *Publizistische Sammlungen zum Acacianischen Schisma* (1934), or *Acta Conciliorum Oecumenicorum* iv 2 (1914); the collectio Avellana in *CSEL* 35; papal letters ed. A. Thiel, *Epistolae Romanorum Pontificum Genuinae* i, 461–523 (Brunswick, 1868). But the documents of the Roman councils during the Laurentian schism are best edited in T. Mommsen's *MGH* edition of the *Variae* of Cassiodorus (1894). Ennodius is edited by Hartel for *CSEL*, by Vogel for *MGH*. Severus of Antioch's letters are partly in E. W. Brooks' edition (1904), partly in *Patrologia Orientalis* xii 2 and xiv 1; *contra impium Grammaticum* is edited and translated into Latin by J. Lebon.

Gerbert's mathematical writings: ed. N. M. Bubnov (Berlin, 1899).

BIBLIOGRAPHY

ABERG, N. *Die Goten und Langobarden in Italien.* Uppsala, 1929.
ABRAMOWSKI, L. 'Trinitarische und christologische Hypostasenformeln', *Theologie und Philosophie* 54, 1979, 38–49.
ACKRILL, J. L. *Aristotle's Categories and De interpretatione.* Oxford, 1963.
ADAMO, L. 'Boezio e Mario Vittorino traduttori e interpreti dell' Isagoge di Porfirio', *Rivista critica di storia della filosofia* 22, 1967, 141–64.
ALFONSI, L. 'De quibusdam locis quos ex antiquis poetis Boethius et Maximianus repetisse videntur', *Aevum* 16, 1942, 86–92.
—— 'Problemi filosofici della Consolatio boeziana', *Rivista di filosofia neoscolastica* 35, 1943, 323–8.
—— 'Studi boeziani', *Aevum* 19, 1945, 142–57; 25, 1951, 132–66; 210–29.
—— 'Romanità e barbarie nell' Apologia di Boezio', *Studi Romani* 1, 1953, 605–16.
ALTANER, B. *Kleine patristische Schriften* = Texte und Untersuchungen 83. Berlin, 1967.
AMANN, E. Articles on Hormisdas: *DTC* 7, 1 (1927), 171–5; Scythes (Moines), *DTC* 14, 2 (1941) 1746–53; Théopaschite (controverse), *DTC* 15, 1 (1946), 505–12.
AMERIO, R. 'Probabile fonte della nozione boeziana di eternità', *Filosofia* 1, 1950, 365–72.
ANASTASI, R. 'Sul processo di Boezio', *Miscellanea di studi di letteratura cristiana antica* 1, 1947, 21–39.
—— 'Boezio e Massimiano', ibid. 2, 1948, 1–20.
—— 'La fortuna di Boezio', ibid. 3, 1951, 93–110.
ANDERSON, J. F. *St. Augustine and Being, a metaphysical essay.* The Hague, 1965.
ANDRE BARBERA, C. 'Arithmetic and geometric divisions of the Tetracord', *Journal of Music Theory* 21, 1977, 294–323.
ANNAS, J. *Aristotle's Metaphysics books M and N.* Oxford, 1976.
ARCARI, P. M. *Idee e sentimenti politici dell'alto medioevo.* Milan, 1968.
ARMSTRONG, A. H. *St. Augustine and Christian Platonism.* Villanova University, 1967.
AUERBACH, E. *Literatursprache und Publikum in der lateinischen Spätantike und im Mittelalter.* Bern, 1958. (Eng. tr. by R. Manheim, London, 1965.)

AUGUSTINE *De Dialectica*, tr. B. Darrell Jackson. Dordrecht and Boston, 1975.
BACH, E. 'Théoderic, romain ou barbare?', *Byzantion* 25–8, 1955–7, 413–20.
BALTES, M. 'Gott, Welt, Mensch in der Consolatio Philosophiae des Boethius', *Vigiliae Christianae* 34, 1980, 313–40.
BARDY, G. *L'église et les derniers Romains*. Paris, 1948.
BARK, W. 'Theoderic vs. Boethius: vindication and apology', *American Historical Review* 49, 1944, 410–26.
—— 'The Legend of Boethius' martyrdom', *Speculum* 21, 1946, 312–17.
—— 'Boethius' fourth tractate, the so-called De fide catholica', *Harvard Theological Review* 39, 1946, 55–69.
BARNES, J. *Aristotle's Posterior Analytics*. Oxford, 1975.
BARRETT, H. M. *Boethius: some aspects of his times and work*. Cambridge, 1940 (repr. New York, 1965).
BECKER-FREYSENG, A. *Die Vorgeschichte des philosophischen Terminus 'contingens': eine Untersuchung über die Bedeutungen von 'contingere' bei Boethius*. Heidelberg, 1938.
BEDNARZ, G. *De syntaxi Boethii*. 3 vols. Striegau, 1892–1910.
BEIERWALTES, W. *Proklos, Grundzüge seiner Metaphysik*. Frankfurt, 1965. (2nd edn. 1979.)
—— *Identität und Differenz*. Frankfurt, 1979.
—— 'Andersheit, Grundriss einer neuplatonischen Begriffsgeschichte', *Archiv für Begriffsgeschichte* 16, 1972, 166–97.
—— 'Pronoia und Freiheit in der Philosophie des Proklos', *Freiburger Zeitschrift für Philosophie und Theologie* 24, 1977, 88–111.
BERGERON, M. 'La structure du concept latin de personne', *Études d'histoire littéraire et doctrinale du XIIIe siècle*. 2nd edn. Paris, 1932.
BERKA, K. 'Die Semantik des Boethius', *Helikon* 8, 1968, 454–9.
BERNHARD, M. *Wortkonkordanz zu Anicius Manlius Severinus Boethius De Institutione Musica*. Munich (Bavarian Academy), 1979.
BERTOLINI, O. *Roma di fronte a Bisanzio e ai Langobardi*. Bologna, 1941.
BEUTLER, R. art. Proklos, PW 23, 1, 1957, 186–247.
BIDEZ, J. *Vie de Porphyre*. Gand, 1913.
—— 'Boèce et Porphyre', *Comptes Rendus de l'Académie des Inscriptions et des Belles Lettres* 1922, 346–50.
—— 'Boèce et Porphyre', *Revue belge de philologie et d'histoire* 2, 1923, 189–201.

BIELER, L. Edition of Boethius, *Philosophiae Consolatio*. Corpus Christianorum 94. Turnhout, 1957.
BISCHOFF, B. 'Die Hofbibliothek Karls des Grossen', *Karl der Grosse* ii. Düsseldorf, 1965.
—— 'Die griechische Element in der abendländischen Bildung des Mittelalters', *Byzantinische Zeitschrift* 44, 1951, 40–7.
—— 'Eine verschollene Einteilung der Wissenschaften', *Archives d'histoire doctrinale et littéraire du moyen âge* 25, 1958, 5–20.
BLIC, J. de 'Les arguments de saint Augustin contre l'eternité du monde', *Mélanges de science religieuse* 2, 1945, 33–44.
BOCHEŃSKI, J. M. *A History of Formal Logic* (tr. I. Thomas). 2nd edn. New York, 1970. (German original, *Formale Logik*, 1956.)
—— *Ancient Formal Logic*. Amsterdam, 1951.
—— *The Logic of Religion*. New York, 1965.
—— *La Logique de Theophraste*. Collectanea Friburgensia n.s. 32, 1947.
BOESE. H. *Procli Diadochi tria opuscula*. Berlin, 1960.
BOISSIER, G. 'Le christianisme de Boèce', *Journal des Savants* 1889, 449–62.
BOLTON, D. K. 'The study of the Consolation of Philosophy in Anglo-Saxon England', *Archives d'histoire doctrinale et littéraire du moyen âge* 44, 1977, 33–78.
—— 'Remigian commentaries on the Consolation of Philosophy and their sources', *Traditio* 33, 1977, 381–94.
BONNAUD, R. 'L'éducation scientifique de Boèce', *Speculum* 4, 1929, 199–206.
BOYANCÉ, P. 'Les Muses et l'harmonie des sphères', *Mélanges F. Grat* i, Paris, 1946, 3–16.
BOWER, C. 'Boethius and Nicomachus, an essay concerning the sources of De Institutione Musica', *Vivarium* 16, 1978, 1–45.
BRAGARD, R. 'L'harmonie des sphères selon Boèce', *Speculum* 4, 1929, 206–13.
—— 'Boethiana: études sur le De Institutione Musica de Boèce', *Hommage à Charles van den Borren*, Antwerp, 1945, 84–139.
BRANDT, S. 'Entstehungszeit und zeitliche Folge der Werke von Boethius', *Philologus* 62, 1903.
—— Edition of Boethius, *In Isagogen Porphyrii commenta*, CSEL 48, 1906.
BRENNAN, R. E. *The Trinity and the Unicity of the Intellect by St. Thomas Aquinas* (Eng. tr. of Thomas' commentary on Boethius, De Trinitate). St. Louis and London (Herder), 1946.
BREZZI, P. and others. *La fine dell'impero romano d'Occidente* Rome, 1978.

BROSCH, H. J. *Der Seinsbegriff bei Boethius*. Innsbruck, 1931.
BRUDER, K. *Die philosophische Elemente in den Opuscula Sacra des Boethius*. Leipzig, 1928.
BRUNHÖLZL, F. *Geschichte der lateinischen Litteratur des Mittelalters* I, Munich, 1975, 25–7.
BRUNNER, F. 'Providence et liberté', *Revue de Théologie et de Philosophie* 26, 1976, 12–24.
BRUNO, L. 'La tradizione platonica nel De Consolatione philosophiae di Boezio', *Giornale italiano di filologia* 15, 1962, 257–8.
BRUYNE, E. de *Etudes d'esthétique mediévale*. Bruges, 1946. (Eng. tr. by E. B. Hennessy, New York, 1969.)
BRUYNE, L. A. de *L'antica serie di ritratti papali della basilica di S. Paolo fuori le mura*. Studi di antichità cristiana 7. Rome, 1934.
BÜCHNER, K. Edition of *Consolatio Philosophiae*. 3rd edn. Heidelberg, 1977.
BURNS T. S. *The Ostrogoths, kingship and society* = Historia, Einzelschriften, 36. 1980.
BURY, J. B. *History of the Later Roman Empire from the death of Theodosius I to the death of Justinian*. London, 1923.
CAMERON, AVERIL. 'A Nativity Poem of the sixth century AD', *Classical Philology* 74, 1979, 222–32.
CAMPENHAUSEN, H. von. *Lateinische Kirchenväter*. Stuttgart, 1960. (Eng. tr. by M. Hoffmann, *The Fathers of the Latin Church*. London, 1964.)
CAPIZZI, C. *L'imperatore Anastasio I*. Orientalia Christiana Analecta 184. Rome, 1969.
CAPPUYNS, M. 'Le plus ancien commentaire des Opuscula Sacra et son origine', *Recherches de théologie ancienne et mediévale* 3, 1931, 237–72.
—— 'The supposed commentary of John the Scot on the Opuscula Sacra of Boethius', *Revue néo-scolastique de philosophie* 36, 1934, 67–77.
—— art. Boèce, *DHGE* 9, 1937, 348–80. (Below, p. 302 n. 7.)
—— 'L'origine des Capitula d'Orange 529', *Recherches de théologie ancienne et mediévale* 6, 1934, 121–42.
CAPUA, F. di. 'Il cursus nel De Consolatione philosophiae e nei trattati teologici di Severino Boezio', *Didaskaleion* 3, 1914, 269–303. (Reprinted in his *Scritti Minori*, Rome, 1959.)
CARTON, R. 'Le christianisme et l'augustinisme de Boèce', *Mélanges Augustiniennes*, Paris 1931, 243–329. (= *Revue de Philosophie* n.s. 30, 1, 1930, 573–659.)
CASPAR, E. *Geschichte des Papsttums* II. Tübingen, 1933.
CELLUPRICA, V. *Il capitolo 9 del De Interpretatione di Aristotele:*

Rassegna di studi 1930–1973. Milan, 1977.
CHADWICK, H. 'The authenticity of Boethius' fourth tractate De fide catholica', *Journal of Theological Studies* n.s. 31, 1980, 551–6.
—— 'Theta on Philosophy's Dress in Boethius', *Medium Aevum*, 1980.
CHAMBERLAIN, D. S. 'Philosophy of Music in the Consolation of Boethius', *Speculum* 45, 1970, 80–97.
CHAMBERS, G. B. 'Boethius De musica, an interpretation', *Studia Patristica* 3, 1961, 170–5.
CHAPPUIS, P. G. 'La théologie de Boèce', *Congrès d'histoire du Christianisme: Jubilé Alfred Loisy* iii, Paris and Amsterdam, 1928, pp. 15–40.
CHARANIS, P. *Church and State in the Later Roman Empire: the religious policy of Anastasius I.* 1st edn. Madison, Wisconsin, 1939; 2nd edn. Thessaloniki, 1974.
CHASTAGNOL, A. *La préfecture urbaine à Rome sous le bas-empire.* Paris, 1960.
—— *Le sénat romain sous le règne d'Odoacre.* Antiquitas, Reihe 3, Band 3. Bonn, 1966.
CILENTO, V. *Medioevo monastico e scolastico.* Milan and Naples, 1961.
CIPOLLA, C. 'Per la storia del processo di Boezio', *Studi e documenti di storia e diritto* 21, 1900, 335–46.
CLAGETT, M. 'The medieval latin translations from the Arabic of the *Elements* of Euclid, with special emphasis on the versions of Adelard of Bath', *Isis* 44 (1953), 16–42.
—— *Greek Science in Antiquity.* 2nd edn. New York, 1963.
CLAUDE, D. 'Universale und partikulare Züge in der Politik Theoderichs', *Francia* 6, 1978, 19–58.
CLOVER, F. M. *Flavius Merobaudes.* Transactions of the American Philosophical Society 61, 1, 1971.
COLLINS, J. 'Progress and Problems in the reassessment of Boethius', *The Modern Schoolman* 23, 1945–6, 1–23.
COOPER, L. *A Concordance of Boethius: the five theological tractates and the Consolation of Philosophy.* Cambridge, Mass., 1928.
COSTER, C. H. *The Iudicium Quinquevirale.* Medieval Academy of America, monograph 10. Cambridge, Mass., 1935.
—— *Late Roman Studies.* Harvard, 1968.
COSTER, C. H. and PATCH, H. R. 'Procopius and Boethius', *Speculum* 23, 1948, 284–7.
COURCELLE, P. 'Boèce et l'école d'Alexandrie', *Mélanges de l'école française de Rome* 52, 1935, 185–223.
—— *Les lettres grecques en occident de Macrobe à Cassiodore.* 2nd

edn. Paris, 1948. Eng. tr. by H. E. Wedeck, *Late Latin Writers and their Greek sources*. Harvard, 1969.
—— *La consolation de philosophie dans la tradition littéraire: antécedents et posterité de Boèce*. Paris, 1967.
—— *Connais toi toi-même de Socrate à S. Bernard*. Paris, 1974–5.
—— 'La survie comparée des Confessions augustiniennes et de la Consolation boécienne', in R. R. Bolgar (ed.), *Classical Influences on European culture AD 500–1500*. Cambridge, 1971.
—— art. Boèce, in *Dictionnaire des Lettres françaises*, Le moyen âge, Paris, 1964, 139–41.
CRACCO-RUGGINI, L. *Economia e società nell' Italia annonaria*. Milan, 1961.
—— 'Come Bisanzio vide la fine dell' impero d'occidente', in *La fine dell'impero romano d'occidente*. Rome (Istituto di studi Romani) 1978.
CRÄMER-RUGENBERG, I. *Die Substanzmetaphysik des Boethius in den opuscula sacra*. Diss. Köln, 1967.
CROCCO, A. *Introduzione a Boezio*. 2nd edn. Naples, 1975.
CURTIUS, E. R. *Europäische Literatur und lateinisches Mittelalter* 1st edn. Bern, 1948; 3rd edn. Munich, 1961. (Eng. tr. by W. R. Trask, London, 1953, repr. 1979.)
DAL PRA, M. (ed.) *Storia della filosofia*, vols. 5–6. Milan, 1975.
DALY, E. 'An early ninth century manuscript of Boethius', *Scriptorium* 4, 1950, 205–19.
DANE, J. A. 'Potestas/potentia: note on Boethius De Consolatione Philosophiae', *Vivarium* 17, 1979, 81–9.
DECELLES, D. 'Divine Prescience and human freedom in Augustine', *Augustinian Studies* 8, 1977, 151–60.
DEGLI' INNOCENTI, M. 'Nota al De Hebdomadibus di Boezio', *Divus Thomas* 42, 1939, 397–9.
DIENELT, K. 'Sprachliche Untersuchungen zu Boethius' Consolatio Philosophiae', *Glotta* 29, 1942, 98–138; 31, 1951, 28–69.
DIESNER, H. J. *Fulgentius von Ruspe als Theologe und Kirchenpolitiker*. Arbeiten zur Theologie 26. Stuttgart, 1966.
DRAAK, M. 'A Leyden Boethius-fragment with old Irish glosses', *Mededelingen der Koninkl. Nederl. Akad. von Wetensch. afd Letterkunde* 11, 3, 1948, 115–27 (on ninth-century fragment of Boethius, *Arithmetica*).
DRÄSEKE, J. 'Über die theologischen Schriften des Boethius', *Jahrbücher für protestantische Theologie* 12, 1886, 312–33.
—— 'Boethiana', *Zeitschrift für wissenschaftliche Theologie* 31, 1888, 94–104.
DUCHESNE, L. Edition of the *Liber Pontificalis*. 2 vols., Paris, 1886,

1892 (repr. 1955). (Supplementary volume by C. Vogel, 1957.)
—— L'église au VIème siècle. Paris, 1925.
DUCHEZ, M. E. *Imago mundi: la naissance de la theorie musicale occidentale dans les commentaires carolingiens de Martianus Capella*. Paris, 1979.
DÜRING, I. *Ptolemaios und Porphyrios über die Musik*. Göteborgs Högskolas Årsskrift 40, 1934.
—— (edition) *Die Harmonielehre des Klaudios Ptolemaios*. Göteborgs Högskolas Årsskrift 36, 1, 1930.
—— *Aristotle in the biographical tradition*. Göteborgs Universitets Årsskrift 63, 1957, no. 2.
—— (edition) *Aristotle's Protrepticus*. Studia Graeca et Latina Gothoburgensia 12, 1961.
DÜRR, K. *The propositional logic of Boethius*. Amsterdam, 1951.
EBBESEN, S. *Anonymus Aurelianensis II: Aristotle, Alexander, Porphyry and Boethius*. Cahiers de l'Institut de moyen-âge grec et latin, 16. Copenhagen, 1976,
ELERT, W. 'Die theopaschitische Formel', *Theologische Literaturzeitung* 75, 1950, 195–206.
—— *Der Ausgang der altkirchlichen Christologie*. Berlin, 1957.
ELSÄSSER, M. *Das Person-Verständnis des Boethius*. Diss. Würzburg, 1970.
ENGELS, J. 'Origine, sens et survie du terme boécien "secundum placitum"' *Vivarium* 1, 1963, 87–114.
ENSSLIN, W. *Theoderich der Grosse*. Munich, 1947. (2nd edn. 1959).
—— 'Papst Johannes I als Gesandter Theoderichs bei Kaiser Justinos I',*Byzantinische Zeitschrift* 44, 1951, 127–34.
—— 'Des Symmachus Historia Romana als Quelle für Jordanes', *Sitzungsberichte der bayerischen Akademie der Wissenschaften* 1948, 3.
—— 'Rex Theodericus inlitteratus', *Historisches Jahrbuch* 60, 1940, 391–8.
EVANS, G. R. 'The sub-Euclidean Geometry of the earlier middle ages up to the mid-twelfth century', *Archive for History of exact sciences* 16, 1976, 105–18.
—— 'More Geometrico: the place of the axiomatic method in the twelfth-century commentaries on Boethius' opuscula sacra', *Archives internationales d'histoire des sciences* 27, 1977, 207–21.
—— 'Introductions to Boethius' Arithmetic of the tenth to the fourteenth century', *History of Sciences* 16, 1978, 22–41.
—— 'A commentary on Boethius' Arithmetic of the twelfth or thirteenth century', *Annals of Science* 35, 1978, 131–41.

―― Old Arts and New Theology: The beginnings of theology as an academic discipline. Oxford, 1980.
FABRO, C. Participation et causalité selon S. Thomas d'Aquin. Louvain, 1961.
―― La nozione metafisica di partecipazione. 3rd edn. Rome, 1963.
FAUST, A. Der Möglichkeitsgedanke. Heidelberg, 1931.
FERRARINO, P. 'Quadruvium (quadrivio di sei arti? La caverna platonica)', Atti del congresso internazionale di Studi Varroniani, Rieti, settembre 1974 ii 358–64.
FLAMANT, J. Macrobe et le néoplatonisme latin à la fin du IVe siècle. Leiden, 1977.
FOLKERTS, M. (Edition) 'Boethius': Geometria altera. Texte und Untersuchungen zur Geschichte der exakten Wissenschaften 9. Wiesbaden, 1970.
FONTAINE, J. art. Ennodius, RAC 5, 1962, 398–421.
FORTESCUE, A. and SMITH, G. D. Edition of Consolatio Philosophiae, 1925.
FRANCISCI, P. de. 'Per la storia del senato romano e della curia nei secoli V e VI', Rendiconti della Pontificia Accademia Romana di Archeologia 22, 1946–7, 275–317.
FRANTZ, A. 'Pagan philosophers in Christian Athens', Proceedings of the American Philosophical Society 119, 1; 1975, 29–38.
FREDE, D. Aristoteles und die Seeschlacht. Hypomnemata 29. Göttingen, 1970.
FREDE, M. Die stoische Logik. Abhandlungen der Akademie der Wissenschaften zu Göttingen, phil. hist. Klasse, Dritte Folge 88, 1974.
GALDI, M. Saggi boeziani. Pisa, 1938.
GEGENSCHATZ, E. 'Die Gefährdung des Möglichen durch des Vorauswissen Gottes in der Sicht des Boethius', Wiener Studien 79, 1966, 517–30.
―― 'Die Freiheit der Entscheidung in der Consolatio Philosophiae des Boethius', Museum Helveticum 15, 1958, 110–29.
GERSH, S. From Iamblichus to Eriugena. Leiden, 1978.
GERVAISE, F. Histoire de Boèce, sénateur romain. Paris, 1715.
GIBSON, M. T. (ed.) Boethius, his life, thought, and influence. Oxford, 1981.
GIGON, O. Edition of Consolatio Philosophiae. Zürich, 1969.
GLORIE, F. Maxentii aliorumque Scytharum Monachorum nec non Ioannis Tomitanae urbis episcopi opuscula. Corpus Christianorum s.l. 85A. Turnhout, 1978.
GOUBERT, P. 'Autour du voyage à Byzance du Pape S. Jean I (523–526)', Orientalia Christiana Periodica 24, 1958, 339–52.

GRABMANN, M. *Die Geschichte der scholastischen Methode*, i. Freiburg-i-B., 1909. (2nd edn. Berlin, 1957.)

GRILLMEIER, A. 'Vorbereitung des Mittelalters, eine Studie über das Verhältnis von Chalkedonismus und Neu-Chalkedonismus in der lateinischen Theologie von Boethius bis zu Gregor dem Grossen', in *Das Konzil von Chalkedon*, eds. A. Grillmeier and H. Bacht, ii, 791–839. Würzburg, 1953.

GRUBER, J. *Kommentar zu Boethius De Consolatione Philosophiae*. Texte und Kommentare 9. Berlin, 1978.

GUITTARD, C. 'Une tentative de conciliation des valeurs chrétiennes et paiennes à travers l'oeuvre de Macrobe: syncretisme et philosophie d'histoire à la fin du IVe siècle', *Actes du IXe congrès de l'association Guillaume Budé*, Rome, avril 1973, ii, 1019–30. Paris, 1975.

GUNDERSDORF VON JESS, W. 'Divine Eternity in the doctrine of St. Augustine', *Augustinian Studies* 6, 1975, 75–96.

GUZZO. A. 'L'Isagoge di Porfirio e i commenti di Boezio', *Annali dell'Istituto superiore di magistero del Piemonte*, 7. Turin, 1934.

HAACKE, W. *Die Glaubensformel des Papstes Hormisdas im Acacianischen Schisma*. Analecta Gregoriana 20. Rome, 1939. [Thereon H. Koch in *Theolog. Literaturzeitung* 65, 1940, 259.]

HADOT, I. *Le problème du néoplatonisme alexandrin: Hieroclès et Simplicius*. Paris, 1978.

HADOT, P. 'Un fragment du commentaire perdu de Boèce sur les Catégories d'Aristote dans de codex Bernensis 363', *Archives d'histoire doctrinale et littéraire du moyen âge* 26, 1959.

—— 'La distinction de l'être et de l'étant dans le De Hebdomadibus de Boèce, in *Miscellanea Mediaevalia* ed. P. Wilpert ii, 147–53. Berlin, 1963.

—— *Porphyre et Victorinus*. Paris, 1968.

—— *Marius Victorinus*. Paris, 1971.

—— 'Forma essendi: interprétation philologique et interprétation philosophique d'une formule de Boèce, *Les Études Classiques* 38, 1970, 143–56.

—— 'L'harmonie des philosophies de Plotin et d'Aristote selon Porphyre dans le commentaire de Dexippe sur les Catégories', *Plotino e il Neoplatonismo in oriente e in occidente* (Accademia dei Lincei 1974, Quaderni 198, pp. 34–7). Rome, 1974.

—— 'Dieu comme acte d'être dans le néoplatonisme', *Dieu et l'être*. Paris: Études Augustiniennes, 1978.

HÄRING, N. M. *Life and works of Clarembald of Arras*. Toronto, 1965.

—— *The commentaries on Boethius by Gilbert of Poitiers*. Toronto,

1966.
—— *Commentaries on Boethius by Thierry of Chartres and his school.* Toronto, 1971.
—— 'Four commentaries on the De consolatione philosophiae in ms. Heiligenkreuz 130', *Medieval Studies* 31, 1969, 287–316.
HAGER, F. P. 'Die Materie und das Böse im antiken Platonismus', *Museum Helveticum* 19, 1962, 73–103.
—— 'Proklos und Alexander von Aphrodisias über ein Problem der Lehre von der Vorsehung', *Kephalaion for C. J. de Vogel*, 171–82. Assen, 1975.
HALLER, J. *Das Papsttum, Idee und Wirklichkeit I*, 1950, corrected edn. 1962.
HANDSCHIN, J. 'Die Musikanschauung des Johannes Scotus', *Deutsche Vierteljahrschrift für Literaturwissenschaft und Geistesgeschichte* 5, 1927, 361–41.
HARNACK, A. VON. 'Der erste deutsche Papst (Bonifatius II, 530/32) und die beiden letzten Dekrete des römischen Senats', *Sitzungsberichte der Berliner Akademie* 1924, 24–42 = *Kleine Schriften* II, 1980, 655–73.
HARTMANN, L. M. art. Boethius, *PW* III, 1, 1899, 596–600.
HEERKLOTZ, A. T. *Die Variae des Cassiodorus Senator als kulturgeschichtliche Quelle.* Diss. Heidelberg, 1926.
HENINGER, S. K. *Touches of Sweet Harmony: Pythagorean cosmology and Renaissance poetics.* San Marino (California): Huntington Library, 1974.
HENRY, D. P. *The Logic of St. Anselm.* Oxford, 1967.
—— *Commentary on De Grammatico: the historical-logical dimensions of a dialogue of St. Anselm's.* Dordrecht, 1974.
HENRY, P. *Plotin et l'occident.* Louvain, 1934.
HILDEBRAND, A. *Boethius und seine Stellung zum Christentume.* Regensburg, 1885.
HINTIKKA, J. *Time and Necessity: studies in Aristotle's theory of modality.* Oxford, 1973.
—— *Aristotle on Modality and Determinism* = Acta Philosophica Fennica 29, 1 (Helsinki, 1977).
HODGKIN, T. *Italy and her Invaders* III. 2nd edn. Oxford, 1896.
—— *Theodoric the Goth: the barbarian champion of civilisation.* New York and London, 1891.
HOFFMANN, E. 'Griechische Philosophie und christliches Dogma bei Boethius', *Pädagogischer Humanismus*, eds. W. Rügg and A. Stein. Zürich, 1955.
HOLLEMAN, A. W. J. *Pope Gelasius I and the Lupercalia.* Amsterdam, 1974.

HUBER, P. *Die Vereinbarkeit von göttlicher Vorsehung und menschlicher Freiheit in der Consolatio Philosophiae des Boethius.* Diss. Zürich, 1976.
HUYGENS, R. B. C. 'Mittelalterliche Kommentare zum O qui perpetua', *Sacris Erudiri* 6, 1954, 373–426.
I Goti in Occidente: problemi = Settimane di studio del Centro Italiano di Studi sull'alto medioevo III. Spoleto, 1956.
INEICHEN-EDER, C. E. 'Theologisches und philosophisches Lehrmaterial aus dem Alkuin-Kreise', *Deutsches Archiv für Erforschung des Mittelalters* 34, 1978, 192–201.
IRMSCHER, J. 'Das Ende des weströmischen Kaisertums in der byzantinischen Literatur', *Klio* 60, 1978, 397–401.
ISAAC, I. *Le Peri Hermeneias en Occident de Boèce à saint Thomas: histoire littéraire d'un traité d'Aristote.* Bibliothèque Thomiste 29. Paris, 1953.
JAHN, O. 'Über die Subscriptionen in den Handschriften römischer Classiker', *Berichte der Sächsische Akademie* 3, 1851, 327–72.
JEAUNEAU, E. 'L'héritage de la philosophie antique', in *La cultura antica nell'occidente latino dal VII all' XI secolo* = Settimane di studio del Centro Italiano Studi sull' alto medioevo XXII, 17–54. Spoleto, 1975.
JOLIVET, J. *Godescalk d'Orbais et la Trinité.* Paris, 1958.
JOLIVET, R. *Le problème du mal chez saint Augustin.* Paris, 1929.
JONES, A. H. M. 'The constitutional position of Odoacer and Theoderic', *Journal of Roman Studies*, 52, 1962, 126–30.
—— *The Later Roman Empire* (284–602). Oxford, 1964.
JONES, L. W. *Cassiodorus Senator, an introduction to divine and human readings.* New York, 1946.
JOSEPH, H. W. B. *An Introduction to Logic.* 2nd edn. Oxford, 1916.
JOURDAIN, C. 'De l'origine des traditions sur le christianisme de Boèce', *Memoires présentés par divers savants à l'Académie des Inscriptions et des Belles Lettres* 6, 1, 1860, 330–60.
KAPPELMACHER, A. 'Der schriftstellerische Plan des Boethius', *Wiener Studien* 46, 1929, 215–25.
KLIBANSKY, R. *The Continuity of the Platonic tradition during the middle ages.* 2nd edn. 1950.
KLIBANSKY, R. and LABOWSKY, C. Edition of Proclus, *in Parmenidem.* Plato Latinus III, 1953. (Contains parts of the commentary, in the Latin version of William of Moerbeke, not found in the Greek of Cousin's edition of 1864.)
KLINGNER, F. *De Boethii Consolatione Philosophiae.* Philologische Untersuchungen, 27. Berlin, 1921.
—— *Römische Geisteswelt.* 4th edn. Munich, 1961.

―― Review of Weinberger's edition of *Consolatio*, *Gnomon* 16, 1940, 26–32.
KNEALE, W. and M. *The Development of Logic.* Oxford, 1962.
KRAFFT, P. 'Apuleius Darstellung der providentia tripertita', *Museum Helveticum* 36, 1979, 153–63.
KUNZ, L. 'Die Tonartenlehre des Boethius', *Kirchenmusikalisches Jahrbuch* 31, 1936, 5–24.
LABRIOLLE, P. DE. *Histoire de la littérature latine chrétienne.* 3rd edn. Paris, 1947. (Eng. tr. by H. Wilson, 1924 repr. 1968.)
LADARIA FERRER, L. F. 'Persona y Relación en el De Trinitate de San Agustín', *Miscelanea Comillas* 30, 1972, 245–91.
LAMMA, P. *Teoderico.* Brescia, 1951.
―― *Oriente e Occidente nell'alto medioevo: studi storici sulle due civiltà* = Medioevo e umanesimo 5. Padova, 1968.
LANGLOIS, P. 'Les oeuvres de Fulgence le mythographe et le problème des deux Fulgences', *Jahrbuch für Antike und Christentum* 7, 1964, 94–105.
LAPIDGE, M. 'A Stoic metaphor in Late Latin poetry: the binding of the cosmos', *Latomus* 39, 1980, 817–37.
LAUFENBERG, H. *Der historische Wert des Panegyricus des Bischofs Ennodius.* Diss. Rostock, 1902.
LEHNERT, G. 'Eine rhetorische Quelle für Boethius' Commentare zu Aristoteles Peri Hermeneias', *Philologus* 59, 1900, 574–7.
LEONARDI, C. 'I commenti altomedievali ai classici pagani: da Severino Boezio a Remigio d'Auxerre', in *La cultura antica nell' occidente latino dal VII all' XI secolo* = Settimane di studio del Centro Italiano di Studi sull' alto medioevo XXII, 459–508. Spoleto, 1975.
LEVIN, F. R. *The Harmonics of Nicomachus and the Pythagorean tradition.* American Classical Association, 1975.
LEWIS, C. S. *The Discarded Image: an introduction to medieval and renaissance literature.* Cambridge, 1964.
LIEBESCHÜTZ, H. 'Boethius and the legacy of antiquity', in A. H. Armstrong (ed.), *The Cambridge history of later Greek and early medieval philosophy.* Cambridge, 1967.
LIPPMANN, E. A. 'The place of music in the liberal arts', *Aspects of medieval and renaissance music in honour of G. Reese.* London, 1967.
LLEWELLYN, P. A. B. 'The Roman Church during the Laurentian schism: priests and senators', *Church History* 45, 1976, 417–27.
―― 'The Roman clergy during the Laurentian schism', *Ancient Society* 8, 1977, 245–75.
―― 'Le indicazioni numeriche del Liber Pontificalis relativamente

alle ordinazioni del V secolo', *Rivista della storia della Chiesa in Italia* 29, 1975, 439–43.
LLOYD, A. C. 'Neoplatonic logic and Aristotelian logic', *Phronesis* i, 1955–6, 58–72 and 146–60.
LÖWE, H. *Von Cassiodor zu Dante*. Berlin, 1973.
—— 'Theoderich der Grosse und Papst Johann I', *Historisches Jahrbuch* 72, 1953, 83–100.
LUDWIG, G. *Cassiodor: über den Ursprung der abendländischen Schule*. Frankfurt/M, 1967.
LUISELLI, G. 'Note sulla perduta Historia Romana di Q. Aurelio Memmio Simmaco', *Studi Urbinati* 49, 1975, 529–35.
—— 'Sul De summa temporum di Jordanes', *Romanobarbarica* I, 83–133. Rome, 1976.
LUMPE, A. 'Ennodiana', *Byzantinische Forschungen* i, 1966, 200–210.
—— 'Die konziliengeschichtliche Bedeutung des Ennodius', *Annuarium historiae Conciliorum* 1, 1969, 15–36.
MCINERNY, R. *A history of western philosophy* III, 52–75. Notre Dame, 1970.
—— 'Boethius and St. Thomas Aquinas', *Rivista di filosofia neoscolastica* 66, 1974, 219–45.
MCKINLAY, A. P. 'Stylistic texts and the chronology of the work of Boethius', *Harvard Studies in Classical Philology* 18, 1907, 123–56.
—— 'The De syllogismis categoricis and Introductio ad syllogismos categoricos of Boethius', *Classical and Mediaeval Studies in honor of E. K. Rand*, ed. L. W. Jones, 209–19. New York, 1938.
MCTIGHE, T. P. 'Boethius on Universals, a reconsideration', *Proceedings of the patristic, mediaeval, and renaissance Congress*, 2, 1977, 113–21.
MAGI, L. *La sede romana nella corrispondenza degli imperatori e patriarchi bizantini, VI–VII sec.* = Bibliothèque de la Revue d'histoire ecclésiastique 57. Louvain, 1972.
MAIOLI, B. *Teoria dell' essere e dell' esistente e classificazione delle scienze in M. S. Boezio*. (Università di Siena, Quaderni dell' Istituto di scienze filosofiche 4.) Rome, 1978.
MAIR, J. R. S. 'A manual for monks: Cassiodorus and the Enkyklios Paideia', *Journal of Theological Studies*, n.s. 31, 1980, 547–51.
—— 'A note on Cassiodorus and the seven liberal arts', ibid. 26, 1975, 419–21.
MANITIUS, M. *Geschichte der lateinischen Literatur des Mittelalters*. 3 vols. Munich, 1911–31.
MARIÉTAN, J. *Problème de la classification des sciences d'Aristote à*

saint Thomas. 1901.
MARROU, H.-I. *S. Augustin et la fin de la culture antique.* Paris, 1938.
—— *Histoire de l'éducation dans l'antiquité.* Paris, n.d. (1948). (Eng. tr. by G. Lamb, 1956.)
MARSHALL, M. H. 'Boethius' definition of Persona and medieval understanding of the Roman Theater', *Speculum* 25, 1950, 471–82.
MARTINDALE, J. R. *The Prosopography of the Later Roman Empire* II, AD 395–527. Cambridge, 1980. (Abbreviated *PLRE*.)
MARTROYE, F. *L'Occident à l'époque byzantine: Goths et Vandales.* Paris, 1904.
MASI, M. 'Manuscripts containing the De musica of Boethius', *Manuscripta* 15, 1971, 89–95.
MASSERA, G. *Severino Boezio e la scienza armonica tra l'antichita e il medio evo.* Parma, 1976.
MATES, B. *Stoic Logic.* Berkeley, 1953.
—— *Elementary Logic.* Oxford, 1965.
MATHIESEN, T. J. 'An annotated translation of Euclid's division of a monochord, *Journal of Music Theory* 19, 1975, 236–58.
MATHON, G. 'Le commentaire du pseudo-Erigène sur la Consolatio Philosophiae de Boèce', *Recherches de théologie ancienne et mediévale* 22, 1955, 213–57.
—— 'La tradition de la Consolation de Boèce', *Revue des études Augustiniennes* 14, 1968, 133–8.
MATHWICH, J. 'De Boethi morte', *Eunomia* 4, Prague, 1960, 26–37.
MAURACH, G. 'Boethiusinterpretationen', *Antike und Abendland* 14, 1968, 126–41; reprinted in *Römische Philosophie*, ed. G. Maurach, 385–410. Darmstadt, 1976.
MERLAN, P. *From Platonism to Neoplatonism.* 3rd edn. The Hague, 1968.
—— 'Ammonius Hermiae, Zacharias scholasticus, and Boethius', *Greek Roman and Byzantine Studies* 9, 1968, 193–203.
MICHEL, P.-H. *De Pythagore à Euclide.* Paris, 1950.
MIEKLEY, G. *De Boethii libri de musica primi fontibus.* Diss. Jena, 1898.
MILIK, J. T. 'La famiglia di Felice III papa', *Epigraphica* 28, 1967, 140–2.
MILLÁN BRAVO, L. 'Die Prägung des Terminus accidenter im Latein durch Boethius', *Vivarium* 5, 1967, 1–7.
MINIO-PALUELLO, L. (ed.). *Aristoteles Latinus*, vols. I, II, III, V, VI. Leiden, 1961–75.
—— *Opuscula: the Latin Aristotle.* Amsterdam, 1972.

—— art. Boethius: *Encyclopaedia Britannica* (1968).
—— art. Boethius: *Dictionary of Scientific Biography* II, New York 1970, 228–36.
MOHRMANN, C. 'Some remarks on the language of Boethius' Consolatio Philosophiae', in J. J. O'Meara and B. Naumann (eds.), *Latin script and letters* AD 400–900: *Festschrift Ludwig Bieler*, 54–61. Leiden, 1976.
—— Introduction to edition of *Consolatio Philosophiae* by O. Dallera (Milan, 1977).
MOMIGLIANO, A. 'Cassiodorus and the Italian culture of his time', *Proceedings of the British Academy* 41, 1955, 207–55, reprinted in his *Secondo Contributo alla storia degli studi classici*, 191–299 (Rome, 1960), and in his *Studies in Historiography*, 181–210 (London, 1969).
—— 'Gli Anicii e la storiografia latina del VI sec. d. C.', *Rendiconti Accad. Lincei* 8, 11, 1956, 279–97, reprinted in his *Secondo Contributo*, 1960.
MOMMSEN, T. 'Ostgothische Studien', *Neues Archiv* 14–15 (1889–90), reprinted in his *Gesammelte Schriften* 6, 1910 repr. 1965.
—— Edition of *Chronica Minora*, 3 vols. (Monumenta Germaniae Historica), 1892–8.
—— Edition of *Liber Pontificalis* (MGH), 1898.
MONCEAUX, P. 'L'Isagoge latine de Marius Victorinus', in *Philologie et linguistique, Mélanges L. Havet*, 291–310. Paris, 1909.
MOORHEAD, J. 'The Laurentian schism: East and West in the Roman church', *Church History* 47, 1978, 125–36.
—— 'Boethius and Romans in Ostrogothic service', *Historia* 27, 1978, 604–12.
MORAUX, P. *Les listes anciennes des ouvrages d'Aristote*. Louvain, 1951.
—— *Le commentaire d'Alexandre d'Aphrodise aux Second Analytiques d'Aristote*. Berlin, 1979.
MOREAU, J. (ed.) *Excerpta Valesiana*. Revised edn. by V. Velkov. Leipzig, Teubner, 1968.
MORROW, G. R. (tr.). *Proclus: a commentary on the first book of Euclid's Elements*. Princeton, 1970.
MÜLLER, G. A. *Die Trostschrift des Boetius, Beitrag zu einer literarhistorischen Quellenuntersuchung*. (Diss. Giessen.) Berlin, 1912.
MÜNXELHAUS, B. *Pythagoras musicus: zur Rezeption der pythagoreischen Musiktheorie als quadrivischer Wissenschaft im lateinischen Mittelalter*. Bonn, 1976.
NAJOCK, D. *Drei anonyme griechische Traktate über die Musik*.

Göttingen, 1972.
NAVARRA, L. 'Contributo storico di Ennodio', *Augustinianum* 14, 1974, 315–42.
NÉDONCELLE, M. 'Les variations de Boèce sur la personne', *Revue des sciences religieuses*, 29, 1955, 201–38.
—— 'Prosopon et persona dans l'antiquité classique', *Revue de science religieuse* 22, 1948, 277–99.
NISTERS, B. *Die Christologie des hl. Fulgentius von Ruspe.* Münsterische Beiträge zur Theologie 16, 1930.
NITZSCH, F. *Das System des Boethius und die ihm zugeschriebenen theologischen Schriften.* Berlin, 1860.
NORIS, H. 'De uno ex Trinitate carne passo', in *Thesaurus theologicus* IX (Venice, 1762), 231–323.
OBERTELLO, L. A. M. *Severino Boezio de hypotheticis syllogismis.* Brescia, 1969.
—— 'Boezio, le scienze del quadrivio e la cultura medioevale', *Atti del' Accademia Ligure di scienze e lettere* 28, 1971, 152–70.
—— *Severino Boezio.* 2 vols. Genoa, 1974.
—— *Boezio: la Consolazione della filosofia, gli opuscoli teologici.* (I classici del pensiero, sezione II, Medioevo e rinascimento.) Milan (Rusconi), 1979.
O'DONNELL, J. J. *Cassiodorus.* Berkeley, 1979.
—— 'The demise of paganism', *Traditio* 35, 1979, 45–88.
—— Review of revised Loeb edition of Boethius by S. J. Tester, in *American Journal of Philology* 98, 1977, 77–9.
OTTO, S. *Person und Subsistenz, die philosophische Anthropologie des Leontios von Byzanz.* Munich, 1968.
OVERBECK, F. *Vorgeschichte und Jugend der mittelalterlichen Scholastik, eine kirchenhistorische Vorlesung*, ed. C. A. Bernouilli. Basel, 1917 (repr. Darmstadt, 1971).
OWEN, G. E. L. (ed.) *Aristotle on Dialectic, the Topics.* Oxford, 1968.
PAGALLO, G. F. 'Per una edizione critica del De hypotheticis syllogismis di Boezio', *Italia Medioevale e Umanistica* 1, 1958, 69–101.
PALERMO, G. 'Cassiodoro, l'anima', *Orpheus* 23, 1976, 41–143.
PATCH, H. R. *The Tradition of Boethius.* Oxford, 1935.
—— 'Fate in Boethius and the Neoplatonists', *Speculum* 4, 1929, 62–72.
—— 'Necessity in Boethius and the Neoplatonists', *Speculum* 10, 1935, 393–404.
—— 'The beginnings of the legend of Boethius', *Speculum* 22, 1947, 443–5.

PATTIN, A. *Le Liber de causis*. Louvain n.d. (1966).
PEIPER, R. Edition of Boethius' *Consolatio philosophiae* and *Opuscula*. Leipzig, Teubner, 1860.
PEPE, L. 'La metrica di Boezio', *Giornale italiano di filologia* 7, 1954, 227–43.
PÉPIN, J. *Augustin et la dialectique*. Villanova University, 1976.
PERRONE, L. *La Chiesa di Palestina e le controversie cristologiche* = Testi e ricerche di scienze religiose 18. Brescia, 1980.
PFEILSCHIFTER, G. *Der Ostgotenkönig Theoderich der Grosse und die katholische Kirche*. Münster, 1896.
—— *Theoderich der Grosse*. Mainz, 1910.
PFLIGERSDORFFER, G. 'Zur Frage nach dem Verfasser der pseudoaugustinischen Categoriae Decem, *Wiener Studien* 65, 1950, 131–7.
—— 'Andronikos von Rhodos und die Postprädikamente bei Boethius', *Vigiliae Christianae* 7, 1953, 98–115.
—— 'Zu Boethius, De Interpr. ed sec. I p. 4, 4 sq. Meiser nebst Beobachtungen zur Geschichte der Dialektik bei den Römern', *Wiener Studien* 66, 1953, 131–42.
PICKERING, F. P. *Augustin oder Boethius? Geschichtsschreibung und epische Dichtung im Mittelalter und in der Neuzeit*. Berlin, 1967.
PICOTTI, G. B. 'Il senato romano e il processo di Boesio', *Archivio storico Italiano* 7, 15, 1931, 205–28.
—— 'Osservazioni su alcuni punti della politica religiosa di Teodorico', *Settimana*... Spoleto III, 1956, 173–226.
—— 'I sinodi romani nella scisma laurenziano', *Studi in onore di G. Volpe* III, 743–86. Florence, 1958.
PIEPER, J. *Scholastik*. Munich, 1960. (Eng. tr. by R. and C. Winston, London, 1961.)
PIETRI, C. 'Le sénat, le peuple chrétien et les partis du cirque sous le pape Symmache', *MEFR* 78, 1966, 122–39.
—— *Roma Christiana*. French school at Rome, 1976.
PIKE, N. 'Divine Omniscience and voluntary action', *Philosophical Review* 74, 1965, 27–46.
—— *God and Timelessness*. London, 1970.
—— 'Divine Foreknowledge, human freedom, and possible worlds', *Philosophical Review* 86, 1977, 209–16.
PIZZANI. U. 'Studi sulle fonti del De institutione Musica di Boezio', *Sacris Erudiri* 16, 1965, 5–164.
—— 'Boezio consulante tecnico al servizio dei re barbarici', *Romanobarbarica* 3, 1978, 189–242.
PLANTINGA, A. *The Nature of Necessity*. Oxford, 1974.
—— *God, Freedom and Evil*. New York, 1974.

PRINZ, K. 'Bemerkungen zur Philosophiae Consolatio des Boethius', *Wiener Studien* 53, 1935, 171–5.
PRIOR, A. N. 'The logic of negative terms in Boethius', *Franciscan Studies* 13, 1953, 1–6.
—— *Formal Logic*. 2nd edn. Oxford, 1962.
RAJNA, P. 'Le denominazioni Trivium e Quadrivium', *Studi medievali* n.s. 1, Turin 1928, 4–36.
RAND, E. K. 'Der dem Boethius zugeschriebene Traktat De fide catholica', *Jahrbücher für classische Philologie*, suppl. 26, 1901, 401–61.
—— 'On the composition of Boethius' Consolatio Philosophiae', *Harvard Studies in classical philology* 15, 1904, 1–28.
—— *The Founders of the Middle Ages*. Cambridge, Mass. 1928.
—— 'The supposed commentary of John the Scot on the Opuscula sacra of Boethius', *Revue néo-scolastique* 36, 1934, 67–77.
—— 'La Rome de Boèce et de Dante', *Revue des cours et conférences* 37, 1, 1936, 450–63.
—— Review of V. Schurr in *Speculum* 11, 1936, 153–6.
RAPISARDA, E. *La crisi spirituale di Boezio*. Florence, 1947. 2nd edn. Catania, 1953.
RASI, P. 'Sulla paternità del c.d. Edictum Theoderici regis', *Archivio Giuridico* 145, 1953, 113 ff.
REICHENBERGER, K. *Untersuchungen zur literarischen Stellung der Consolatio Philosophiae*. Cologne, 1954.
REIFFERSCHEID, A. *De Latinorum codicum subscriptionibus commentariolum*. Bratislava, 1873.
RICHÉ, P. *Education et culture dans l'occident barbare VIe–VIIe siècle*. Patristica Sorbonensia 4. Paris, 1962.
—— *Les écoles et l'enseignemenent dans l'occident chrétien de la fin du Ve siècle au milieu du XIe siècle*. Paris, 1979.
RIJK, L. M. de. *Logica Modernorum*, 2 vols. Assen, 1962, 1967.
—— 'On the chronology of Boethius' works on logic', *Vivarium* 2, 1964, 1–49, 125–62.
RINTELEN, F. JOACHIM VON. 'Augustine, the ascent in value towards God', *Augustinian Studies* 2, 1971, 155–78.
RIST, J. M. *Stoic Philosophy*. Cambridge, 1977.
ROBINSON, D. M. 'The Wheel of Fortune', *Classical Philology* 41, 1946, 207–16.
RODA, S. 'Alcune ipotesi sulla prima edizione dell' epistolario di Simmaco', *La Parola del Passato* 184, 1979, 31–54.
ROGER, M. *L'enseignement des lettres classiques d'Ausone à Alcuin*. Paris, 1905.
ROHLS, J. *Wilhelm von Auvergne und der mittelalterliche Aristote-*

lismus. Münchener Monographien zur historischen und systematischen Theologie, 5. Munich, 1980.
ROLAND-GOSSELIN, M.-D. *Le de ente et essentia de S. Thomas d'Aquin*. Bibliothèque Thomiste 8. Le Saulchoir, 1926.
ROUSSEAU, P. 'The death of Boethius: the charge of maleficium', *Studia Medievalia*, 3rd series, 20, 1979, 871–89.
RULAND, H.-J. *Die arabischen Fassungen von zwei Schriften des Alexander von Aphrodisias, Über die Vorsehung und über das liberum arbitrium*. Diss. Saarland, 1976.
SALAMON, M. 'Priscianus und sein Schülerkreis in Konstantinopel', *Philologus* 123, 1979, 91–6.
SAN MARTIN, J. 'La prima salus del papa Hormisdas', *Revista española de teología* 1, 1941, 767–812.
SASSEN, F. 'Boethius Leermeister der middeleeuwen', *Studia Catholica* 14, 1938, 97–122 and 216–30.
SCHANZ, M., HOSIUS, C. and KRÜGER, G. *Geschichte der römischen Litteratur bis zum Gesetzgebungswerk des Kaisers Justinian*, IV 2. Munich 1920.
SCHEIBLE, H. *Die Gedichte in der Consolatio Philosophiae des Boethius*. Heidelberg, 1972.
SCHEPSS, G. *Handschriftliche Studien zu Boethius De consolatione philosophiae*. Progr. Würzburg, 1881.
—— 'Geschichtliches aus Boethiushandschriften', *Neues Archiv* 11, 1886, 121–41.
—— 'Subscriptionen in Boethiushandschriften', *Blätter für das bayerische Gymnasialschulwesen* 24, 1888, 19–29.
—— 'Zu Boethius', *Commentationes Woelfflinianae*, 277–80. Leipzig, 1891.
—— 'Zu Boethius De consolatione', *Philologus* 52, 1893, 380–1.
—— 'Zu pseudo-Boethius De fide catholica', *Zeitschrift für wissenschaftliche Theologie* 38, 1895, 269–78.
—— 'Zu König Alfreds Boethius', *Archiv für das Studium der neueren Sprachen* 94, 1895, 149–60.
SCHLIEBEN, R. *Christliche Theologie und Philologie in der Spätantike: Die schulwissenschaftlichen Methoden der Psalmenexegese Cassiodors*. Arbeiten zur Kirchengeschichte 46. Berlin, 1974.
SCHMID, W. 'Philosophisches und Medizinisches in der Consolatio des Boethius', *Festschrift Bruno Snell*, 1956, 113–44 (reprinted in *Römische Philosophie*, ed. G. Maurach, Darmstadt, 1976, 341–84).
—— 'Boethius and the Claims of Philosophy', *Studia Patristica* 2 = Texte und Untersuchungen 64, 1957, 368–75.

SCHMIDT-KOHL, V. *Die neuplatonische Seelenlehre in der Consolatio Philosophiae des Boethius*. Beiträge zur klassischen Philologie 16. Meisenheim, 1965.
SCHNEIDER, A. M. 'Gotengrabsteine aus Konstantinopel', *Germania* 21, 1937, 175–7.
SCHRADE, L. 'Music in the philosophy of Boethius', *Musical Quarterly* 33, 1947; 188–200.
—— 'Die Stellung der Musik in der Philosophie des Boethius als Grundlage der ontologische Musikerziehung', *Archiv für Geschichte der Philosophie* 41, 1932, 368–400.
SCHRIMPF, G. *Die Axiomenschrift des Boethius (de Hebdomadibus) als philosophisches Lehrbuch des Mittelalters*. Leiden, 1966.
SCHURR, V. *Die Trinitätslehre des Boethius im Lichte der 'Skythischen Kontroversen'*. Forschungen zur christlichen Literatur und Dogmengeschichte 18, 1. Paderborn, 1935.
SCHWARTZ, E. *Publizistische Sammlungen zum Acacianischen Schisma*. Abhandlungen der bayerischen Akademie der Wissenschaften, Phil. hist. Abt. NF 10, 1934.
SCIUTO, F. 'Il dualismo della Consolatio di Boezio', *Acta Philologica* 3, 1964, 361–71.
SEECK, O. art. Symmachus (30) in *PW* IVA, 1932, 1160.
SEMERIA, G. 'Il cristianesimo di Severino Boezio rivendicato', *Studi e documenti di storia e diritto* 21, 1900, 61–178.
SHARPLES, R. W. 'Aristotelian and Stoic conceptions of necessity in the De fato of Alexander of Aphrodisias', *Phronesis* 20, 1975, 247–74.
—— 'Responsibility, chance and not being (Alex. Aphr. Mantissa 169–72)' *Bulletin of the Institute of Classical Studies*, University of London, 22, 1975.
—— 'Alexander of Aphrodisias De fato: some parallels', *Classical Quarterly*, 28, 1978, 243–66.
SHIEL, J. 'Boethius and Andronicus of Rhodes', *Vigiliae Christianae* 11, 1957, 179–85.
—— 'Boethius' commentaries on Aristotle', *Mediaeval and Renaissance Studies* 4, 1958, 217–44.
—— 'Boethius the hellenist', *History Today* 14, 1964, 478–86.
—— 'Boethius and Eudemus', *Vivarium* 12, 1974, 14–17.
SILK, E. T. 'Boethius' Consolation of Philosophy as a sequel to Augustine's Dialogues and Soliloquies', *Harvard Theological Review* 32, 1939, 19–39.
SILVESTRE, H. 'Grégoire de Tours avait-il lu Boèce?' *Latomus* 9, 1950, 437.
—— 'Le commentaire inédit de Jean Scot Erigène au mètre IX du

Livre III du De consolatione philosophiae', *Revue d'histoire ecclésiastique* 47, 1952, 44–122.
—— 'Loci paralleli entre l'Alethia de C. M. Victorius et la Consolation de Boèce, *Sacris Eruditi* 13, 1962, 517–18.
—— 'Note sur la survie de Macrobe au moyen âge', *Classica et mediaevalia* 24, 1963, 170–80.
SODANO, A. R. Edition of Porphyry, *in Timaeum*. Naples, 1964.
SOLIGNAC, A. art. Marius Victorinus, in *Dictionnaire de Spiritualité* 10, 1978, 616–23.
SOLMSEN, 'Platos Einfluss auf die Bildung der mathematischen Methode', *Quellen und Studien zur Geschichte der griechischen Mathematik*, B Studien I, 1931, 93–107.
—— *Die Entwicklung der aristotelischen Logik und Rhetorik*, 1929.
—— 'Boethius and the Organon', *American Journal of Philology* 31, 1944, 69–74.
SORABJI, N. *Necessity, Cause and Blame*. London, 1980.
STAHL, W. H. *Martianus Capella and the seven liberal arts*, 2 vols. New York, 1971–7.
STANGL, T. 'Pseudoboethiana', *Jahrbücher für classische Philologie* 29, 1883, 193–208 and 285–301.
—— 'Zu Boethius', *Philologus* 51, 1892, 483.
—— *Boethiana vel Boethii commentariorum in Ciceronis Topica emendationes ex octo codicibus haustas*. Gotha, 1882.
—— *Tulliana et Mario-Victoriniana*. Progr. Munich, 1888 (edition of Victorinus, *De definitionibus*, reprinted in P. Hadot, *Marius Victorinus*, 1971).
STEIN, E. *Histoire du bas-empire* II. Paris, 1949.
STEWART, H. F. *Boethius, an essay*. Edinburgh, 1891.
—— 'A commentary by Remigius Autissiodorensis of the De consolatione philosophiae of Boethius', *Journal of Theological Studies* 17, 1915, 22–42.
STEWART, H. F. and RAND, E. K. Edition of *Consolatio* and *Opuscula* in Loeb Classical Library. 1st edn. 1918. Revised edition by S. J. Tester 1973.
STÖBER, F. 'Quellenstudien zum Laurentianischen Schisma (498–514)', *Sitzungsberichte... Wien*, Phil. hist. Kl, 112, 1886, 269–347.
STUMP, E. *Boethius de topicis differentiis*. Ithaca, NY 1976.
—— 'Boethius' works on the Topics', *Vivarium* 12, 1974, 77–93.
SULLIVAN, M. W. *Apuleian Logic: the nature, sources, and influence of Apuleius's Peri Hermeneias*. Amsterdam, 1967.
SULOWSKI, J. 'Les sources du De consolatione philosophiae de Boèce', *Sophia* 25, 1957, 76–85.

―― 'The sources of Boethius' De consolatione philosophiae', *Sophia* 29, 1961, 67–94.
SUNDWALL, J. *Abhandlungen zur Geschichte des ausgehenden Römertums*. Helsingfors, 1919 (repr. 1980).
TATEO, F. art. Boezio in *Enciclopedia Dantesca* I. Rome, 1970.
TAYLOR, A. E. *A commentary on Plato's Timaeus*. Oxford, 1928.
THEILER, W. *Forschungen zur Platonismus*. Berlin, 1966.
THOMAS, A. and ROQUES, M. 'Traductions françaises de la Consolatio Philosophiae de Boèce', *Histoire littéraire de la France* 37, 1938, 419–88.
THOMAS, I. 'Boethius: locus a repugnantibus', *Methodos* 3, 1951, 303–7.
TIXERONT, J. *Mélanges de Patrologie et d'histoire des dogmes*. 2nd edn. Paris, 1921.
TRÄNKLE, H. 'Philologische Bemerkungen zum Boethiusprozess', *Romanitas et Christianitas, Studia J. H. Waszink*, 1973, 329–39.
―― 'Ist die Philosophiae Consolatio des Boethius zum vorgesehenen Abschluss gelangt? *Vigiliae Christianae* 31, 1977, 148–56.
TOTOK, W. *Handbuch der Geschichte der Philosophie* I, 349–53. Frankfurt, 1964. (Bibliography.)
ULLMANN, W. *Gelasius I: das Papsttum an der Wende von der Spätantike zum Mittelalter*. Stuttgart, 1981.
USENER, H. 'Der römische Senat und die Kirche in der Ostgothenzeit', *Commentationes philologicae in honorem Mommseni*. Berlin, 1877.
―― *Anecdoton Holderi, ein Beitrag zur Geschichte Roms in ostgothischer Zeit*. Bonn, 1877 (repr. 1969).
VAN DEN DRIESSCHE, R. 'Sur le De syllogismo hypothetico de Boèce', *Methodos* 1, 1949, 293–307.
VAN DER VYVER, A. 'Clovis et la politique méditerranée', *Études à la mémoire de H. Pirenne*, 1937, 367–87.
―― 'Les étapes du developpement philosophique du haut moyen-âge', *Revue belge de philologie et d'histoire* 8, 1929, 425–52.
―― 'Cassiodore et son œuvre', *Speculum* 6, 1931, 244–92.
―― 'Les Institutions de Cassiodore et son fondation a Vivarium', *Revue Bénédictine* 54, 1941, 59–88.
―― 'Les traductions du De consolatione philosophiae en littérature comparée', *Humanisme et Renaissance* 6, 1939, 247–73.
―― Edition of Abbo of Fleury's logical treatises: *Abbonis floriacensis opera inedita* (ed. R. Raes). Brugge, 1966.
VAN GERVEN, J. 'Liberté humaine et préscience divine d'après saint Augustin', *Revue philosophique de Louvain* 55, 1957, 317–30.
VARADY, L. 'Jordanes Studien: Jordanes und das Chronicon des

Marcellinus Comes—die Selbständigkeit des Jordanes', *Chiron* 6, 1976, 441–87.
—— *Die Auflösung des Altertums*. Budapest, 1978.
VASILIEV, A. A. *Justin the First*. Dumbarton Oaks Studies I. Cambridge, Mass., 1950.
VERBEKE, J. and MONCHO, J. R. *Némésius d'Emèse De Natura Hominis: Traduction de Burgundio de Pise*. Leiden, 1975 (especially Introduction, pp. lxii/lxxxv).
VERNET, F. art. Boèce, in *Dictionnaire de spiritualité* I, 1937, 1739–45.
VISCARDI, O. 'Boezio e la trasmissione e conservazione della cultura greca in Occidente', in *I Goti in Occidente, Settimana ... Spoleto*, 1956, 323–43.
VISMARA, G. 'Romani e Goti di fronte al diritto nel regno ostrogoto', ibid. 409–63.
—— 'El Edictum Theoderici', *Estudios visigoticos* 1, 1956, 49–89.
VOGEL, C. J. DE. 'Boethiana', *Vivarium* 9, 1971, 59–66; 10, 1972, 1–40.
—— 'Amor quo caelum regitur', *Vivarium* 1, 1963, 2–34.
—— 'The problem of philosophy and Christian faith in Boethius' Consolatio', in *Romanitas et Christianitas: Studia J. H. Waszink* (Amsterdam, 1973), pp. 357–70.
—— 'The concept of personality in Greek and Christian thought', in *Studies in philosophy and the history of Philosophy*, ed. J. K. Ryan, ii, Washington, 1963.
VOLBACH, W. F. *Elfenbeinarbeiten der Spätantike und des frühen Mittelalters*. 3rd edn. Mainz, 1976.
WALLIS, R. T. *Neoplatonism*. London, 1972.
WARTELLE, A. *Inventaire des manuscrits grecs d'Aristote et de ses commentateurs*. Paris, 1963.
WASZINK, J. H. Edition of Calcidius' commentary on the Timaeus, London and Leiden, 1962.
WEINBERGER, G. Edition of *Consolatio Philosophiae*, CSEL 67, 1934.
WES, M. A. *Das Ende des Kaisertums im Westen des römischen Reiches*. 's-Gravenhage, 1967.
WESTENBÜRGER, G. *Der Symmachusprozess von 501*. Tübingen, 1939.
WESTERINK, L. G. *Anonymous Prolegomena to Platonic Philosophy*. Amsterdam, 1962.
WESTERINK, L. G. and SAFFREY, H. D. Edition of Proclus' *Theologia Platonica* (Budé collection). Paris, 1968–.
WIELAND, W. *Offenbarung bei Augustinus*. Tübinger theologische

Studien 12. Mainz, 1978.
WILHELM, F. 'Maximianus und Boethius', *Rheinisches Museum* 62, 1907, 601–14.
WILLE, G. *Musica Romana: die Bedeutung der Musik im Leben der Römer*. Amsterdam, 1867.
WILMART, A. *Analecta Reginensia* = Studi e Testi 59, 1933.
WILTSHIRE, S. F. 'Boethius and the Summum Bonum', *The Classical Journal* 67, 1972, 216–20.
WINTERBOTTOM, M. 'Quintilian and Boethius', *Bulletin of the Institute of Classical Studies*, University of London, 14, 1967, 83.
WOLF, C. 'Untersuchungen zum Krankheitsbild in dem ersten Buch der Consolatio Philosophiae des Boethius', *Rivista di cultura classica e medioevale* 6, 1964, 213–23.
WOLFRAM, H. *Geschichte der Goten von den Anfängen bis zur Mitte des sechsten Jahrhunderts: Entwurf einer historischen Ethnographie*. Munich, 1979.
WOLFSKEEL, C.-W. 'Christliches und Neuplatonisches im Denken Augustins', *Kephalaion for C. J. de Vogel*, 195–203. Assen, 1975.
WOTKE, F. art. Boethius, *RAC* ii, 1954, 482–8.
WURM, K. *Substanz und Qualität*. Berlin, 1973.
ZEILLER, J. 'Les églises ariennes de Rome à l'époque de la domination gothique', *MEFR* 24, 1904, 17–33.
—— 'Etude sur l'arianisme en Italie à l'époque ostrogothique et à l'époque lombarde', *MEFR* 25, 1905, 127–46.
ZIMMERMANN, F. W. *Al-Farabi's commentary and short treatise on Aristotle's De interpretatione*. British Academy, 1981.
ZINTZEN, C. *Damascii Vitae Isidori Reliquiae*. Hildesheim, 1967.
ZUM BRUNN, E. *Le dilemme de l'être et du néant chez saint Augustin*. Paris, 1969.

NOTES

CHAPTER I   Pages 1–3

1. Ennodius, *Paraenesis didascalica*, ed. Vogel *(MGH)* p. 314, 40 f.; ed. Hartel *(CSEL* 6), p. 409, 8. His name Severinus may point to a family connection with the consul of this name (for 461, see *PLRE* ii, p. 1001) whose attendance at an imperial banquet in Arles is described by Sidonius Apollinaris *(ep.* i, 11, 10–16). A connection with Severinus the apostle of Noricum, who died about 482, is unlikely.
2. Procopius, *BG* i, 1, 5–8.
3. Cassiodorus, *Variae* ii, 24.
4. A. H. M. Jones, 'The Constitutional Position of Odoacer and Theoderic,' *Journal of Roman Studies* 52 (1962), 126–30.
5. *Avell.* 114, 1 *(CSEL* 35 p. 508) = Hormisdas, *ep.* 14, p. 768 Thiel.
6. Boethius, *In Cat.* iii, *PL* 64, 264A.
7. Avitus, *C. Eutych.* i, p. 16, 1 Peiper *(MGH)* = *PL* 59, 203B1. Cf. ibid. ii, p. 22, 14 = *PL* 59, 210 C10, where Anastasius is 'rex orientis'.
8. *CSEL* 35, p. 509, 20 = Hormisdas, *ep.* 14, 2 p. 769 Thiel. So also Jordanes, *Getica* 29, 146 and 49, 257. The usage goes back to the division by Theodosius I in 395 *(Epitome de Caesaribus* 48, 19–20), but the source may reflect later custom. During the Acacian schism Pope Felix III tells the emperor Zeno 'hoc expedit ut si utraque Roma pro mutuo pignore nuncupatur, fiat utriusque [utraque Thiel] una fides illa Romanorum . . . ' *(ep.* 15, 3 p. 272 Thiel; critical edn. in Schwartz, *Publizistische Sammlungen zum Acacianischen Schisma,* Abh. Bayer. Akad. NF 10, 1934, p. 84). This anticipates Gelasius' declaration to Anastasius 'sicut Romanus natus Romanum principem amo' *(ep.* 12, 1 p. 350; Schwartz, p. 19), remarkable in view of Gelasius' African origin; and the bitter remonstrance of Symmachus to the same emperor *(ep.* 10, 14 p. 707; Schwartz, p. 157) 'nec viventes in iure Romano lacerare conveniat Romanis', both being rejoinders to imperial demands that Rome and the West conform to the orthodoxy recognized by the East Roman emperor. In 520, the schism being two years ended, Epiphanius patriarch of Constantinople turned the argument back on Hormisdas with suggestions unwelcome to Rome: 'dum una utraque sit ecclesia, procul dubio et bona, quae per vigilantiam eveniunt, communis exinde laudis gloria utrisque patriarchalibus sedibus rimatur,' carrying the implication of sister patriarchates. Hormisdas, *ep.* 130, 2 p. 949.
9. *Utilis* at this date may mean good, brave, worthy, honest (Löfstedt, *Late Latin* p. 102), but here means rich as the contrast with *miser* shows; so J. C. Rolfe in the Loeb translation, supported by J. N. Adams, *The Text and Language of a Vulgar Latin Chronicle* (Bulletin of

University of London Institute of Classical Studies, suppl. 36, 1976), p. 108.
10. *Anon. Vales.* 61 and 79; Procop. *BG* i, 2, 16. The story is more plausible of Justin than of Theoderic: Procop. *Anecdota* vi, 11; Malalas XVII, 410; Lydus, *Mag.* iii, 51; Zacharias, *Hist. Eccl.* vii, 14; viii, 1; Suda A 1470; I 449.
11. *Anon. Vales.* 58. Jordanes, *Get.* 52, 289, calls her Erelieva; Gelasius, frag. 36 p. 502 Thiel (from the eleventh-century canon-collection of Deusdedit, but probably authentic) Hereleuva regina.
12. Theodorus Lector ii, 14 (463 p. 131 Hansen) says Theoderic sent him to execution.
13. *Anon. Vales.* 65. Gelasius, frag. 12 p. 489 (from Gratian, *Decretum* I 10, 12), asks Theoderic to extend the validity of Roman law to include reverence for papal authority. Frag. 13 p. 490 (from Deusdedit) speaks of the king as 'vir praecellentissimus filius meus Theodericus rex.' Caution is obviously needed in using fragments of Gelasius, whose name enjoyed authority for the makers of medieval canon-collections; each has to be judged on its inherent merits, suspicion surrounding any piece that could easily have been shaped or forged to serve medieval controversies.
14. The medallion is recently discussed by M. R. Alföldi, 'Il medaglione d'oro di Teodorico,' *Rivista italiana di Numismatica e scienze affini* 80 (1978), 133–41.
15. Symmachus, *ep.* i, 52 (ed. Seeck). For Byzantine pressure on Odovacar and Theoderic to favour Roman senators see Procopius, *BG* ii, 6; Cassiodorus, *Var.* iii, 43.
16. *CIL* v, 8120 = Dessau *ILS* 1301. In interpreting NAR as Nonius Arrius I follow R. Delbrück, *Die Consulardiptychen* (1929), no. 7, 103, and W. F. Volbach, *Elfenbeinarbeiten des Spätantike und des frühen Mittelalters* (3rd edn. Mainz, 1976), no. 6 p. 32 with plate 3.
17. E. A. Lowe, CLA iii, 296; A. Chastagnol, *Le sénat romain sous le règne d'Odoacre* (Bonn, 1966), pp. 50, 82. Asterius also produced an edition of Sedulius. *PLRE* ii p. 173.
18. *In cat.*ii, PL 64, 201B. Cf. Cic. *De divin.* i, 1.
19. On Symmachus see H. Usener, *Anecdoton Holderi* (Bonn, 1877), pp. 17–36; Otto Seeck in *PW* IV A (1932), 1160; M. A. Wes, *Des Ende des Kaisertums im Westen des römischen Reichs* (The Hague, 1967); prosopographic matter in J. Sundwall, *Abhandlungen zur Geschichte des ausgehenden Römertums* (Helsingfors, 1919), pp. 159–62, correcting Usener; Chastagnol, op. cit., p. 83. *PLRE* ii p. 1044.
20. Dessau, *ILS* 8955.
21. Keil, *Grammatici Latini* iii, 405.
22. *Paraenesis didascalia*, ed. Vogel (*MGH*), pp. 310–5; ed. Hartel, *CSEL* 6, pp. 401–10; Migne, *PL* 63, 249–56. Date: Vogel, praef. p. xxii.
23. The brief Latin text is reprinted in (e.g.) Mommsen's *MGH* edition of Cassiodorus, *Variae*, p. v; or the edition of the *Variae* in *Corpus Christianorum* S.L. 96 (1973), p. v; or T. Hodgkin, *The Letters of Cassiodorus* (1886), p. 74. The most recent discussion of it is by J. J.

O'Donnell, *Cassiodorus* (Berkeley, 1979). Passages on Cato as moral example are gathered by A. Hermann, *RAC* 2 (1954), 927–42. In Cassiodorus allusions to Cato are very common.

24. Rome is often 'sacratissima urbs' in Cassiodorus' *Variae* (iii, 45, 1; vi, 15, 2 etc.). The epithet seems a Christian coinage of Pope Damasus' time, 366–84; see Ambrosiaster, *Quaest.* 115, 16 (*CSEL* 50, 232); cf. *C. Th.* xiv, 3, 12 (370).
25. *Getica*, 15, 83–8. For speculative reconstruction of Symmachus' history see W. Ensslin, 'Des Symmachus Historia Romana als Quelle für Jordanes,' *SB. Bay. Akad.* 1948, Heft 3; Wes, *Das Ende des Kaisertums im Westen*, pp. 110–22; reserve towards their theory in A. Demandt, *Byz. Zeits.* 62 (1969), pp. 96–101; G. Luiselli, 'Note sulla perduta Historia Romana di Q. Aurelio Memmio Simmaco', *Studi Urbinati* 49 (1975), p. 529; id. 'Sul De summa temporum di Jordanes,' *Romanobarbarica* i (Rome, 1976), pp. 83–133; J. J. O'Donnell, *Cassiodorus* (1979), pp. 271 ff.
26. Greg. M. *Dial.* iv, 14. On Galla, Fulgentius, *ep.* ii, 16, 32; 18, 34. Monastery of St. Stephen 'cata Galla patricia': *Lib. Pont.* ii, 28. Proba: *PLRE* ii p. 907. From the circle of Fulgentius and his fellow-exiles in Sardinia there survives the codex of Hilary of Poitiers at St. Peter's Rome (Basilicanus D 182: Lowe, *CLA* i 1 ab), written at Cagliari in 509–10 (fo. 288 'contuli in nomine domini iesu christi aput karalis constitutus anno quarto decimo trasamundi regis').
27. Avitus, *ep.* 35 (*MGH*) = 31 Migne, *PL* 59, 248–9. E. Caspar, *Geschichte des Papsttums*, ii, p. 104 influentially misreads Avitus as assuming the senator Symmachus to be already supporting his namesake as pope. Likewise *PLRE* ii, p. 1045. I do not think Avitus is asking Faustus and Symmachus to do something they are committed to doing already. The letter is an essay in persuasion, not congratulation. See further above, p. 41. J. Schurr, *Die Trinitätslehre des Boethius* (1935), pp. 113–16, thinks Boethius sided with Pope Symmachus.
28. C. Pietri, *Roma Christiana* (French School at Rome, 1976).
29. Leo, *Sermo* 82; cf. 3, 4; 36, 3. The contrast Peter/Romulus is already in Augustine, *En. ps.* 44, 23. On Leo's imperial sense see P. A. McShane, *La Romanitas et le pape Léon le grand* (Montreal, 1979). On his juristic ideas J. Fellermayr, *Tradition und Sukzession im Lichte des römischantiken Erbdenkens, Untersuchungen zu den lateinischen Vätern bis zu Leo dem Grossen* (Munich, 1979).
30. Augustine, *Sermo* 296, 6 'Men say, Peter's body lies at Rome, Paul's body lies at Rome, Laurence's body lies at Rome, the bodies of other holy martyrs lie at Rome. And Rome is wretched, Rome is sacked, afflicted, burnt'.
31. Leo, *ep.* 7; *Sermo* 16, 4; Nov. Val. 18 = Leo, *ep.* 8.
32. *Variae* iv, 51.
33. Anon. *Vales.* 70 'erat amator fabricarum et restaurator civitatum'. Cassiodorus' *Chronicle* (Mommsen, *Chronica Minora* ii, 160) says that in Theoderic's happy reign many cities were renovated, including the old Ravenna aqueduct. On restorations in Rome see *Variae* iii, 29–31 and x,

30 (AD 535) where Theodahad orders repair of the bronze elephants by the Via Sacra.
34. Gelasius, *ep.* 10, 7 p. 346 Thiel; critical ed. Schwartz, *Publizistische Samml. z. Acac. Schisma*, p. 18.
35. Gelasius, *Tract.* 6 p. 598 Thiel; critical ed. Günther, *GSEL* 35, 453. See A. Chavasse, 'Messes du pape Vigile dans le sacramentaire léonien', *Ephemerides Liturgicae* 64 (1950), 161–213 at 212; G. Pomarès, *Gélase 1er, lettre contre les Lupercales et dix-huit messes du sacramentaire léonien* (Paris, 1959); A. W. J. Holleman, *Pope Gelasius I and the Lupercalia* (Amsterdam, 1974). Andromachus: *PLRE* ii, p. 89.
36. Other ancient evidence in H. Chadwick, *Priscillian of Avila* (Oxford, 1976) p. 52 n. 3.
37. Boethius, *In Cat.* iii, *PL* 64, 263A; cf. Livy 25, 12, 8 ff.; Macrobius, *Sat.* i, 17, 27 ff.; Filocalus' Calendar of 354 in *CIL* I² p. 268.
38. S. Roda, 'Alcune ipotesi sulla prima edizione dell' epistolario di Simmaco', *La Parola del Passato* 184 (1979), 31–54.
39. Boethius, *Arithm.* praef. 'utrarum peritissimus litterarum'.
40. P. Courcelle, *Les lettres grecques en occident*², p. 259 n. 2 = *Late Latin Writers* p. 275 n. 16.
41. R. T. Wallis, *Neoplatonism* (London, 1972); I. Hadot, *Le problème du néoplatonisme Alexandrin: Hieroclès et Simplicius* (Paris, 1978); P. Merlan in A. H. Armstrong, *The Cambridge History of late Greek and early mediaeval philosophy* (1967).
42. Cassiodorus, *Variae* i, 45; ii, 40; i, 10 (denarii, once 6000 to the gold solidus, now drastically devalued so that soldiers and court officials resent being paid in them). This last move may be Theoderic's baffled reaction to the decision of the eastern emperor Anastasius that the government would control the exchange rate and not leave it to be bargained in the market: Marcellinus Comes, *Chron. Min.* ii, 95; Malalas XVI 400; thereon D. M. Metcalf, *The Origins of the Anastasian Currency Reform* (Amsterdam, 1969); P. J. Alexander, *The Oracle of Baalbek*, Dumbarton Oaks Studies 10 (1967), pp. 95–6.

Intellectual contact of a kind between Ostrogothic Italy and the Franks is illustrated by the extant treatise by Anthimus, *vir inlustris*, a Greek physician living in Italy, who wrote for the Frankish king Theoderic I (511–33) advising the Franks to avoid a high fat diet: *Corpus Medicorum Latinorum* viii, 1.
43. *Cons. Phil.* i, 4, 12. On 'coemptio' see E. Stein, *Histoire du bas-empire* ii (Paris, 1949), pp. 199–203.
44. The best guides remain L. Duchesne, *L'église au VIe siècle* (Paris, 1925); E. Stein, *Histoire du bas-empire* ii (1949); E. Caspar, *Geschichte des Papsttums* ii (1933); E. Schwartz, *Publizistische Sammlungen zum Acacianischen Schisma* (1934) with important edition of documents other than those in the *Avellana* collection (*CSEL* 35). On the Laurentian schism: G. B. Picotti, 'I sinodi romani nello scisma laurenziano,' *Studi storici in onore di G. Volpe* (Florence, 1958) pp. 743–86; C. Pietri, 'Le sénat, le peuple chrétien et les partis du cirque sous le pape Symmache,' *MEFR* 78 (1966), pp. 122–39; P. A. B. Llewellyn, 'The Roman Church

during the Laurentian Schism: priests and senators,' *Church History* 45 (1976), pp. 417–27; id. 'The Roman Church during the Laurentian Schism: a preliminary analysis,' *Ancient Society* 8 (1977), pp. 245–75; J. Moorhead, 'The Laurentian Schism: East and West in the Roman Church,' *Church History* 47 (1978), pp. 125–36.

Hormisdas' negotiations are studied by W. Haacke, *Die Glaubensformel des Papstes Hormisdas im Acacianischen Schisma*, Analecta Gregoriana 20 (Rome, 1939).

45. *Cons. Phil.* iii, 4, 4. Decoratus' career in Sundwall, op. cit. pp. 112–13; *PLRE* ii, p. 350.
46. Hormisdas, *ep.* 104, p. 905 Thiel = *Avell.* 173, 1. *Lib. Pont.* I 263. *PLRE* ii p. 51.
47. Ammianus Marcellinus xiv, 1, 2; xix, 12, 8–15; xxviii, 1; xxix, 1. Zosimus iv, 13–16. Cf. Chadwick, *Priscillian of Avila*, pp. 139–42. Gelasius' treatise on the Lupercalia tells Andromachus that recent drought and plague in Campania, Africa, and Gaul are a visitation for sins, especially for Christian resort to 'magic horrendous even to pagans' (p. 602 Thiel).
48. C. H. Coster, *The Iudicium Quinquevirale* (Medieval Academy of America, Monograph 10, Cambridge, Mass., 1935). Coster's treatment of the trial of Boethius in this monograph is much modified in his paper 'The Fall of Boethius: his character', *Mélanges Henri Grégoire* IV(= *Annuaire de l'Inst. de Philol. et d'Histoire Orientales et Slaves*, 1952), pp. 45–81, reprinted with further changes in his *Late Roman Studies* (Harvard, 1968), pp. 54–103, where he abandons his earlier chronology (dating Boethius' death in 526) in favour of that long conventional, viz, that Boethius was arrested in 523 and executed in 524. See also Coster's paper 'Procopius and Boethius', *Speculum* 23 (1948), 248–87, reprinted in *Late Roman Studies*, pp. 46–53. Whatever may be the faults in Coster's studies, they do not merit the contempt accorded to them by Stein, *Bas-empire* ii p. 258 n.1. I think Coster right at least in one point, that Boethius' Catholic friends thought at the time that religion had something to do with his execution.
49. Cassiodorus, *Variae* v, 40; viii, 21. The careers of Cyprian and Boethius' other accusers are set out in *PLRE* ii.
50. Marius of Aventicum (Avenches), *Chronica Minora* ii, 234, 522, ed. Mommsen.
51. Laterculus regum Vandal., *Chronica Minora* iii, 459. Procop. *BV* i, 9, 1; Vict. Tonn. chron. ad ann. 523, *Chron. Minora* ii, 196–7.
52. Diehl, *ILCV* 1046; Hartel's edition of Ennodius (*CSEL* 6) p. 609.
53. *Liber Pontificalis* i, 104–5 (272).
54. *Anon. Vales.* 87 'rex vero vocavit Eusebium praefectum urbis *Ticini*' (which should be emended with Mommsen to *Ticinum*). The correct interpretation of Boethius' account, *Cons. Phil.* i, 4, 36, is by H. Tränkle, 'Philologische Bemerkungen zum Boethiusprozess', *Studia J. H. Waszink* (1973), 329–39, at p. 334.

On the legend of his martyrdom, the fourteenth-century Pavia chronicle is printed by L. A. Muratori, *Rerum Italicarum Scriptores* XI

(Milan, 1727); esp. ch. iv. The story in *Anonymus Valesianus* 87 of Albinus and Boethius being taken to a baptistery is strange, since one would expect them to have fled to the font for asylum (for an analogy see Collectio Avellana 186, 5, *CSEL* 35 p. 643), only to be dragged away.
55. Procopius, *Anecdota* xvi, 26. Dr. A. D. Smith has advised me on the medical aspects of this unpleasant subject, and I owe him thanks for his expert opinion.
56. *Anon. Vales.* 92. Agnellus, *Liber Pontificalis Ecclesiae Ravennatis* 39 (MGH ed. Holder-Egger, p. 304) records in the ninth-century that a sarcophagus containing the bones of Symmachus and Boethius was still at Ravenna.
57. Ammianus Marcellinus xxvii, 7, 5.
58. *Variae* ii, 27 (*religionem imperare non possumus, quia nemo cogitur ut credat invitus*). In 523–26 Theoderic promises protection to the Jews of Milan on condition that they avoid provoking the local Christians (*Var.* v, 37).
59. *Anon. Vales.* 81–2. Magnus Maximus forfeited massive support when he ordered restitution after a synagogue in Rome was burnt in 388; Ambrose, *ep.* 40, 23; cf. H. Chadwick, *Priscillian of Avila*, p. 125.
60. J. Zeiller, 'Etude sur l'arianisme en Italie à l'époque ostrogothique et à l'époque lombarde', *MEFR* 25 (1905), 127–46, notes that Agnellus records six Arian churches in Ravenna, their dedications in the ninth century being to SS. Eusebius, George, Sergius, Zeno, Theodore, and Martin in Coelo aureo (= S. Apollinare Nuovo). A sixth century papyrus (Marini 119 = Tjäder 34) mentions an 'ecclesia legis Gothorum Sanctae Anastasiae'. Probably some of these antedate the rule of Odovacar and Theoderic. Cf. F. W. Deichmann, *Ravenna* II (Wiesbaden, 1974), pp. 243–45.

Vibo Valentia in Calabria had a 'basilica barbarorum' in which a certain Felix sought asylum in Gelasius' time (frg. 42 p. 506 Thiel).
61. Greg. M. *Dial.* iii, 30 says that the church was situated *in Suburra*. So also *Liber Pontificalis* i, 312 'eodem tempore dedicavit ecclesiam Gothorum quae fuit in Subora in nomine beatae Agathae martyris'. Gregory (*ep.* iv, 18 of 594) entrusts the church's revenues to Leo an acolyte. As St. Agatha is a Sicilian martyr, of Catania, the endowment may have been drawn from Sicilian estates. The Ricimer inscription was legible at the church of S. Agata dei Goti in Baronius' time (*Mart. Rom.* 5 Feb.); Rossi, *Inscr. Chr. Rom.* II, i, p. 438 no. 137; Diehl, *ILCV* 1637. The second Arian church: Greg. M. *ep.* iii, 19 of 593. Discussion by J. Zeiller, 'Les églises ariennes de Rome à l'époque de la domination gothique,' *MEFR* 24 (1904), 17–33.

The *Liber Diurnus* 24 has a Latin formula for the transfer of a church building to Catholic use. About 560 Justinian assigned the revenues formerly attached to Arian churches in Ravenna for the Catholic church there: Agnellus, *Liber Pontificalis Ecclesiae Ravennatis* 85; J. O. Tjäder, *Die nichtliterarischen lateinischen Papyri Italiens aus der Zeit* 445–700 (Lund, 1955) i, pp. 178–83, pap. 2 (Marini, 87).
62. Procopius, *Anecdota* xi, 16.

Pages 59–66   Notes   291

63. Anon. Vales. 90; Liber Pontificalis i, 104–5 (275); Caspar, Geschichte des Papsttums ii, 185. The mosaic of Ecclesius: F. W. Deichmann, Ravenna III (1969), plate 353. Foundation of S. Vitale: Diehl, ILCV 1795; Agnellus, 57. Ecclesius is portrayed also at S. Apollinare in Classe: Deichmann, plates 400–1.
64. Cassiodorus, Variae ii, 6; Hormisda, ep. 122 p. 925 Thiel = Avell. 228. PLRE ii p. 31.
65. Chronica Minora ii, 102. On Pope John's reception at Constantinople: Theophanes, AM 6016 p. 169 de Boor; Nicephorus Callistus, H.E. xvii, 9 (PG 146, 291 BC). W. Ensslin, 'Papst Johannes I als Gesandter Theoderichs bei Kaiser Justinos I,' Byzantinische Zeitschrift 44 (1951), 127–34, interprets the emperor's salute as a kiss rather than a deep prostration. This minimises Lib. Pont. i, 105 'humiliavit se pronus et adoravit beatissimum Johannem papam.' If a kiss, it was a kiss of death.
66. Demonstrated by H. Löwe, Hist. Jahrb. 72 (1953), 83–100, using Merovingian evidence for this formula collected by R. Köstler, Huldentzug als Straffe (1910), p. 12 n. 4.
67. Some scholars have maltreated the Anonymus Valesianus as if the chronicler had used two contrasting sources, one favourable to Theoderic, then mindlessly switching to a second, hostile account of the latter part of his reign. The antithesis of light and dark is essential to the chronicle's edifying purpose; to regard him merely as an evident case of source-criticism is simply to miss the point of his work, that Theoderic was a great king upon whom Arianism brought catastrophe (like Ate). The chronicler's estimate is strikingly similar to the modern scholar E. Stein's assessment of Anastasius as the emperor who made possible the sixth century apogee of Byzantine power and civilisation but whose Monophysite sympathies were more responsible than any other cause for the religious crisis which tore the empire apart (Hist. du Bas-empire ii p. 192).
68. Procopius, BG i, 1, 32–9.
69. Duchesne, Liber Pontificalis i, 278 with iii, 91. The Cambridge University manuscript, Kk. 4. 6 (2021), s. xii, is a text of the Liber Pontificalis into which are inserted many Roman inscriptions. The verses (from fol. 238r) are printed by W. Levison in Neues Archiv 35 (1910), p. 352. The text runs on without break to give two more distichs recording Pope Symmachus' dedication to St. Andrew of the Theodosian mausoleum beside St. Peter's, sadly destroyed to make room for the sacristy (Duchesne, LP i p. 265 n. 16). If these four lines are part of the same inscription (a possible but not necessary deduction), then a reference to John I is excluded.
70. Procopius, BG i, 2, 4–5; iii, 21.
71. de Rossi, Inscr. Urb. Rom. II 79. 429. Her epitaph at St. Peter's is preserved in manuscript collections. Three late medieval mss. of the Consolation of Philosophy claim her as Boethius' wife. See PLRE ii pp. 537–8.
72. Greg. M. Reg. ii, 27; ix, 72; xi, 26. Sundwall, Abhandlungen zur Geschichte des ausgehenden Römertums, p. 104.

73. Riese, *Anthol. Latina* I 2, 494 c; de Rossi, *Inscr.* II i, 63 p. 109. See Averil Cameron, 'A Nativity Poem of the sixth-century AD', *Classical Philology* 74 (1979), pp. 222–32.

CHAPTER II

1. *In Cat.* ii, 230C.
2. *In Porph. Isag.* II (*CSEL* 48, 294, 11 = *PL* 64, 137C); *Perih.* ii, 79 Meiser (= *PL* 64, 433C); *Intr. ad syll. cat.* 762C.
3. H. Jäger, *Die Quellen des Porphyrios in seiner Pythagoras-Biographie* (Diss. Zürich, 1919).
4. Iamblichus' commentary is edited by H. Pistelli (Teubner, 1894); Asclepius' commentary by L. Tarán, *Transactions of the American Philosophial Society* n.s. 59/4 (1969); Philoponus' work by Hoche (Progr. Wesel, 1864/5; Berlin, 1867), now a very rare book.
5. Marinus, *V. Procli* 28; Suda, s.v. Proklos (3).
6. Edited by C. Jan, *Musici Scriptores Graeci* (Teubner, 1895).
7. Some manuscripts of the *Institutio Arithmetica* have the subscription 'legi opusculum meum', i.e. the archetype had been revised by Boethius himself. See G. Schepss in *Blättern f.d. Bayer. Gymnasialwesen* 24 (1888), 28. Some early mss. give the title 'incoeptio arithmetica'.
8. On the tradition of Philolaus' fragments see Burkert, *Lore and Science in Ancient Pythagoreanism* (1972), pp. 238–77, on this fragment, pp. 250 f. which is fuller in Stobaeus i, 21, 7a. Proclus alludes to its doctrine of the world as a harmony of opposites (*In Tim.* i, 176, 27 Diehl). Similarly Macrobius, *In Som. Scip.* i, 14, 19 (of the soul). Theon of Smyrna writes (p. 12, 10 Hiller) 'The Pythagoreans, whom Plato often follows, say that music is the harmony of opposites and the unity of multiplicity and the concord of dissidents, not only concerning rhythms and melody but of everything absolutely.'
9. *PL.* 64, 162. See H. Thesleff, *The Pythagorean Texts of the Hellenistic Period* (Åbo, 1965) p. 22. On these Archytas apocrypha cf. Burkert, op. cit., p. 222.
10. Philolaos is cited by Nicomachus for this view, Boethius drops the allusion. The distinction between the three types of mean is incisively set out by Proclus, *In Tim.* ii, 171, 21 ff.
11. See W. Burkert, *Lore and Science in ancient Pythagoreanism*; B. L. van der Waerden, 'Die Harmonielehre der Pythagoreer', *Hermes* 78 (1943), 163–99.
12. *Som.* i, 36–37; *Q. Gen.* iii, 3 (cf. Plato, *Phaedrus* 259c).
13. *In de Caelo*, 469, 18–20 Heiberg.
14. *Hexaemeron* iii, 3, *PG* 29, 57C.
15. *Hexaemeron* ii, 2, 7, *CSEL* 32/1 p. 45. Ambrose combines Cicero, Philo and Basil. There has been some disagreement about Ambrose's sources in this passage. P. Courcelle (*Rev. ét. latines* 34, 1956, 232–9) proposed Basil, Cicero, and Macrobius, but did not convince M. Fuhrmann (*Philologus* 107, 1963, 301–8) who prefers the hypothesis of Origen's lost commentary on Genesis. This hypothesis may be supported from

Ambrose, *De Abr.* ii, 8, 54 (*CSEL* 32/1, p. 608) where he says that 'our Origen' affirms the music of the spheres, but he hesitates to accept his authority since 'his writings show him to allow much to the tradition of the philosophers', and Ambrose prefers to be timid with St. Paul than learned with the Platonists. Courcelle's proposal to date Macrobius before Ambrose has found no following: cf. J. Flamant, *Macrobe et le néo-platonisme latin à la fin du IVe siècle* (Leiden, 1977), p. 139.

16. *Enarr. in Psalmos* 42, 7. It will be evident that Augustine and Simplicius would have felt some mutual rapport.
17. *De Doctrina Christiana* ii, 16, 26; ii, 38, 56.
18. *In Somn. Scip.* ii, 1–4.
19. *The Merchant of Venice*, v, 1.
20. Alex. Aphr. *In Metaph.* A 5 (p. 40 Hayduck, *CAG* I, 1891). The passage is reckoned to be in substance a fragment of Aristotle by P. Wilpert, 'Reste verlorenen Aristotelesschriften bei Alexander von Aphrodisias,' *Hermes* (1940), 369–96.
21. Claudius Ptolemaeus, *Harmonica* (ed. Düring) iii, 8–16.
22. Macrobius, *In Somn. Scip.* ii, 4, 11. 'To give even a short account of the *nete* and *hypate* and the other strings and to discuss intricate matters about tones and semitones... is ostentatious... Cicero's mention of music does not justify one in going through the endless treatises on the subject.'
23. Ptolemy, *Harm.* iii, 5–7 (Pythagorean mattins, p. 100, 7).
24. C. Bower, *Vivarium* 16 (1978), 43 f. thinks Boethius wrote seven books in all, the last three dependent on Ptolemy. This is plausible.
25. Aristotle, frag. 25 Ross = 47 Rose³, from Ps. Plutarch, *De musica* 25, 1140AB.
26. Aristides Quintilianus is edited in the Teubner library by R. P. Winnington-Ingram (1963). His Neoplatonic milieu is discussed by L. Zanoncelli, 'La filosofia musicale di Aristide Quintiliano,' *Quaderni Urbinati di cultura classica* 24 (1977), 51–93; A. J. Festugière, 'L'âme et la musique d'après Aristide Quintilien', *Trans. Amer. Philol. Assoc.* 85 (1954).
27. C. von Jan, *Musici Scriptores Graeci* (Teubner, 1895), pp. 210–82 edits the *Enchiridion* and a series of excerpts from Nicomachus' longer work, both texts offering many parallels to Boethius i–ii, so that there is no doubt of his careful following of his Greek authority. On Boethius' main source there is a recent study by F. R. Levin, *The Harmonics of Nicomachus and the Pythagorean Tradition* (American Classical Association, 1975), almost wholly confined to the *Enchiridion*, and making negligible use of Boethius. There is a study of all Boethius' sources, certain or probable, by Ubaldo Pizzani, 'Studi sulle fonti del "De Institutione Musica" di Boezio', *Sacris Erudiri* 16 (1965), 5–164; but weighty corrections are proposed by Calvin Bower, 'Boethius and Nicomachus, an essay concerning the sources of De Institutione Musica', *Vivarium* 16 (1978), 1–45. The originality and independence of Boethius is vehemently but unconvincingly asserted by H. Potiron, *Boèce théoricien de la musique grecque* (Paris, 1961); though he offers little

argument, he rightly sees that Boethius on Music must be interpreted in relation to ancient Greek music, not from interpretations put upon him by medieval musicologists. He seems to be over-reacting to Gevaert's rhetorical view (*La Melopée antique*, 1870, pp. 25–6) that Boethius' stupid misunderstandings of his sources made the survival of the treatise a misfortune for the art from which it took many centuries to recover.

28. The apparatus in Pistelli's edition of Iamblichus' commentary on Nicomachus'*Arithmetic* (Teubner, 1894) carefully notes several parallels with Boethius' *De musica*. These are also recorded in Pizzani's article mentioned in the preceding note.

29. Some mss. add after 'nusquam una' three words ('proportio vincat duas') to restore sense. Bruges 531 s. xi ends 'explicit musica boecii nondum finita italorum invidia'. See R. Bragard's study (in the next note).

30. A list of manuscripts of *De institutione musica* is given by M. Masi in *Manuscripta* 15 (1971), 89–95; cf. M. Huglo in *Scriptorium* 27 (1973), 401–2. Masi has also discussed iconography in illuminated manuscripts of Boethius in *Latomus* 33 (1974), 57–75. The manuscripts in Belgium (Bruges 531 s. xi; Brussels 5444–6 s. x–xi; 10114–6 s. xi; 18397 s. xiii; II 6188 s. xv) are examined by R. Bragard, 'Boethiana—études sur le De Institutione Musica de Boèce', *Hommage à Charles van den Borren* (Antwerp, 1945), pp. 84–139.

31. Aristotle, *Politics* viii (1339a–1342b) concedes that practical music has educational value if it is not done to professional standard and does not include the pipe or exciting modes.

32. This assumption is denied by the Epicureans for whom all sound is morally neutral. The sole question is whether it is pleasant or unpleasant. See L. P. Wilkinson, 'Philodemus on Ethos in Music', *Classical Quarterly* 32 (1938), 174–181.

33. Aristoxenus' *Elementa harmonica* are edited and well translated by H. S. Macran (Oxford, 1902, repr. Hildesheim 1974), and re-edited by Rosetta da Rios (Rome, 1954). See also F. Wehrli, *Die Schule des Aristoteles* II *Aristoxenos* (2nd ed. 1967). On his achievement see especially R. P. Winnington-Ingram, 'Aristoxenus and the Intervals of Greek Music', *Classical Quarterly* 26 (1932), 195–208, and Louis Laloy, *Aristoxène de Tarente disciple d'Aristote et la musique de l'antiquité* (Paris, 1904). A critique of the Platonic theory, probably written prior to Aristoxenus, appears in Hibeh papyrus 13 (s. iii BC) discussed by W. Crönert in *Hermes* 44 (1909), 503–21; W. D. Anderson, *Ethos and Education in Greek Music* (1966), pp. 147–52.

34. See Boethius, *de Musica* i, 17–18; ii, 28–9; iii, 1–4. The basic calculation comes from Plato, *Timaeus* 36 b.
    Cf. Plutarch, *De animae procreatione in Timaeo* 12 (1017F); Theon of Smyrna, 69 Hiller.

35. With this calculation Boethius, *Mus.* iv, 2, concludes his adaptation of the Euclidean text. On the extent of Boethius' additions to and divergences from the Euclid see Calvin Bower in *Vivarium* 16 (1978), 12–14, who plausibly suggests that Boethius found the *Sectio Canonis* in

36. Nicomachus to whom it would obviously have been highly congenial. See also T. J. Matheisen, 'An annotated translation of Euclid's division of the Monochord', *Journal of Music Theory* 19 (1975), 236–58.
36. Plato *Republic* 587a–588a, observes that 27^2 is the number of days and nights in the year.
37. Boethius, *Mus.* i, 10; Nicomachus, *Enchiridion* 6, pp. 245 f. Jan; Iamblichus, *In Nicom. Arithm.* 110, p. 121, 13 ff. Pistelli; V. *Pythag.* 26; Macrobius, *In Som. Scip.* ii, 1, 9 ff.; Gaudentius, *Introd. Harm.* 11, p. 340 Jan; Elias, *Prolegomena Philosophiae* 11 (CAG XVIII p. 29, 22). The physical impossibility of the alleged experiment was shown by Mersenne in 1634: see Burkert, *Lore and Science in ancient Pythagoreanism* (1972), p. 375.
38. Speusippus observed this in his book on Pythagorean numbers: *Theol. Arithm.* p. 82 Falco; Burkert, op. cit. p. 72.
39. Boethius, *Mus.* v, 4, from Ptolemy, *Harm.* i, 3.
40. The Pythagoreans believed Pythagoras to be inventor of the monochord (Diogenes Laertius viii, 12). Nicomachus (*Ench.* 4) says that monochords are called 'canons' by the Pythagoreans, 'phandouroi' by others.
41. Boethius, *Mus.* v, 5; Ptolemy, *Harm.* i, 4.
42. Augustine holds this view in a letter to Jerome: *ep.* 166, 13.
43. Boethius, *Mus.* i, 1.
44. The opinion, shared by Plato with Aristotle (e.g. *Politics* viii) and even with Aristoxenus, that music and morality are linked was denied by the Epicureans. Epicurus' book on music (Diog. Laert. x, 28) is lost. But parts of Philodemus on music survive through fragments found at Herculaneum, attacking the classical theory: Melody, being irrational, cannot rouse the soul from tranquillity, or quieten it when aroused; moreover, different individuals react in divergent ways to the same music, so that no objective character can be ascribed to music itself. See L. P. Wilkinson, *CQ* 32 (1938), 174–81; H. Abert, *Die Lehre vom Ethos in der griechischen Musik* (1899); W. D. Anderson, *Ethos and Education in Greek Music, the evidence of poetry and philosophy* (Harvard, 1966); E. A. Lippman, *Musical Thought in Ancient Greece* (New York and London, 1964), ch. 2.
45. Similarly Ammonius' commentary on Porphyry's *Isagoge*, CAG IV, 3, p. 13, 25; and Elias, *Prolegomena Philosophiae* 11 (CAG XVIII, p. 31, 11).

In Friedlein's text 'subphrigii modi sono' (p. 185, 1) is an error for 'sub phrigii modi sono' (as p. 185, 6). The correction is noted by C. Bower, *Vivarium* 16 (1978) p. 44, n. 118, as invalidating an argument used by Pizzani that the prefatory matter in Boethius is based on a Latin source.
46. CAG XVIII, p. 31, 8. Proclus, *In Eucl. Elem. I*, praef. p. 24 Friedlein, says that mathematical order is morally beneficial.
47. Dio Chrysostom 68, 7.
48. *In Categ.* 120, 6–9 Busse; Porphyry is echoed by Simplicius, *In Categ.* 192, 11 Kalbfleisch. In the sixth-century Olympiodorus remarks that while the remains of classical Greek arithmetic, geometry, and astro-

nomy survive, those of ancient music are lost: cited by David, *Prolegomena Philosophiae* 20 (CAG XVIII, 2, 1904), 64, 32 Busse.
49. *In Som. Scip.* ii, 4, 13. (Pseudo-)Plutarch, *Mus.* 38–9, complains that modern musicians reject the enharmonic quartertone as too small an interval to be heeded by the ear; yet they like the sound of irrational intervals within the tetrachord.
50. Boethius, *Mus.* v, 16 (Ptol. i, 12) after Aristoxenus. Much of our understanding of the three methods of tuning depends on Aristoxenus' discussion, masterfully elucidated by Winnington-Ingram, in *CQ* 26 (1932), 195 f.
51. There is good elucidation of this passage by C. Andre Barbera, 'Arithmetic and Geometric Divisions of the Tetrachord', *Journal of Music Theory* 21 (1977), 294–323.
52. D. Najock (ed.), *Anonyma de musica scripta Bellermanniana* (Teubner, 1975), section 67, p. 19. See also Najock's *Drei anonyme griechische Traktate über die Musik* (Göttinger Musikwissenschaftliche Arbeiten 2, 1972).
53. *PL* 143, 433B. Gerbert, *Script. Mus. Sacr. Potiss.* II (1784), p. 143 also prints the text.
54. Ptolemy, *Harm.* ii, 10, p. 63, 7 Düring. L. Kunz, 'Die Tonartenlehre des Boethius', *Kirchenmusikalisches Jahrbuch* 31 (1936), 13, concludes from this difference that Boethius is here independent on Ptolemy, an opinion rejected by Pizzani, art. cit. p. 135, n.1. Bower, however, has recently suggested that throughout book iv, and especially on Modes, Boethius is using Nicomachus who also had Ptolemy before him; i.e. Boethius' divergencies from Ptolemy (which are numerous) are explained on the hypothesis that what he knows of Ptolemy on Harmony comes to him through Nicomachus, not directly: *Vivarium* 16 (1978), 31.
55. When Pizzani's critical edition appears in *Corpus Christianorum*, all should be at least as clear as it was to Boethius himself. Meanwhile any account of this controversial topic must necessarily be provisional. Pizzani produces a working diagram in his article, p. 135.
56. Aristoxenus i, 20 p. 112, 16–21 Macran = i, 20, 16–23 de Rios; cf. ii, 45.
57. This question is also discussed by Proclus, *In Tim.* ii, 168, 6 and especially 183, 23 ff. where he refuses to decide for or against Ptolemy because Plato does not mention the matter.
58. *Cons.* i m. 5, 1–24.
59. *Cons.* ii m. 8; iv m. 6.
60. *Cons.* iii m. 9, 1–17.
61. *Arithm.* i, 1 ('ad cumulum perfectionis').
62. See David S. Chamberlain's illuminating essay 'Philosophy of Music in the Consolation of Boethius', *Speculum* 45 (1970), 80–97.

CHAPTER III

1. The contrary is asserted, on a wafer-thin basis, by G. Pfligersdorffer in *Wiener Studien* 66 (1953), p. 152.

2. P. Courcelle, *Les Lettres grecques en occident*[2] (1948), p. 272 = *Late Latin Writers* (1969), p. 288.
3. Boethius, *de Trinitate* 2, has been attacked for gross confusions by P. Merlan, *From Plato to Neoplatonism*[3] (1968), but mistakenly. See for a counter-attack R. McInerny in *Rivista di filosofia neoscolastica* 66 (1974), pp. 219–45.
    Aristotle (*Metaph*. A 6, 987b 14–22) ascribes the tripartite division to Plato (cf. *Republic* 511bc and 533e–534c); *Physics* B 2, 193b 23–37. Ps. Alex. Aphr. *in Metaph*. E, 1, 1025b 18–1026a 6 (*CAG* I, 446, 35 ff. Hayduck). Proclus, *In Tim*. ii, 153, 18 (Aristander and Numenius).
    Concerning the relation between astronomy and physics (on one side) or pure mathematics (on the other), Simplicius' commentary on *Physics* B 2 (*CAG* IX, 290–3) illustrates the Neoplatonic via media between Plato's removal of astronomy beyond the realm of sense-perception and Aristotle's insistence that the astronomer and the 'physicist' deal with the same objects but with different methods.
4. Ammonius, *in Porph. Isag*. *CAG* IV 3 p. 38, 14 Busse; *Perih*. *CAG* IV 5 p. 47, 20; Elias, *in Isag*. *CAG* XVIII p. 42, 1 ff.
5. Boethius, *Isag*. ii, p. 177, 21; 178, 6 Brandt; cf. *C. Eutychen* 3, 96 Rand (*ecclesiasticus loquendi usus*); cf. 4, 4 (*ecclesiastica locutio*). Anselm's *De grammatico* is the subject of more than one detailed study by D. P. Henry, e.g. *The Logic of St. Anselm* (Oxford, 1967) and a full *Commentary on De grammatico* (Dordrecht, 1974) with much Boethian matter.
6. *Syll. cat.* i, 793CD.
7. *Syll. hyp.* i, 846B.
8. Ammonius, *In Cat.* p. 4, 29; Simplicius, *In Cat.* p. 5.
9. M. W. Sullivan, *Apuleian Logic* (Amsterdam, 1967) urges Boethius' direct use of Apuleius against the hypothesis of a common source favoured by J. Isaac, *Le Peri Hermeneias en occident de Boèce à saint Thomas* (Paris, 1953). Sullivan defends Apuleius' authorship of the tract, as also G. Pfligersdorffer, 'Zu Boethius De Interpr. Ed. Sec. I p. 4, 4 sqq. Meiser, nebst Beobachtungen zur Geschichte der Dialektik bei den Römern,' *Wiener Studien* 66 (1953), pp. 131–54, at 130–4.
10. *Cons.* i m. 7. 21 f. 'Lumine claro/Cernere verum.' Cf. Mart. Cap. ii, 125, v. 10 ff. 'lumine claro . . . cernere vultus.' *Cons.* ii m. 8, 3 'pugnantia semina', as Mart. Cap. i, 1 v. 3. Cf. p. 235.
11. Eriugena is evidently familiar with the *Decem Categoriae* as a work of Augustine. Except for the *Arithmetica*, it is not easy to be confident how much of Boethius is known to him. Allusions to the *Arithmetica* are frequent (*PL* 122, 498BC, 505B, 651B ff., 655AB). His doctrine that the Liberal Arts are created by God (748D–749A, etc.) is not directly anticipated by Boethius. But music and harmonic principles are for him part of the structure of the cosmos, exemplified in the harmony of the spheres. It is hard to affirm or to deny that he had read Boethius' *Institutio musica*, to which he makes no explicit reference. In ideas the kinship is obvious, and ignorance is unlikely.
12. J. A. Fabricius, *Bibliotheca Graeca* III (1793), p. 211; Schanz/Hosius, *Gesch. d. röm. Litt.* IV 2 (1920), pp. 412, 414. Minio-Paluello's opinion

is rejected in favour of the old view by G. Pfligersdorffer, 'Zur Frage nach dem Verfasser der pseudo-augustinischen Categoriae Decem,' *Wiener Studien* 65 (1970), pp. 131–7, who has also (surprisingly) persuaded P. Hadot, *Marius Victorinus* (Paris, 1971), p. 197 n. 33.
13. Cf. Flamant, *Macrobe*, pp. 58–65.
14. J. Pépin, *Augustin et la dialectique* (Villanova University, 1976).
15. *Inst.* ii, 3, 13 p. 119 Mynors.
16. Diehl, *ILCV* 104. On Victorinus, Hadot's monograph (above n. 12) is of high authority.
17. Aug. *Conf.* viii, 2, 3.
18. *Isag.* i p. 4, 12 Brandt (= *PL* 64, 9B).
19. Victorinus, *De defin.* p. 25, 13 Stangl = *PL* 64, 896D. (Stangl's critical text is reprinted by Hadot, op. cit., pp. 331–62.) The demonstration that this tract printed among Boethius' works is by Victorinus is in Usener, *Anecdoton Holderi* (Bonn, 1877). One tenth-century manuscript of Boethius' first commentary on Porphyry (Avranches 229) has a subscription recording 'Marii Victorini de xv speciebus definitionum' (*CSEL* 48 p. 132).
20. *CSEL* 48 p. 23, 17 (*PL* 64, 18C).
21. *CSEL* 48 p. 135 (*PL* 64, 71A). Cf. *Syll. cat.* i, 794C 'non enim eloquentiae compositiones sed planitiem consectamur'. Genus: *CSEL* 48 p. 34, 17 (*PL* 64, 23C). The contrast between Victorinus' rhetorical and Boethius' logical interests is examined by Luigi Adama, 'Boezio e Mario Vittorino traduttori e interpreti dell' Isagoge di Porfirio', *Rivista critica di storia della filosofia* 22 (1967), 141–64.
22. *CSEL* 48 p. 173 (*PL* 64, 88AB). Similarly *Perih.* ii, 345, 2–4 Meiser.
23. Hadot, op. cit. pp. 313–21 reconstructs the remnants of Victorinus' commentary on Cicero's *Topics* from these three sources.
24. Hadot, op. cit. p. 196.
25. *PL* 64, 1109D, 1147B. These two small fragments pass unmentioned in Vollmer's edition of Merobaudes, *MGH AA* XIV (1905) and in Lenz's article, *PW* xv (1932), 1039–47, but are noticed by F. M. Clover, *Flavius Merobaudes*, Transactions of the American Philosophical Society 61, 1 (1971), p. 9.
26. T. Stangl, 'Pseudoboethiana', *Jahrbücher für classische Philologie* 29 (1883), 193–208 and 285–301. The text in question is printed by J. C. Orelli and J. G. Baiter, appended to their edition of Boethius' commentary on Cicero: *M. Tullii Ciceronis Opera Omnia* V, 1 (Zürich, 1833).
27. *Isag.* i, *CSEL* 48, 94–95; *In Cic. Top.* 1055C, 1098A–C.
28. *Def.*, *PL* 64, 895B.
29. Ammonius, *Isag.* *CAG* IV 3 p. 39, 4 Busse. He too defends the utility of philosophy as useful to rhetoricians (p. 8, 4 ff.).
30. *In Cic. Top.* iii, 1098D ff.; vi, 1165BC; Victorinus, *Def.* 901D–907C (pp. 16–29 Stangl).
31. *CSEL* 48 p. 149, 12 from Victorinus, *Def.* 906B. Victorinus also discusses the term 'necessary' in his *Explanationes in Ciceronis rhetoricam* i, 29 (ed. Halm, *Rhetores latini minores*, 1863, p. 32): 'Necessarium est,

inquit, quod aliter ac dicitur nec fieri nec probari potest. . . . Necessarium porro tale est argumentum: . . . 'Si natus est morietur. Si peperit, cum viro concubuit . . . ' Alioqui, secundum Christianorum opinionem non est necessarium argumentum. . . . Non apud eos manifestum est sine viro natum et non mortuum.'

32. *In Cic. Top.* i, 1048D, 1050B. *De topicis differentiis* is well translated with valuable introduction and notes by E. Stump (Cornell University Press, 1978).
33. Critics of Boethius: *In Cic. Top.* ii, 1063B; iv, 1107C; v, 1152AB; vi, 1153B–D; 1157A. *Top. diff.* ii, 1182D; *Divis.* 877A.
34. Porphyry's title does not explain what he is introducing. School convention took the book as a preface to the *Categories*, already standing first in the ordered edition of Aristotle's logical writings: *CSEL* 48, p. 15, 20; 146, 27. A list of Greek manuscripts of the *Isagoge* has been made by A. Wartelle (1963).
35. Particulars of these versions are in Minio-Paluello's introduction to *Aristoteles Latinus* i, 6–7 (1966).
36. *Arithm.* i, 1 (*PL* 64, 1081D1) inserts it into Nicomachus' framework. Cf. *Isag., CSEL* 48, p. 226, 2 'scientia infinita esse non potest'; *Cat.* i, 160C 3. Aristotle (*Metaph.* 994ab) argues that the infinite is unknowable.
37. Elias, *Proleg.* 15 (*CAG* XVIII p. 39, 7); Suda, s.v. Porphyrios.
38. R. Walzer in *Entretiens Hardt* 12 (1966), at pp. 286–7. Al-Farabi wrote on the harmony of Plato and Aristotle.
39. H. J. Blumenthal, 'Themistius, the last peripatetic commentator on Aristotle?', in *Arktouros: Hellenic Studies presented to B. M. W. Knox on his 65th birthday* (Berlin, 1979), pp. 391–400.
40. First printed by J. Nolle, the text is reprinted in Thesleff's *Pythagorean Texts of the Hellenistic Period* (1965), and again, with full discussion, by T. A. Szlezák, *Pseudo-Archytas über die Kategorien* (Berlin, 1972).
41. F. Klingner, *De Boethii Consolatione Philosophiae* (Berlin, 1921), pp. 38–67.
42. J. Shiel, 'Boethius' commentaries on Aristotle', *Mediaeval and Renaissance Studies* 4 (1958), 217–44, a paper containing much valuable matter even if its central thesis fails to convince.
43. *CSEL* 48 p. 164, 4 'nos Alexandro consentientes'.
44. *CSEL* 48, pp. 140–2; Ammonius, *In An. Pr.* 8, 15 ff.; 10, 36 ff. Ammonius does not use Boethius' argument about the limits or frontiers of the various parts of philosophy. At p. 142, 25 Boethius uses an argument rejected by Ammonius' pupil Philoponus, *In An. Pr.* (*CAG* XIII, 2), 8, 30.
45. Boethius' translations of Porphyry's *Isagoge, Categories, Interpretation, Prior Analytics, Topics,* and *Sophistici Elenchi* have been edited in exemplary fashion by L. Minio-Paluello (the last treatise by B. Dod) in *Aristoteles Latinus* i, ii, iii, v, and vi (1961–75). The versions printed in Migne are misleading. The Latin introductions by Minio-Paluello contain fundamental information.
46. *Cat.* ii, 225A1; *Perih.* ii, 172, 20; 194, 1; 218, 26. On Plotinus: *Divis.* 875D.

47. *Aristoteles Latinus* iii 1–4 (1962).
48. *Dial.* ii, 1 (*PL* 188, 1163). L. Minio-Paluello, 'Jacobus Venetus Graecus: canonist and translator,' *Traditio* 8 (1952), 215–304, reprinted in his *Opuscula* (Amsterdam, 1972), pp. 189–228. James' translation of the *Posterior Analytics* made possible John of Salisbury's account of this work, *Metalogicon* iv, 6–9. Minio-Paluello suggests identifying this James with the unnamed translator of Aristotle concerning whose skill John of Salisbury voices doubts in *ep.* 201 (II 294 ed. W. J. Millor and C. N. L. Brooke, Oxford Medieval Texts, 1979). James seems to have accompanied his translation by some annotations, a trace of which survives in a 13th century commentary on *Sophistici Elenchi* in the Bodleian ms. Laud. misc. 368, noted by S. Ebbesen, *Cahiers de l'Institut de Moyen-Age grec et latin* 21 (1977), pp. 1–9.
49. *In Cic. Top.* iii, 1092D; Aug. *Sermo* 241. *City of God* xiii, 16.
50. The best discussion of the dates is by L. M. de Rijk, 'On the Chronology of Boethius' works on Logic,' *Vivarium* 2 (1964), 125–162. Elements of conjecture cannot be excluded. Some scholars (e.g. E. K. Rand and Obertello) have wanted to date the first *Isagoge* commentary before the *Arithmetica*. This is unlikely because it is not the Platonic order.
    Reliability in deciding the relative order depends on the uncertain assumption that, unlike Proclus who added cross-references when later revising his works, Boethius left his original text intact.
51. 'Est vero in mente de tribus olim quaestionibus disputare, quarum una est quid praedicamentorum velit intentio . . .' Attention was first drawn to this reading of the manuscripts, against the traditional printed text, by G. Schepss in *Blätter für das bayerische Gymnasialschulwesen* 33 (1897), 252, followed by S. Brandt in *Philologus* 62 (1903), 275. I have not as yet seen a manuscript corresponding to the printed text in Migne.
52. P. Hadot, 'Un fragment du commentaire perdu de Boèce sur les Catégories d'Aristote dans le Codex Bernensis 363,' *Archives d'histoire doctrinale et littéraire du moyen âge* 26 (1959), 11–27.
53. The evidence is collected by P. Moraux, *Les listes anciennes des ouvrages d'Aristote* (Louvain, 1951) pp. 58–59. The Migne text of Boethius 263BC is seriously misleading. A critical text of this passage is provided by J. Shiel, 'Boethius and Andronicus of Rhodes,' *Vigiliae Christianae* 11 (1957), 179–85, whose discussion brings important corrections to the study by G. Pfligersdorffer, 'Andronikos von Rhodos und die Postprädikamente bei Boethius,' *Vigiliae Christianae* 7 (1953), 98–115.
54. I. Düring, 'Aristotle in the biographical tradition,' *Göteborgs Universitets Årsskrift* 63 (1957), 2 p. 449, thinks this scheme pre-Neoplatonic.
55. P. Courcelle, *Lettres grecques*, p. 269 = *Late Latin Writers*, p. 286.
56. Philoponus, *Cat.* (*CAG* XIII 1) 8, 27 ff. Otherwise Olympiodorus, *Prolegomena* 18, 27–22, 2 (*CAG* XII 1). Boethius, *Perih.* ii, 7, 25–27.
57. Porphyry's Question and Answer commentary has a lacuna at this point, parallel to Boethius 241D7–245B2. But the story is not his style. Boethius 244A6–7 is paralleled in Simplicius 231, 8.
58. Courcelle, *Lettres grecques* p. 273 = *Late Latin Writers*, p. 289, on Ammonius, *Cat.* 106 and Simplicius, *Cat.* 430. Boethius' form of figure is as Philoponus, *CAG* XIII, 1 p. 203.

59. J. Shiel, 'Boethius and Eudemus,' *Vivarium* 12 (1974), 14–17.
60. H. Usener suggested this (in an otherwise disappointing review of Meiser's edition, *Deutsche Literaturzeitung* 1880, 369). It is rejected by de Rijk, *Vivarium* ii (1964), 37–8. I think the possibility open.
61. de Rijk, *Logica Modernorum* (1962), pp. 24–43, examines Boethius' doctrine of fallacy, and brings out where it diverges from Ammonius'. It may be noted that Boethius' power to detect logical error is not great: *Perih.* ii 388 reports an 'acute' observation of Theophrastus about impossible (= necessary) and non-necessary (= possible), described by Bocheński (*Logique de Théophraste*, pp. 87–9) as 'gross error'.
62. *An. Pr.* i, 13–22, subjected to critical dismemberment by A. Becker, *Die Aristotelische Theorie der Möglichkeitsschlüsse* (Berlin, 1933), who thinks the passage interpolated by early editors in the Peripatetic school.
63. Victorinus' translation of the *Isagoge*, cited by Boethius, *CSEL* 48 p. 101, 18. See P. Hadot, *Marius Victorinus* (1971), pp. 189–90; A. Becker-Freysing, *Die Vorgeschichte der philosophischen Terminus 'contingens': einer Untersuchung über die Bedeutungen von 'contingens' bei Boethius* (Heidelberg, 1938).
64. J. Hintikka, *Time and Necessity* (Oxford, 1973), pp. 147–78, with a bibliography of modern discussions. See also R. Sorabji, *Necessity, Cause and Blame* (London, 1980).
65. See Benson Mates, *Stoic Logic*^{2} (1961), p. 37.
66. Boethius, *Divis.* 877B. Alexander of Aphrodisias, *In Topica*, CAG II 2 p. 532, 20 'Division is of a genus into species, a whole into parts, a word into its meanings.' Similarly *In An. Pr.*, CAG II 1 p. 161, 33 f.
67. Albinus, p. 156, 29 ff. Hermann; Sextus Empiricus, *PH* ii, 213 f.; Clem. Alex. *Strom.* viii, 19, 1–8; Joh. Dam. *Dialectica*, ch. vi pp. 64 ff. Kotter; PG 94, 545–59.

    P. Moraux, *Der Aristotelismus bei den Griechen von Andronikos bis Alexander von Aphrodisias* I (Berlin, 1973), pp. 120–32.

    A commentary on Boethius *On Division* was written by Albert the Great, and was edited by P. M. v. Loe (Bonn, 1913).
68. This is explained by Apuleius, *Perih.* p. 193, 5 Thomas. Its significance is not grasped by Ammonius, CAG IV, 6 p. 68, 25.
69. Dedication to Patricius is favoured by de Rijk, *Vivarium* ii, p. 147, and by Obertello, A. M. Severino Boezio, *De hypotheticis syllogismis* (Brescia, 1969), pp. 131–35.
70. Cassiodorus, *Inst.* ii, 3, 13 p. 119, 10–12 Mynors; *Exp. Psalm.* vii, line 137 p. 82 Andriaen = *PL* 70, 68C–69A. Discussion of the work's probable content in Hadot, *Marius Victorinus*, pp. 143–61.
71. M. Kneale, *The Development of Logic*, p. 180, observes that, to become valid, the seventh should read 'Not both not the first and not the second; but not the first, therefore the second'.
72. The monograph on the hypothetical syllogism has attracted more interest than any other part of Boethius' logical work. See Karl Dürr, *The Propositional Logic of Boethius* (Amsterdam, 1951); R. van den Driessche, 'Sur le De syllogismo hypothetico de Boèce', in *Methodos* i (1949), 293–307; I. M. Bocheński, *A History of Formal Logic* (Eng. transl. 1961), p. 139; Ivo Thomas, 'Boethius: locus a repugnantibus',

Methodos iii (1951), 303-7; Obertello's introduction to his edition (1969).

Theophrastus' work on the hypothetical syllogism is discussed by I. M. Bocheński, *La Logique de Théophraste*, Collectanea Friburgensia n.s. 32 (1947), pp. 105 ff.

73. According to Simplicius, *In de Caelo*, CAG VII, 552, 31–553, 4, Theophrastus distinguished between 'if' (to be used when the antecedent is true) and 'when' (to be used when it is both true and evident). Although this is not really a point in logic, it suffices to show that ancient logicians were aware of ambiguities surrounding 'if'.

CHAPTER IV

1. Horace, *Carm*. iii, 30; Verg. *G*. i, 42; *A*. viii, 67. I owe these two observations to Dr. A. M. Crabbe.
2. A long list of Augustinian echoes is given by E. K. Rand, 'Der dem Boethius zugeschriebene Traktat de fide catholica', *Jb. f. class. Philologie*, suppl. 26 (1901), 421–4.
3. Augustine does not deny that envy was an important element in the devil's motivation (*Enarr. in Ps*. 58, 5, etc.).
4. Cf. Aug. *City of God* xv, 8 for Adam's survival after Abel's death; but Augustine makes nothing of Adam's remorse on contemplating the fearful consequences of his sin.
5. Cf. Aug. *Sermo* 67, 7 'simul Christus et in coelo et in terra'.
6. *PL* 59, 406AB.
7. E. K. Rand, *Founders of the Middle Ages* (Harvard, 1928), pp. 156–7. Like H. F. Stewart who at first rejected the authenticity of *De fide catholica* (with the dangerous sentence 'a single reading of it is sufficient to convince one that this is no work of Boethius', *Boethius, an Essay*, 1891, p. 139), Rand came soon to abandon his earlier view that *De fide catholica* is spurious (*Jb. f. class. Philologie*, suppl. 26 (1901), pp. 401–61). In 1918 the first edition of Stewart and Rand's Loeb edition of the Tractates and Consolation (p. 52) made the change of mind of both scholars explicit. *De fide catholica* is accepted as genuine by M. Cappuyns in his important article 'Boèce' in *Dictionnaire d'Histoire et de Géographie Ecclésiastique* ix (1937), 371–2. Though most scholars concur, it was not accepted by P. Courcelle, *Les lettres grecques en Occident* (2nd ed. Paris, 1948), p. 301; nor by Helen M. Barrett, *Boethius, some aspects of his times and work* (Cambridge, 1940), pp. 148–50; nor by the best German study of the Opuscula, Viktor Schurr, *Die Trinitätslehre des Boethius im Lichte der 'skythischen Kontroversen'* (Forschungen zur christlichen Literatur—und Dogmengeschichte, XVIII, 1, Paderborn 1935), pp. 8–9. Against this weight of opinion L. Obertello first argued that the tract is either by Boethius or by John the deacon: *Severino Boezio* (1974) i pp. 252–85. He has now come to think it certainly Boethius' work; see the notes to his translation of *Gli Opuscoli Teologici* (Milan: Rusconi, 1979). I have independently concluded from the diction that *De fide catholica* is certainly from his

pen: 'The authenticity of Boethius' fourth tractate, De fide catholica', *JTS* 31 (1980), 551–6, written before Obertello's 1979 translation was available.

8. W. Bark, 'Boethius' fourth tractate, the so-called De fide catholica,' *Harvard Theological Review* 39 (1946), 55–69, at 68. Bark's argument for authenticity is the consistency of the theology of the fourth tractate with that of Tr. i, ii, and v.

9. Courcelle, *Lettres grecques*² p. 299 n. = *Late Latin Writers* p. 317, proposed the impossible conjecture that Boethius is expressing surprise at the western Catholic definition which he heard for the first time at this meeting in Rome; and that he was brought up as a Monophysite, his father being identified with the prefect of Alexandria of the same name mentioned by Zacharias' *Church History*. Courcelle is also mistaken in claiming that the name Boethius is otherwise unparalleled in this period (it appears for bishops of Cahors and Carpentras). No part of this hypothesis can stand a moment's scrutiny.

10. Gelasius, *De duabus naturis*, is critically edited by E. Schwartz, *Publizistische Sammlungen zum Acacianischen Schisma* (1934), 85–106. A text also in Thiel 530–57; not in Migne.

11. Nephalius: Evagrius III, 22; 33; Zachariah VI, 2; C. Moeller in *RHE* 40 (1944–5), 73–140.

12. Text of Proclus in *ACO* IV, 2 (1914), 187–95 = *PG* 65, 856–73. (Grumel, *Regestes* 78.) M. Richard, 'Proclus de Constantinople et le théopaschisme', *RHE* 38 (1942), 303–31.

13. In 431 seven delegates from Antioch submitted a complaint to the emperor Theodosius II that some corrupt the *hagiasmos* which the angels offer to God: *ACO* I, i, 7, p. 72.

14. Ephrem of Amid, patriarch of Antioch 526–44, explains this in a letter to an ultra-Monophysite lawyer of Emesa named Zenobius, summarised by Photius, *Bibliotheca* 228 (245a 24 ff.).

15. Marcellinus Comes, a. 512 (*Chronica Minora* ii, 97). An astonishing account of July 518 in *ACO* III, 71–76 (Mansi VIII, 1058–66); Trishagion, 76, 17.

16. On Vitalian see *PLRE* II s.v. Texts of Maxentius and several pieces by Dionysius Exiguus are edited and discussed by E. Schwartz, *ACO* IV 2 (1914); some corrections in F. Glorie's introduction to his edition of Maxentius in *Corpus Christianorum*, s. l. LXXV A (1978). See also B. Altaner's two papers reprinted in his *Kleine patristische Schriften* = *TU* 83 (1967), 375–91; 489–506; E. Amann, art. Scythes (Moines), *DTC* XIV, 2 (1941), 1746–53. New ground was broken by V. Schurr, *Die Trinitätslehre des Boethius im Lichte der 'Skythischen Kontroversen'* (Forschungen zur christlichen Literatur- und Dogmengeschichte 18, 1, Paderborn, 1935), whose book remains indispensable. Faustus of Riez: see P. Viard in *Dict. de Spiritualité* v, 113–18 (1964).

17. Trifolius' letter, first printed by Labbe, is edited by Schwartz, *Publ. Samml. z. Acac. Schisma*, 115–17, from a ninth-century Berlin ms. (79, once Phillips 1776); not in Thiel or Migne. Eutychian monk at

Chalcedon: *Act. Chalc.* iv, 107–08 (*ACO* II, i, 316). Maxentius claimed Chalcedon's general approbation of Proclus: *Libellus fidei* x, 17 p. 15 Glorie = *ACO* IV, 2 p. 6, 26.
18. Dioscorus to Hormisdas: *Avell.* 216, *CSEL* 35, 2, p. 675. Cf. 224 p. 686. (Hormisdas, *epp.* 75 and 98 Thiel.)
19. Fulgentius, *ep.* 17, 6, 13.
20. Ferrandus, *ep.* 5, 9 (*PL* 67, 919AB, cf. 921D).
21. John II's letter, first edited by Sichard, is in *ACO* IV, 2, pp. 206–10 (Mansi VIII, 803).
22. Ferrandus, *ep.* 5, 11 (*PL* 67, 921C); Facundus i, 3 (*PL* 67, 534).
23. Severus of Antioch, *C. impium grammaticum* iii, 29.
24. Cyril of Scythopolis, *V. Sabae* 38, p. 127 Schwartz.
25. Sev. Ant. *ep.* 22 (*PO* XII, 2, 215).
26. Sev. Ant. *Select Letters* i, 63 (i p. 199 E. W. Brooks tr.); J. Lebon, *Le Monophysisme Sévérien* (Louvain, 1909), p. 247.
27. E. zum Brunn, *Le dilemme de l'être et du néant chez saint Augustin* (Paris, 1969).
28. *Perih.* ii, 70, 22–71, 3. Cicero, *Tusc.* ii, 15, 35.
29. P. Hadot, 'La distinction de l'être et de l'étant dans le De Hebdomadibus de Boèce', *Miscellanea Mediaevalia*, ed. P. Wilpert, ii (Berlin, 1963), 147–53.
30. A classified list of texts from Proclus on this point is given by H. D. Saffrey and L. G. Westerink's note, *Proclus, Théologie Platonicienne* I (Paris, 1968), pp. 159–61.
31. Augustine (*De moribus* ii, 11, 24) has 'quo esse aut cogitari melius nihil possit'. The formula approximates to that of Aristotle, as quoted by Simplicius, *In de caelo*, CAG VII, 289, 7 (= Arist. frg. 16); above, p. 235.
32. *ACO* IV, 2, p. 197, 1.

CHAPTER V

1. The monographs of Klingner (1921), Courcelle (1967), and Gruber (1978) have amassed much essential material for interpreting the *Consolation of Philosophy*, on which I have constantly tried to draw in this chapter. Gruber's detailed, sentence-by-sentence exegesis has been particularly valuable, and his book makes it superfluous to provide this chapter with full annotation.
2. Proclus, *In Tim.* i, 167, 22, interprets it to mean intellectual wisdom. Celsus (in Origen, *Contra Celsum* vi, 42) shows that there is a long history to the Platonic exegesis of the peplos of Athene.
3. I have discussed this in *Medium Aevum* (1980). Professor J. A. W. Bennett calls my attention to Thomas Browne's *Christian Morals* i, 22 'There is a natural standing court within us, examining and acquitting, and condemning at the Tribunal of our selves, wherein iniquities have their natural Thetas, and no nocent is absolved by the verdict of himself.'
4. Michael Lapidge, 'A Stoic metaphor in Late Latin poetry: the binding of the cosmos', *Latomus* 39 (1980), 817–37.

5. A. Cabaniss has suggested that Boethius should be regarded as the earliest witness to the great Antiphon: *Speculum* 22 (1947), 221 f. This is possible but not perhaps probable.
6. Boethius' definition of eternity is akin to, not identical with, that of Plotinus iii, 7, 3. On the transience of the present, Calcidius 106.
7. Bovo is edited by R. B. C. Huygens, 'Mittelalterliche Kommentare zum O qui perpetua...', *Sacris Erudiri* 6 (1954), 373–427.

PRESERVATION AND TRANSMISSION

1. G. Schepss, 'Subscriptionen in Boethiushandschriften', *Blätter für das bayerische Gymnasialschulwesen* 24 (1888), pp. 19–29, at p. 28.
2. Maximian is edited by E. Baehrens, *Poetae latini minores* (Teubner) vol. 5, p. 316. Text with annotations by R. Webster (Princeton, 1900). F. Wilhelm, 'Maximianus und Boethius,' *Rheinisches Museum* 62 (1907), 601–14. A good recent monograph is mainly concerned with the textual criticism: W. Schetter, *Studien zur Ueberlieferung und Kritik des Elegikers Maximian* = Klass. philol. Studien 36 (Wiesbaden, 1970).

   If the allusion in *Eleg.* 5, 1 to an embassy from the West to the East were securely autobiographical, and if Maximian the poet could be identified with the Maximian who appears in Cassiodorus, *Variae*, then he could have known Boethius personally. But much here is precarious and conjectural. To Ennodius (*epigr.* 132) Boethius was an erotic poet.
3. Orléans 267; Paris, Bibl. Nat. nouv. acq. 1611 (Libri 31), saec. x–xi.
4. This stands on fo. 51r of the Paris portion of the manuscript.
5. Orléans 267, fo. 88r.
6. Montfaucon, *Bibliotheca bibliothecarum* II (Paris, 1739), 1130d, no. 481, to which attention was drawn by Schepss, art. cit. p. 24.
7. Keil, *Grammatici Latini*, vols. ii–iii contain the text of Priscian. An inaccurate account of the subscriptions may be found in Pauly-Wissowa, s.v. Priscianus, Band XXII, 2, col. 2329, with the error 'memorabilis' for 'memorialis'.
8. Instances in papyrus 6 of J. O. Tjäder, *Die nichtliterarischen lateinischen Papyri Italiens aus der Zeit 445–700* (Lund, 1955), i p. 222.
9. *PL* 59, 397–408. The text is reedited from Vatic. Reginensis 1709A, fol. 24–31 by A. Wilmart, *Analecta Reginensia* = Studi e Testi 69 (1933), 170–9. The Migne text is reprinted from Mabillon, *Museum Italicum* (1786). At *PL* 59, 401C 5 for 'fuit' read 'fiat'; 405B 7 'hoc est' before 'quia' has fallen out; 406D 12 read 'secundam'.

INDEX

Abelard 195
Acacius of Constantinople 30, 44, 182; schism 12, 29–45, 57
Acephali 185
Achilles bp of Spoleto 32
Adam 177–8, 201–2
Ado of Vienne 54
Adrastus 121
Agapetus, Pope 40, 65
Agapitus (cos. 517) 6, 60
Agapitus, patricius 60, 62
Agnellus of Ravenna 4, 290
Agorius 114
Akoimetae 184
Alan of Lille 252
Alaric 11
Albinus, Platonist 164
Albinus on *artes* 84, 104, 113
Albinus, senator 48–9, 55, 58, 62
Alcuin 107, 136, 251–2
Alexander of Aphrodisias 16, 81, 105, 109 f., 126, 129, 133–4, 139, 205; future contingents 246; *Categories* 145–6, 193; *Interpretation* 152; *fate* 159, 162; *providence* 161; Theophrastus 171
Alexandria 17–20, 121; see 30
Amalafrida 53
Amalasuintha 4, 51, 62, 66
Amantius 43–4
Ambrose of Milan 6, 215; music of spheres 80, 292–3
Ambrose and Beatus 6
Amiri, Al- 125
Ammianus 83
Ammonius, philosopher 19–20, 105–6, 111 ff., 125 ff., 139 f., 191, 197, 208, 220, 244; astrolabe 102; *Categories* 147 ff.; *Interpretation* 153 ff.; hypothetical syllogism 167–9; question of Boethius' debt 20, 108–9, 146, 154
Anastasius II, Pope 30–1, 38–40, 42, 183
Anastasius, emperor 2, 30–46, 60, 185, 291 n. 67
Andromachus 12–14, 249
Andronicus of Rhodes 121, 126, 143, 151, 164

angels 177, 242
Anonymus Valesianus 3, 50, 52, 61; verdict on Theoderic 63
Anselm 112; 235–6
Anselm of Havelberg 140
Anthemius, W. emperor 20
Anthimus, physician 288
Antiphon, Advent 237
Apollo 14, 159
Apion 66
Apuleius 21, 70, 113, 156, 166, 232
Aquinas 17, 175, 195, 203, 223
Archimedes 82, 103, 105, 149
Archytas 77–8, 87, 89–90, 99, 127, 143 f.
Areobindus 46
Arianism 3, 57–9, 62, 177, 200, 213, 216
Arigern 49
Aristarchus 69
Aristides, Aelius 61
Aristides Quintilianus 22, 83–4
Aristotle 16–21, 69, 73, 108–73; brevity 112; on goodness 208; non-being 207; man 122, 227; honour 231; nobility 233; chance 244; music of spheres 79; numbers 81; music 83, 86; geometry 104–5; the one 227; hierarchy of sciences 109 f.; Latin translations 133–40; *Metaphysics* 150, 244; *Ethics* 214; *Protrepticus* 233; *on Philosophy* 235 f.; *on the Soul* 153; 'heresy' 121; on coming to be and on passing away 150, 199; *Physics* 139, 150, 191 f., 244
Aristoxenus of Tarentum 87–101
Arnold, G. 174
Asclepius of Tralles 71
Aspasius 121, 126, 155
Asterius 5, 7
astronomy 102–7, 110; zodiac 82
asylum 32, 51, 289 n. 54
Athalaric 52, 62–3, 66
Athens 17–20
Augustine 117, 121, 131, 175 ff., 187, 191 ff., 197, 199 ff., 211 ff.; God 215, 237–7, hub 242; God's

service freedom 227; goodness 206–7; faith and reason 251; music of heaven 80; intellectual/intelligible 111; Platonism 16, 249–50; harmony of Plato and Aristotle 141; liberal arts 114; *De musica* 87–7, 101; Muses 86, 226; reminiscence 106; past happiness 230; prisons 226; relics at Pavia 54; parallels to Boethius 250
Ausonius 224
Avienus 6
Avitus of Vienne 2, 9–10, 41, 184

Barbara 6
Bark, W. 180
Basil, accuser 51
Basil, senator 49
Basil, prefect 57
Basil bp of Caesarea 80
bedbugs 228
Belisarius 255
Bellermann, F. 96
Bhutto, Z. A. 226
Bible 178, 237 f.
Boethius: birth 1; death 54–5, 66–9, 225 f.; wife 6; ancestry 5; education 19; consul 24; sons' consulate 45–7, 229; master of the offices 46 ff.; poet 23; *solamen* of philosophy 168; Consolation 1, 54, 128–9, 140, 162–3, 173–4, 209, 220 ff., 222 ff; Bible allusions 238; quadrivium 73 ff.; panegyric on Theoderic 46; plan to translate Plato 135, 140; prolix 120; critics 120
Boniface II, Pope 65
Bovo 247
Brandt, S. 135
Brescia diptych 5
Burgundians 23, 52
Burgundio of Pisa 139

Calcidius 21, 70, 81, 191, 203, 242, 246
calendar of 354 12, 16, 35–6
Calvenzano 55
Capella, Martianus XII, 15, 21f., 24, 70, 84, 92, 102, 113, 116, 121, 169, 224, 232, 235
Cassiodorus 117; master of the offices 54; *Anecdoton Holderi* 7, 23, 46, 175, 225; chronicle 41, 51f.; *Institutiones* 70, 102, 115–16; 118, 139,

168–9, 254–5; consul 41
Castor and Pollux 13 f.
Cato 7, 243
Censorinus 84
Cethegus 6
Chalcedon 25, 29–45
Chaldaean Oracles 204, 235, 243, 248
chance 119, 158, 244, 250
Charlemagne 60
chromatic genus 93–4
Cicero 5, 24, 68, 105, 148, 241; wrong on chance 119; *Tusculans* 228; *pro Cluentio* 229; *pro Archia* 231; *ep. ad Brutum* 230; *Divination* 241, 250; *Topics* 113, 168 f.; *Timaeus* 141
Clovis 2, 23
coemptio 24, 41
comet 50
Constantine Porphyrogenitus 60
consulate 4–5, 24
contingent 157 ff.
Corinth 60–1
coronation 60, 67
Courcelle, P. 20, 140, 153, 303
Cresconius of Todi 39
Cunigast 47
Cyprian, referendarius 48, 51
Cyril of Alexandria 18, 183, 185
Cyril of Scythopolis 189

Damascus 18–20, 157
Damasus, Pope 10–11, 287 n. 24
Dante 40, 223
deification 211, 236
determinism 157–63; 245f.
Devil 178
Diodorus Cronus 159
dialectic 108 ff.
Dionysius Areopagita 221
Dionysius Exiguus 186, 212 f.
Dioscorus bp of Alexandria 44, 184
Dioscorus, deacon 28, 37, 188; antipope 65
division 164
Donatus, grammarian 69, 116
Dorotheus of Thessalonica 182
dream poems 225

Easter 31–3, 36
Ecclesius bp of Ravenna 60
Elias 92, 112, 145
enharmonic genus 83, 93–4
Ennodius: on Boethius 1, 23; Theoderic

4, 41; ambitions 6–7; career 15;
   related to Senarius 27; Pope Symmachus 32, 37; legate 42; death 53;
   prosimetric genre 6, 224
Epictetus on silence 231; Simplicius on,
   20
Epicureans on music 294 n. 32; 295 n.
   44
Epiphanius of Constantinople 285
Equitius 49 f.
Ereliliva 3
Eriugena, see John the Scot
eschatology 240–1
eucharist 184, 219
Euclid 22, 74, 89 f., 103, 105, 208
Eudemus 127, 153, 166 f.
Eudokia 52
Eugippius 9, 40, 255
Eusebius of Fano 60
Eusebius, prefect 53
Eutharic Cillica 4, 51–2
Eutyches 25–6, 30, 44, 178, 180–202
evil 222 ff., 239 ff.

Faber Stapulensis 136
Facundus 189
fallacy 156
Farabi, Al- 126, 128, 152
fate 49–50, 228 ff., 242 ff., 250
Faustus bp of Riez 186, 188, 201
Faustus Albus 9, 12, 41
Faustus Niger 6, 9–10, 40–1, 188
Felix III, Pope 11, 30, 285 n. 8
Felix IV, Pope 64–5
Ferrandus 189, 199
Festus 6, 38, 41
Filioque 176, 219
Filocalus 10, 12, 35–6
Flavian 256
form and matter 214–5
fortune 119, 229
Franks 2, 288 n. 42; see Clovis
Fulgentius 9, 15, 40, 188, 201, 217
future contingents 157–63, 245f.

Gaius 119
Galen 112, 167, 228
Galla 9, 15, 40, 287 n. 26
Gaudentius on music 84
Gaudentius, accuser 51
Gelasius 12–14, 41–2, 45, 183–4, 190,
   198, 249, 285–6
Gellius, Aulus 75, 193, 203

geometry 70, 73, 77, 102–7, 110, 132,
   208, 210, 214
Gerbert of Aurillac 76, 102–3, 255
Gilbert of Poitiers 203
Glareanus 138
God 210, 236 ff.; universal belief 156,
   207; Augustine on 215, 235–7, 242;
   the One 215 f., 227, 236; no accidents
   216–17
Goths 1–68; prefer harsh modes 92
grammar 116; see also Donatus, Priscian
Gregory the Great 9, 11 f., 33, 40, 49 f.,
   62 f., 190
Gregory of Tours 64
Gruber, J. 23, 234

Hadot, P. 135, 207
Hebdomads 203
Helpis 66
Henoticon 30 ff., 65, 182
Hermannus Contractus 98
Herminus 126
Herold 181
Hierocles 17–18, 107, 125, 211, 224,
   229, 241, 244, 247
Hilary of Poitiers 219, 287 n. 26
Hilderic 52–3
Hippocrates 112, 203
Hippolytus 82
Historia Augusta 8
Hobbes 11
Horace 176
Hormisdas 25, 28, 41–5, 53, 57–8, 60,
   181 f.; 187 ff.; formula 44 f.
horoscopes 50, 107
Hypatia 18
Hypatius 43

Iamblichus 19, 157, 246, 253; future
   contingents 163; authority 134;
   God and time 163, 246; *Life of
   Pythagoras* 71; Nicomachus 17,
   71 f., 90; *Protrepticus* 233;
   Categories 16, 78, 129, 142–5.
imaginationes 131, 214, 220
imperfection 210, 236
implication 172
Importunus, senator 60
induction 151
infinite 125; no infinite regress 210
Isidore of Seville 114

James of Venice 140

Jerome 69, 115, 117, 224
Jews 58, 290
John the deacon 26–9, 168, 179–81, 202–3, 255; perhaps identical with John I, Pope 29, 53, 60–4, 67, 248
John II, Pope 65, 189
John of Damascus 164
John of Salisbury XI, 161, 300 n. 48
John the Scot 107, 225, 297 n. 11
John Talaia 30
Jordanes 8–9, 63
Julian, defensor 62
Juliana, Anicia 46
Justin I, emperor 3, 43 ff., 48, 50, 55, 58, 60
Justinian 43, 55, 58, 190; church policy 25, 50; Athens school 18; Gothic war 66–8; murder of Vitalian 186

Klingner, F. 234
know thyself 227

Laurentius 9–10, 26, 31–41
law, Roman 35, 119, 286 n. 13
Leo I, Pope 11–12; Tome 26, 30 ff., 192, 200
Leo XIII, Pope 68
Leontius, monk 186
lethargy 227–8
Lewis, C. S. 251
Liber Pontificalis 9–10, 39–40, 48, 60–2, 291 n. 69
liturgy 251; baptismal 27; Paternoster 202
Lombards 66
love 232, 244
Lucan 232, 243
Lucian 224
Lupercalia 12–14, 249
Lupus bp of Troyes 107
Lydian mode 92, 95–6

Macedonius 182
Macrobius 7–8, 14, 21, 70, 90, 102, 107, 114, 132–3, 231; music of spheres 80–2
Macrobius Plotinus Eudoxius 7
magic 49–50, 227, 289 n. 47
Manichees 11, 57, 177
Marcellinus Comes 8, 37, 60
Marcellus, Tullius 114
Marinus 121, 204
Marius of Aventicum 55

Martial 225
Martianus, *see* Capella
martyrs 227, 230, 249, 287 n. 30
Mary 178, 188; Theotókos 179
mathematics 70 ff.
matter 191, 199, 229
Maxentius 186 ff., 211
Maximian 254 f.
Menippos 224
Merobaudes 117
Minio-Paluello, L. 113 f., 129, 132, 135 ff.
modal logic 157 ff.
modes 83, 91–3, 96–9
Monophysites 25, 29–45, 50, 58, 180 ff.
Montfaucon, B. de 256
More, T. 253
Muses 86, 117, 226, 238, 250
Music: Boethius' introduction 78 ff.; therapy 92; ratios 78–9; spheres 79–81; in *Consolation* 101
Mutianus 84

names 239; names of names 123
Napoleon 3
nature 191 ff.
necessity 157, 162, 245
Nephalius 185
Nestorius 26, 30, 44, 178, 180–202
Nicomachus XII, 17, 21, 70–101, 120
Nitzsch, F. 174
nothing 190 ff., 244
Numenius 110

Obertello, L. 168
Odovacar 1–5, 12, 47
Olybrius 46
Olympiodorus 121, 141, 295 n. 48
Opilio 51, 189
oracles 159
Origen: comets 50; slow medication 228; silence 231; freedom 162
Orpheus 240
Ostia temple 13
Ovid 225

Palladio 84
papacy 9–12; Laurentian schism 29 ff.; divine right 31, 65; free of error 40; jurisdiction 43–5; above synods 34–5, 41. *See* Leo, Anastasius II, Gelasius, Symmachus, Hormisdas, John, Rome.

Papinian 230
Parmenides 239. *See* Plato
parts of speech 116
Paschasius 40
Patricius 103, 117, 119, 168
Paulinus, senator 48
Paulinus of Nola 232
Pavia 1, 53–4, 59, 68
Pelagius 178
persona 149, 190 ff., 218–20, 253
Peter, S. 10–12: S. Peter's Rome 3, 31–2; 35–7, 57, 64; opp. Romulus 11
Peter bp of Altinum 26, 33–9, 57
Peter Fullo bp of Antioch 44
Peter Mongos 30, 185
Peter of Poitiers 195
Petronius 257
Philo 79–80
Philo of Megara 159–60
Philocalus, *see* Filocalus
Philodemus 86, 295
Philolaus 77, 89
Philoponus 19–20, 71, 106, 133, 138, 147–9, 191, 197, 216
Photius 72
planets 81
Plato 16–21, 108 ff., 204, 233; cave 240; reminiscence 106, 237; transmigration 240; soul's wings 240; triadic cosmos 83; mathematics 70–1, 77–9, 88, 111; modes 91–2, 96; *Gorgias* 240–1; *Parmenides* 219, 227; *Republic* 109; *Sophist* 108–9, 164; *Theaetetus* 109; *Timaeus* 233 ff., 239; *Meno* 106
Plotinus 16, 205, 211, 216 ff., 239–40, 242–3, 247; logic 109, 197; authority 134
Plutarch (Pseudo-) *Music* 83, 97; *Consolation to Apollonius* 228
Plutarch of Athens 17
Polemius Silvius 14
Pons Asinorum 147
porisma 106–7, 211
Porphyry 16, 19, 21, 194, 217, 240; authority 134; tree 192; harmony of Plato and Aristotle 16, 125, 141, 163; Life of Pythagoras 71, 79; *Timaeus* 81; *Sophist* 126, 164; Ptolemy 78, 92; Life of Plotinus 16, 87; *Isagoge* 18, 21, 121 ff., 131 ff.; *Categories* 94, 125–6

Posidonius 232
Praetextatus, Vettius Agorius 120
Praetextatus, senator 49
prefect of the annona 230
Priscian 5, 116, 256; panegyric 43
Proba (Symmachus' daughter) 9, 15, 40
Proba (exegete of Aristotle) 152
Probinus 6, 41
Probus 6
Proclus of Constantinople 185, 188
Proclus Diadochus, of Lycia 17–21, 111, 125, 145–6, 191, 203–11; quoted by Boethius 129; verbosity 112; hierarchy of sciences 110; on Aristotle 18, 121; providence 129, 242 ff.; Euclid 17, 105–7; Ptolemy 17, 102; Nicomachus 72; *Timaeus* 17, 94, 110, 129, 197, 234 ff.; *Republic* 150–1, 224; *Parmenides* 109, 216, 218, 236; opuscula 162, 224; biography 17, 121; prolix 112
Procopius 3, 55, 59, 63, 66, 67
proportionality 77–8, 88 ff., 110, 234
propositions 166 ff.
providence 158 ff., 222 ff.
Ptolemy 81–103, 231
Ptolemy I, king 105
purgatory 179, 240
Pythagoras 71; ratios 90; therapy 92; Pythagoreanism 71 ff., 142, 144

quadrivium 70–107
Quintilian 70, 92

Rand, E. K. 176, 302 n. 7
Ravenna: Arian churches 59, 290; S. Vitale 60; S. Apollinare Nuovo 59; synagogues 58; Theoderic's palace 4; mausoleum 62; sarcophagus with Boethius and Symmachus 290 n. 56; Pope John I's funeral 61; corruption at court 32, 47
Reginbert 175
relation 149, 196, 218
relativism 155–6, 220
Remigius 203
Renatus 27, 168, 189, 255–6
rhetoric 112 ff.
Richard of S. Victor 195
Ricimer 59
Rijk, L. M. de 165, 300 n. 50
Rome 10–14; 'royal city' 35; Sacred city 8; S. Peter's 3, 31–2, 35, 57, 64;

S. Paul's 3, 37; S. Sebastiano 35; S.
  Agata 79, 290; S. Severinus 59; S.
  John Lateran 33, 35; S. Croce in
  Gerusalemme 39; Sessorian palace
  39; synagogues 58; Theodosian
  mausoleum 57, 291 n. 69; patronal
  feast (29 June) 37; title churches 31,
  36; Arian churches 59, 290; calendar
  (354) 12, 36; papal schism (418) 32;
  Laurentian schism 31–41; games for
  Apollo 14; *Roma Invicta* coins 13;
  fall to Totila 66; ruined buildings 12;
  Via Sacra elephants 287 n. 33
Romulus Augustulus 1, 18
Rota, J. M. 136, 143, 258
Rusticiana 6, 9, 15, 56, 66, 254–5
Rusticus 195

Sabinus bp of Canosa 60
scholasticism XIV
Scythian monks 29, 185 ff., 211 f.
seafight 158
sede vacante 33
Sedulius 286 n. 17
Senarius 27
Seneca 227–8, 230, 244
Severinus of Cologne 54, 59
Severinus of Noricum 40; 285 n. 1
Severus bp of Antioch 25, 27, 182, 189–90, 257, 260
Severus, Acilius 224
Severus, Messius Phoebus 20
Sextus Empiricus 164, 166
Sextus the Pythagorean 149
Shiel, J. 129–31, 153
Sidonius Apollinaris 107, 224, 285 n. 1
Sigeric 52
Sigibuld 65
Sigismund 52
Simplician bp of Milan 16, 70
Simplicius, Pope 30, 57
Simplicius, philospher 19–20, 78–9,
  102, 111, 125, 127, 206; uses
  Iamblichus 144, 235, 244; on
  Epictetus 199; *Physics* 139, 146; *De
  caelo* 139–40; *Categories* 143–5,
  148, 216, 220
sorcery, *see* magic
soul, immortal 230, 247; mathematical
  111; musical 86; wings 240; returns
  to itself 131, 221, 227, 237; inferior
  to mind 151
speculatio 131

spheres, revolving 242; music 79–81
stars 22, 50, 162; zodiac 82; horoscopes 107; fate 242; Boethius'
  astronomy 102–7, 227
Stephania 6
Stephanus 152
Stoicism 108–73, 151, 228–33
Sylvester II, Pope: *see* Gerbert
Symmachus, Pope 9, 26, 31–45, 48, 57,
  181
Symmachus, Q. Aurelius (fourth-cent.
  senator) 5, 9, 14–15
Symmachus, Q. Aurelius Memmius
  (Boethius' father-in-law) 5–10, 12,
  16, 23, 40–1, 56, 69, 103, 116, 168,
  181, 213, 226, 229; executed 56, 67;
  haunts Theoderic 63; drops him into
  hell 63
Synesius 234
Syrianus 17, 111, 121, 125, 128, 139,
  153–4, 156–7, 191, 197, 203

Talleyrand 3
Taylor, T. 243
Teles 229
Themistius 78, 114, 120, 127–8, 140
Theodora 55
Theoderic 24, status 2, 30, 42–3;
  medallion 3–4; at S. Peter's 3; care
  for *Romanitas* 4; for law 119;
  civilitas 35; toleration 56 ff.;
  dynastic marriages 52; restores cities
  12; golden age 63, 66; death 62;
  mausoleum 62; Arianism 3, 27, 34,
  52 ff., 63, 179; tyranny 227 ff., 240,
  248
Theodorus, senator 60
Theodorus, scribe 27, 256
Theologoumena Arithmeticae 72, 142
Theophrastus 126, 166–7, 171; 301 nn.
  61, 72
Thrasamund 52–3; 287 n. 26
theta 1, 225
Thierry of Chartres 203
Tiberianus 235
Ticinum, *see* Pavia
time 163, 177, 217–8, 242 ff.
Timothy Aelurus 44
Totila 63, 66
transmigration 240
Trifolius 188
Trigguilla 47
Trishagion 185 ff.

Ulfila 2
Ulpian 119
universals 124, 130, 133, 147–8, 215
Usener, H. 7, 157, 241

Valla, L. XI
Vallinus 175
Vandals 21, 32, 52–3, 56
variables 164
Varro XII, 21, 203, 224
Vergil 5, 23, 176, 235, 243, 245; *Aeneid* allegorised 15
Verona 48, 53; Euclid 103–4
via media 182–3
Victorinus, Marius 16, 21, 70, 115–18, 134–5, 158, 168–70, 209, 216

Victorius of Aquitaine 31, 36
Vigilius, Pope 195
Vitalian 43, 186
Vitruvius XII, 84

Webster, R. 255
wisdom: Solomon 237; *sapientia* through *scientia* 131

Xystus III, Pope: alleged adultery 36

Zacharias: *Ammonius* 19; *Church History* 303 n. 9
Zeno, emperor 9, 30, 285; *see* Henoticon